ERRATA

Due to unexpected difficulties in typesetting, there are, we regret, a number of printing errors in this volume. Among them the following should be noted especially:

p. 19, line 28 – "on the part of"
p. 39, line 12 – "worldly" for "wordly"
p. 66, line 21 – "antichrist"
p. 90, line 20 – "had been"
p. 95, line 12 – "continuous"
p. 109, line 19 – "Chaucer"
p. 133, line 11 – "Woodford"
p. 134, note 110, *add*: "Quotation here is from the version edited by Conrad Lindberg, *MS. BODLEY 959: GENESIS-BARUCH in the Earlier Version of the Wycliffite Bible* (Stockholm, 1959-73), vol. 5 (1969), 103-104."
p. 135, line 16 – "The Wycliffite Prologue insists, following Jerome..."
p. 135, note 112 – "*De Veritate* I, 80; 103 ff; cf. Wycliffite Prologue, 225."
p. 162, note 57 – "Donovan"
p. 201, line 6 – "literalism"
p. 213, note 10 – "Delaney"
Index – "Benedetti"; "Brusendorff, Aage"; "Davis, Charles T."; "Koonce, B.G."

Chaucer
and
scriptural
tradition

By the same Author:

By Things Seen: Reference Recognition in Medieval Thought, *Edited by David Lyle Jeffrey*, University of Ottawa Press, 1979.

Chaucer
and
scriptural
tradition

compiled and edited by
David Lyle Jeffrey

University of Ottawa Press

Canadian Cataloguing in Publication Data

Main entry under title:
Chaucer and scriptural tradition

Includes bibliographical references and indexes.
ISBN 0-7766-4826-8

1. Chaucer, Geoffrey, d. 1400—Criticism and interpretation—Addresses, essays,
lectures. 2. Bible and literature—Addresses, essays, lectures. I. Jeffrey, David
L., 1941-

PR1924.C42 1984   821'.1   C84-090084-8

for
ROBBIE

Quod adhuc multi meminerunt senes,
quorum relatu haec solemus audire.
Quod ideo credendum est, quia nunc
quoque si quis theatrum talium nugarum
imperitus intraverit, nisi ei dicatur ab
altero quid illi motus significent,
frustra totus intentus est.

St. Augustine,
De doctrina christiana

CONTENTS

Acknowledgements

Contemporary doctors of literature, no less than Chaucer's "doctour of phisik," have usually followed curricula in which their "studie was but litel on the Bible." Yet many have wished some remedy for the misfortune, since we cannot but sense that much of Chaucer's poetry is rooted in the biblical literature he so easily employs. The present book of essays is a response by eleven scholars to this evident and lively relationship. While the book does not pretend to a systematic treatment of so large a subject, each essay attempts to be evaluative, as well as suggestive, and to offer a kind of preliminary mapping of territory. The patient reader will discover, I trust, the effort toward a modest *compilatio* rather than simple *collectio* on the subject: though imperfect, the whole should compose a considered invitation to further, more extensive explorations.

As editor it has been my pleasure to work with keen and thoughtful contributors. I am especially grateful to Russell Peck and John Fleming, whose chapters were first essayed as much shorter papers for an MLA session on this subject which I chaired in New York, in 1978, and to Chauncey Wood, Douglas Wurtele, and David C. Fowler for subsequent encouragement in the development of the volume. Above all, a debt of acknowledgement is due to Professor D. W. Robertson, Jr., not merely for his substantial contribution to this book, but for the pioneer work with which he has made all of us, willingly or unwillingly, awake to the scriptural richness of Chaucer's texts. Even where some of us have been provoked to vigorous disagreements concerning insight or emphasis, we have usually found the energy generated by the insistent challenge of his thought and scholarship to be an invaluable source of direction and sustentation for our own enterprise.

David Lyle Jeffrey
University of Ottawa
March 1, 1983

Introduction

Few modern readers of the *Wife of Bath's Tale* fail to notice that a significant proportion of its jokes are literary, and that many of these depend on some familiarity with Scripture and its "familiar" controversies of interpretation. Other of Chaucer's tales too—*Melibee,* the *Miller's, Canon's Yeoman's, Nun's Priest's,* and *Maunciple's* among them—carry this explicit suggestion in both overt and covert aspects of their "narrature." Despite a variety of significant efforts to retrain the modern reader according to what might be judged a better approximation of Chaucer's own literary education, many modern readers can still feel a slight discomfiture with the recurrence of biblical narrative and aphorism in Chaucer's text: it is almost, we may think, as if a part of the "literary" joke could be on us.

Some of the intimidation, clearly, has to do with the superposition of a substantial library of patristic scholia and scholastic commentary between Chaucer and his Scripture texts. Not that these many examples of *accessus* are without value, as was sometimes argued in the past, or merely an accretion of scholarly impedimenta, a kind of academic impertinence. Few of us any longer doubt that the complex intellectual texture of Chaucer's poetry demands reference for historical understanding to that rich storehouse of medieval patristic and encyclopedic learning to which critics such as Robertson and others have skillfully directed our attention. But some have wondered why it is we should automatically turn—for however valid and useful a point of reference—to commentators as distant as St. Bruno Astensis or Hildegard of Bremen, when it may be that the idea we pursue is much nearer to the surface than that—and thus more plausibly convincing as a suggestion of Chaucer's imaginative context in the first place. If the ultimate source of a Chaucerian formulation is as close as St. Paul, or Jeremiah, or the Gospel according to St. Matthew, then it may be the text of the Bible which should first be examined. If a valid tradition of interpretation still seems to need consideration, perhaps we should be paying closer attention to transmitters of that tradition more proximate to Chaucer, such as Bradwardine, Fitzralph, or Wyclif. If exegetical sources other than those most commonly available (e.g., in the margins of texts of Scripture, such as comprise the *Glossa ordinaria* or the *postillae* of Nicholas of Lyra) are rightfully to be considered in attempting to establish the historical meaning of Chaucer's vocabulary, it may make good sense to turn, at least in the beginning, to important and accessible contemporary authors, rather than to works, however well indexed, which would have been rather difficult or even impossible for Chaucer to find.

To these considerations the specific exercises of late medieval exegesis are thus, however necessary, in this instance secondary. They are a kind of grammar for texts which, once encountered, naturally lead to issues of rhetoric and logic, as from the question "what" to the questions "how" and "why." In general terms we may still say that the exegetical method most familiar to the fourteenth century is, as de Lubac, Spicq, de Bruyne, Robertson, and others have shown, largely Augustinian in character. [1] Deriving from Augustine's distinction between things *(res)* and signs *(signa)* in his *De doctrina christiana*, it concerns itself with the principle of lexical and symbolic reference, with the *double entendre* of things in a world in which the literal significance of a word or its object is but an index to its various possible levels of spiritual or inner meaning. We see the world itself as a created book, analogous in some respects to the "Book of God's Word," in which meaning is revealed as God is seen to write with a larger lexicography of persons, creatures, and events.

It has been extensively argued that Chaucer largely accepted the main outlines of this method; that, in fact, he owes to no writer in this area so much as to St. Augustine, nor to any book of his so much as *De doctrina christiana*. Most critics of medieval poetry now agree that at least some understanding of medieval exegetical method is indispensable for an historical understanding of the language of medieval poetry. What is opened to us, in various medieval categories of those references, is the spiritual lexicography available to a medieval poet, and with it we may pursue the significance of his choices of vocabulary in a more reliable way. On the other hand, some basic questions remain unsatisfied by this method alone.

We recognize that what makes Chaucer different (and from some points of view more attractive) than, let us say, Gower or Lydgate, is not that he employed a significantly different typology, lexicography, or even symbology: what sets him apart as a poet is the high drama of his dialectical method, and, above all perhaps, the radically new land of doubts and second guesses into which he thrusts the reader with respect to this question of the authority and the meaning of texts—even his own texts.

In mapping Chaucer's world of readers and interpreters, typology is one, and in time perhaps even the first, level of understanding. But the fundamental questions which engage the poet, which prompt his writing in the first place, and which often create the unique artistic character of his works, are surely entered upon only as we master, then surpass, this level of method in interpretation, embarking on a journey into the larger questions of principle which govern the whole composition. By turning certain

---

1. Henri de Lubac, *Exégèse médiévale* (Paris, 1959-1964), 4 vols.; C. Spicq, *Esquisse d'une histoire de l'exégèse latine au moyen âge* (Paris, 1944); Edgar de Bruyne, *Études d'esthétique médiévale* (Bruges, 1946); D. W. Robertson, Jr., *A Preface to Chaucer: Studies in Medieval Perspectives* (Princeton, 1962) and *Essays in Medieval Culture* (Princeton, 1980).

questions back on Chaucer, so as to see him in the act of interpreting texts, particularly scriptural texts, as also by examining those common tools for scriptural exegesis and the formulation of largely hermeneutic questions most accessible to him, we may hope to acquire further prospect on these "how" and "why" questions.

In setting ourselves to further this task, the contributors of this volume build gratefully on the "good grammar" established by others—extensive and fruitful explorations of textual traditions and textual method such as have become a central feature of modern Chaucerian scholarship. Recently, this scholarship has been added to substantially by Dudley R. Johnson and Graham D. Caie, whose dissertations compose indispensable reference for further study in this area, and by the still more recent work of Alistair Minnis and Judson B. Allen on traditions of exegesis and literary theory.[2]

The essays in the present volume are organized in five sections. First, there is an essay of contextualization by the modern pioneer in this field of study, D. W. Robertson, Jr. This section composes an introduction to some of the questions to be asked, and a review of Chaucer's relationship to the *corpus christianorum* as it might bear upon these questions.

In the second, Chauncey Wood and Edmund Reiss address some of the general and historical questions attendant upon placing Chaucer with respect to the interaction between his own texts and texts from Scripture and Christian tradition.

The third section of the volume attends to the tradition of textual glossing, to Chaucer's own activity as a kind of glossator, to his attitude toward glossing, and to the principal tools he could be expected to employ—glosses on Sacred Scripture such as could be found in the margins of the scriptural text itself. These essays, by Lawrence Besserman, Graham D. Caie, and Douglas Wurtele, provide valuable insight into literary method and textual matters. What they discover is that there is considerable evidence that Chaucer actually did consult such glosses, and that he self-consciously acknowledged them—possibly even in his own textual correction of copy received from the scrivener. To these I have added an introduction to the literary approach to Scripture of Chaucer's famous contemporary, John Wyclif. Wyclif's hermeneutic, his ideas on interpretation and reading theory, have a lively complementarity to Chaucer's thoughtful

---

2. Dudley R. Johnson, "Chaucer and the Bible," *DAI*, 31 (1971), 3506A (Yale), and Graham D. Caie, "The Significance of Glosses in MSS of *The Canterbury Tales*" (Ph. D. dissertation, McMaster University, 1974); also Caie's article "The Significance of the Early Chaucer Manuscript Glosses (with special Reference to the *Wife of Bath's Prologue*)," *Chaucer Review*, 10 (1975-76), 350-60. For literary theory see the articles of Alistair J. Minnis, especially "'Authorial Intention' and 'Literal Sense' in the Exegetical Theories of Richard Fitzralph and John Wyclif," *Proceedings of the Royal Irish Academy*, 75, Sec. C (1975), 1-31. Prof. Minnis has promised a full book on the subject of the influence of exegetical theory in the fourteenth century upon Gower and Chaucer. See also Judson B. Allen's *The Ethical Poetic of the Later Middle Ages* (University of Toronto Press, 1982).

explorations in *The House of Fame* and *The Canterbury Tales*, and suggest an important contemporary source for insight into his response to scriptural tradition.

The fourth section regards Chaucer's poetry, especially *The Canterbury Tales*, in relationship to the text—as well as the "poetics"—of the Bible, moving through the issues of creation and subcreation, wisdom literature, revelation and history, spiritual obedience and observance, to Pauline epistola on the vagaries and pragmatics of ordinary ethical life. In this section Russell A. Peck, Theresa Coletti, John Fleming, and John Alford concern themselves with Chaucer's handling of issues arising from biblical text, as well as specific traditions of biblical interpretation.

The last essay in this volume recurs to the *House of Fame*, where some of Chaucer's most difficult questions about authority and the use of literary tradition in general are put to us sharply by his analytical (as well as poetic) fourteenth-century mind. This essay, directed to aspects of Chaucer's own "theoretical" and "hermeneutic" concerns, discovers that even in despair of the definitive authority of literary texts, scriptural tradition distils itself as the form for an answer to the poet's dilemma.

Collectively, these chapters make three central points about Chaucer's use of Scripture and traditions of its interpretation. First, it becomes clear that Chaucer's handling of the biblical materials, themselves often simple and direct, can be surprisingly sophisticated and self-conscious with respect to interpretation and interpretative method. Further, in his confident use of Scripture Chaucer reveals that kind of easy familiarity of the savant which lends itself to knowledgeable parody, textual counterpoint, and the elaboration of far-reaching enquiry into matters raised by biblical texts. These matters may be of an ethical as well as epistemological character. Finally, Chaucer is not interested in scriptural tradition merely as a repository of typologies, nor in using it merely to signal a kind of fideistic self-accrediting. He is interested in the largest questions of interpretation, in the reliability of text and textual tradition, and in the recovery of truth from the written word.

I

Context

Chaucer and Christian Tradition

D. W. ROBERTSON, Jr.

Princeton University

I. INTRODUCTION

The medieval use of Scripture and scriptural tradition generally—that is, of the Bible and its accessory literature and commentary—can only be understood adequately when the textual materials are contextualized within the relevant social history of medieval Christian tradition. This becomes particularly apparent when we consider the case of Geoffrey Chaucer. Chaucer was eminently a 'textual' man, but he was preeminently a moral, social, and political man, a statesman committed to the ethical well-being of his community, and it was these concerns which directed—even dictated—his attention to scriptural tradition.

Medieval European Christianity was not primarily a metaphysical system, a superstitious regard for the supernatural, a chimerical escape from the burdens of existence, nor an authoritarian and oppressive set of shackles imposed on the "innocent" and "natural" freedoms of humanity. It is true that during the thirteenth century a metaphysical system, based on Aristotle and largely, though not entirely, academic, did develop; that a hope for a better life hereafter was often inculcated, although medieval people devoted far more attention to ways of facing the problems of this life than they did to dreams about the next; and it is also true that Christian thought, although humane, was not characterized by the kind of sentimental humanitarianism that grew up during the later eighteenth century and has since come to dominate modern thought. "Man," wrote St. Augustine, "is a great thing, made in the image and likeness of God, not in that he is encased in a mortal body, but in that he excels the beasts in the dignity of a rational soul." But he went on to quote with approval the warning of Jeremiah, "Cursed be the man that trusteth in man." [1] Man's great gift, and the "image of God" within him, was reason, and when he abandoned it for the sake of passion, he lost his "likeness," becoming something other than a man. Our fellow men are to be loved, he thought, not for themselves, but for the virtues reflected in them, or for the source of those virtues, God.

---

1. *On Christian Doctrine*, 1. 22. 20.

Christians inherited from Antiquity a mode of thought, not so much a "system" as a fundamental attitude, that envisioned the existence of "intelligible" (intangible) realities, whose existence was available to the reason but not immediately to the senses, calling them for their own purposes after St. Paul "the invisible things of God." Although these are to be understood, as St. Paul said (Romans 1:20), "through the things that are made," they are not "abstractions" derived from observing the qualities of concrete particulars, or from "experiment upon things seen"; they are rather external realities, "natural" in their own right. Among them were the virtues, which were the gift of God's grace, available to those who loved them and Him. And God was Himself the apex of a hierarchy of such realities. The efficacy of the virtues, when they were reflected in men, was thought to be a matter of common experience, for they protected men from the ill consequences of their "natural" inclinations. [2] Thus St. Augustine was able to say, quite reasonably under the circumstances, that every Christian has an obligation in his "pilgrimage" through the created world "to comprehend the eternal and spiritual" by his observation of "corporal and temporal things." Such things, as Hugh of St. Victor was to put it later, are "the voice of God speaking to man." [3] The Trinity was a mystery, difficult to comprehend, but faith did not involve a mystical leap into the realm of the "supernatural." Most educated Christians regarded "magic" as an illusion. The miracles of Christ and his Saints were not magical, but were manifestations of God's grace. The idea of the "supernatural" was introduced into Europe by the scholastic philosophers in the mid-thirteenth century. [4] To confuse a sense of the reality of the "intelligible" with ordinary superstition, as Cain does in the Wakefield *Mactacio Abel*, [5] is to demonstrate both irrationality and what St. Augustine calls "the crime of malevolence." However we, with an entirely different universe of discourse, may wish to evaluate this old mode of thought, we must seek at least to understand it if we wish to understand those who shared it, their behavior, and the products of their culture.

Although medieval thinkers were able to make Christian beliefs and attitudes rationally coherent, medieval Christianity was not a "system" but essentially a way of life supported by ideals that, because of human weakness, were not often observed consistently. No one expected that they would be, but everyone was urged to seek, and if possible to find, the grace made available to him through Christ to wish to do what he should do. Human beings were expected to be sinners, and the fact that a man was a sinner did not make him either a "pagan" or a "hypocrite" (unless he

---

2. That is, such inclinations were "natural" after the Fall, although not "natural" to man as he was created. The words "Nature" and "natural" as applied to man are thus ambiguous.

3. *On Christian Doctrine*, 1. 4. 4.

4. See Johann Auer, "In wieweit ist im 13. Jahrhundert der Wandel des Begriffs "Supernaturalis" bedingt durch den Wandel des Naturbegriffs?" in *La filosofia della Natura nel Medioevo* (Milan, 1966), pp. 331-49.

5. Ed. A. C. Cawley, *The Wakefield Pageants in the Towneley Cycle* (Manchester, 1958), p. 8, line 297.

professed innocence); it simply implied that he was among those whom the great crusading bishop Adhemar de le Puy called *exsules filii Evae*. Rousseau had not yet made humanity basically innocent, and common experience taught that left to himself man might well anticipate Freud's "polymorphous perverse infant." Christianity was cherished because it had what we should call beneficial psychological, economic, social, and political functions, restraining people from the immediate satisfaction of their physical appetites or worldly ambitions at the expense of others, and concerning them with the welfare of their communities. It was an "ecologically sound" feature of medieval culture. [6] Its basis was the Bible regarded in a certain way, a way indicated in the writings of the Fathers of the Church that were often thought of as a necessary extension of the scriptural text.

As time passed and the structures of medieval society changed, emphases on various principles of Christian thought changed also, along with "styles" in the arts and in literature itself. A verbal statement may be quoted with approval for centuries, but the "meaning" of the statement, which is something that exists not in words but in people, changes as societies and people change, and may indeed vary from place to place at a given time in different "cultures." When we talk about "semantic change" we are actually talking about changes in people and their ways of doing things. Ways of doing things changed more rapidly during the Middle Ages and varied more from place to place than most people suppose, and it is wrong to use the word *medieval* as though we were talking about a static culture without sharp local differences. Nevertheless, certain principles, varying in their implications for different communities, remained constant.

St. Augustine, pausing to consider cultural diversity in a discussion of the *mores* revealed in the Old Testament, observed that "Some, as it were somnolent, who were neither in the deep sleep of folly nor able to awaken in the light of wisdom, misled by the variety of innumerable customs, thought that there was no such thing as absolute justice but that every people regarded its own way of life as just. For if justice, which ought to remain immutable, varies so much among different peoples, it is evident that justice does not exist." There is nothing new, we notice, about the lure of "situational ethics," and the fact of cultural diversity has long been recognized. But St. Augustine continues, "They have not understood, to cite only one instance, that 'what you do not wish to have done to yourself, do not do to another' (cf. Matt. 7:12, Luke 6:31) cannot be varied on account of any diversity of peoples," and he goes on to call attention to "charity (or the love of God and of one's neighbor for the sake of God) and its most just laws." [7] The catechism of Queen Elizabeth I, composed many years later in a different world, contains the statement: "My duty towards my neighbor is to love him as myself: And to do to all men as I

---

6. I refer to human ecology, although the general attitude that the world was to be "used" for the sake of God probably contributed to reasonably sound "ecological" practices.

7. *On Christian Doctrine*, 3. 14. 22.

would they should do unto me.'' And Alexander Pope, still later, could write in his *Essay on Man* that "all Mankind's concern is Charity," adding that "where Faith, Law, Morals all began, / All end, in Love of God and Love of Man.'' St. Augustine is in fact typical of the whole "Christian era" in regarding charity, or love, as the basic message of the Scriptures. Its implications vary from place to place and from time to time, so that each generation requires new verbal elaborations to make it vivid and understandable.

The general outlook we have briefly sketched, except for the Christian addition of the "laws of charity," is an adaptation of classical attitudes in Pythagorean and Platonic traditions, and it continued to influence European thought, with some exceptions especially toward the end of the period, down through the early eighteenth century, providing a certain cultural continuity. Before considering the variety of ways in which it was applied, it may be useful to inquire into the literary assumptions that accompanied it. St. Augustine advised his friend Licentius to keep his poem on Pyramus and Thisbe, but to arrange it in such a way that it would praise divine love,[8] and he defined a fable as a lie composed for utility and delight.[9] He thought that figurative language made truths hidden beneath its surface more pleasant and memorable when they were discovered with some effort, and that such discovery aided in the comprehension of the intelligible.[10] These views are reflected in numerous statements about the usefulness of fabulous narratives from the early Middle Ages to the defenses of poetry written by Petrarch, Boccaccio, and Salutati.[11] In general, therefore, although there are in the Middle Ages many explicitly doctrinal poems and narratives, there are many others whose doctrine is concealed beneath a pleasing surface. The tendency among scholars, eager to find support for "enlightened modern attitudes" in medieval literature, to read such works literally has led to some curious interpretations. Some figurative language, like "the sleep of folly," or the "light of wisdom" in the passage from St. Augustine quoted above, is more or less inherent in the general intellectual posture, and some of it, more obscurely derived from "the things that are made" or from classical sources often requires research to discover. The following very brief survey should help to explain why students of Chaucer should be interested in scriptural and patristic materials, and at the same time introduce some of the more important general sources for such study.

---

8. *On Order*, 1. 8. 24.
9. *Soliloquies*, 2. 10. 18 and 19.
10. *On Christian Doctrine*, 2. 6. 7-8. Cf. 4. 8. 22, and Letter 50. 7. 13 to Januarius: "And in like manner, whensoever illustrative symbols are borrowed, for the declaration of spiritual mysteries, from created things . . . this is done to give the doctrine of salvation an eloquence adapted to raise the affections of those who receive it from things seen, corporeal and temporal, to things unseen, spiritual and eternal." See the Rev. J.G. Cunningham, *Letters of St. Augustine* (Edinburgh, 1872), I, 215. A more eloquent and striking statement of this principle, since it involves amatory imagery, may be found in St. Gregory's Preface to his commentary on the Canticle of Canticles.
11. See D. W. Robertson, Jr., *A Preface to Chaucer* (Princeton, 1962), pp. 337-65.

II. MILITIA EST VITA HOMINIS SUPER TERRAM

Turning now to the general changes in medieval culture that led to varying emphases on "the laws of charity"—and here we shall content ourselves with a very brief account, ignoring many variations and emphasizing the close of the period—we find that Christianity in the earlier Middle Ages stressed the abandonment of superstitious worship (of various kinds from locality to locality) and pagan ritual, and the importance of controlling violence. Thus St. Caesarius of Arles, whose eloquent and effective sermons enjoyed wide circulation, especially since they were sometimes confused with the sermons of St. Augustine, pointed to the evils of sacrilege, homicide, adultery, false testimony, theft, rapine, pride, envy, avarice, wrath, drunkenness, and detraction. [12] Similar transgressions likely either to disturb the peace or to lead to disturbances of the peace were emphasized in the Old German *Beichten,* which were probably influenced by the sermons. [13] Peace could not be maintained without the motivation supplied by faith, so that an effort was made to see to it that everyone knew the Paternoster and the Creed; and the *abrenuntiatio* at Baptism often included specific renunciation of pagan beliefs. [14] As St. Gregory's famous letter to Mellitus indicates, Augustine of Canterbury was urged not to destroy pagan temples but to transform them into churches. [15] In much the same way the songs of the pagans were transformed. Aldhelm is said to have composed verses in English in order to lead his listeners "to health by interweaving among the foolish things, the words of Scripture," and our first English poet of record, Caedmon, sang songs of great skill and subtlety to his vernacular audience. [16] The vanity of worldly ease and glory and the necessity for the wise man to maintain his *militia* are celebrated in short poems like "The Wanderer" and "The Seafarer"; and longer poems, in military ("epic") terms, from *Beowulf* and the "Christian Epics" to *The Song of Roland,* portray the struggle to maintain wisdom and to combat vice, stressing the dangers of fraternal discord. The *Psychomachia* of Prudentius, which affected iconography in the arts for centuries, and the *Beatus* page of the St. Albans Psalter reflect a common concern. This general idea persisted throughout the Middle Ages, and is well illustrated, for example, in a letter by Elizabeth's faithful and longsuffering counsellor William Cecil to Nicholas White in 1570. Cecil, we should notice, loved the virtues "settled in" his friend, and he himself was armed against the "darts and pellets" of the world by faith. His words paraphrase St. Paul:

---

12. Sermo 169 in *Opera,* ed. D. G. Morin (Maretioli, 1937), I, 684. There are similar lists in other sermons. It is not difficult to find a similar emphasis in St. Gregory's account of the armies of the vices in *Moralia,* 31. 45. 87-88, *PL,* 76, cols. 620-21.

13. See Franz Hautkappe's dissertation, *Uber die altdeutchen Beichten und ihre Beziehungen zu Cäsarius von Arles* (Munster, 1927).

14. E.g., see W. Braune, *Althochdeutsches Lesebuch,* 9th ed. (Halle, 1928), p. 170.

15. Bede, *Ecclesiastical History,* 1. 30.

16. See B. F. Huppé, *Doctrine and Poetry* (New York, 1959), p. 69, and Chapter IV. For an account of Aldhelm's life and work, see W. F. Bolton, *A History of Anglo-Latin Literature* (Princeton, 1967), pp. 68-100.

I do contynue and will not desist to love hartily the honest virtues which I am persuaded are settled and rooted in you, and so will, except you make the change. I am as you have known me if not more tormented with the blasts of the world, willing to live in calm places, but it pleaseth God otherwise to exercise me, in sort as I cannot shun the rages thereof, though his goodness perserveth me as it were with the targett of his providence, from the dangers that are gaping uppon me. *Vita hominis est militia super terram.* I use no armour of proofe agaynst the darts or pellets, but confidence in God by a cleare conscience. [17]

During the later Middle Ages it was thought that one achieved strength for this battle through the sacrament of confirmation.

III.   DEUS CARITAS EST

Local strife by no means disappeared during the early twelfth century, as the successful preaching of St. Norbert, who sought to calm it, well illustrates. But a new *militia Christi* arose with the establishment of the crusading orders, directed against paganism in the Holy Places across the sea, first with the transformation of the Order of the Knights of the Hospital of St. John of Jerusalem into a military order (1113) and then with the establishment of the Knights of the Temple of Solomon (1118), whose aims and ideals were set forth in a rule under the aegis of St. Bernard, providing the foundation for the European cult of chivalry. The ascetic ideals of these orders and the demand for self-sacrifice in chivalric doctrine illustrate once more the fact that the two kinds of *militia* could be combined. One was an inspiration to the other, and both were inspired by love. More settled conditions generally, especially within the confines of monastic and cathedral schools, permitted renewed attention to the central doctrine of Christian belief, love. The Canticle of Canticles, upon which the most influential and distinguished commentary had long been that of St. Gregory the Great, received new attention. Five commentaries on this book were produced in the ninth century, one in the tenth century, six in the eleventh, and thirty-three by writers who died between 1115 and 1215. [18] Of the last, six treated the Bride as the Blessed Virgin, whose cult developed steadily during the century, so that in 1198 Odon de Soliac, Bishop of Paris, added the *Ave* to the Paternoster and the Creed as formulas to be recited daily by Christians. [19] Among the authors of the commentaries were such distinguished figures as St. Bernard, Alanus de Insulis, Honorius of Autun, William of St. Thierry, Hugh of St. Victor, Richard of St. Victor, and Ailred of Rievaulx, whose commentary, unfortunately, has been lost. Meanwhile, treatises on love, both human and divine, proliferated, and included the extremely influential transformation of Cecero's *De amicitia* into a work *On Spiritual Friendship* by Ailred of

---

17.   Thomas Wright, *Queen Elizabeth and her Times* (London, 1838), II, 364-65.

18.   John C. Gorman, S. M., *William of Newburgh's Explanatio sacri epithalamii in matrem sponsi* (Fribourg, 1960), pp. 42-43.

19.   H. Leclercq, "Sur la Salutation angélique," in C. J. Hefele and H. Leclercq, *Histoire des Conciles* (Paris, 1907-38), V, App. IV, p. 1747.

Rievaulx, and the same author's *Mirror of Charity*. Abelard had written a love story, *The History of My Calamities*, to illustrate the vulnerability of sexual love to the whims of Fortune (Providential justice misunderstood), a theme still flourishing in Chaucer's *Troilus* and in Shakespeare's *Romeo and Juliet*, and he explores the possibility of its transformation into divine love. [20] This last possibility, elaborated by Ailred, [21] was to have far-reaching consequences in the works of Dante and Petrarch, in Castiglione's *Courtier*, where it received a "Platonic" decor, and even in Elizabethan sonnet sequences. [22]

Tags from the Canticle had long been used to illuminate Latin poems, like the famous "Levis exsurgit Zephirus" from *The Cambridge Songs*, which concludes with an echo of Cant. 3:1. Spring in the Canticle is the *tempus putationis*, or time of penance during Lent, and the contrast between the burgeoning of the earth, the mating of the birds and animals, with the penitential duties of the Christian or the scholarly duties of the schoolboy moved by another love became a popular subject for song, and there is indeed a reflection of this theme at the opening of *The Canterbury Tales*, whose pilgrims are, presumably, setting out on a penitential journey. In the schools of the twelfth century new poetic material was provided by a renewed interest in the Classics, especially in the poetry of Ovid. Although both St. Caesarius and Rabanus had warned against hearing "wicked" or "lecherous" songs, [23] a warning that continued to echo in later confessional manuals, masters in the schools, like Hildebert du Lavardin, and their students who learned Latin and plainsong simultaneously, [24] became especially interested in Ovid, not because he was regarded as a "lecherous poet," but because he was read as a "mocker of light loves," offering vivid and amusing illustrations of their consequences. Mythographers like "the Third Vatican Mythographer," and commentators like Arnulf of Orléans both summarized traditional teachings and offered aid to new students seeking moral instruction in the Classics. If a verse from Ovid could serve Alanus de Insulis as a "theme" for a sermon, [25] and if Ovid could offer useful quotations for a commentary on the Canticle, [26] there was no reason why he could not serve as a model for schoolboys, most of whom were in any event thoroughly familiar with sexual activity, partly because of a lack of privacy and squeamishness in medieval homes, and partly because they came from a prevailingly agricultural environment. A kind of Ovidian wit, reinforced by scriptural allusions, flashes through some poems in the *Car-*

---

20. See D. W. Robertson, Jr., *Abelard and Heloise* (New York, 1972), pp. 99-118.

21. *PL*, 195, cols. 659-702.

22. See the forthcoming study of sonnet sequences now in preparation by Thomas P. Roche, Jr.

23. Caesarius, *Opera*, I, Sermo I, pp. 10-12; Rabanus, *Homeliae* (First Series), *PL*, 110, col. 34. The homilies of Rabanus often reflect the sermons of Caesarius.

24. Cf. Nicholas Orme, *English Schools in the Middle Ages* (London, 1973), p. 63. Song was an aid in learning Latin pronunciation.

25. See Marie-Thérèse d'Alverny, *Alain de Lille: Textes inédits* (Paris, 1965), pp. 136-37.

26. See the commentary by Thomas the Cistercian, *PL*, 206, cols. 22-862.

mina Burana,[27] while others explore various amorous inclinations and ex-periences, usually suggesting, if only by mentioning Venus, the ill conse-quences of her delights. The basically Ovidian inspiration and clerical wit that many of these poems display also appears in the famous *De amore* of Andreas Capellanus.[28]

If love, which as St. Augustine said, "moves the pilgrim's feet" in the road of this life, was a popular subject in the schools, it was also a popular subject in vernacular literature. The troubadours explored its ramifications in crusading songs like those of William IX of Aquitaine, who was famous for entertaining his military followers in songs often reflecting Ovidian techniques, or Marcabru, who castigated noblemen for indulging in adul-terous affairs while their obligations demanded a struggle against the in-roads of the pagans, or Jaufré Rudel, who found the Blessed Virgin, of whom he spoke rather openly in amatory terms reminiscent of the Canticle, an inspiration to valor overseas. A kind of Ovidian wit even permeated the romances that were beginning to vie with the "feudal epics" in popularity.[29] As the cult of chivalry developed it became obvious that faith to one's overlord, an aspect of faith in God,[30] could not be maintained except by a tie of love, a tie that naturally extended in court circles to the overlord's wife and to the ladies of his court. As John of Salisbury said, discussing the need for love between the prince and his subjects, "That battle wedge that is bound by a tie of love is not easily broken."[31] But the greatest enemy of military effectiveness, he said, was luxury,[32] which leads to the weaknesses of lust.[33] Conventionally, the *militia Veneris* was the worst enemy of any form of that *militia* that is a part of every man's obligation, whether in chivalric enterprise or in the conduct of life.[34] Chrétien's Erec has to learn to subdue his venereal preoccupations before he can set out on his quest for wisdom, and in Chaucer's *Parliament* the speaker is taught by that model of valor and chastity Scipio Africanus[35] to link "brekers of the lawe" and "likerous folk."[36] The Blessed Virgin, the highest and most striking exemplar of chastity, now being adorned with

---

27.   E.g., see D. W. Robertson, Jr., *Essays in Medieval Culture* (Princeton, 1980), pp. 131-50.

28.   Cf. Robertson, *Preface*, Chapter V, and *Essays*, pp. 257-72.

29.   Cf. Robertson, *Essays*, pp. 173-201.

30.   See John of Salisbury, *Policraticus*, 6. 9, who argues that a man who cannot keep faith with God cannot keep faith with his overlord.

31.   *Ibid.*, 4. 3.

32.   *Ibid.*, 6. 11.

33.   *Ibid.*, 8. 6; cf. 8. 15.

34.   See Robertson, *Preface*, pp. 408-10.

35.   The hero of Petrarch's *Africa* was, like his Laura, noted for chastity and his dis-couragement of lechery in Massinissa.

36.   By Chaucer's time many schoolboys in England were reading a poem called *Cartula* (*PL*, 184, cols. 1307-14), recommending love for Christ and condemning worldly love, including prominently at the outset "the filth of carnal love." See Orme, *op. cit.*, pp. 104-5. Bishop Bradwardine's *Sermo Epinicius* delivered in 1346 to celebrate English victories against the Scots and French attributed the defeat of the French, among other things, to their "militia Veneris," calling them "milites Epicuri." See the edition of H. A. Oberman and J. A. Weisheipl, *Archives d'histoire doctrinale et littéraire du moyen age*, 33 (1958), 323-24.

increasing frequency with imagery from the Canticle, was especially venerated by St. Bernard.[37] She was celebrated in some of the most beautiful Latin sequences ever written, and she became increasingly an inspiration to chivalry and courtesy as well as an object of popular devotion.[38] Geoffrey of Monmouth's King Arthur, the model for English chivalric *pietas*, carried her image on his shield and called to her as he rode into battle, foreshadowing that later model of chivalric reform in a decadent "Arthurian" court, Sir Gawain in *Sir Gawain and the Green Knight*. Toward the close of the thirteenth century the last of the great troubadours, Giraut Riquier, addressed her in moving terms, and in his final song, "Be'm degra de chantar tener," he realized that through their pride and malice, "far from the commandments and love of our Lord," Christians had been cast out of God's Holy Place across the sea. The holy *militia* had failed because of "disordered will," so that Christians, raging at one another, should be driven into the earth. The song concludes with a prayer to Mary:

> Dona, Maires de caritat,
> acepta nos per pietat
> de ton filh, notra redeptor,
> gracia, perdon, et amor.

Notable men, still moved by what were then regarded as Christian ideals of military valor, turned to her in fourteenth-century England. Sir John Chandos, famous for valor and wisdom, wore a surcoat embroidered with her image; that image often adorned English swords and breastplates, and Garter Knights bore it on their right shoulders during Divine Service.[39] Visual testimony of the devotion of Richard II survives in the Wilton Diptych. The beauty and grace of the Virgin were widely heralded, and it was natural that Chaucer should surround another inspiration to chivalric conduct, Blanche of Lancaster, with her imagery,[40] having written, presumably, one of his earliest surviving poems, the "ABC," for her devotion to Mary. Later on, he would close his great poem shadowing the failure of English chivalric ideals with a prayer to the Trinity for defense against both visible and invisible foes and to Jesus for mercy.

> For love of mayde and moder thyn benigne!

This is no mere rhetorical flourish, no empty convention, but in the context of its time a powerful appeal for a redirected love that might free Chaucer's contemporaries from the attacks of "invisible enemies" of the kind that produced the "disordered will" of Giraut's Christian crusaders, and that brought Troilus (and Troy) to destruction. The success of enemies within invited attacks by visible enemies without.

---

37. See the attractive and useful volume, *Saint Bernard et Notre Dame*, edited by P. Bernard (Abbaye de Sept-fons, 1953).

38. See the reference in note 19, above.

39. Edmund Walerton, *Pietas Mariana Britannica* (London, 1879), pp. 41-46. I wish to thank my colleague Gail M. Gibson for calling my attention to this volume.

40. James I. Wimsatt, "The Apotheosis of Blanche in *The Book of the Duchess*," *JEGP*, 66 (1967), 26-44.

As European governments grew more complex and written documents multiplied in their administrations, there were new demands for
"practical" literacy among lay officials.[41] In England, the rise in the
number of such documents was especially impressive during the reign of
Henry II, who was himself notable for his love of learning.[42] M. T. Clanchy writes that "an educated layman in 1300 . . . like Henry de Bray was
probably familiar with some writing in three literary languages (Latin,
French, and English)."[43] John of Salisbury, following (but modifying) the
Institutio Traiani attributed to Plutarch, held that there are four things that
should be inculcated in rulers of commonwealths: "a reverence for God,
self-discipline, the learning of officials and those in power, the affection of
their subjects, and their protection."[44] The learning of officials, and this
means administrators of all degrees, was an important matter for John, who
thought that all learning had as its end the promotion of charity.[45] Among
officials, he thought avarice, an aspect of the love of the tangible, to be the
worst of vices,[46] and this idea was to become more important with the
passage of time and the increasing complexity of both secular and ecclesiastical administration. The "political" theory of the day (actually a
part of moral theory, as it had been in Aristotle's *Politics*) was based on the
assumption that the commonwealth was an integrated whole whose health
depended on the virtue of all of its members, including the prince. "If,
then, everyone were to labor in self-cultivation," John said, "and were to
regard external things as alien to him, the state of individuals and of the
whole would straightway become the best, virtue would flourish and reason
would rule, with mutual charity everywhere prevailing, so that the flesh
would be subjected to the spirit and the spirit would, in complete devotion,
become as a servant to God."[47] A new aggressiveness inspired by a love
for wealth gained by peaceful but underhand means was beginning to re-
place the aggressiveness of the sword, in spite of clerical attacks on it.

How were the literate able to learn "the laws of charity"? As Clanchy notes, "The sacred Scriptures, which had dominated literate culture
since before 1066, still stood in pride of place, of course, but they were
surrounded and overlaid from the twelfth century onwards by the glosses
and summaries of the schoolmen."[48] Among the summaries of the schoolmen the most important was the *Four Books of Sentences* of Peter the

---

41. See the stimulating and useful book by M. T. Clanchy, *From Memory to Written
Record* (Cambridge, Mass., 1979).
42. W. L. Warren, *Henry II* (London, 1973), p. 208. On documents, see Clanchy's
table, *op. cit.*, p. 44. Feeling that he lacked time to read all of St. Gregory's *Moralia*, Henry
had Peter of Blois compile a compendium on Job known as the *Gregorianum* (*PL*, 207, cols.
777-92), so that he could master it quickly.
43. *Op. cit.*, p. 86. For Henry de Bray, see *The Estate Book of Henry de Bray*, Cam-
den Third Series, 27 (1916).
44. *Policraticus*, 5. 3.
45. *Ibid.*, 7. 11.
46. *Ibid.*, 8. 5.
47. *Ibid.*, 6. 29. Cf. Aegidius Romanus, *De regimine principum*, 1. 2. 10 (Rome, 1607),
p. 72. This work was extremely popular in fourteenth-century England.
48. *Op. cit.*, p. 259.

Lombard, produced in Paris around the middle of the century. This was largely a series of selected quotations from the Fathers (and some of their notable successors) arranged in systematic fashion so as to form a work of easy reference suitable at the same time for systematic study. It remained, in fact, a basic theological textbook for many years and a standard introduction to the Scriptures. [49] Students of theology gained their reputations by lecturing on it and writing commentaries on it. It remains, with some few exceptions, the best source for standard doctrines during the later Middle Ages. Patristic opinions became available also in a variety of glosses. The most important of these, which often accompanied the scriptural text in the margins, was the *Ordinary Gloss*, now usually attributed to the "school" of Abelard's old enemy Anselm of Laon. [50] Lombard's *Commentaries on the Psalms of David* offered a verse by verse account of all the Psalms with quotations from Jerome, Augustine, Chrysostom, Cassiodorus, Alcuin, and Remigius of Auxerre. [51] More influential, however, was his great *Collection in All the Epistles of St. Paul*, [52] which contained "questions" of the kind used later in the *Sentences*. These two glosses together were called the *Major Glossatura* since they provided a much more thorough treatment than the *Ordinary Gloss*. There were other commentaries, treatises, and sermon collections that afforded materials useful to an understanding of the sacred text, not to mention sermons delivered in churches, and the writings of the Fathers themselves continued to be copied and made available in libraries. For the entire Middle Ages the standard introduction to what we should call the "method" of scriptural study was St. Augustine's *On Christian Doctrine*, supplemented at times by *On the Education of Clerics* by Rabanus Maurus, which often repeats whole passages from St. Augustine. The twelfth century produced another such guide, the *Didascalicon* of Hugh of St. Victor (who was often hailed as "the second Augustine") which became, like the works just mentioned, a standard school text. [53] For perspectives on scriptural history, the *Scholastic History* of Peter Comestor, also a standard text, is useful for commonplace historical opinions. The influence and popularity of *The Consolation of Philosophy* of Boethius (who was venerated as a saint), which had been adapted for English readers by King Alfred, continued to

---

49. In the Preface to his *Laws of Ecclesiastical Polity* Hooker observed that among the Reformed, Lombard had been replaced by Calvin as a standard reference, implying that the "unreformed" were still using him.

50. A partial version is available in *PL*, 113 and 114, cols. 9-752. Migne attributed it (falsely) to Walahfrid Strabo. This edition omits some books and often gives only the beginning and conclusion of a gloss available elsewhere in *PL*.

51. *PL*, 191, cols. 55-1296. The great *Ennarationes in Psalmos* of St. Augustine, however, retained its prestige, and was much admired by Boccaccio and Petrarch. Meanwhile, the commentary by St. Ambrose was often consulted.

52. *PL*, 191, cols. 1297-1696; 192, cols. 9-520.

53. Ed. C. H. Buttimer (Washington, 1939) and available in an annotated English translation by Jerome Taylor (New York, 1961).

grow, and a very influential commentary on it was provided by William of Conches, who had assisted in the education of King Henry II of England. [54]

Were laymen interested in works of this kind? Henry II was an avid reader, and other noblemen shared his enthusiasm for books. The Beaumont twins, Robert and Waleran (b. 1104), are said to have astonished Pope Calixtus and the Cardinals with their learning at the age of 15 during a conference at Gisors. In Britanny, Abelard, whose father, he says, had some knowledge of letters, encouraged his education; and he abandoned his inheritance for learning. Many younger sons of noblemen went to school, seeking clerical careers. Preachers like Robert of Arbrissel, St. Norbert, and St. Bernard were astonishingly popular. Not all noblemen could read and write Latin as Henry de Bray could, but even those who did not often had access to the new learning. Thus Baudoin of Guisnes, who was knighted by Thomas of Canterbury, was not a "mute auditor" of theological writings, but listened eagerly to readings in the Scriptures, demanding not only the literal but the spiritual sense. He enjoyed disputation with his clerks and had translations made, including one of the Canticle of Canticles, along with a gloss on the text. His library contained a variety of books, including the Life of St. Anthony, a work on physics, a work on the nature of things, books of noble deeds, songs, and fabliaux. [55] It is true, however, that his son preferred stories about Roland, Oliver, and King Arthur, and romances. [56] Generally, the literary abilities and tastes of noblemen in the twelfth century are difficult to assess, but modern historians may have been over-cynical about this matter. Clanchy, referring to the next century, observes somewhat acerbically that "by and large the knights of thirteenth-century England, and their families too, probably had a wider and deeper knowledge of language than those historians who have adopted a patronizing tone towards them because they were not highly literate." [57] Among vernacular writers in England we should include Marie de France, who probably belonged to a noble family and who indicates in the Prologue to her *Lais* that she could translate Latin. Her *Lais* were said, by a somewhat prejudiced contemporary observer, to have been especially popular among the ladies. They were undoubtedly designed to produce lively discussion and varied interpretation among the members of their audience, and they are, as might be expected, largely concerned with varieties of love.

---

54. *PL*, 198, cols. 1053-1722. All Chaucerians should, of course, have a firsthand familiarity with standard texts used in the schools during Chaucer's time if only to acquire an understanding of prevailing attitudes.

55. Lambert d'Ardres, *Chronicon* (Paris, 1855), pp. 173, 175. Baudoin was a vigorous man. After the death of his wife, Chrétienne, in 1177, he developed a taste for virgins, and there were said to have been 33 children at his funeral. Lambert, who was a priest, laments his lechery but does not call him either a "pagan" or a "courtly lover," either of which would have been an absurdity. Looking at the matter calmly, however, we can see that Baudoin did not have to be spectacularly lecherous to produce some twenty-odd children in twenty-odd years. Nor were lecherous inclinations confined to men. See the account of the Countess Yde de Boulogne, *ibid.*, 205, 207.

56. *Ibid.*, pp. 215, 217.

57. *Op. cit.*, p. 261.

IV. ALTISSIMUS DE TERRA CREAVIT MEDICINAM

Chaucer's *Canterbury Tales* concludes with a sermon on penance. Perhaps a brief glimpse of historical developments will assist our understanding of why this arrangement was appropriate. In the first place, it was widely held that the Old Law was a law of strict justice, but that the New Law fulfilled the Old with charity, so that under Christ the law of justice became a law of justice tempered with mercy, not to everyone, but to those who are repentant, or, to put it in another way, to men of good will. Thus St. Augustine said, "the mercy of God is never to be despaired of by men who truly repent." [58] How does one "truly repent"? It was clearly necessary for the Church to devote special attention to the penance of its members and to provide formal means for its expression. In the early Roman church confession was public, but in the Celtic church secret confession to a priest rather than public confession was customary, and "Penitentials," or long lists of sins and crimes, were compiled along with the penances to be administered for each. [59] When Theodore of Tarsus came to England, he decided to continue the Celtic system he found there, a decision that had profound repercussions throughout Western Christendom, for under his influence the custom of private confession spread throughout Europe. Penitentials, which emphasized penances to be imposed—and these were often severe—were not uniform, a fact that gave rise to complaints about injustices, so that some Frankish synods sought to abolish them. They continued to be used, however. In the early eleventh century Burchard of Worms produced a kind of standard Penitential, his famous *Corrector*, which was widely circulated and continued to be influential for many years. [60] This, like its predecessors, has little schematic organization and contains no account of general principles to be followed in questioning penitents and in estimating the gravity of their sins.

During the later eleventh century there developed an interest in the general theory of penance. Certain basic guidelines were set forth in a treatise *On True and False Penance* which seemed so reasonable and authoritative that it was attributed to St. Augustine, [61] and it is usually printed among the Appendices to his works in modern times. Principles from this text were incorporated in Lombard's *Four Books of Sentences*. In the early Middle Ages little differentiation was made between sacraments and sacramentals, but Lombard described a series of seven sacraments, all of which could be said to have been established by Christ, and penance was among them. A decisive impetus to the spread of the new doctrines con-

---

58. *Enchiridion*, 65.
59. For accounts of these works, see John T. McNeill and Helen M. Gamer, *Medieval Handbooks of Penance* (New York, 1938), pp. 25-50, and Adrian Morey, *Bartholomew of Exeter* (Cambridge, 1937), pp. 168-71.
60. This work is described at length in P. Fournier and G. Le Bras, *Histoire des collections canoniques* (Paris, 1931, 1932), I, 364-421.
61. For the importance of this work see Dom D. A. Wilmart, "Une opuscule sur la confession composée par Guy de Southwick vers la fin du XIe siècle," *Recherches de théologie ancienne et médiévale*, VII (1935), p. 339. Cf. Morey, *op. cit.*, p. 71.

cerning the sacraments and penance especially was provided by the decrees of the Fourth Lateran Council of 1215, as the reactions of local bishops clearly indicate.[62] The Profession of Faith at the opening of the Council endorsed, for the first time officially, the doctrine of transubstantiation, and the decree on penance demanded that everyone participate in Communion at least once a year.[63]

The decree itself is worth quoting:

> Every one of the faithful of either sex [utriusque sexus], after he arrives at the age of discretion [i.e., seven years], should confess all of his sins faithfully in private, to his own priest, at least once in the year, and should seek to fulfill the penance enjoined to him before men, receiving reverently at least at Easter the sacrament of the Eucharist, unless, indeed, on the advice of his own priest, for some rational cause, he should abstain from taking it at that time. Otherwise, if he is alive, he should be denied entrance in the church [i.e., suffer minor excommunication]; and if he is dead, he should be denied a Christian burial.[64]

Here the requirements for an annual participation in the Sacrament of the Altar and annual confession are combined, for it was thought participation in the former might be inefficacious, or even noxious, if the individual were in a state of sin. However, it was recognized that the proper administration of penance would require considerable skill on the part of priests, and the decree went on to urge that the priest be discreet and cautious "so that in the manner of a skilled consecrated physician, he may administer wine and oil to the wounds, diligently inquiring of the circumstances, both of the sinner and of the sin, by means of which inquiry he may prudently judge how he should counsel the sinner and what kind of remedy he should apply, using varied evidence in curing the sick."[65] If the decree were to be properly implemented, an enormous program of clerical and lay education would be necessary. With reference to the latter the Council had already recognized the need for more efficacious preaching, observing that "the food of the word of God is known to be most necessary" for the Christian people, "for even as the body is nourished by material food, so is the spirit nourished by spiritual food," so that bishops should appoint "preachers to assist them profitably in the office of preaching, men powerful in deed and word, who shall visit the people committed to them in their places . . . and edify them by word and example."[66] We may recognize in the distinction

---

62. E.g. in England, see David Wilkins, Conciliae Magnae Brittaniae et Hiberniae (London, 1737), I, 593, 650. For the Continent, see G.D. Mansi, Sacrorum Conciliorum . . . Collectio (Paris, 1903-27), 23, cols. 929-30, 1051, 1186-1203; 24, cols. 903-1056. Dates and attributions in Wilkins should be checked in C.R. Cheney, English Synodalia in the Thirteenth Century (London, 1941). English episcopal statutes offer many interesting insights into the life of the times.

63. For the Profession of Faith, see Hefele and Leclercq, op. cit., V, 1325. The decree on the Eucharist was echoed in episcopal statutes throughout the thirteenth century. One bishop, Peter Quivil of Exeter, urged his priests to explain the doctrine of Transubstantiation to laymen with exempla, reasoning, and miracles. See Wilkins, op. cit., II, 133.

64. Hefele and Leclercq, V, 1350.

65. Cf. Chaucer's Parson's Tale (ed. Robinson), lines 958-80. Cf. D.W. Robertson, Jr., "A Note on the Classical Origin of 'Circumstances' in the Medieval Confessional," SP, 43 (1946), 6-14.

66. Hefele and Leclercq, V, 1340.

between "material" and "spiritual" food a prevailing theme in *Piers Plowman*, and in the demand for preachers "powerful in deed and word" a foreshadowing of Chaucer's Parson. In England the most famous response to this demand was the decree of Archbishop Peckam (1281) specifying a series of sermons on seven topics that would assist parishioners in an understanding of their penitential obligations. Preachers were to explain the following subjects four times a year: (1) the fourteen articles of the faith, (2) the Commandments, (3) the two precepts of charity, (4) the seven Works of Mercy, (5) the seven capital sins and their progeny, (6) the seven virtues, (7) the seven Sacramental graces. They were to do this simply and clearly without any "fantastic elaboration." [67]

Generally the response to the Council was astonishing. Bishops both in England and on the Continent echoed it in their Constitutions, sometimes supplying manuals of instruction for their priests to enable them to become skilled physicians. [68] Meanwhile, the Council repeated a decree of the Third Lateran Council, which now acquired a new significance, that there should be a master in every Cathedral Church to teach grammar and other subjects to the local clergy and to "other poor scholars" free of charge, and that there should be a master of theology in every metropolitan church. [69] Insofar as the Eucharist is concerned, enthusiasm for its efficacy became widespread, leading eventually to the establishment of the Feast of Corpus Christi with its attendant processionals, sometimes under guild auspices, and to the cycles of mystery plays. [70] In addition, the necessity for confession to be complete and circumstantial stimulated the production of confessional manuals both in Latin and in the vernaculars. One such manual by the Lincolnshire scholar William de Montibus, written before the Council but resembling a miniature "Parson's Tale," became a standard school text in the fourteenth century. [71]

It had been customary to compose sermons for special social groups known as *sermones ad status*. Society was, as John of Salisbury insisted, an interrelated whole, somewhat like the human body, and its health depended on the proper functioning of all of its parts, or on the virtues of all of its members and, since society was hierarchical, on the fidelity of each member to his superiors and the charitable treatment of inferiors. Fidelity was ideally insured by love, for, as St. Augustine had said, Christ binds His Church (Christian society), which is His body, "which has many members performing diverse offices, in a bond of unity and charity." [72] To endanger this bond was to offend against "the laws of charity." The "diverse offices" exposed men to various temptations, some peculiar to each

---

67. Wilkins, II, 54.
68. See Cheney, *op. cit.*, pp. 40-43, and Robertson, *Essays*, pp. 116-25.
69. Hefele and Leclercq, V, 1341.
70. See most recently V. A. Kolve, *The Play Called Corpus Christi* (Stanford, 1966), esp. pp. 44-49.
71. See Orme, *English Schools*, pp. 103-4. The text is by the Lincolnshire scholar William de Montibus (d. 1213), *PL*, 207, cols. 1153-56.
72. *On Christian Doctrine*, 1. 16. 15.

office. The great Cardinal Jacques de Vitry preached special sermons to prelates, to priests in synods, to regulars, to scholars, to pilgrims and crusaders, to merchants, to farmers and craftsmen, to servants, to virgins, and to widows. [73] Similarly, in his manual for Dominican preachers, Humbert de Romans, fifth Master of the Order, presented his followers with materials for one hundred such sermons, ranging from *"ad omnes homines"* to *"ad mulieres meretrices."* [74] Manuals of confession were sometimes organized in the same way, suggesting that priests inquire of their penitents specifically concerning the obligations of each group. For example, of monks, whether they have observed the rule; of priests concerning simony, the proper expenditure of church funds, and the observance of the offices; of merchants concerning cupidity; of lords and their officers concerning unjust tallages; of burgesses concerning lying, guile, usury, pledges, barratry, and unjust weights and measures; of agricultural laborers concerning theft, tithes, the eradication of boundaries, encroachments on the lands of others, and of faithfully maintaining their works and services. [75] It is not often recognized by historians that oppressive lords, greedy merchants, and slothful peasants were alike violators of fidelity, and that confessors questioned them on these matters and required penances for them. However, surveys of the social order like that near the beginning of *Piers Plowman* or that in the General Prologue to *The Canterbury Tales* probably owed a great deal to the habit of thought engendered both by preachers and by confessors in their attention to specific social groups.

Humbert de Romans was, as indicated above, a Master of the Dominicans, and Archbishop Peckam was a Franciscan. The Friars, especially the Franciscans and Dominicans, helped enormously, both in their theoretical studies and in their pastoral work, to implement the decree of the Lateran Council. The Dominicans arrived in England first in 1221, establishing a convent at Oxford. Their numbers increased rapidly, and by the end of the century Blackfriars in London, with its great church two hundred and twenty feet long, was well established and had close connections with the royal court, which it retained throughout the next century. The Franciscans' great London church Greyfriars, even larger than Blackfriars, adorned with marble columns and a marble floor not entirely consistent with Franciscan ideals of poverty, did not arise until the next century, but meanwhile the order had established itself in towns throughout England. Bishop Grosseteste, who lectured to the Franciscans at Oxford, was impressed by their zeal, and they won the hearts of townsmen with their evangelical fervor and popular preaching, which often included the employment of songs. [76] They became active in such civic matters as the construction of waterworks for towns, and the wealthy who wished to reward

---

73. T. F. Crane, *The Exempla of Jacques de Vitry* (London, 1890), p. xxxix.
74. *Maxima bibliotheca veterum patrum* (Lyons, 1677), 25, pp. 456-67. Cf. Lecoy de la Marche, *La chaire française au moyen âge* (Paris, 1886), p. 341.
75. E.g., see Mansi, 24, col. 528; cf. cols. 987-88.
76. See David L. Jeffrey's study, *The Early English Lyric and Franciscan Spirituality* (Lincoln, Nebraska, 1975). On Franciscan literature generally, see John V. Fleming, *An Introduction to Franciscan Literature of the Middle Ages* (Chicago, 1977).

them often resorted to use of enfeoffments, stimulating the growth of that arrangement.[77] Their contribution to the style and content of the Middle English lyric can hardly be exaggerated, and they also exerted an influence on the development of the vernacular drama.[78] Unfortunately the Friars did not agree on basic doctrinal matters, and they quarreled among themselves. Meanwhile, under the leadership of William of St. Amour at Paris a controversy between the Friars on the one hand and the "secular" clergy on the other, sometimes aided by traditional regulars, raged in the universities and spread to popular literature, especially in the later fourteenth century when the Friars had become very influential, very numerous, and often seemingly more interested in their own wealth than in the souls of the people. They became rivals of the secular clergy rather than their supporters, and were accused of standing on street corners like so many Pardoners, preaching for monetary contributions, and of offering easy penances for money. These activities, it was alleged, diverted funds from parish priests and their churches.[79]

Although some Friars, like Nicholas Trivet, who wrote a very full commentary on *The Consolation of Philosophy*, had "humanistic" leanings, many persons regarded Friars as being "enemies of poetry," at least of the humanistic variety. Chaucer was influenced by the *Roman de la Rose*, which espoused the cause of William of St. Amour, and probably by Boccaccio, as well as by anti-fraternal preaching and writing in England, the latter well exemplified in the *Philobiblon* of Richard de Bury. And it is undoubtedly true that the Friars were subjected to the same kind of pressures and temptations in late medieval England that affected the population as a whole. Chaucer's tales of the Friar and the Summoner do not leave us much to choose from between the abuse of penance on the part of the Friars and the administration of canonical correction on the part on the secular hierarchy. It is true, nevertheless, that the *animus* against the Friars still echoes in the pages of Erasmus, St. Thomas More, and Rabelais. There are still faint echoes in Shakespeare.

The sermons delivered by the Friars in their hall churches, designed more for preaching than for liturgical ceremonies, were often enlivened by *exempla* or entertaining and instructive stories as well as by adaptations of popular songs or by lyrics composed for the purpose. Exemplary narratives or descriptions became common in popular sermons during the thirteenth century,[80] and in the fourteenth century the tendency toward increasingly specific and sometimes localized exemplification became a feature of both

---

77. J. H. Baker, *An Introduction to English Legal History* (London, 1971), p. 130, and A. W. B. Simpson, *An Introduction to the History of the Land Law* (Oxford, 1961), p. 164.

78. See David L. Jeffrey, "Franciscan Spirituality and the Rise of Early English Drama," *Mosaic*, 8 (1975), 17-46.

79. Another complaint involved the zeal of the Friars in the profitable business of burying the dead. See, for example, F. M. Powicke and C. R. Cheney, *Councils and Synods with Other Documents Relating to the English Church*, II, Part II (Oxford, 1964), pp. 1255-64.

80. For the history of the *exemplum* see the monumental study by J.-T. Welter, *L'exemplum dans la littérature religieuse et didactique du moyen âge* (Paris, 1927).

verbal and visual art, producing an impression of "realism," although *verisimilitude*, a term current at the time, would be a better word for it. [81] Jacques de Vitry had said that in addressing rustics the preacher should use such "corporal and palpable things" as they knew most frequently "by experience," since they are more moved by "external examples" than by profound doctrines. [82] Etienne de Bourbon, a Dominican, found them to be valuable, however, in addressing men of "all states." [83] As time passed the Friars became famous for their stories, although some of their opponents, like Wyclif, thought them to be more entertaining than edifying and objected to their use. In *The Canterbury Tales* Chaucer's characters frequently either grossly misinterpret the *exempla* they use or amusingly disregard their implications, creating a humorous effect that may reflect the inept use of stories among preachers, fraternal and otherwise. And the tales told by the less worthy of his pilgrims often cause them to comment inadvertently on themselves as they are described in the General Prologue. On the other hand, it is but a step from an elaborate *exemplum* to a Canterbury Tale, except that the Tale conceals its *sentence* under what Petrarch called a "veil" of fiction, instead of employing an elaborate moralization at the close. The technique of the "fabulous narrative" was by no means new in the fourteenth century, but Chaucer's heavy dependence on various kinds of exemplification was a feature of the general "style" of his time, and it allowed him opportunities for especially incisive satire. There is thus a sense in which the character of Chaucer's literary artistry owes something to the Lateran decree and its effects.

The more obvious literary consequences of the decree are not difficult to detect, especially in England. M. Dominica Legge, in her study of Anglo-Norman literature, wrote that it produced "a remarkable series of manuals, treatises, and encyclopedias of religious knowledge designed for the laity, or for the parish clergy who were to prepare them for confession," [84] adding that "all sorts of people wrote these books, from an archbishop and an earl to a chaplain and a friar." They include St. Edmund's *Merure de Seinte Eglise*, clearly influenced by the decrees of Bishop Richard Poore of Salisbury, who was among the first English bishops to respond to the recommendations of the Council in his own statutes. [85] The *Merure* survives in numerous Anglo-Norman, Latin, and English manuscripts, and it contains the lyric Carleton Brown called "Sunset on Calvary." [86] The manual of confession called the *Manuel des péchés* attributed to William of Wadington enjoyed a fairly substantial audience. Its English adaptation, Robert Mannyng's *Handlyng Synne* has become famous in modern times for its skillful use of *exempla*. A more popular

---

81.   Cf. Robertson, *Essays*, pp. 99, 222, 232.
82.   Crane, *op. cit.*, p. xlii.
83.   A. Lecoy de la Marche, *Anecdotes historiques d'Étienne de Bourbon* (Paris, 1877), p. 12.
84.   *Anglo-Norman Literature and its Background* (Oxford, 1963), p. 106.
85.   For Poore's interest in penitential material and a general discussion of the sources of his statutes and their influence, see Cheney, *English Synodalia*, Chapter III.
86.   *English Lyrics of the Thirteenth Century* (Oxford, 1933), no. 1, p. 1.

work was the *Lumere as lais* based on the *Elucidarium* of Honorius of Autun and the *Sentences* of Peter the Lombard, indicating once more an interest on the part of laymen in problems of doctrine. Grosseteste's *Chasteau d'Amour*, probably directed to a noble audience, is an indication of the same kind of interest. For other works in the same tradition, which extends into the next century, Legge's chapter "The Interdict and the Fourth Lateran Council" forms a useful guide. [87] The "earl" she mentions was Henry of Lancaster, father of Chaucer's Blanche, whose *Seyntz Medicines* describes his own penitential experience, and offers, at the same time, a remarkable illustration of the effects of the new penitential doctrines on a distinguished layman. There is, in fact, a close relationship between literature describing the need for penance and devotional literature, as W. A. Pantin has observed. [88] True penance was inspired by love, not by fear. Love for Christ and the Virgin and sympathy for their sufferings at the Crucifixion, portrayed in many English lyrics, was thus a very proper inspiration to contrition, the basis for true penance. Among thirteenth-century English works the *Ancrene Wisse*, which contained sections on Confession, Penance, and Love, including an account of the seven sins, became, as Geoffrey Shepherd said, a "manual of counsel" cherished by "many gifted Englishwomen and Englishmen of the last medieval centuries." [89] The spirituality of the twelfth century, as the *Merure* of St. Edmund also demonstrates, blended well with the new doctrines following the Lateran decree, and the latter undoubtedly contributed to the renewed interest in the former, which grew as the Middle Ages progressed toward the Renaissance. [90] The "medicine" of the new pastoral theology was thus in part a logical development of the doctrines of love that flourished in the twelfth century, and it helped to reinforce and preserve them.

V. NON VENI PACEM MITTERE, SED GLADIUM

During the thirteenth century the population of England, as of Europe generally, experienced rapid growth, possibly as a result of the increasing consumption of meat. [91] The vills of England and the manorial organizations associated with them (for vill and manor did not always coincide) became integrated into tightly knit communities whose social interests were supported by centers of two kinds, the local courts and the parish churches. Speaking generally, the courts were of three kinds: manorial courts representing the community of the manor; honor courts to which freemen had access in some areas; and the county court with its sub-

---

87. Legge, *op. cit.*, pp. 206-42.
88. *The English Church in the Fourteenth Century* (Cambridge, 1955), pp. 248-50.
89. *Ancrene Wisse: Parts Six and Seven* (Manchester, 1972), p. ix.
90. See Giles Constable, "The Popularity of Twelfth-Century Spiritual Writers in the Late Middle Ages," reprinted from *Renaissance Studies in Honor of Hans Baron* (Florence, 1971).
91. Vern Bullough and Cameron Campbell, "Female Longevity and Diet in the Middle Ages," *Speculum*, 55 (1980), 317-25.

sidiaries in the hundreds or on manors which enjoyed the "View of Frank-pledge." The towns had courts of various kinds of their own, differing somewhat from locality to locality. The county court represented the community of the shire, which was the *patria* of its inhabitants.[92] These were all social, and sometimes "political," as well as legal institutions. There were also less popular ecclesiastical courts administered by bishops, archdeacons, and rural deans.[93] But the local social center for all ranks of society was the parish church whose parson or vicar shared in the agricultural life of the community in rural areas and was closely associated with guilds and fraternities in the towns. He sponsored processionals (where he was not being superseded by the Friars), pilgrimages to local shrines and holy places, which often had the atmosphere of community "picnics," and the celebration of festivals, including the popular festivities on St. John's Eve ("Midsummer Night"), commemorating the passing of the Old Law, represented by "witches" or fairies, and the coming of the New, and on Maundy Thursday, all of which have left their literary traces in such works as Adam de la Halle's *Le jeu de la feuillée* and *The Tournament of Tottenham*. As some of the liturgical plays and many of the cyclic plays reveal, medieval religious festivities were not necessarily "solemn" in the modern sense, and we should not assume that the reverence for Christian attitudes implied a somnolently serious attitude. The Good Lord was to be served with joy.

In the countryside many agricultural families had occupied the same lands for generations. There was a close tie between families and the lands they tilled, and manorial communities depended for their welfare on close ties between lord or manorial steward and tenants acting to further their mutual interests.[94] As the population grew, the necessity for the full use of all economic resources, both physical and human, became evident. "Assarts," or newly cleared lands, expanded the arable areas, new towns or vills were established, and in the parish churches the new teachings concerning the sacraments brought even closer ties between a man and his church, and, consequently, between a man and his fellow communicants. Bishops appointed confessors, including Friars, to circulate in the parishes during Lent to hear confessions and to remind folk of the evils of transgressions against their neighbors or lapses in fidelity. The churches supplied the ideals that fostered mutual interest in communities and sought to deter self-aggrandizement at the expense of neighbors or of the community as a whole, assisted by manorial customs, royal laws enforced at the

---

92. For the community of the shire generally, see Helen M. Cam, *Liberties and Communities in Medieval England* (New York, 1963), pp. 245-47; and on county courts in the fourteenth century, see J. R. Madicott, "The County Community and the Making of Public Opinion in Fourteenth-Century England," *TRHS*, Fifth Series, 28 (1978), pp. 27-43.

93. See Jean Scammel, "The Rural Chapter in England from the Eleventh to the Fourteenth Century," *EHR*, 86 (1971), 1-21.

94. The community spirit of manorial life has often been commented on, especially on open field manors. See, for example, C. S. and C. S. Orwin, *The Open Fields*, 2nd ed. (Oxford, 1954), pp. 173-74, and, more recently, W. O. Ault, *Open Field Husbandry and the Village Community, TAPS*, New Series, 55.7 (1965), pp. 40-54.

"View," borough regulations, and guild regulations. In the towns merchants developed a keen sense of local "patriotism," a jocular and humorous but nevertheless sincere manifestation of which may indeed survive in *Havelok the Dane*, which is easily envisioned as entertainment for a festive gathering of fishmongers at Grimsby. Close ties developed between merchant guilds, or groups of prominent individual guilds, and town governments. Many guilds were outgrowths of parish fraternities when groups of persons engaged in the same trade attended the same parish church, and such fraternities or guilds sought to control the moral as well as the commercial behavior of their members, to settle differences among them, and to provide for aged and impoverished members. When a man looked from the fields toward a town or village, the steeples or towers of the churches that met his eye did not represent something separate from the ordinary conduct of his affairs, but an integral part of his community life. His ancestors and those of his friends, close relatives, and neighbors rested there. The fragmentation of modern life, demanding separate demeanors for different groups and occasions (multiple "personalities") was as yet unknown.

The fourteenth century witnessed a series of events that severely strained community relationships of all kinds. The disastrous crop failures of 1315-1322, accompanied by human and cattle disease, dampened the rise in population, led to spectacularly high prices for grain, and encouraged crime in the countryside. [95] The prevailing intellectual attitudes of the time suggested a need for penance and moral reform, and Archbishop Reynolds of Canterbury ordered the clergy to go barefoot on processionals carrying the Sacrament and the sacred relics, ringing bells and chanting the Litany, urging the people to atone for their sins, and to devote themselves to prayer, fasting, and the performance of good works. [96] The economy generally seems to have recovered fairly well from this disaster, or series of disasters, but royal taxation and the activities of voracious and unscrupulous purveyors and local commissioners of array (some of whom apparently outdid Shakespeare's Falstaff) during the early years of Edward III certainly represented a burden, especially on the poor, as a poem on the subject indicates:

Unquore plus greve a simple gent collectio lanarum,
Que vendre fet communement divicias earum. [97]

The poem goes on to complain about the scarcity of coinage, so acute that many were unable to sell their cloth, grain, pigs, or sheep. For one historian these things all represented a very serious situation, reaching a peak in the years 1336-1341, when many thought that the people would rebel. [98]

---

95. The situation has been studied by Ian Kershaw, "The Agrarian Crisis in England in 1315-22," in R. H. Hilton, *Peasants, Knights, and Heretics* (Cambridge, 1976), pp. 85-132.
96. *Ibid.*, p. 89.
97. Isabel S. T. Aspin, *Anglo-Norman Political Songs* (Oxford, 1963, rpr. N. Y., 1971), X. 5. 21-22. Cf. the Harley lyric "Ich herde men upon mold make muche mon."
98. J. R. Madicott, *The English Peasantry and the Demands of the Crown, 1294-1341*, Past and Present Supplement I (1975).

Another, however, has pointed out that although taxation was sometimes disastrous locally, the economy as a whole, as wool exports indicate, remained vigorous, and that the nation as a whole did not share the economic woes of the government. [99] Whatever we may conclude about this period, when the Exchequer "seal of the green wax" became an object with which to terrorize simple people, [100] and a sensitivity to taxation developed which was to hamper foreign policy and lead to "tyrannical" measures in the next reign, a disaster of devastating proportions struck the land in 1348-49, the Black Death, which, according to some estimates, wiped out between a third and a half of the population, although its effects were not uniform throughout the country. [101]

Chaucer was only a small boy in London when this happened, but he must have witnessed some of the devastation and panic and heard harrowing tales about it during his early youth, especially since plagues were recurrent, in 1354, 1361, 1369, and again in the seventies. In the countryside the "wrath of God" was felt keenly, inspiring a new interest in themes from *The Consolation of Philosophy* which began to appear with increasing frequency in wall paintings in parish churches, along with representations of St. Christopher, whose influence was thought to be helpful in protecting potential victims of the disease. Barbara Harvey observes that on manors "the family sense of association with a particular holding, which had been so marked a feature of rural society in the early Middle Ages, weakened; indeed, in some places it almost disappeared." [102] This effect was sometimes delayed until after the plague of 1361, or even later, so that Cecily Howell, examining inheritance customs in the Midlands, writes that "there was a sharp decline in hereditary continuity between 1350 and 1412." [103] As families disappeared, peasant holdings increased in size, and landlords seeking ready cash began to lease their demesne lands on a large scale and to substitute money rents for customary services on villein holdings generally. Naturally, these developments tended to encourage a new kind of landholder chiefly interested in making profits beyond his rent without regard for the maintenance of the land and its buildings, [104] but it also tended to increase productivity on the larger holdings that could be managed more

---

99.   A. R. Bridbury, "Before the Black Death," *EcHR*, Second Series, 30 (1977), 303-410.

100.   The green seal of the Exchequer was still a frightening object many years later, since its appearance on a document could be used to extort money from illiterate persons who recognized it but could not read. See the Wakefield play of the Last Judgment, ed. David Bevington, *Medieval Drama* (Boston, 1975), p. 647, lines 283-84, although the editor's note misconstrues the word *green*.

101.   On some manors the effects were not serious. See, for example, Judith A. Brent, "Alciston Manor in the Later Middle Ages," Sussex Archaeological Collections, 106 (1968), 89-102. Cf. Francis M. Page, *The Estates of Crowland Abbey* (Cambridge, 1934), pp. 120-25.

102.   *The Estates of Westminster Abbey in the Late Middle Ages* (Oxford, 1977), pp. 318-19.

103.   "Peasant Inheritance Customs in the Midlands, 1280-1700," in Jack Goody, Joan Thirsk, and E. P. Thompson, *Family and Inheritance* (Cambridge, 1976), p. 127.

104.   Cf. E. M. Holcrow, "The Decline of Demesne Farming on the Estates of Durham Cathedral Priory," *EcHR*, Second Series, 7 (1955), pp. 351-54.

efficiently. [105] However, the new situation weakened community ties. A new spirit of personal ambition, stimulated by rising wages as the demand for agricultural labor increased, developed throughout the realm. And plagues seem to have been followed by significant rises in crime, especially after 1361. [106]

A further decline is evident in the social functions of local courts. The shires, except in the north and the south where somewhat different procedures were followed, were divided into "hundreds," traditionally supervised by bailiffs under the sheriff or by manorial lords who held the "View of Frankpledge." The population was divided into groups called "tithings," originally groups of ten (although the numbers varied), including everyone reaching the age of 12 except women, members of the clergy, noblemen, and wealthy freeholders presumably under the jurisdiction of their lords. The members of these "tithings" under one or two "chief pledges" were responsible for one another's behavior, and the pledges insured their appearance at court, where minor offenses ("trespasses") were tried. The mobility of agricultural workers after the Black Death tended to disrupt the frankpledge system, injuring another form of mutual responsibility among neighbors, although some landlords continued to maintain it throughout the fifteenth century and a few even later. [107] The government, meanwhile, sought to control wages and prices in the Ordinance of Labourers of 1349 and the Statute of 1351. In 1352 the Keepers of the Peace were given power to enforce the Statute, and this function was later assumed by the Justices of the Peace. The activities of the Justices diminished the importance of the shire courts, but efforts to control wages and prices were not successful. An especially good harvest in 1375 brought agricultural prices down, but there was no corresponding decline in wages, a fact that stimulated parliamentary agitation. [108] A more determined effort to control wages may have been partly responsible for the Revolt of 1381.

The royal courts generally had been suffering from a failure to observe an ordinance of 1346 that stipulated that the royal justices execute the laws for rich and poor alike, that they should take no robes and fees from anyone except the King, and no gifts beyond food and drink of small value. In spite of it magnates frequently retained justices and sergeants on a regular basis, a fact that led to widespread discontent. The judicial process was being corrupted on a large scale, affecting not only justices of

---

105. Cf. Howell, *op. cit.*, p. 139. D. L. Farmer, "Grain Yields on the Winchester Manors in the Later Middle Ages," *EcHR*, Second Series, 30 (1977), 555-56, finds a substantial increase in productivity after 1381.

106. E.g., see J.A. Raftis, "An English Village After the Black Death," *Med. Stud.*, 29 (1967), 163-64. Cf. the same author's *Warboys* (Toronto, 1974), p. 220. The conditions described here were widespread. John Bellamy, *Crime and Public Order in the Later Middle Ages* (London and Toronto, 1973), p. 6, reports that "in 1362 there was a great clamour about the committing of felonies and trespasses and the excesses of officials." There were said to be congregations or warlike vagabonds in Staffordshire and many felons abroad in Devon. The chronicler Knighton reported a wave of theft in 1364.

107. See D. A. Crowley, "The Later History of Frankpledge," *BIHR*, 48 (1975), 1-15.

108. A. R. Bridbury, "The Black Death," *EcHR*, Second Series, 26 (1973), 584-85.

assize and jail delivery, but also justices of the peace and local sheriffs, not to mention the central courts themselves. Chaucer's Sergeant of the Law with his "fees and robes," and his extensive holdings in land held in fee simple, which were readily alienable, together with his companion the Franklin, who had been both a sheriff and a justice of the peace, with his own extensive lands and epicurean tastes, and capacity for offering lavish entertainment to influential men of the county, are vivid exemplifications of this corruption. The situation undoubtedly contributed to the unrest that burst forth in 1381, for the rebels displayed special *animus* against lawyers. [109] The connection between the corruption of justice and the revolt was pointed out at the Parliament of 1381 (November) by Sir Richard de Waldgrave, the speaker for the Commons, a distinguished Suffolk knight whose career is said to have resembled that of Chaucer's Knight. He had been associated with Joan of Kent, who was surrounded by men who showed a strong interest in reform, and served as a Knight of the Household and as a member of the Council. [110] It is quite likely that Chaucer knew him. He said in effect that maintenance and embracery were so common in the countryside that no justice could be done. [111]

To return for a moment to the manors of England, which functioned as the basis for the national economy, the disruption in local communities we have discussed was further aggravated by the development of industries that offered wages by the day and hence ready cash of a kind that could not be obtained on traditional holdings. Here local conditions determined what trades were most attractive. In Cornwall the proximity of agriculture and tin mining had been beneficial to both, creating a ready market for produce and maintaining a demand for land. [112] But this situation, assisted by the system of seven-year leases on the lands of the Duchy and the enlightened policies of the Black Prince and his council, was unique. As new trades developed elsewhere the effect was to cause agricultural workers to demand higher wages by the day for labor in the fields that could most readily be obtained from the new class of leaseholders with extensive holdings on manors. [113] At the same time, trade attracted many people away from the land. The cutlery trade at Thaxted in Essex offers a good example that has been studied in detail. [114] But the most rapidly developing industry was the

---

109. See J. R. Madicott, *Law and Lordship: Royal Justices and Retainers in Thirteenth and Fourteenth Century England*, Past and Present Supplement 4 (1978). Cf., on commissions of oyer and terminer, Richard W. Kaeuper, "Law and Order in Fourteenth-Century England: The Evidence of Special Commissions of Oyer and Terminer," *Speculum*, 54 (1979), 734-84. For the connection between judicial corruption and the Revolt, cf. Madicott, pp. 61-64.

110. See J. S. Roskell, *The Commons and their Speakers* (Manchester, 1965), p. 127.

111. Madicott, *Law and Lordship*, p. 64.

112. John Hatcher, "A Diversified Economy: Later Medieval Cornwall," *EcHR*, Second Series, 22 (1969), 208-27. See also the same author's detailed study, *Rural Economy and Society in the Duchy of Cornwall* (Cambridge, 1970).

113. See Elizabeth Chapin Furber, *Essex Sessions of the Peace, 1351, 1377-79*, Essex Archaeological Society, Occasional Publications, 3 (1953), p. 68.

114. Norah Ritchie, "Labour Conditions in Essex in the Reign of Richard II," in E. M. Carus-Wilson, *Essays in Economic History*, II (London, 1962), 91-111.

cloth industry, which spread to rural areas where convenient streams for fulling mills were readily available and where tradesmen would not be restricted by guild regulations. [115] The last factor is in itself a manifestation of the general tendency to seek to avoid community obligations for the sake of profit. Even persons in villein tenure who held fulling mills might become wealthy in an industry that relied heavily on cheap labor, mostly female, readily available in the countryside. It is not surprising that one of Chaucer's most spectacular characters who vehemently attacks accepted views of hierarchy and glorifies wealth should be a female clothier. At the same time, tradesmen in the towns, motivated by the growing general desire for money, were making what authorities both royal and civic regarded as outrageous profits, often by dubious means. [116]

The ecclesiastical hierarchy was not immune from the temptations that beset other members of society. As we have seen, the Friars were becoming wealthy, and in many instances greedy and unscrupulous, and archdeacons and their officials, never popular, were becoming more and more burdensome to their communities. The Black Death impoverished parishes and monastic communities and left many small chapels in the countryside without support. In her study of the church in Lincolnshire Dorothy Owens writes that "the rolls of the justices of the peace for 1360 and 1375 are full of accusations of theft and violence committed by chaplains." But such accusations were confined neither to Lincolnshire nor to those years. [117] Moreover, similar offenses were committed by other members of the hierarchy. Parsons were not all like Chaucer's Parson. Thus in 1372 the Parson of Rothwell with others stole crops of 5 acres valued at 5s. an acre at Cuxwold. Shortly thereafter Walter the Parson of Scoter harbored a female felon and raped her, extorted 6s. 8d. from a man, stole 20 pigs belonging to the Abbot of Peterborough, and 19 other pigs, and assaulted a man. In 1375 another Parson is said to have stolen a black bull belonging to the Master of the Temple. [118] In the same year the Parson of Witton in Norfolk is said to have raped a man's wife and stolen goods

---

115. This situation is discussed at length in an article on the Wife of Bath by the present author soon to appear.

116. To cite an illustrative example, one Henry Souter of a town in Lincolnshire is said to have bought all the shoes made by William Brid and his men for 5 ½d. a pair on 11 Oct. 1372 and then, on 28 March and later during the next year sold them for 8d. a pair "to the serious oppression of the people." See Rosemund Sillem, *Records of Some Sessions of the Peace in Lincolnshire, 1360-75*, Lincoln Record Society, 30 (1936), pp. 198-99.

117. *Church and Society in Medieval Lincolnshire* (Lincoln, 1971), p. 133. Cf. during the period 1355-59, E. G. Kimball, *Sessions of the Peace for Bedfordshire*, Bedfordshire Historical Record Society, 48 (1969), pp. 52, 55, 57, 57-8, 63; and the same author's *Rolls of the Gloucestershire Sessions of the Peace*, Transactions of the Bristol and Gloucestershire Archaeological Society, 62 (1942), pp. 65, 66, 72, 75, 78, 87, 115, 115-16, 117-118, 119, 122-23, 123, 124-25 (in which instance the chaplain broke into a man's house, raped his wife, and stole goods valued at 10s., but the Dean of Hawkesbury, having discovered this misdeed, extorted 26s. 8d. from him for adultery, for which he in turn was indicted, as he was in a later case of extortion), 130, 154. Chaplains seem to have especially enjoyed raping wives and stealing the husband's goods, sometimes, indeed, taking the wives with them also.

118. Rosemund Sillem, *op. cit.*, pp. 55, 205, 209.

worth 20s. [119] These are merely illustrative cases, and it would be possible to compile substantial lists of vicars and clerks accused of similar offenses. To judge from the peace rolls, ecclesiastical officials were often given to extortion. The extortionate practices of archdeacons and their officials were notorious, [120] but others were also accused of similar offenses. The Dean of Manly is said to have extorted £20 in the wapentake of Manly, and he excommunicated one Henry of Walsham, forcing him to pay £10 and later threatened to kill him. [121] The Registrar of the Bishop of Winchester was brought before the King's Bench for a series of extortions. [122] And Henry of Wakefield, Bishop of Worcester, whom Chaucer undoubtedly had known at court where he had been Keeper of the Wardrobe and later Treasurer of the Exchequer, was indicted, together with his suffragan, for extorting money for consecrating chapels and altars. [123] The same bishop was brought before the King's Bench for an especially unsavory double rape. He is said to have raped a young woman twice and subsequently raped her mother whom he abducted along with goods valued at 40s. [124] Monastic estates were subject to economic strains, relaxed discipline, and a dwindling population of monks. The necessity to glean as much profit as possible from their tenants naturally encouraged increasingly worldly concerns. [125] It is not surprising that the author of *Piers Plowman* should have envisioned the ecclesiastical hierarchy succumbing to the charms of Lady Meed or questioned the possibility of finding the true priesthood of God on earth, or that Wyclif should have doubted the rights of sinners in the hierarchy to spiritual dominion. But of more importance was the fact that the most cherished social center of English communities, the parish church, was suffering from moral decay. This does not mean that all parishes everywhere lacked good shepherds. It does mean that enough of their clergy were corrupt to give rise to uneasiness and a growing desire for reform.

After 1369 the "Sword of Castigation" was considerably assisted by the French and their allies, and the period between that date and the nineties was one of gloom and disillusionment, creating demands for reform. To put this in another way, the years of Chaucer's maturity during which he produced his major works were haunted by memories of former glories in an atmosphere of what appeared to be almost continuous deterioration. [126] Edward III had been spectacularly successful as a military

---

119.   Bertha Haven Putnam, *Proceedings before the Justices of the Peace in the Fourteenth and Fifteenth Centuries* (Ames Foundation, 1928), p. 120.
120.   E.g., see Margaret Aston, *Thomas Arundel* (Oxford, 1967), pp. 92-94.
121.   Kimball, *Lincolnshire*, II, Lincoln Record Society, 56 (1952), p. 157.
122.   G. O. Sayles, *Select Cases before the Court of the King's Bench*, VII (Selden Society, 1971), pp. 82-83.
123.   E. G. Kimball, *Some Warwickshire and Coventry Sessions of the Peace, 1377-97*, Dugdale Society, 16 (1939), pp. 105-6.
124.   Sayles, *Select Cases*, VII, 53-54.
125.   Chaucer's Monk well illustrates the prevalent weaknesses of monks in this respect, but this does not mean that he is "typical."
126.   It has been vigorously argued that the economic effects of the Black Death were ultimately beneficial and that the new spirit of enterprise was basically healthy. See, for ex-

leader, often compared with King Arthur, and the Order of the Garter had become the most prestigious chivalric center in the West. But after the Plague bereft Edward of his Queen in 1369 he began to spend more and more time on his estates, hunting and enjoying his unedifying relationship with Alice Perrers. A brief look at just some of the succeeding events in the period should help us to understand the general mood. There were disastrous floods in 1370, followed by a series of plagues. The French adopted a strategy of avoiding confrontation on the battlefield, so that Gaunt's march through France, from Calais to Bordeaux, although it represented a military feat of astonishing proportions and helped to demoralize the enemy, produced no famous victories to hearten the people at home. Overseas trade, especially the cloth trade, suffered a depression from which it did not recover until 1379. The Black Prince, who was the hope of English chivalry, died in 1376, and in that year the town of Southampton asked the government to take over its defenses. Edward III died in 1377, leaving a minor, Richard II, to assume the crown. The south coast was heavily attacked by the French, including the towns of Hastings, Rottingdean, Dartmouth, and Plymouth. Rye was burned, and the Scots attacked in the north. The city of London was hastily fortified. Meanwhile, the French were making headway in Gascony. In 1378 Gaunt unsuccessfully attacked St. Malo, returning home in disgrace. In the next year the expedition of John of Arundel, who is said to have abducted nuns as companions for his followers, was destroyed in a storm at sea. In 1380 Thomas of Woodstock unsuccessfully invaded France, Spaniards attacked the south coast, and Winchelsea was taken by the French. The unsuccessful efforts of the government to defend the south coast were probably a contributing factor to the unrest that broke forth in the "Peasants' Revolt" of the following year. As M.M. Postan has explained, the actual facts of the revolt do not support the traditional picture of a "working class revolt against oppression." [127] The moral outrage of John Gower probably represents a widespread reaction at court. In 1382 an earthquake rocked London (ominously) during the trial of Wyclif. In the following year the Bishop of Norwich launched his unsuccessful and misdirected crusade (probably reflected in the portrait of Chaucer's Squire). The court was torn by factionalism, and an unsuccessful attempt was made to kill Gaunt in a tournament in 1385 while a great French fleet was assembling to attack England. The threat of invasion created panic throughout the realm during the next year, and some lords, complaining about the decay of chivalry, threatened to depose the King.

The continuing influence of the Lateran decree was probably stimulated by the general decline in *mores* that accompanied social change in the

---

ample, F. R. H. Du Boulay, *An Age of Ambition: English Society in the Late Middle Ages* (London, 1970). But the actual process must have appalled contemporaries whose ideas of value were traditional and who had no means of rationalizing the kind of behavior that produced a new kind of wealth for individuals and at the same time denied financial support for chivalric action abroad.

127. M. M. Postan, *The Medieval Economy and Society* (Berkeley and Los Angeles, 1972), p. 153.

fourteenth century in England, as well as by natural disasters and setbacks overseas. The century produced numerous manuals for priests, religious instruction books for laymen, and devotional works, the last probably made more popular in part by disillusionment with the ecclesiastical hierarchy. There was at the same time, as Pantin indicates, a rise in lay literacy especially in the towns, providing a ready and often eager audience. [128] There were reform movements at court. Chaucer, who was probably associated closely with the Chamber, and clearly sympathetic with men like Sir Lewis Clifford, Sir John Clanvowe, and Sir Richard Sturry, all of whom were accused (falsely) of being "Lollards" because of their interest in reform, [129] read the revised version of his first great poem, Troilus, to a court audience at a time when "New Troy" seemed about to be invaded by its enemies. The fact that modern critics, swayed by attitudes stemming from the literary traditions of the late eighteenth century, should have turned this poem into a lament over the "tragic beauty of human love" or "courtly love" is one of the ironies of history. As the ending of the poem clearly indicates, and as the Boethian reflections throughout the poem, not to mention the structural use of the traditional three steps in the progress of sinful conduct, imply, [130] it is a clear warning against the substitution of self-indulgent passion for chivalric self-sacrifice of the kind that had been demanded ever since the ideals of chivalry were first developed in the twelfth century. English reverses during this period, as John Barnie tells us, "were explained as a punishment visited by God on the sins of his

---

128.   Op. cit., Chapters IX, X, XI. It is not difficult to detect the influence of the decree in works of a more "literary" character as well. If The Canterbury Tales closes with a sermon on penance, the B and C Texts of Piers Plowman conclude with the complaint that the Friars have "enchanted" the people and "plastered" them easily (or in C given them an opiate for their "wounds") so that they do not fear sin. That is, Chaucer reminds his audience of basic principles whereas Langland assumes a desire for the proper administration of the Sacrament. The latter also attributes the difficulty to the Friars, whereas Chaucer, although he attacks them on similar grounds in the General Prologue, finds similar kinds of corruption throughout the fabric of society, perhaps taking a fairer view. The works of the Pearl poet show somewhat less striking but nevertheless obvious traces of the same influence. That is, Pearl praises that "innocence" (or freedom from sin) that is restored through penance; Purity praises chastity, or the maintenance of proper love; Patience recommends patient obedience to authority (Cf. Chaucer's Clerk's Tale); and Sir Gawain not only celebrates the fortitude necessary to the militia Christi, but closes with a recommendation for penance (represented by the wearing of the girdle) when that fortitude is weakened through "cowardice and covetousness."

129.   Du Boulay observes in his essay "The Historical Chaucer" in Derek Brewer, Geoffrey Chaucer (London, 1974), p. 46, that "it remains possible that as a group they (the "Lollard Knights") showed in exaggerated form the sentiments felt by many orthodox contemporaries." K. B. McFarlane's argument for actual Lollardy in Lancastrian Kings and Lollard Knights (Oxford, 1972), Part II, seems to me, except in one instance, unconvincing. The interest in Crusading evinced by Clifford, Clanvoe, and Nevill, for example, is hardly consistent with literal Lollard views. And Clanvoe complains openly in his moral treatise that persons who refrain from worldliness are called "Lollards."

130.   Cf. Robertson, Preface, pp. 477. The pattern is adumbrated in Book I, which emphasizes the first step; the second step is exemplified in Book II, and the third, the abandonment of reason, in Book III. The whole procedure is decorated with the kind of wit that had characterized literate attacks on Venerian pursuits since the twelfth century.

people."[131] If Chaucer had read the poem modern readings have attributed to him he would have disgraced himself before his friends. At about this time Clifford began to show an interest in the Order of the Passion founded by Philippe de Mézières, who had been Chancellor to the great crusading leader Peter of Lusignan. Philippe attributed the decline of chivalry to pride, avarice, and luxury (whose tutelary spirit was Venus), reflecting a variation on the traditional three temptations that brought down Adam and that Christ overcame in the wilderness,[132] and hoped to unite the French and English in a new crusade against the Turks, strongly urging that Christians not fight among themselves. If Christians were to escape the sword of God's wrath a new *militia* was required, both against vices at home and against physical attacks on Christian territory. The idea was an old one, but the implications were new. Philippe had a very strong and genuine influence on both the French and English courts.[133] Chaucer's open admiration for one of his ambassadors, Oton de Grandson, is well known, and he made the fictional Knight of his *Tales* a participant in some of Peter of Lusignan's campaigns.[134] The principles of ordered social life laid down by John of Salisbury had by no means been forgotten. Philippe urged Charles VI to read the *Policraticus* as well as St. Augustine's *City of God*,[135] and when Sir Arnold Savage, who supervised the election in which Chaucer obtained his seat in Parliament and who served as executor for his friend Gower, addressed Parliament himself as speaker in 1401, he pointed out that the new king was indeed a rich man, as well as being a man of sense and humanity, for he had the greatest treasure that any king may have, "le coer de son poeple."[136]

To literate persons at court, of whom there were many during the time that Chaucer was writing *The Canterbury Tales*, it must have seemed that "charity and its most just laws" were being blatantly disregarded throughout the kingdom by individuals of all ranks, and that "the love of money" was disrupting communities, great and small. The inherited ideals of the past were being abandoned for the sake of personal gain, and the institutions they had brought forth were being systematically corrupted for money. And all this was happening while England was losing its holdings overseas and the frontiers of Christianity were being attacked by pagans. It was obvious that a new *militia* was required involving the patience, constancy, and fortitude necessary to face disaster with equanimity and to

---

131. *War in Medieval Society* (Ithaca, 1974), p. 103.
132. *Sentences*, 2. 21. 5.
133. See J. J. N. Palmer, *England, France, and Christendom* (London, 1972), pp. 186-91.
134. It has been alleged that the Knight is suspect because he fought under one of Peter's pagan allies, and this allegation has found its way into a popular school text. However, John of Salisbury insists that it does not matter if a Christian knight fights under a pagan, so long as he maintains his faith. See *Policraticus*, 6. 9. It is clear that Chaucer knew this work.
135. For a summary of Philippe's recommendations to the king, see G. W. Coopland, ed., *Philippe de Mézières, Le Songe du vieil pèlerin* (Cambridge, 1969), II, 18-20.
136. See Roskell, *op. cit.*, p. 362; *Rotuli parliamentorum*, III, 456a. Under "sense" and "humanity" the Speaker referred to the competence of Henry's ecclesiastical and lay associates.

maintain the coherence of English society. New lessons in love, like those afforded by *The Consolation of Philosophy*, seemed desirable to shift men's affections away from "sensible" goods toward those goods that are "eternal and spiritual." Boethius was a potent supporter of Augustinian ideals of responsibility and of freedom from that slavery of the spirit that subjects men to the whims of Fortune. Finally, if the wrath of God were to be appeased, the clear remedy was penance, and through it a new dedication to "the common profit." Chaucer had translated Boethius for his friends and patrons, and had written *Troilus*, further enforcing the contemporary relevance of Boethian ideas. In *The Canterbury Tales* he offered trenchant and amusing criticisms of the weaknesses of social groups, along with vivid reminders of the ideals that were being disregarded. He begins with the Knight's jocular portrayal of the evil effects of the concupiscible and irascible passions and the desirability of harmony with "the fair chain of love"; and he closes with a very salutary sermon on the practical means of achieving that harmony on the "way" to what Christians regarded as their "home," from which, as Boethius had reminded them, they can be exiled forever only by themselves. It is not the purpose of this essay to examine patristic and scriptural materials in the *Tales* specifically, but simply to suggest that Chaucer's narratives would have been impossible without the traditions of patristic and scriptural teachings as they were adapted and elaborated to meet the needs of medieval life. To understand Chaucer it is, I believe, important to discover as much as we can about those traditions, so that we can recognize them when Chaucer employs them; and, at the same time, to discover as much as we can about the actual lives of people living in his time, so that we can understand the relevant application of those traditions. Otherwise, we shall be in no position to account for his success nor to appreciate the craftsmanship he employed in saying what he wished to say vividly and effectively to his own audience.

II

The Bible and Chaucer's Text

Artistic Intention and Chaucer's Uses of Scriptural Allusion

CHAUNCEY WOOD
McMaster University

As even the most casual inspection of bibliographic materials will show, scholars writing on Chaucer have not often been concerned with Chaucer and Scripture. When they have been, their primary goal has usually been to identify a hitherto unnoticed specific biblical allusion, while their secondary goal has been to describe that allusion's significance in its literary context. Overviews of Chaucer's use of the Bible, such as Grace W. Landrum's 1924 article on Chaucer's use of the Vulgate, are relatively rare, and it is worth noting that there is no separate chapter on Chaucer and the Bible in Beryl Rowland's *Companion*, although some specific references are discussed under the rubric of imagery or are subsumed under the larger topics of the church and religion. [1] A slightly different kind of article is one like that of Professor Richard Hoffman, which takes a biblical reference noted without comment in Robinson's edition of the text, and demonstrates the significance and usefulness of the reference in understanding the text in which it is embedded. [2]

The result of this piecemeal approach is that we know a good deal more today than we did previously about what Chaucer used from the Bible, and for a pleasing number of instances we have had suggested an interpretation of how he used his specific allusions to Scripture. Several deficiencies remain. In this essay I want to call attention to how Chaucer's biblical allusions vary in kind. That is, some are paraphrases, some are

---

1. Grace W. Landrum, "Chaucer's Use of the Vulgate," *PMLA*, 39 (1924), 75-100; *Companion to Chaucer Studies*, ed. Beryl Rowland, rev. ed. (New York, 1979). Some typical articles on hitherto unnoticed biblical allusions are R. E. Kaske, "The Summoner's Garleek, Oynons, and eek Lekes," *MLN*, 74 (1959) with reference to Numbers 11: 5; the same author's "The *Canticum Canticorum* in the *Miller's Tale*," *SP*, 59 (1962), 479-500; U. C. Knoepflmacher, "Irony through Scriptural Allusion: A Note on Chaucer's Prioresse," *ChauR*, 4 (1970), 180-83, with reference to Matthew 23: 25-26. A Chaucerian use of Ecclesiasticus 38: 26-39 is interestingly analyzed in the closing paragraphs of an article mainly on a larger topic. See R. E. Kaske, "The Aube in Chaucer's *Troilus*," in *Chaucer Criticism: Volume II: Troilus and Criseyde and the Minor Poems*, ed. Richard J. Schoeck and Jerome Taylor (Notre Dame, Ind., 1961), 167-79.

2. "Two Notes on Chaucer's Arcite," *ELN*, 4 (1967), 172-75, with reference to Joshua 9: 21.

direct quotations with the biblical reference supplied, some are un-specified brief citations, some are misquotations, some are proper cita-tions in inappropriate contexts, and some appear to be deliberately dis-guised for artistic effect. Not surprisingly, I shall argue that Chaucer's ar-tistic intention varies with his several kinds of uses of biblical materials. Secondarily, I should like to examine what might be called covert or im-plicit non-specific biblical allusions, with a view to determining to what degree such elusive entities can legitimately be discussed. They are the biblical 'quarks' of humanistic scholarship.

Clearly, the place to start with such a survey is with the most explicit biblical reference in Chaucer in order to examine both its nature as a quota-tion of Scripture and the artistic use to which Chaucer puts it. When, at the beginning of the *Parson's Tale*, Chaucer introduces a quotation from Jeremiah, he labels it, quotes it, translates it, and glosses it:

> Jer. 6°. State super vias, et videte, et interrogate de viis antiquis que sit via bona, et ambulate in ea; et inuenietis refrigerium animabus vestris, etc.
>   Oure sweete Lord God of hevene, that no man wole perisse, but wole that we comen alle to the knoweleche of hym, and to the blisful lif that is perdurable, / amonesteth us by the prophete Jeremie, that seith in thys wyse: / Stondeth upon the weyes, and seeth and axeth of olde pathes (that is to seyn, of olde sentences) which is the goode wey, / and walketh in that wey, and ye shal fynde refresshynge for youre soules, etc. / Manye been the weyes es-pirituels that leden folk to oure Lord Jhesu Crist, and to the regne of glorie. / Of whiche weyes, ther is a ful noble wey and a ful convenable . . . and this wey is cleped Penitence . . . .[3]

The passage, and Chaucer's treatment of it, are worth some consideration; he is seldom as explicit as he is here. In the first place, this is one of the few biblical references in Chaucer's work that is labeled—if not by chapter and verse at least by chapter and book. Moreover, Chaucer adds to the prophet Jeremiah's recounting of the Lord's injunction to the residents of Jerusalem a clearly typological exegesis. That is, the Lord's exhortation to the Jerusalemites to return to the true path of worship becomes in Chaucer an invitation to consider various spiritual paths and to follow the sacramental way of Penitence. It is likely that Chaucer added all of this to whatever source or sources he used, but it does not really matter.[4] Artisti-cally we have here something he either invented or was willing to keep: a scriptural reference that is repeated for emphasis, interpreted for clarity, and referred for identification.

Chaucer's artistic goal in his citation of the sixth chapter of Jeremiah appears to be persuasion. One presumes that by citing an authority, by making clear what the authority is, by quoting the verse both in Latin and in English, and by supplying a typological gloss, Chaucer is interested in introducing the Parson's sermon on Penance with a single image of the

---

    3. The *Parson's Tale*, 1. 75, in *The Works of Geoffrey Chaucer* ed. F. N. Robinson (Boston, 1957). Subsequent quotations will be from this edition and will be cited in the text.
    4. As Landrum points out, it is assumed by scholars that the biblical quotations were taken by Chaucer from an unknown source. But what kind of source is an unknown source?

crossroads that both sums up all his pilgrimage imagery to this point, and opens the way for the penitential message that leads to the spiritual pilgrimage that both accompanies and supersedes the earthly one.[5] Had Chaucer used a vague reference, say to "Paul," or to "the apostle," or "the prophet," or "hooly writ," the effect would be very different, even if, in the case of one of those possibilities, the reader might in fact think of the same quotation from Jeremiah. By doing what he does, Chaucer has used an overt as opposed to a covert scriptural reference, one that is to a specific, singular verse rather than to a repeated idea or theme, and in all this he has been as explicit as possible.

He is not always so—because, one presumes, his artistic intentions are often different. For example, in another overt scriptural reference just a few lines earlier in the Prologue to the *Parson's Tale*, Chaucer has the Parson glance at an idea in passing, but although there is some specificity, the sources are in fact multiple.

> This Persoun answerde, al atones,
> "Thou getest fable noon ytoold for me;
> For Paul, that writeth unto Thymothee,
> Repreveth hem that weyven soothfastnesse,
> And tellen fables and swich wrecchednesse." (*Pars Prol*, 30-34)

Although the reference to Paul who writes to Timothy sounds specific enough, in fact there are three different occasions in Paul's two letters to Timothy in which he inveighs against fables.[6] Chaucer does not cite any of the three verses or even note that Paul writes to Timothy about fables more than once, because the scriptural reference is subsumed in a larger artistic strategy in which fables are contrasted with the Parson's own "myrie tale in prose." Thus in this case Chaucer's scriptural reference is once again overt, but not to just one passage, hence multiple rather than singular. Since it does not cite an actual text it is not very explicit. Both artistically and textually the reference to Paul on fables is subordinate.

Neither of these references to Scripture puts very much of a strain on the reader. The audience does not need to know the biblical verse or idea in question because the narrative either repeats the words or rehearses the idea. There are, however, many cases in which even overt biblical allusions demand some specific knowledge of the text in order for the sense of the allusion to be clear. For example, Professor D. W. Robertson has examined some of the Wife of Bath's quotations of Scripture and has shown that some of them are sufficiently wrenched from context as to constitute misquotations. To take just one example, the Wife argues that the Apostle Paul "bad oure housbondes for to love us weel" (*WBProl*, 161). While this is a fairly close rendering of Ephesians 5:25 ("Husbands, love your wives") as Robinson's notes point out, Robertson makes a good case that the reference applies equally well to Colossians 3:19 ("Husbands, love

---

5. On the artistic implication of the imagery see further Chauncey Wood, *Chaucer and the Country of the Stars* (Princeton, 1970), pp. 289-90.
6. 1 Tim. 1:4; 1 Tim. 4:7; 2 Tim. 4:4.

your wives") which is introduced by the important injunction to wives, "Wives, submit yourselves unto your own husbands." Since the Wife wishes to have mastery in marriage, it is probable that Chaucer had in mind the partial text of Colossians for her source. Thus the reader is supposed to realize that the Wife is not merely quoting Scripture but is, like the devil, quoting it for her own purposes.

The matter of partial or erroneous biblical quotation by Chaucer's characters is difficult to prove conclusively, since it is one of the many cases in which the critic is forced to argue that what the text says is not an authorial *lapsus mentis* (or *calami*) but an artistic device, and that in other cases what the text 'says' is the opposite of what it 'means.' Those who, like Robertson, have argued for this possibility, derive some support from a clear-cut case of this sort of biblical game-playing in *Piers Plowman*. In the third *Passus* of the B-Text, Mede the maid attempts to defend gift-giving in general—overlooking her own misuse of the practice in order to subvert—by citing Scripture. Solomon, she avers, writes in the book of Wisdom, "*Honorem adquiret qui dat munera.*" [7] Conscience grants that her Latin is accurate, but rebukes Mede for partial citation:

> Ac thow art like a lady · that redde a lessoun ones,
> Was *omnia probate* · and that plesed here herte,
> For that lyne was no lenger · atte leues ende.
> Hadde she loked that other half · and the leue torned,
> She shulde haue founden fele wordis · folwyng therafter,
> *Quod bonum est tenete* · treuthe that texte made! (11. 334-39)

Conscience then goes on to supply the other half of Mede's original text. While the giver of gifts acquires honor, the soul receiving them is under an obligation. Even though the Piers poet attributes the citation incorrectly to Wisdom rather than to Proverbs 22:9, the idea of partial quotation as a device to undercut the reliability of a literary character is very clearly illustrated here.

Chaucer's use of Jeremiah in the *Parson's Tale*, Paul's letters to Timothy in the Parson's Prologue, and the allusion to either Ephesians or Colossians in the Wife of Bath's Prologue may all be called overt and explicit, yet they function in very different ways. Some demand more of the reader, some less, not because of the degree of their obscurity, but rather because of the literary situation in which they are involved. In some ways, though, it is the biblical allusions without explicit reference that are most interesting to the critic. A good instance of this kind of biblical allusion is afforded by the Summoner's fondness for spicy foods:

> Wel loved he garleek, oynons, and eek lekes,
> And for to drynken strong wyn, reed as blood. (*Gen Prol*, 634-35)

As Professor Kaske noted, the Summoner's dietary preferences are not what earlier critics liked to call "individualizing touches," nor are they to be construed as evidence of the reportorial Chaucer—the poet who de-

---

7. *The Vision of William Concerning Piers the Plowman*, ed. Walter W. Skeat (Oxford, 1954), I, 98.

scribes life as he sees it in fourteenth-century England.[8] Rather, the garlic, onions, and leeks are among the foods mentioned in Numbers 11:5. Some of the Israelites who have left Egypt complain to Moses that the manna that has been provided for them is unsatisfactory; they miss the melons and cucumbers, the garlic, onions, and leeks of Egypt.

Chaucer's artistic employment of this image of backsliding Israelites is particularly interesting because of its dissimilarity from his overt biblical references. Not only is this allusion covert as opposed to overt, but it is sufficiently covert that it escaped detection in modern times for a very long while. As I have argued elsewhere, Chaucer may have been inspired to use this particular reference for purposes of characterization by a passage in John Gower's *Vox Clamantis*, in which a wordly prelate is described as preferring onions and leeks to manna.[9] By suppressing the reference to manna, Chaucer makes his biblical allusion less readily identifiable, but by adding garlic to Gower's onions and leeks he seems to be trying to give the reader enough material to make the allusion ultimately if not immediately identifiable. Had Chaucer had the same artistic intentions Gower had he probably would have used the same form of reference. Since manna did not exist as a fourteenth-century item of diet the reader knows immediately that Gower is alluding to the Bible. Chaucer's decision to suppress the reference to manna while adding the allusion to garlic suggests a different artistic goal. Chaucer is not hortatory in his description of the Summoner but rather iconographic. That is, he does not wish to *tell* us that the Summoner is depraved, but rather to *show* us. Whereas Gower supplied us with a recognizable biblical image and then immediately told us what it meant—"Such are the people the bosom of the Church now nourishes—people who seek after earthly vanities instead of things divine"—Chaucer stresses the image and leaves the meaning implicit.[10] By passing over the manna and complementing the Summoner's diet of garlic, onions and leeks with a beverage of strong red wine, Chaucer simultaneously gives us an illusion of reality while nevertheless supplying us with images that have meaning—in this case biblical meaning. Since both John Gower and Peter Riga use the contrast between leeks and onions on the one hand and manna on the other, the modern reader can assume that in Chaucer's day Numbers 11:5 was an easily recognizable text. What Chaucer does is to disguise it slightly in order to permit it to fit in naturally with the other details of the portrait: the garland on the Summoner's head, his buckler of a cake, the whelks on his cheeks, his ignorant use of Latin tags.

While not nearly so covert as the allusion to Numbers 11:5 just examined, the glance at Luke 7:32 in the Prologue to the *Reeve's Tale* is another covert biblical allusion that needs more and better explanation than

8. *Op. cit.*, note 1.

9. "The Sources of Chaucer's Summoner's 'Garleek, Oynons, and eek Lekes,'" *ChauR*, 5 (1971), 240-44.

10. *The Major Latin Works of John Gower*, trans. Eric W. Stockton (Seattle, Wash., 1962), p. 119.

it has received. The Summoner's dietary preferences were identified and put into a correct biblical context by Kaske, who attempted to investigate further Chaucer's particular artistic use of the allusion. The occurrence of Luke 7:32, however, has been identified but wrenched from its biblical context, and thus far no attempt to examine Chaucer's use of the allusion has been made. The Reeve, we remember, is angry about the Miller's references to carpenters and grumbles that he could tell a bawdy tale too, if it suited him, but he is old and does not wish to indulge in such games. He then discourses on the more unattractive aspects of old age, into which Chaucer weaves a glancing reference to the idea of dancing to the world's tune from Luke:

> But ik am oold, me list not pley for age;
> Gras tyme is doon, my fodder is now forage;
> This white top writeth myne olde yeris;
> Myne herte is also mowled as myne heris,
> But if I fare as dooth an open-ers,—
> That ilke fruyt is ever lenger the wers,
> Til it be roten in mullok or in stree.
> We olde men, I drede, so far we:
> Til we be roten kan we nat be rype;
> We hoppen alwey whil the world wol pype.
> For in oure wyl ther stiketh evere a nayl,
> To have an hoor heed and a grene tayl,
> As hath a leek; for thogh oure myght be goon,
> Oure wyl desireth folie evere in oon.
> For whan we may nat doon, than wol we speke;
> Yet in oure asshen olde is fyr yreke. (3867-82)

As far as one can tell, Grace W. Landrum in her 1924 article mentioned above was the first to note this allusion, but her goal was to collect evidence that Chaucer knew the Bible firsthand, so she merely notes that it is a reference to "Christ's beautiful simile of the children in the market-place . . . ."[11] The first task, therefore, is to place the allusion in its biblical context. This is not easy, because the text is difficult to understand. In Luke 7 (the story and parable also occur in Matthew 11), Christ is commenting on the present generation, which has rejected both John the Baptist and himself. He asks, rhetorically, what the present generation should be compared with, and responds with a parable:

> They are like unto children sitting in the marketplace, and calling one to another,
> and saying, We have piped unto you, and ye have not danced; we have mourned
> to you, and ye have not wept.

To most modern readers, it would seem that the men of the present generation are better compared with the children who do not respond than with the children who pipe and weep. Recently, however, Olof Linton has brilliantly argued that the correct reading of the text has to do with John the Baptist's call for penitential fasting and Christ's call to his wedding feast. Both of these invitations break with Judaic tradition, wherein the precise times for fasting and rejoicing are spelled out. Thus the pharisees, the men

---

11. Landrum, p. 96.

of this generation who deny John and Jesus, are like children playing at games of dancing (at a wedding) or mourning (at a funeral) who ask John and Jesus to join in to play at their time and place. When they do not, the peevish "children" say that John has a devil and Christ is a glutton (Luke 7: 33-34). [12]

It is doubtful that our medieval ancestors interpreted the passage this way. In the *Glossa ordinaria* we find the children who pipe and weep styled as humble doctors whose exhortations to those who abandon the law are scorned. Thus the "other children" are those whose hearts are not raised up to God, indicated by the dance, and who are not converted to penance by the lamentations of the prophets. [13] In this sense, then, it is better to listen to the children who call out than not to listen to them. Well, the Reeve seems to listen, for he notes that he is an old man who will hop when the world pipes. The echo of Luke 7 or Matthew 11 would probably be noticed by a medieval audience, but if noticed, surely the differences in both form and meaning would have been noticed as well. For with the Reeve's citation it is not children who pipe to other children, but the world which pipes to an old man. His willingness to dance to the world's tune does not sound like someone willing to listen to a call to raise one's heart to God or to be penitent, but sounds very much like a willingness to join in the dance of the flesh—the "olde daunce" (*Gen Prol*, 476) so well known by that other carnal oldster on the pilgrimage, the Wife of Bath.

Viewed in this light, the Reeve's enthusiasm for carnality even when his potency is fading makes him an embodiment of Paul's old man of the flesh who is contrasted with the new man of the spirit (Ephesians 4: 22-24). Unlike Paul himself, who willed to do the good and failed (Romans 7: 18 ff.), the Reeve wills himself to be like a leek but his tail as well as his head remains white. The whole passage bristles with vaguely biblical or patristic echoes. The Reeve's grass time is done, and we remember that flesh is grass (Is. 40: 6; 1 Peter 1:24). The Reeve compares his aging rottenness to the ripening of the open-ers or medlar pear, and we are reminded of the pear as symbol of the flesh in St. Augustine's *Confessions*, in the medieval French *Romance of the Pear*, as the goal of lusty May's appetites in the *Merchant's Tale*, and in numerous other contexts. The leek itself, the unattainable goal of the Reeve's aspirations, is one of the foods already discussed as characteristic of the yearning for the fleshpots of Egypt. Remarkably, for all its superficial immediacy and "Englishness," the passage as a whole owes a great deal to religious and biblical sources. What Chaucer has done in this covert reference to Luke 7 is to wrench the idea with sufficient forcefulness to arrest our attention. The image of dancing while the world pipes is not there, as Grace Landrum seems to have thought, to add a touch of beauty, but rather to make us think.

---

12. "The Parable of the Children's Game," *New Testament Studies*, 22 (1975-76), 159-79.
13. *Patrologia Latina*, 114, cols. 121, 271. Much the same sense is to be found elsewhere. See, for example, Hilary of Poitiers, *Sur Matthieu*, ed. Jean Doignon (Paris, 1978), 262-65.

Thus far we have concerned ourselves only with Chaucerian allusions to specific biblical verses, whether to one or several similar verses. We should not, though, overlook Chaucer's references to biblical stories—stories which are sometimes developed over several verses or which have versions in different biblical books. Noah's Flood is a good example of this kind of allusion. The flood is hypocritically promised in the *Miller's Tale*, by the self-serving clerk Nicholas, and the gullible carpenter John foolishly believes it will arrive. Because of the irony of a story about a false Noah's Flood being told on April 17—the traditional date of the biblical flood—Chaucer uses the absence of water rather than the excess of it to punish the characters in the tale. The squeamish Absolon, himself modeled on a biblical character noted for pride, places his misdirected kiss and is forced to rub his mouth "with sond, with straw, with clooth, with chippes" (*MillT*, 3748), for there seems to be no water; Nicholas, who is burned, as it were in the seat of his passions, cries out vainly "Help! water! water! help, for Goddes herte!" (*MillT*, 3815), and hearing the call for water old John cuts the rope holding his tub near the ceiling, and falls and breaks his arm on the dry floor below. [14] It is worth noting that while the story of the flood is used in the *Miller's Tale*, the significance of it is explained in the *Parson's Tale*. Because it is said openly in the latter place that the flood was sent to punish the sin of lechery, (*ParsT*, 839), Chaucer's artistic use of the story in his ribald *Miller's Tale* is easier to understand. Whereas the flood would be thought by most modern readers to have been sent down to punish sin in general, our medieval ancestors thought of the flood as having been sent to punish the very sin that is so rampant in the *Miller's Tale*. John wants Alison, Nicholas wants Alison, and Absolon wants Alison. Alison herself seems happy enough to accept the embraces of her husband and Nicholas, and her lack of interest in Absolon is perhaps the only instance of a lack of lecherous instinct in the entire tale. Thus with the false promise of a flood on the anniversary of the actual one, both a biblical story and its meaning are played upon for several kinds of ironic literary effect.

If the story of Noah's Flood is an illustration of a biblical allusion that is overt rather than covert, specific rather than general, it nevertheless is best understood when we interpret its appearance in the *Miller's Tale* in light of what we learn about its significance in the *Parson's Tale*. The question then arises: what can we say about presumably covert allusions that are overt elsewhere? For example, the biblical flood is overt in two tales, but I have argued elsewhere that the April opening of *The Canterbury Tales*, with its emphasis on vernal showers and rebirth, may well contain a covert allusion to the biblical story. [15] If the allusion is indeed there, it is so completely covert that it might better be called tacit, implicit, or concealed. It may be that in "finding" such things we are reading into Chaucer's text something that he did not put there. However, when we consider the range and flexibility of his overt and covert allusions, it does not seem far-fetched

14. See further *Chaucer and the Country of the Stars*, pp. 161-72.
15. *Ibid*.

to argue that an idea could be worked into his text as well as a verse of Scripture. If Chaucer felt, like Boccaccio, that one of the pleasures of poetry was the intellectual effort occasioned by the search for meaning, then his covert glances at Scripture are more understandable aesthetically, and there is an implicit case for believing in implicit, tacit, or concealed biblical allusions. [16] If we think we have found them, and if they have remained undiscovered for a number of years, that does not necessarily mean that we have found something not really there; it could as well mean we have found something that was deliberately well-concealed because of medieval ideas about poetry.

A case in point is Chaucer's probable multiple allusions to Zechariah 9: 9-10, which have been very intelligently developed by Rodney K. Delasanta. [17] The prophecy of Zechariah, that the King of Jerusalem would come to the city riding upon an ass, is quoted by Chaucer's Parson as part of an exhortation against pride (*ParsT*, 432-35). Thus in the *Parson's Tale* the allusion is overt and specific, yet Delasanta uses the biblical passage and its New Testament counterparts describing Palm Sunday in order to illuminate the significance of the various horses in the General Prologue, where no specific biblical allusion, overt or covert, can be specifically identified. Delasanta's article has been in print for a dozen years now, and no one has been sufficiently outraged by its assumptions to venture a contradiction in print. The case is a good one: Chaucer knew and used the passage from Zechariah in one place, and his audience knew Zechariah's prophecy or its fulfillment in the New Testament, for there is ample sermon literature about the horse and rider generally; therefore it is a probable assumption that Chaucer's numerous uses of horses in his descriptions of his pilgrims were neither journalistic nor accidental, but were implicitly based on some biblical texts that help us to judge as well as to visualize the pilgrims.

From this, it is an easy enough step to what I have called a biblical quark: the biblical allusion to a verse or story that is not named where it is used, not named elsewhere in Chaucer, not quoted or misquoted, but which nevertheless when called to our attention transforms the literary text by a kind of catalytic magic and adds spiritual meaning to what seems at first reading only physical description. Like the quark of modern physics, it is a hypothetical elemental particle with a certain charge. Once again, we must assume that Chaucer's literary goal with this sort of heavily veiled or deeply submerged allusion is to exercise one part of our minds while simultaneously entertaining another. An excellent example of this kind of allusion is afforded by Grace Landrum's comment many years ago that the diet of two characters in Chaucer could best be explained by an unnamed, un-

---

16. "Surely no one can believe that poets invidiously veil the truth with fiction, either to deprive the reader of the hidden sense, or to appear more clever; but rather to make truths which would otherwise cheapen by exposure the object of strong intellectual effort and various interpretation, that in ultimate discovery they shall be more precious" (*Boccaccio on Poetry*, trans. Charles G. Osgood [New York, 1956], p. 60).

17. "The Horsemen of the *Canterbury Tales*," *ChauR*, 3 (1968), 29-36.

mentioned biblical text. When the Friar in the *Summoner's Tale* says that "I am a man of litel sustenaunce;/ My spirit hath his fostryng in the Bible" (*SumT*, 1844-45), the text is given proper dimension when read in light of Matthew 4: 4, "Man shall not live by bread alone, but by every word that proceedeth out of the mouth of God." [18] The same biblical passage, she suggests, also explains the peculiar "gap in thought" in the General Prologue between the description of the Physician's diet and his reading habits:

> Of his diete mesurable was he,
> For it was of no superfluitee,
> But of greet norissyng and digestible.
> His studie was but litel on the Bible. (*Gen Prol* 435-38) [19]

Matthew 4: 4 is not mentioned here nor anywhere else in Chaucer's works, yet the submerged, hypothetical allusion is potentially as helpful as the physicist's quark in that it can explain something that might otherwise not make much sense. The sense of the two passages, though, is perhaps not precisely what Professor Landrum has suggested.

The heavy and multiple ironies in the Friar's claim that he is a man whose spirit is nourished by the Bible are best understood in the context of the scene in which he makes his claim. Having called upon Thomas and his wife, the Friar is asked if he wishes to dine. He says that he would have what might be nowadays called an elegant sufficiency if only a few odds and ends were set out for him, and adds that his body is so habituated to sleeplessness that his appetite has been destroyed, which is the complement of his claim that his spirit is nevertheless well nourished by his biblical reading. While the Friar is making these claims, however, there is an undercurrent in the text flowing in an opposite direction. The bits and pieces he says would suffice turn out to include a sliver of the soft, i.e., fine bread, the liver, i.e., one of the choicest parts of a capon, and the entire head of a roast pig—scarcely a tidbit.

> "Now dame," quod he, "now *je vous dy sanz doute*,
> Have I nat of a capon but the lyvere,
> And of youre softe breed nat but a shyvere,
> And after that a rosted pigges heed—
> But that I nolde no beest for me were deed—
> Thanne hadde I with yow hoomly suffisaunce.
> I am a man of litel sustenaunce;
> My spirit hath his fostryng in the Bible.
> The body is ay so redy and penyble
> To wake, that my stomak is destroyed." (*SumT*, 1838-47)

The Friar's claim to be a man of little sustenance is given the lie by his request for capon liver and a roasted pig's head, while his claim that his spirit is nourished by the Bible is given the lie by his blatant rejection of

---

18. It is interesting to note that Robinson's edition ignores Landrum's very apposite citation and mentions only John 4: 34 ("My meat is to do the will of him that sent me, and to finish his work"), and Job 23: 12 ("I have esteemed the words of his mouth more than any necessary food"), both advanced by Skeat long ago.

19. No scriptural allusion is mentioned in Robinson's notes.

Luke 10: 3-9, in which the Apostles, the supposed spiritual forerunners of the Friars, were enjoined to eat and drink only what was offered them rather than what they might choose. [20] And, of course, his hypocritical claim to be fostered or nourished in spirit by the Bible not only brings to mind the overlooked prescriptions of Luke 10, but also Christ's reminder in Matthew 4: 4 that man does not live by bread alone. Professor Landrum's contention that the Friar discourses "delightfully" on the "contrast" between his "easy satisfaction in such food as capons and roasted pig and his zest for spiritual nourishment" takes him too much at face value. He has, in fact, no real zest for spiritual nourishment at all, so the issue is a different kind of contrast from what Landrum imagines. With some biblical passages in mind, it is easy enough to see not only that the Friar is not a man of little sustenance as he claims, but also that his claim to be spiritually nourished by the Bible is also false. The contrast, then, is not so much between the zest for both physical and spiritual food as it is between what is said and what should be understood.

Matthew 4: 4 on mankind's different diets is scarcely the only biblical passage on the subject. I Corinthians 6: 13 says that meats are for the belly and the belly for meats, but God will destroy both; Romans 14: 17 says very similarly to Matthew 4: 4 that the kingdom of God is not meat and drink but righteousness and peace; the Sermon on the Mount abjures Christians to take no heed of food or drink, for life is more than meat (Matthew 6: 25); while Mark 6: 8, like the instructions in Luke already discussed, commands the apostles not to carry bread with them. The direction of all of these—and more passages could be adduced—is clear enough. Even though Chaucer does not quote any of these texts in the *Tales*, nevertheless it is hard to imagine that a medieval audience would not have thought these texts somehow to be implicit in Chaucer's descriptions of people's diets, just as biblical remarks about horses are implicit in his descriptions of a wide variety of appropriate and inappropriate steeds, jades, mares, and so forth. Thus in Chaucer's descriptions of his regular clergy as overweight, there is not only an irony in that all are breaking their vows about diet, but a further irony in that all are ignoring biblical injunctions about spiritual nourishment while concentrating on the flesh. The Prioress has enough roast meat and fine bread to give the leftovers to her dogs, the Monk is fat himself and favors a fat swan for his meals, the Friar frequents taverns and knows the sellers of victuals, while in contrast the Clerk, who does not live under a rule, is nevertheless so thin as to arouse the narrator to comment "he nas nat right fat, I undertake,/ But looked holwe, and therto sobrely" (*Gen Prol*, 288-89). Just as Christ coupled food with raiment in the Sermon on the Mount and urged his followers to pay no heed to either, Chaucer follows his description of the Clerk's emaciated frame with a reference to his threadbare cloak. When Chaucer describes his Parson as being able "in litel thyng to have suffisaunce" while at the

---

20. On Chaucer's uses of antifraternal commonplaces see Arnold Williams, "Chaucer and the Friars," *Speculum*, 28 (1953), 499-513, and John V. Fleming, "The Antifraternalism of the *Summoner's Tale*," *JEGP*, 65 (1966), 688-700.

same time being "riche . . . of hooly thoght and werk" (*Gen Prol*, 490; 479), that there are therein echoes of numerous passages from the New Testament is difficult to deny.

Chaucer's artistic goal in using details in his narrative that are ultimately, if not immediately, biblically derived, is surely to combine instruction with delight in Horatian fashion, adapted for a medieval Christian audience. It is quite far removed both in form and in intention from his overt, formal, rhetorical use of Jeremiah in the *Parson's Tale*. But even allowing for differences, surely we must grant that the biblical quarks exist as truly as the biblical passages for which Chaucer gives us chapter and verse, for without them the text is sometimes left senseless. As Grace Landrum long ago pointed out, the bizarre rhyme of "Bible" with "digestible" in Chaucer's description of the Physician cries out for an explanation, and that explanation can be obtained from Matthew 4: 4. Artistically, though, there is more than just a "gap in thought" between the two lines as Professor Landrum suggested. We must remember that unlike the swan-eating Monk or the Franklin in whose house it snowed meat and drink, the Physician is cautious about his diet, which is nourishing, digestible, and "of no superfluitee." Thus in physical or medical terms it is in fact a good diet, and it is only the recollection of biblical verses about diet that explain how a proper diet can nevertheless be a concomitant of insufficient biblical study. The Physician is not a glutton, but in his concentration on "phisik and surgerye" (*Gen Prol*, 413), his reading of medical texts, his fondness for gold and taffeta-lined garments, he has forgotten that whatever the propriety of his diet for his belly, God will destroy both. In his concern to prolong life, he has forgotten how properly to live it. Man cannot, after all, live by bread alone, but must be nourished "by every word that proceedeth out of the mouth of God." And the place to find the word of God is in the Physician's neglected Bible. By confining his diet so that it did not contain any superfluity the Physician—probably unknowingly—rejected Christ's injunction to take no thought for what we eat or drink, for as St. Augustine commented, food and drink can cause the heart to be divided "even when nothing superfluous is sought after . . . ."[21] In the wide range of Chaucer's uses of biblical allusions the references that cannot be "found" but must be adduced can serve to illuminate Chaucer's text as surely as a glossed text.

---

21. *Commentary on the Lord's Sermon on the Mount...*, trans. Denis J. Kavanaugh, O.S.A. (New York, 1951), p. 157.

Biblical Parody:
Chaucer's 'Distortions' of Scripture

EDMUND REISS
Duke University

We have seen that quotations from and allusions to the Bible fill Chaucer's writings, and sometimes in such a way that the biblical text takes its revenge on those of Chaucer's characters who misuse it. It is possible to develop this point, suggested by John Alford in a later chapter, in such a way as to widen our perspective on Chaucer's actual practices in citing Scripture. [1]

We should remind ourselves that Chaucer was not particularly avant-garde in the mere fact of his employing a significant body of Scripture in his poetry. By the fourteenth century, biblical paraphrase was an established part of vernacular literature in English. As David Fowler has noted, biblical paraphrase was commonly juxtaposed against the kinds of narratives found in romances and popular tales. Clerical authors not infrequently began by asserting that their religious compositions, of Christ not of Charlemagne, were designed to turn men from romance. As the prologue to the vast, influential verse rendering of Scripture known as the *Cursor Mundi* (c. 1300) implies, whereas the fool wishes to hear of Alexander, Arthur, and Tristan and Isolt, the wise man turns to Scripture. On the other hand, as the late thirteenth-century *Iacob and Iosep* and the late fourteenth-century *Susannah* would seem to indicate, professional writers themselves by the fourteenth century had already turned to the Bible for narrative materials. [2]

While recognizing that in Chaucer's England it was possible for so-called secular authors to use scriptural material, we should also realize that these Ricardian authors had no prescribed or standard way of employing this material, and that Chaucer's uses of the Bible are significantly different from these of Langland, the Gawain-Poet, and even of John Gower. Although these differences—as well as Chaucer's possible involvement in the controversy surrounding the translation of the Bible into English—need to

---

1. See W. Meredith Thompson, "Chaucer's Translation of the Bible," *English and Medieval Studies Presented to J. R. R. Tolkien* (London: Allen & Unwin, 1962), p. 183, for an important pioneering enquiry into this subject.

2. David C. Fowler, *The Bible in Early English Literature* (Seattle: University of Washington Press, 1976), pp. 133 ff.

be studied, it is enough here to understand that Chaucer's handling of Scripture reflects his own artistic method, and that it may profitably be examined by itself.

A few generalities concerning the body of material used by Chaucer should provide a perspective for understanding something of his procedure. Biblical allusions and quotations fill Chaucer's writings from his early *ABC to the Virgin* to his Retraction to *The Canterbury Tales*. Whereas the list of biblical references provided by W. W. Skeat numbers approximately 250 items, the notes in F. N. Robinson's edition add substantially to these. Moreover, Dudley Johnson has counted over 400 quotations, Bert Dillon cites approximately 500 references, and a recent dissertation notes approximately 700 biblical quotations and allusions.[3] About three-fifths of these come from the Old Testament, including the Apocrypha; the most frequently cited books are Proverbs, Ecclesiasticus, and Matthew—in that order—then Genesis, Psalms, Canticles, and John, followed by Job, Ecclesiastes, Luke, and 1 Corinthians. In the Old Testament, the books of wisdom—the source for the bulk of Chaucer's proverbs—are most cited, and those of prophecy least cited; and in the New Testament, references are divided about equally between the Gospels and the Epistles. Of all these biblical references, almost nine-tenths appear only once and reveal no obvious pattern in Chaucer's writings, though by far the majority of them appear in *The Canterbury Tales*. While questions concerning this distribution should be posed, those about Chaucer's actual use of the Bible must take precedence.

The simplest use of Scripture by Chaucer reflects the medieval predilection for using the Bible—along with experience, reason, and scholarly authority—as one of the standard ways of establishing proof. Chaucer cites such biblical *auctoritees* as Solomon, Jesus Sirach, and Saint Paul sometimes by name alone and sometimes in conjunction with a quotation. As we might expect, such references appear most noticeably and consistently in *Melibee*, where they give support to Prudence's teachings, and in the *Parson's Tale*, where they document the words on repentance. Important as these citations of authority may be, far more striking—and more literary—are the scriptural figures and details Chaucer alludes to in bringing out special qualities in his characters, and in giving additional significances to his episodes.

More metaphoric than authoritative, such biblical citations rely on exegetical principles that sometimes suggest a plethora of significances. Chaucer's awareness of multivalent allusion may be seen in his using

---

3. See *The Complete Works of Geoffrey Chaucer*, ed. Walter W. Skeat (Oxford: Clarendon, 1894), VI, 381-84; *The Works of Geoffrey Chaucer*, ed. F. N. Robinson, 2nd ed. (Boston: Houghton Mifflin, 1957); Dudley R. Johnson, "Chaucer and the Bible," *DAI*, 31 (1941), 3506A; Bert Dillon, *A Chaucer Dictionary: Proper Names and Allusions, Excluding Place Names* (Boston: Hall, 1974), pp. 27-39; Theodore B. Buermann, "Chaucer's 'Book of Genesis' in *The Canterbury Tales*: The Biblical Schema of the First Fragment," *DA*, 28 (1968), 5009A. See also Grace Landrum, "Chaucer's Use of the Vulgate," *PMLA*, 39 (1924), 99; and Thompson, pp. 187-90.

Judith in the *Man of Law's Tale* to suggest how with God's help so un-likely a person as Custance can prevail (B 939), and in *Melibee* to show that good women have actually existed (B [2] *2288). Similarly, he cites Job in the *Friar's Tale* to show how through perseverance man may be saved (D 1491) and in the *Clerk's Tale* to give additional meaning to Griselda's patience (E 932). Even when Chaucer recounts a biblical story more exten-sively, he is conscious of various possibilities of meaning and is likewise less concerned with telling the story for its own sake than with applying it to a character or situation.

These allusions tend to occur when we might least expect them and in distinctly profane contexts. The reference in the portrait of the Summoner in the *General Prologue* to his love for garlic, onions, and leeks—foods of Egypt preferred by the backsliding Hebrews of Numbers 11: 5—may catch us unawares. Similarly, we may be surprised by the echo of Canticles in Absolon's love song to Alisoun in the *Miller's Tale* (A 3698 ff.) and in January's *aube* to May in the *Merchant's Tale* (E 2138). [4] But, surprising or not, such allusions pervade Chaucer's writings. Occasionally we may sense biblical figures behind certain Chaucerian characters—the Samaritan woman at the well behind the Wife of Bath, "the Unjust Steward behind the Reeve, the ubiquitous Sadducee, Scribe, and Pharisee behind the un-holy ecclesiasts." [5] Or we may be aware of biblical events being echoed in particular Chaucerian episodes—Noah's Flood in the *Miller's Tale*, the Jonah story in the *Man of Law's Tale*, the Sacrifice of Isaac in the *Physician's Tale*, as well as the Testing of Job in the *Clerk's Tale*. [6] At other times, these biblical echoes may be more general and elusive—the Fall of Man in the *Nun's Priest's Tale*, the Annunciation in the *Miller's Tale*, the Resurrection in the *Shipman's Tale*, and Pentecost in the *Summoner's Tale*. [7]

---

4. See especially R. E. Kaske, "Patristic Exegesis: The Defence," *Critical Ap-proaches to Medieval Literature* (New York: Columbia University Press, 1960), pp. 49 ff.; and D. W. Robertson, Jr., "The Doctrine of Charity in Medieval Literary Gardens: A Topical Approach through Symbolism and Allegory," *Speculum*, 26 (1951), 43-45. See also James I. Wimsatt, "Chaucer and the Canticle of Canticles," *Chaucer the Love Poet* (Athens: Univer-sity of Georgia Press, 1973), pp. 84-90; and Douglas Wurtele, "Ironical Resonances in the *Merchant's Tale*," *ChauR*, 13 (1978), 66-79.

5. See Rodney Delasanta, "And of Great Reverence: Chaucer's Man of Law," *ChauR*, 5 (1971), 307.

6. See especially Margaret Schlauch, "Constantine, Jonah, and the *Gesta Romanorum*," *Kwartalnik Neofilologiczny*, 20 (1973), 305-306; Anne Lancashire, "Chaucer and the Sacrifice of Isaac," *ChauR*, 9 (1975), 320-26; and Lawrence L. Besserman, *The Legend of Job in the Middle Ages* (Cambridge: Harvard University Press, 1979), pp. 111-12.

7. See especially Bernard S. Levy and George R. Adams, "Chauntecleer's Paradise Lost and Regained," *MS*, 29 (1967), 178-92; Thomas W. Ross, "Notes on Chaucer's Miller's Tale, A 3216 and 3320," *ELN*, 13 (1976), 256-58; Gail McMurray Gibson, "Resurrection as Dramatic Icon in the *Shipman's Tale*," *Signs and Symbols in Chaucer's Poetry* (University, Ala.: University of Alabama Press, 1980), pp. 102-12; and Bernard S. Levy, "Biblical Parody in the Summoner's Tale," *TSL*, 11 (1966), 45-60; also Roy Peter Clark, "Doubting Thomas in Chaucer's *Summoner's Tale*," *ChauR*, 11 (1976), 164-78. At least one student of Chaucer has seen in these echoes a deliberate attempt on Chaucer's part to parallel the story of the Bible from Creation to Last Judgment; see Buermann, *DA*, 28 (1968), 5009A-10A.

While recognizing the possibility of all of these echoes, we should also be aware of their purpose. While some of them may function to suggest that the tale at hand is an *imitatio* of the biblical narrative, others call attention to obvious differences between the Bible and Chaucer's narrative. For example, in the *Miller's Tale* the flood that Nicholas conjures up for John is hardly a second Deluge, and John is certainly not a second Noah. Such instances—and they seem to be the majority—suggest that Chaucer's biblical echoes can be designed to create incongruity, as well as to provide additional perspective for his fiction.

Chaucer's attitude toward Scripture was "not that of a scholar, theologian, or preacher," but rather "that of a professional writer to whom all experience and all books, including the Bible, were grist for the mill." [8] Instead of overtly distinguishing between the sacred and the profane, Chaucer purposely links biblical and non-biblical material. In particular, he blends the biblical with the mythological, sometimes apparently to give a sense of completeness—as in the balade in the Prologue to the *Legend of Good Women*, where Absalon, Esther, and Jonathan are joined by figures from classical legend (F 249 ff.), and as in the book of the Wife of Bath's fifth husband, where the accounts of the Fall of Man and the deception of Samson are linked to stories from classical antiquity likewise demonstrating the wickedness of women (D 1713 ff.). At other times these blends seem designed to create a sense of incongruity, as in the *Book of the Duchess*, where Samson's dying "for" Delilah is equated with Echo's dying "for" Narcissus and with Dido's dying "for" Aeneas (730 ff.), even though the biblical death is obviously different in kind from the others. The incongruity is surely intentional in the *Merchant's Tale* when references to Solomon and Jesus Sirach on marriage are put into the mouths of Pluto and Proserpine (C 2242 ff.).

At times, as we might expect, Chaucer's choice of allusion seems to be related to the kind of narrative he is writing. Just as biblical references are understandably prominent in both the sermon represented by the *Pardoner's Tale* and the sermon-like treatise on sin and repentance that is the *Parson's Tale*, so they are understandably lacking in the *Troilus* and the *Knight's Tale*, narratives set in classical antiquity, as well as in the early dream visions, which have as their starting points stories from Ovid, Virgil, and Cicero. Still, it would be simplistic, even misleading, to assert that genre or setting is the determining factor in Chaucer's decision to cite the Bible. Although we might well expect to find a profusion of scriptural echoes in the overtly religious tales of the Prioress and Second Nun, these tales actually offer few such references, emphasizing instead the legendary, with its sense of the miraculous. Conversely, the *Squire's Tale*, set in Genghis Khan's Asia, contains allusions to Moses and Solomon (F 250), as well as to Lamech (who is joined to Jason and Paris, 550); the Manciple's fable from Ovid ends with references to the Psalms of David and to Solomon (H 345), as well as perhaps an imitation of Proverbs (314 ff.); and the

---

8. Thompson, pp. 192-93.

Physician's Tale not only draws from Livy, but, representing the words of a Canterbury pilgrim whose "study was but litel on the Bible" (A 438), alludes to Jephtha and his daughter (C 240).

Along with the straightforward citations of Scripture and those where incongruity is possible are scores—if not hundreds—of others that clearly alter, pervert, or in some way misapply the biblical original. Some of these distortions involve simple wordplay, such as when the Pardoner in his tale uses the term "Sampsoun, Sampsoun" to refer to the sound the drunken man makes through his nose (C 553 ff.). The addition, "And yet, God woot, Sampsoun drank nevere no wyn," far from disclaiming the biblical association, in fact ensures that the connection between the sound and the hero of Judges is clear. [9] Similar play may be seen in the *Summoner's Tale* when Friar John criticizes pompous and gluttonous clerics—"Whan they for soules seye the psalm of Davit;/ Lo, 'buf!' they seye, '*cor meum eructavit!*'" (D 1933-34)—and focuses on the literal significance of *eructavit* as belch. [10] This play is linked to a more blatant mis-statement of Scripture in another assertion of Friar John: "Fro Paradys first, if I shal nat lye,/ Was man out chaced for his glotonye;/ And chaast was man in Paradis, certeyn" (D 1915-17). The witty joining of "chaced" and "chaast" cannot keep us from wondering about the simplistic and dubious assertions that gluttony was the cause of man's Fall and that chastity was man's prelapsarian condition. And we have an increasing sense that Friar John is more concerned with using Scripture as the vehicle for his wit than with stating it accurately.

Other distortions of Scripture are even less innocuous than these. In the *Miller's Tale*, for instance, Absolon is hardly the figure of beauty his biblical name would suggest; his love of Alisoun is scarcely the ideal love suggested by the several allusions to Canticles; and notwithstanding Nicholas's singing the "*Angelus ad virginem*" (A 3216), he is no more the angel Gabriel than Alisoun is the Virgin Mary. More particularly, Alisoun's words to Absolon when he is intruding upon her adultery with Nicholas—"Go forth thy wey, or I wol caste a ston" (3712)—are but a grotesque reversal of Christ's words in John 8: 7 concerning the woman taken in adultery; and Gerveys' sharpening plowshares and making what amount to weapons out of them (3762) acts as an ironic negation of the famous words in Isaiah 2: 4 about turning swords into plowshares. [11] Given such topsy-turvy echoes as these in the *Miller's Tale*, we may well wonder about Chaucer's purpose in including such biblical distortions in his writings.

---

9. See Joseph E. Grennen, "'Sampsoun' in the *Canterbury Tales*: Chaucer Adapting a Source," *NM*, 67 (1966), 119-20.

10. See Paul E. Beichner, "*Non Allelulia Ructare*," *MS*, 18 (1956), 135-44; also Marie P. Hamilton, "The Summoner's 'Psalm of Davit'," *MLN*, 57 (1942), 655-57. The quotation is from the beginning of Psalm 45 (Vulgate 44).

11. See W. F. Bolton, "The 'Miller's Tale': An Interpretation," *MS*, 24 (1962), p. 93; and Edmund Reiss, "Daun Gerveys in the *Miller's Tale*," *PLL*, 6 (1970), 122-23. Joel 3: 10 speaks of "beating ploughshares into swords, hooks into spears . . . ."

By and large these distortions cannot be explained away as accidental, as the result of confusion on Chaucer's part, or as the product of some
unknown exegetical account. Indeed, Chaucer's mishandlings are all most
likely purposeful and may well be the principal way he uses the Bible for
literary, rather than for authoritative, purposes. While, on the one hand,
Chaucer's poetry reflects the truths of his faith, on the other hand, it demonstrates his more immediate concern with entertaining his court audience. Moral as he is, he should hardly be considered a preacher *manqué*;
and for all his *doctryne* we cannot ignore his concern with *mirth*. It is as a
craftsman of language and as a creator of fictions that Chaucer mainly uses
the Bible, and here he is not at all in competition with the clerics at the
court. When he refers to Scripture, it is hardly to teach the Bible to his
court audience. Rather, Chaucer is more likely relying on their previous
knowledge of Scripture; and when he, through his characters, mis-states
and misapplies it, he would seem to be counting on the audience's ability to
recognize the distortion. Aware of his manipulation of the material and the
discrepancies between the original and his treatment of it, they would give
the necessary corrective. Providing a body of familiar material and traditional meaning, the Bible, like classical myth, offered standard references
that would exist no matter how distorted the allusions might be.

Rather than think that the point of Chaucer's distortions was to poke
fun at the Bible, we should realize that for him and his audience the truth
of Scripture was real, irrefragable and thereby impervious to man's playing
with its expression. Moreover, this playfulness is not at all blasphemous or
sacrilegious. Rather, it functions as parody in the sense that the mis-stated
and misapplied texts contrast with their biblical originals. Through garbling
biblical references, Chaucer makes us aware simultaneously of both the
truth and its false manifestation. Or, to rephrase this point, parody comes
about when the false words and hypocritical actions of Chaucer's characters are held against the moral and spiritual meanings of the biblical
phrases, figures, events, and themes alluded to by them. [12]

Thus in the *Miller's Tale* the scriptural allusions act as an ironic
comment on man's aberrant behavior. For all of its humor, the distortion of
Scripture provides a level of meaning that would otherwise be lacking. The
echoes not only suggest that John, Nicholas, and Absolon demonstrate the
Three Temptations (1 John 2: 16), but the cupidity of all the characters
makes pertinent the allusion to the Deluge, which represents precisely the
cleansing that is needed for this world. Similarly, the Song of Songs provides both a context for evaluating the wrong loving ubiquitous in the tale,
and a depth and quality of love that is the corrective to the false loves. [13]

---

12. This view of parody is discussed more fully in Edmund Reiss, "Chaucer's
Parodies of Love," *Chaucer the Love Poet* (Athens: University of Georgia Press, 1973), pp.
27-28. See also Levy, *TSL*, 11 (1966), 58, n. 4; and Robert R. Black, "Sacral and Biblical
Parody in Chaucer's *Canterbury Tales*," *DAI*, 35 (1975), 6090A. Thompson makes the point
that "unintentional mistranslation . . . is rare" in Chaucer (p. 193, n. 1).

13. See especially R. E. Kaske, "The *Canticum Canticorum* in the *Miller's Tale*," *SP*,
59 (1962), 479-500.

Chaucer's procedure may be further understood by referring to the detail at the end of the *Friar's Tale* where the speaker, having concluded his tale proper, urges his pilgrim audience to be watchful so that "the temptour Sathanas" will not take them unawares. Beware, he says, citing Psalm 10(Vulgate 9): 9, "The leoun sit in his awayt alway / To sle the innocent, if that he may" (D 1656-58). Notwithstanding the conventional appeal to vigilance, the biblical allusion is here misused. Though with it the Friar urges his audience to watch out for the fiend, the passage in Psalms actually concerns not the devil but the wicked man who as the adversary lurks in secret "like a lion in his den" waiting to seize man (cf. 1 Pet. 5: 8). Whereas it is the Friar who is here most immediately dangerous to the other pilgrims, in the totality of his fiction Chaucer casts himself in the role of devil's advocate through his deliberate mis-statement and misapplication of Scripture. Recognizing that in this world appearance is frequently very different from actuality, Chaucer's audience must be constantly alert to ambiguity and distortion. In particular, they must carefully assess everything Chaucer says, even when he offers the highest authority to validate it, and make the necessary corrections. In making this demand, Chaucer not only provides his audience with an intellectual challenge, he adds to the depth of meaning of his work.

One obvious result of Chaucer's creating a gap between Scripture and the allusions to it is the exposure of human folly. "From beak of bird and gap-tooth widow pours forth an eloquence of scriptural allusion . . . recklessly out of context, variously misapplied . . . admixed with high bawdry and low comedy." [14] This may be demonstrated by the Physician's allusion to Jephtha and his daughter. Occurring when Virginia asks her father for some time to lament her imminent death—"For, pardee, Jepte yaf his doghter grace / For to compleyne, er he his slow, allas!" (C 240-41)—the reference seems out of place. But not only does it appear inappropriate to the Physician who is telling the tale; it also has implications not in accord with the ostensible action or point of the story. While Jephtha's sacrifice of his only child was sometimes interpreted as a type of Christ's sacrifice, it also suggested an illegitimate sacrifice, and in this sense was in opposition to the more familiar sacrifice of Isaac by Abraham, which was viewed as legitimate. Chaucer's allusion to the killing of Jephtha's daughter would have as its corollary the sacrifice of Isaac, and together the two biblical stories would serve to give alternative possibilities for assessing the sacrifice of Virginia. Moreover, Chaucer continues referring to traditional exegesis when he has Virginia ask in distinctly New Testament language, "is ther no grace, is ther no remedye?" (236-37). Notwithstanding the importance of grace in the medieval Christian view of the Abraham-Isaac story, for her there is none. Along with suggesting the folly of Virginius and reflecting the Physician's lack of understanding of Scripture, the detail of Jephtha and his daughter serves to complicate the

---

14. Thompson, p. 193.

implicit questions of the tale concerning the relationship between intentions and actions and between judgment and mercy. [15]

A similar ironic use of Scripture may be seen in one of the few biblical allusions in the *Prioress' Tale*, when the sorrowing mother of the "litel clergeoun" is referred to as "this newe Rachel" (B[2] *1817). This allusion to Matthew 2: 18—which itself cites Jeremiah 31: 15—may seem to provide a natural comparison by relating two grieving mothers, and, inasmuch as the Gospel passage was part of the liturgy for the Feast of the Holy Innocents, may seem to offer an appropriate context for viewing the death of the little innocent of the tale. [16] However, in the context of the Prioress' denigrating references to the "cursed folk of Herodes" and to the "Hebrayk peple" in whose heart Satan resides (B[2] *1750, *1764), any reference to an Old Testament figure—even Rachel—must seem out of place. Moreover, a standard medieval interpretation takes the reference to Rachel's weeping for her lost children and refusing to be comforted to represent one who, instead of seeking comfort in this present life, fixes her eye in contemplation of God and transfers all her hope and comfort to the life to come. [17] The projected comparison between this Rachel and the mother in the *Prioress' Tale* who literally refuses to be comforted, is without real significance, and would seem designed to produce a sense of irony, like that unmistakable in the subsequent episode of the tale, where the Christian judge, who incongruously cites the Hebrew *lex talionis* (B[2] *1822), slaughters all the Jews who knew anything about the plan to kill the child. As out of place as the appeal to mercy in the concluding lines of the tale that invoke Hugh of Lincoln to pray for us sinners that "of his mercy, God so merciable / On us his grete mercy multiplie" (*1878-79), the comparison of the mother to Rachel makes meaningful the lack of sensitivity of the Prioress, and the inadequacy of the childlike understanding of Christianity brought out in the tale.

The allusions to the Bible in the *Man of Law's Tale* would seem to function in a quite different way from those in the tales of the Physician and the Prioress. Providing a basis for understanding the significance of Custance's trials and tribulations, the references serve to identify Custance with biblical figures. Still, when Chaucer relates her preservation to that of Daniel in the lions' den, Jonah in the whale, the Hebrews passing through the Red Sea, and the Miracle of the Loaves and Fishes (B 470 ff.), his point is to do more than make a vivid comparison with familiar material. It is also to make her story a modern instance, as it were, of the same kind of miracle found in the biblical narratives, and to demonstrate God's continuing care for man. Moreover, when Chaucer links Custance's strength in

---

15. See Richard L. Hoffman, "Jephtha's Daughter and Chaucer's Virginia," *ChauR*, 2 (1967), 20-31; and Lancashire, p. 323.
16. See Robinson, p. 735, n.; and Sherman Hawkins, "Chaucer's Prioress and the Sacrifice of Praise," *JEGP*, 63 (1964), 609, 614, n. 48.
17. See *Glossa ordinaria*, *PL* 114: 77; and Richard J. Schoeck, "Chaucer's Prioress: Mercy and Tender Heart," *Chaucer Criticism: The Canterbury Tales* (Notre Dame: University of Notre Dame Press, 1960), pp. 253-54.

defending her chastity to David's power against Goliath and Judith's hardiness against Holofernes (932 ff.), his point, again emphasizing how even the weakest person may prevail when supported by God, is to affirm providential order. The typological value of the Old Testament figures is clearly of interest to Chaucer here, and he would seem to use it simply to make Custance herself an exemplar for his audience.

Notwithstanding appearance here, the biblical allusions in the *Man of Law's Tale* are also distorted, though in ways different from what has so far been seen. Most likely representing Chaucer's own additions to the story he took from Nicholas Trivet, they reveal what has been termed a "spate of mini-errors"—for instance, that, as opposed to Daniel 6: 16 ff., Daniel was accompanied by others in the lions' den: "Ther every wight save he, maister and knave, / Was with the leon frete er he asterte" (474-75). [18] These allusions also all appear in passages of overt pathos, where the contrived pulpit rhetoric of the speaker is so dominant that we cannot help but be most aware of the rhetoric itself. Rather than simply add meaning to the folk tale, these additions—including the biblical references—also add a distinct sense of hyperbole, and give the impression that for all the standard and correct *doctryne* at hand, the tale itself, coming from the mouth of the Man of Law, is overblown and without real substance. For all of their figural associations—especially revealing that which is known as the Help of God [19]—these references exist primarily as figures of rhetoric, as devices in a tale where manner is in conflict with matter; and, whether or not erroneous, they function to call attention more to the ostensible rhetorical skill of the literary poseur who tells the tale than to exegetical significance.

In his citations of biblical women in the *Merchant's Tale*, Chaucer distorts Scripture in still another way. To illustrate the point that women are "so trewe and therwithal so wyse," January cites Rebecca, Judith, Abigail, and Esther, all of whom, he says, worked "by good conseil" (E 1358 ff.). Whereas these Old Testament heroines are common types for man's deliverance, [20] Chaucer is using them here in a rather unusual way. To see this, we may compare this passage with one in *Melibee*, which cites the same four women and their "good conseil" to show that many women are indeed good, and that their counsels may well be "ful hoolsome and profitable" (B^2 *2284 ff.). Notwithstanding the obvious similarities of the two passages—both come from Albertano of Brescia—there are at least two notable differences between them. Whereas Prudence cites the four heroines to counter Melibee's rash statement that "alle wommen been wikke" (B^2 *2245), January holds up these same women as admirable wives; and, moreover, each of them was responsible for the deception, if

---

18. See Delasanta, pp. 294-96.
19. See Robert T. Farrell, "Chaucer's Use of the Theme of the Help of God in the *Man of Law's Tale*," *NM*, 71 (1970), 239-40; also Hope Phyllis Weissman, "Late Gothic Pathos in *The Man of Law's Tale*," *JMRS*, 9 (1979), 133 ff.
20. See Charlotte F. Otten, "Proserpine: *Liberatrix Suae Gentis*," *ChauR*, 5 (1971), 278 ff.

not the death, of a man. It seems clear that "if we focus on their behavior toward their husbands or lovers . . . we find nothing to justify honorable mention. Or worse, we find negative evidence." [21] Here then it is the misapplication of the Bible that creates the distortion. In recognizing this, we see further January's inadequate understanding, and become aware of the ideals that are later parodied by May's delivering January from blindness.

A more extensive misapplication of scriptural references may be found in the *Monk's Tale*. It is not just that Chaucer may have chosen for the Monk "the less edifying, more savage and sensational scriptural episodes," [22] he has also used the biblical accounts among the hundred tragedies the Monk knows to carry the burden of irony and incongruity in a variety of ways. The stanza on Adam at the beginning of the tale is not only simplistic in its eight-line condensation of the Creation and Fall, it is ironically joined to the previous stanza, which details the fall of Lucifer. Establishing the pattern of tragedy of the entire tale, this stanza stresses that Lucifer fell "from heigh degree . . . Doun into helle," and will never "twynne / Out of miserie" (B^2 *2003 ff.). Similarly, the point emphasized about Adam is that he was driven from "hye prosperitee" not only to "labour" and to "meschaunce" but also to "helle," where, apparently because there is likewise no remedy for him, he will remain. The reference to hell here, along with the concomitant denial of grace, would seem to be Chaucer's purposeful addition to the story—the account of the Fall of Man in the *Pardoner's Tale*, for instance, says only that Adam was driven "to labour and to wo" (C 506)—and suggests the misunderstandings and distortions of both tragedy and Scripture still to come. [23] From this denial of man's redemption, the Monk turns to Samson, in what is the longest of the biblical tragedies; but in celebrating "this noble almyghty champioun" (*3213)—whose prison in Gaza was often cited as a type of hell—the Monk mainly laments that Samson told his secret to women (*3242 ff.). The moral at the end—different from that in the other tragedies, which stress Fortune—is "Beth war by his ensample oold and playn / That no men telle his conseil til his wyves" (*3281-82).

The paired accounts of Nebuchadnezzar and Belshazzar are likewise odd in avoiding essential matter. Belshazzar's act of profaning the sacred vessels—so important in the Middle English *Cleanness*, and actually

---

21. L. L. Besserman, "Chaucer and the Bible: The Case of the *Merchant's Tale*," *HUSL*, 6 (1978), 19. See also Emerson Brown, Jr., "Biblical Women in the Merchant's Tale: Feminism, Antifeminism, and Beyond," *Viator*, 5 (1974), 387-412; and W. Arthur Turner, "Biblical Women in *The Merchant's Tale* and *The Tale of Melibee*," *ELN*, 3 (1965), 93-95. Cf. the later reference to Esther and Kevin J. Harty, "The Reputation of Queen Esther in the Middle Ages: The Merchant's Tale IV (E) 1742-45," *BSUF*, 19.3 (1978), 65-68. For other biblical allusions in the tale, see A. L. Kellogg, "Susannah and the Merchant's Tale," *Speculum*, 35 (1960), 275-79; and Douglas Wurtele, "The Figure of Solomon in Chaucer's Merchant's Tale," *RUO*, 47 (1977), 478-87.
22. Thompson, p. 193.
23. See George B. Pace, "Adam's Hell," *PMLA*, 78 (1963), 25-26. While seeing the two stanzas forming "an effective and related pair," Pace does not consider any ironic linking.

brought out earlier in the Monk's account (*3416 ff.)—is totally ignored in the moral at the end: "Lordynges, ensample heerby may ye take / How that in lordschipe is not sikernisse" (*3429-30). Similarly, the brief story of Holofernes—only three stanzas long—places its emphasis on the incongruity of this proud and mighty man's being killed by a woman, not on sin. The Monk tells his audience to "taak kep of the deth of Oloferne," and, instead of offering a moral, the last two lines state that after Judith cut off Holofernes' head while he slept, "Ful pryvyely she stal from every wight, / And with his heed into hir toun she wente" (*3763-64). The great victory of the original is completely lacking in this account; and replacing it is the secret—one might be tempted to say shameful—act of Judith.

And finally, in the story of Antiochus, from 2 Maccabees 9, the Monk completely ignores the final repentance of this mighty king and the letter he writes before his death assuring the Jews of the kindness of his successor. Rather, the Monk focuses on the "stynk" that comes from his body and on his wretched end: "And in this stynk and this horrible peyne, / He starf ful wrecchedly in a monteyne" (*3816 ff.). In showing only how Antiochus received "swich gwerdoun as bilongeth unto pryde," and in omitting the repentance, the Monk neglects what may be the most effective as well as the most significant part of the story. [24]

We have seen that biblical references served to undercut the tales of the Physician and the Prioress, that the Man of Law's rhetoric altered the significance of his scriptural references, that the Merchant's misapplication of biblical figures made them appear ludicrous, and that the Monk's focus on the wrong details invariably resulted in his failure to bring out what was most meaningful in his biblical examples. Joining these distorters of Scripture is the Wife of Bath, whose particular error is the twisting of actual lines and teachings from the Bible in an attempt to make them support her own outrageous positions.

In the course of perverting Jerome's arguments in the *Adversus Jovinianum*, the Wife blatantly misuses both the Old and New Testaments. When she claims that Saint Paul says "to be wedded is no synne; / Bet is to be wedded than to brynne" (D 51-52), she misrepresents the words on virginity and marriage in 1 Corinthians 7: 8-9; though she rejects the bigamy of Lamech, she gladly embraces the marital examples of Solomon, Abraham, and Jacob (35, 53-56); and though she is full of proverbs herself, she rejects those that Jankyn reads to her from Ecclesiasticus: "I sette noght an hawe / Of his proverbes n'of his olde sawe" (659-60). The entire performance of the Wife reveals strikingly how overtly ironic Chaucer can be in his misapplications of Scripture, and he seems to have reserved for her some of his most ludicrous distortions. For example, when she compares herself to Christ in being able to refresh men (145 ff.), she not only creates an amusing grotesquerie, she completely turns around the Miracle

---

24. See also Dudley R. Johnson, "The Biblical Characters of Chaucer's Monk," *PMLA*, 66 (1951), 827-43.

of Loaves and Fishes in John 6:9—not Mark, the authority she states—and the whole New Testament sense of spiritual nourishment.

The Wife's mistreatment of Scripture reveals her inability to see beyond the letter to the spiritual sense. She shows this myopia when she makes it clear that although "men may devyne and glosen, up and doun" as to how many husbands the Samaritan woman at the well could have—which is hardly the issue at all in John 4: 17-19—she herself will follow God's "expres"—that is, explicit—command "to wexe and multiplye" (26 ff.). Besides apparently being blind to the fact that she is not waxing and multiplying, the Wife, by preferring the Old Testament words of Genesis 1: 28 to those of the New Testament, in effect reverses the proper relationship between the two parts of the Bible. Whereas the Man of Law was at least concerned with the typological significance of Scripture, though it was submerged in his rhetoric, the Wife of Bath tends to deny this significance. [25]

Like the Wife, Friar John in the *Summoner's Tale* blatantly misuses biblical allusion, though his aberration is in the opposite direction to the Wife's. In celebrating the gloss at the expense of the letter of Scripture—"Glosynge is a glorious thyng, certeyn, / For lettre sleeth, so as we clerkes seyn" (D 1793-94)—he too misapplies the Pauline notion of spiritual nourishment (2 Corinthians 3: 6). Moreover, in stating that even without Scripture he can produce a gloss (1919-20), he virtually rejects the biblical text. Whereas the special pleading of the Wife was to celebrate marriage—or at least her view of it—that of Friar John is to celebrate friars, whom he links not only to the Poor in Spirit of the Beatitudes (1922 ff.) but also to the Apostles and Christ's chosen. In his view friars are the successors of Peter and Paul and enjoy, like Moses, Elijah, and Aaron, a special and intimate relationship with God (1818 ff., 1881 ff., 1904 ff.).

Friar John's particular allusions show not only that he uses Scripture for his own purposes but that he mis-states its literal significance. Although, according to him, Moses "fourty dayes and fourty nyght / Fasted" before God would speak with him (1885 ff.), the point of the account of the renewal of the Covenant in Exodus 34: 28—the earlier account of the initial Covenant on Mount Sinai is even less relevant—is that while Moses was with the Lord he had no need for physical food. Even more at variance with the letter of Scripture is Friar John's assertion that before Elijah spoke with God on Mount Horeb, "He fasted longe, and was in contemplaunce" (1893). Actually, the biblical narrative makes it clear that although Elijah asks for death—hardly a form of "contemplaunce," or contemplation—God insists that he remain alive and, to provide for him, even sends an angel who twice commands Elijah to arise and eat (1 Kings 19: 4 ff.). In fact, the explicit precondition for Elijah's meeting God on

---

25. On the Wife as scriptural exegete, see especially D. W. Robertson, Jr., *A Preface to Chaucer: Studies in Medieval Perspectives* (Princeton: Princeton University Press, 1962), pp. 317-31.

Mount Horeb is that he eat and drink sufficiently to have strength for the journey.

In his final example of the need for fasting, Friar John mis-states the Bible by citing only part of a reference while ignoring the rest. He refers to Aaron and the priests who, as is stated in Leviticus 10: 8-9, should abstain from wine and strong drink when they enter the temple to pray (1894 ff.). Not only does Friar John pass over the fact that the biblical passage concerns drink alone—with the prohibition being for a limited period of time—it ignores the command that follows in Leviticus that Aaron and the priests should take the offerings of food for themselves and eat fully (Leviticus 10: 12 ff.). This kind of incomplete biblical citation is used again in the *Summoner's Tale* when the lord to whom the friar goes after his misadventure of groping behind Thomas says, "Ye been the salt of the erthe and the savour" (2196). Along with the obvious irony of linking "savour" to the olfactory details of this part of the tale is the more subtle irony resulting from an awareness of the passage in the Sermon on the Mount being alluded to here. In its entirety it reads as follows: "You are the salt of the earth, but if salt has lost its savour, how shall its saltiness be restored? It is no longer good for anything except to be thrown out and trodden under foot by men" (Matthew 5: 13). What is not said of Friar John here, but what is alluded to by Chaucer, represents his essential condition and indicates how he should be viewed. [26]

We should look at still one other instance of Chaucer's deliberate distortion of Scripture. For all the irony inherent in the Pardoner's sermon against cupidity being in the mouth of one who may be rightfully considered a personification of cupidity, we might think that the sermon itself with its good words against lechery, gluttony, gambling, and swearing, is without irony. However, the biblical allusions in this sermon are surprisingly suspect even though the speaker here—more than anywhere else in Chaucer's writings—urges his audience to read the Bible and see for themselves the validity of what he is saying (C 578, 586; see also 483).

When, to show that "luxerie is in wyn and dronkenesse," the Pardoner cites how "Dronken Looth, unkyndely / Lay by his doghtres two, unwityngly" (C 484 ff.), he garbles the account of Genesis 19: 30 ff. in several ways. First, the biblical passage explicitly states that Lot's daughters made their father drunk, and, moreover, that they "lay with their father." Though the Pardoner uses the adverb "unwityngly" as a reinforcement of Lot's drunken state, the Bible in effect exonerates Lot. But the most serious misuse of Scripture here is the Pardoner's term "unkyndely," for in the Bible it is clear that Lot's daughters commit incest so "that we may preserve offspring through our father." That is, their action is wholly in accord with nature, as well as with God's command to be fruitful and multiply, in contrast with the unnatural sexuality of the Sodomites.

---

26. See also the interesting view of Roy Peter Clark, "Wit and Witsunday in Chaucer's Summoner's Tale," *AnM*, 17 (1976), 48-57.

The Pardoner's second illustration of the evils of drunkenness—how Herod, "whan he of wyn was repleet," ordered the death of John the Baptist (C 488 ff.)—is out of accord with the story in any of the Gospels or in Peter Comestor's *Historia scholastica*, for none of these texts mentions drunkenness, a detail that might even lessen Herod's responsibility for his action.[27] Similarly, the Pardoner claims without qualification—as Friar John does in the *Summoner's Tale* (D 1915-16)—that gluttony was responsible for Adam and Eve's being driven from Paradise (505 ff.). According to the Pardoner, in what is an addition to the Genesis story, while Adam fasted, he remained in Paradise. A more proper statement of the relationship of gluttony to the Fall of Man may be found in the *Parson's Tale*, where the corruption it brought about is said to be evident in the sin of Adam and Eve (I 819).

The Pardoner's misuse of the Bible is not limited to the Old Testament. His examples against gluttony alter the essence of the Pauline original. Whereas in citing Paul on the corruptibility of the stomach and food (521 ff.), the Pardoner intends to curse the body as foul, the main point of 1 Corinthians 6: 13 ff. is to show that the body, that is, the entire person, belongs to God. Similarly, when the Pardoner goes on to cite Philippians in admonishing man not to make his belly his god (529 ff.), his point is again to curse the uncleanness of the body—"O wombe! O bely! O stynkyng cod. / Fulfilled of dong and of corrupcioun!" (534-35)—and to condemn cooks (purveyors of earthly food) for perversely striving to "turnen substaunce into accident" (539). None of this appears in the *Parson's Tale*, which cites the same quotation in reference to gluttony (I 820). And the passage from Philippians itself (3: 18 ff.) is quite different in that it goes on to emphasize how through Christ the body will be transformed and be like His glorious body. Though the Pardoner's reversal may well be an allusion to contemporary controversies about transubstantiation,[28] its immediate function here is to make the scriptural references seem perverse.

Another kind of misuse of Scripture occurs when to show the evils of drunkenness, the Pardoner asserts that all the acts resulting in victory in the Old Testament "were doon in abstinence and in preyere" (574 ff.). Not only does he fail to account for the scores of battles where abstinence and prayer are not even mentioned, he ignores others in which, for all the abstinence and prayer, the result is defeat—as in Saul's final battle against the Philistines, where though he fasted and prayed, God would not give him victory (1 Samuel 28). It may not be accidental that only seven lines later in his tale the Pardoner calls his audience's attention to what may be the book of Samuel. In citing Lemuel on the evils of drunkenness, he says, rather gratuitously, "Not Samuel, but Lamuel, saye I" (C 585). The actual Lemuel reference, Proverbs 31: 4 ff.—that wine is not for kings to drink but rather for those who are perishing or miserable—is hardly the

---

27. See Robinson, p. 730, n. Cf. Matthew 14: 1-12; Mark 6: 14-29; Luke 9: 7-9; and Peter Taitt, "In Defence of Lot," *N & Q*, 216 (1971), 284-85.
28. See Robinson, p. 730, n.

Pardoner's point, and in the light of his words that this "was commaunded unto Lamuel," it may be worth noting that in the Bible this advice is offered to Lemuel by his mother.

Finally, in his words against swearing (C 631 ff.), the Pardoner passes over the passage in Matthew 5: 34, which prohibits all swearing, to concentrate on Jeremiah's words about how to swear properly. In the *Parson's Tale*, on the other hand, the Matthew reference is quoted and put properly in the context of the Third Commandment (I 586 ff.). Only then does the Parson make the qualification, "if so be that the lawe compelle yow to swear," you should follow Jeremiah. Such is completely lacking in the *Pardoner's Tale*, which focuses on the Old Testament citation and which moves quickly from "gret sweryng" to concentrate on "fals sweryng" (C 631-32). Neglecting the admonition in Matthew about not swearing at all, the Pardoner stresses what he calls swearing "in special" and gratuitously exhibits for his audience precisely what he urges them to avoid: "'By Godes precious herte,' and 'By his nayles,' / And 'By the blood of Crist that is in Hayles'" (651-52).

Whether or not these errors and misapplications are conscious on the part of the Pardoner, they are certainly conscious on the part of Chaucer. And they make it clear that for all of the Pardoner's emphasis on his audience's looking at the Bible, his citation of it should be regarded as suspect. In spite of his sly argument that even a "ful vicious man" is able to tell "a moral tale" (459-60), the Pardoner's venomous words, delivered "under hew / Of hoolynesse" constitute a perversion rather than mere citation of Scripture. [29]

What the Pardoner thus reminds us, once again, is that when we speak of the pervasive presence of the Bible in Chaucer's text, we refer not only to straightforward allusions but to purposeful 'distortions' as well. While recognizing that Chaucer's biblical references "elude any pat system of classification or reductive theory of interpretation," [30] we may understand that biblical parody plays an important role in Chaucer's fiction and is a distinctive feature of his literary art.

---

29. Cf. my earlier wrongheaded defense of the Pardoner's sermon in Edmund Reiss, "The Final Irony of the *Pardoner's Tale*," *CE*, 25 (1964), 260-66. See also Robert P. Miller, "Chaucer's Pardoner, the Scriptural Eunuch, and the Pardoner's Tale," *Speculum*, 30 (1955), 180-99.

30. Besserman, *HUSL*, 6 (1978), 30.

III

Glosses and Contemporary Commentary

Glosynge is a Glorious Thyng:
Chaucer's Biblical Exegesis

LAWRENCE BESSERMAN
Hebrew University

Ryȝtwysly quo con rede,
He loke on bok and be awayed . . . .

(Pearl, 709-10)

Among early Christian writers on Scripture the term *glossa* (Gr. γλῶσσα) meant an explanation of a verbal difficulty. Consisting of a single word, a gloss was easily written between the lines of the scriptural text or in the margin opposite the word it explained. Collections of glosses, "glossaries" of hard words in the Bible, were frequently compiled. Isidore of Seville's *Etymologiae*, completed in 632 A.D., was probably the most influential of such glossaries (it was sometimes referred to as *Liber glossarum*), bringing much classical learning to bear on the sense of words in the Vulgate Bible. Subsequently the term *glossa* came to designate expository comments on a word or phrase in Scripture, and finally a running commentary on one or more entire biblical books. Among dozens of scriptural commentaries of this type, it was the *Glossa ordinaria*, compiled in the twelfth century by Anselm of Laon and others, that emerged as the leading exegetical work of its day and for a long time to come. In the twelfth and thirteenth centuries it was often referred to simply as *Glosa*; 'the Gloss.' Its influence persisted undiminished in Chaucer's day, and we find it regularly in printed Bibles well into the seventeenth century. [1]

No wonder, then, that Professor Robertson, in his illuminating discussion of the Wife of Bath as exegete, repeatedly cites the *Glossa ordinaria* to point out how the Wife's literal interpretations of the Bible are mistaken, even perverse. [2] His reasoning is convincing, as far as it goes: the Wife interprets the Bible literally, for her own selfish purposes; in Chaucer's day all Christian writers (and all true believers) knew that, when reading the Bible, "the letter killeth, but the spirit quickeneth." The most

---

1. On the early history of biblical glosses, see F. Vigouroux, in *Dictionnaire de la Bible*, ed. F. Vigouroux, III. 1: 252-58; and on the *Glossa ordinaria*, see Beryl Smalley, *The Study of the Bible in the Middle Ages* (Oxford, 1952; rpt. 1964), pp. 46-66.
2. D. W. Robertson, Jr., *A Preface to Chaucer* (Princeton, 1962; rpt. 1969), pp. 317-31.

widely used "spiritual" interpretation of the Bible in Chaucer's day—firmly based on the writings of the Church Fathers—was the *Glossa ordinaria*; accurate historical criticism of the Wife's exegesis thus demands that we refer to the *Glossa ordinaria* and other standard biblical commentaries of the late fourteenth century as "control" texts.

I say this is convincing as far as it goes because Chaucer was not a fourteenth-century exegete, and his allegiance to the orthodox view of biblical interpretation (in so far as there was a single view) needs to be proved, not merely assumed. To be sure, the fundamental premise of biblical exegesis was, as Professor Robertson asserts, that the letter kills and the spirit gives life (2 Cor. 3: 6). From New Testament times, and especially with regard to the Old Testament, this was unchallenged orthodoxy. To Chaucer's Wycliffite contemporaries, however, this first premise of exegesis was no guarantee of true piety; it seems to have been the slogan of parties they regarded as corrupt. As one Wycliffite document puts it: "These be the arms of Antichrist's disciples against true men: *And the letter slayeth.*" [3] When the friar in Chaucer's *Summoner's Tale* declares, "For lettre sleeth, so as we clerkes seyn" (III 1794) he is angling to cheat a sick man out of his money; it seems as if Chaucer has placed the biblical phrase in the mouth of the friar according to the Wycliffite formula, to flesh out his portrait of a disciple of antichirst.

This same friar, whom I quote in my title, proves to be a master of the self-enhancing gloss:

> But herkne now, Thomas, what I shal seyn.
> I ne have no text of it, as I suppose,
> But I shal fynde it in a maner glose,
> That specially oure sweete Lord Jhesus
> Spak this by freres, whan he seyde thus:
>   'Blessed be they that povere in spirit been.'
> And so forth al the gospel may ye seen,
> Wher it be likker oure professioun,
> Or hirs that swymmen in possessioun. [4]

(III 1918-1926)

Chaucer's opinion about this sort of "spiritual" interpretation of Scripture is not in doubt.

We can be less certain, I think, about the exegetical labors of another character in *The Canterbury Tales*, Proserpyna in the *Merchant's Tale*. Fighting back against her husband Pluto's anti-feminist tirade, Proserpyna rebuts his appeal to Solomon by glossing a crucial offending verse. Pluto cites Eccles. 7: 28: "'Amonges a thousand men yet foond I oon, / But of wommen alle foond I noon.'" (IV 2247-2248). Proserpyna counters: "I prey yow take the sentence of the man [i.e., Solomon]; / He mente thus, that in sovereyn bontee / Nis noon but God, but neither he ne she" (IV

---

        3. Quoted in Margaret Deanesly, *The Lollard Bible* (Cambridge, 1920; rpt. 1966), p. 273.
        4. This and all subsequent quotations from Chaucer are from the 2nd ed. of F. N. Robinson, *The Works of Geoffrey Chaucer* (Boston, 1957).

2288-2290). Though she doesn't mention it, Proserpyna here alludes to the *Glossa ordinaria*, which comments on Eccles. 7: 28: "Quacunque rem vel discretionem inter homines et eorum mores: quis perfecte bonus nisi solus Christus? . . . Christum qui caput est omnium bonorum; quod figuratur per millenarium qui perfectus numerus" (*PL*, 113: 1124). The situation is, to say the least, unusual: the Queen of Hell expounds a biblical verse in an orthodox fashion to rebut an anti-feminist charge and to defend her intention to allow a mismatched young bride to commit adultery and get away with it. A superbly Chaucerian moment.

Proserpyna's use of the *Glossa ordinaria* and the abuse of *glosynge* by the friar in the *Summoner's Tale* do not prove that Chaucer rejected orthodox scriptural exegesis. What these two cases illustrate is Chaucer's awareness that in his day there were fraudulent exegetes afoot. His fellow Englishmen were aware of this too. According to the *Middle English Dictionary*, in the latter half of the fourteenth century the verb *glosen* meant: (1) 'to gloss, interpret, explain; interpret (a text) falsely; to explain or describe (sth.)'; (2) 'to falsify'; (3) 'to flatter, deceive.' Illustrative quotations in the *MED* indicate the term was most often pejorative. A brief look at the use of *glose* and *glosynge* by the pilgrims in *The Canterbury Tales* will show that they were in step with their real-life contemporaries.

In the *Summoner's Tale*, as we saw earlier, *glose* and *glosynge* are used to denote 'gloss, interpret, explain,' but context shows they are meant pejoratively, for the friar's interpretations are patently deceitful. In the Epilogue to the *Man of Law's Tale* the Shipman objects to the Host's plan to have the Parson "prechen . . . somwhat." He fears that if the Parson is allowed to "gloss" the Gospel he will spread heresy—*glosen* here means 'to interpret falsely' (II 1180). Next the Wife of Bath twice asserts her trust in the literal meaning of things, no matter how much men try to *glose* that meaning away (III 26, 119). And once she rhymes *glose* with *bele chose*, as she relates how her fifth husband would cajole her to make love (III 509-510). When the Merchant so graphically describes May's adultery with Damian in the pear tree, he apologizes for his frankness: "I kan nat glose, I am a rude man" (IV 2351). Similarly, when the "strange knight" in the *Squire's Tale* lists the magical properties of his sword, he asserts: "This is a verray sooth, withouten glose" (V 166). In the latter two cases *glose* comes close to meaning 'to lie.' The Monk and the Manciple, too, use *glosen, glose* pejoratively, roughly with the sense of 'to flatter, deceive' (VII 2140, IX 34).

How revealing of Chaucer's own view are these instances of *glosynge* as 'false interpretation, lying, flattery, deceit'? The fictional speakers quoted so far are not ideal types; they are all without official connection to the Church, "rude" men and women. My last example, however, is more conclusive. For the last pilgrim to take a stand against *glosynge* is the Parson, Chaucer's "good man of religioun":

"Thou getest fable noon ytoold for me;
For Paul, that writeth unto Thymothee,
Repreveth hem that weyven soothfastnesse,

And tellen fables and swich wrecchednesse.
Why sholde I sowen draf out of my fest,
Whan I may sowen whete, if that me lest?
. . . .
I kan nat geeste 'rum, ram, ruf,' by lettre,
Ne, God woot, rym holde I but litel bettre;
And therfore, if yow list—I wol nat glose—
I wol yow telle a myrie tale in prose
To knytte up al this feeste, and make an ende.

(X 31-36, 43-47)

Not willing to tell a tale in verse, alliterative or rhymed, the Parson declares that he will speak prose. His reference to St. Paul (1 Tim. 1: 4, 4: 7 and 2 Tim. 4: 4) is straightforward, and it doesn't require any glossing to see how it supports his stand against "fables." In context, his "I wol not glose" seems to mean "I won't deceive people with poetic fables."

Because the Parson uses *glose* in much the same way as the Wife of Bath and other pilgrims, it seems to me that Professor Robertson's totally unsympathetic view of the Wife's "carnal" exegesis of Scripture is open to question. Chaucer lived at a time when glossing the Bible was acquiring a very bad name, as the "spiritual" sense was being stretched by the likes of the friar in the *Summoner's Tale* for purely selfish ends. I am not saying that the Wife of Bath is Chaucer's answer to fraudulent *glosynge*. Her ends are selfish too. But I think Chaucer had more respect for her carnal, i.e., literal, exegesis than Professor Robertson is willing to allow.

In his tale the Parson quotes the Bible more than any other character in *The Canterbury Tales*, even expanding some of the biblical quotations that were in his sources. [5] Chaucer goes out of his way, it seems, to make the Parson a translator of the Bible into English. As Professor Robertson himself remarks: "It is true that most of his authorities are clear on the surface without exposition, and this is as it should be in a manual addressed to laymen; but it is also true that insofar as it is exegetical, it makes no departures from the traditions of Pauline allegory." [6] This passes lightly over an important point: the *Parson's Tale* is far more "literal" than "exegetical." Chaucer's ideal churchman presents numerous biblical verses in English to a lay audience, concentrating most often on the literal level of interpretation. The Parson holds true to the promise of his portrait in the *General Prologue*:

He was also a lerned man, a clerk,
That Cristes gospel trewely wolde preche;
His parisshens devoutly wolde he teche.
. . . .
This noble ensample to his sheep he yaf,
That first he wroghte, and afterward he taughte.
Out of the gospel he tho wordes caughte . . .
. . . .

---

5. See Siegfried Wenzel, "The Source of Chaucer's Seven Deadly Sins," *Traditio*, 30 (1974), 378.
6. Robertson, p. 336.

But Cristes loore and his apostles twelve
He taughte . . . .

(I 480-482, 496-498, 527-528)

The Parson's use of the Bible is faultless. By contrast, the Wife of Bath reveals in an amusing and entertaining way that the direct, literal approach to Scripture can be abused. Most of her distortions of biblical authority, however, are easily corrected by putting the verses or fragments of verses she quotes back into their context. The friar's false *glosynges* are not so easily exposed. Chaucer's presentation of these and other characters who are exegetes reveals a serious concern for the uses and abuses of biblical authority. We have only begun to appreciate how that concern informs the aesthetic of *The Canterbury Tales*.

* * *

Two strong currents in fourteenth-century English intellectual life that bear heavily on Chaucer's attitude to exegesis and the Bible need to be mentioned here. The first is the anti-fraternal movement of the late four-teenth century and the second, related to the first, is the movement to translate the Bible into English. Both of these movements were of great concern to John Wyclif and his followers, but they were by no means the exclusive preserve of the Wycliffites.

In a recent article, Penn R. Szittya has shed a great deal of light on the anti-fraternal tradition, from its origins to the time of Chaucer. [7] He has shown how from the middle of the thirteenth century and on into Chaucer's day, friars and secular clergy waged a war of mutual recrimination. On both sides the Bible served as ammunition. In Paris it was William of St. Amour (fl. 1250) who, in his *De periculis*, developed what was to become a series of exegetical commonplaces used by later writers against the friars. His work was a refutation of Gerard da Borgo San Donnino's *Introduc-torius ad evangelium aeternum*, an apocalyptic approach to the Bible with a bias in favor of the friars. In England the friars and Wycliffites continued the battle with much the same biblical ammunition. If Chaucer and his contemporaries grew weary of polemical exegesis it may well have been in response to this exegetical Battle of the Book between friars and refor-mers.

Margaret Deanesly's *The Lollard Bible* prints several important documents relating to the question of vernacular Bible translation. [8] Once again the two main camps represented are the mendicants and the secular clergy, in particular the Wycliffites. The friars opposed vernacular Bibles because they worried about errors creeping into a translation (Jerome's Vulgate they regarded as a one-time miracle, not a precedent); and they feared that the literal sense of Scripture might mislead the laity. The

---

7. Penn R. Szittya, "The Antifraternal Tradition in Middle English Literature," *Speculum*, 52 (1977), 287-13.
8. See Deanesly, Appendix II, pp. 399-67.

Wycliffites argued that the Bible had been translated before, many times, as God willed, and that a common-sense reading of Scripture would reveal the shortcomings of the friars to one and all, and mislead no one. In 1378 Wyclif in his *De veritate*, even declared that it was the duty of all Christians to have firsthand knowledge of the Bible. The following passage from Wyclif's *De officio pastorali* gives the flavor of the debate:

> Sum men seyn þat freris trauelen, and þer fautours, in þis cause [i.e., against vernacular Bibles] for þre chesouns.... First þey wolden be seun so nedeful to þe Englizschmen of oure reume þat singulerly in her wit layz þe wit of Goddis lawe, to telle þe puple Goddis lawe on what maner euere þey wolden. And þe secound cause herof is seyd to stonde in þis sentense: freris wolden lede þe puple in techinge hem Goddis lawe, and þus þei wolden teche sum, and sum hide, and docke sum. For þanne defautis in þer lif shulden be lesse knowun to þe puple, and Goddis lawe shulde be vntreweliere knowun boþe bi clerkis and bi comyns. þe þride cause þat men aspien stondiþ in þis, as þey seyn: alle þes newe ordris dreden hem þat þer synne shulde be knowun, and hou þei ben not groundid in God to come into þe chirche; and þus þey wolden not for drede þat Goddis lawe were knowun in Englizsch....[9]

The *Summoner's Tale* leaves no doubt that Chaucer was opposed to the friars' having a monopoly on the Bible. At the same time, his portrait of the Wife as a self-interested, unreliable wielder of biblical quotations suggests he had his reservations about the Wycliffite position, too. It seems that Chaucer stood clear of both camps, but was engaged by the issues that divided them. As Anne Hudson has recently shown, the conflict over Bible translation may have boiled up in the late fourteenth century, but it was not until later that an orthodox versus an heretical position was clearly defined:

> In 1401 the question of biblical translation could be debated openly, without accusations of heresy being levelled against defenders of the view, and without identification of the proponents of translation as *Wycliffistes*. The fact that later in the fifteenth century ... ownership of vernacular scriptures became a piece of primary evidence in cases of suspected Lollardy, should not be interpreted retrospectively.[10]

Neither Professor Robertson nor any other recent commentator on Chaucer's use of the Bible has given sufficient weight to the effect on Chaucer of (1) the fanciful exegetical flights of fourteenth-century friars and their opponents and (2) the rise of the English Bible.[11] I have merely hinted at the relationship of Chaucer and his poetry to these two developments in fourteenth-century intellectual life. It is a relationship that needs to be studied in detail. It may be said at once, however, that Chaucer himself was a gifted translator of the Bible, not relying on the Wycliffite versions

---

9. The text is that printed in Kenneth Sisam, *Fourteenth Century Verse & Prose* (Oxford, 1921; rpt. 1970), pp. 118-19.

10. Anne Hudson, "The Debate on Bible Translation, Oxford 1401," *EHR*, 90 (1975), 17.

11. Professor Robertson mentions the Wycliffe Bible only to say that the Prologue defends the four-level exegetical approach. One might add that the early Wycliffite version included an English gloss on the Gospels. But this is to overlook the real impact of vernacular Bibles on exegesis.

but working independently from the Vulgate, which he must have owned. This much has been noticed before, but not often enough repeated. [12] What has not been noticed is that Chaucer appears in his poetry as an exegete in his own right, and of a most unconventional sort—one who uses the Bible as a kind of gloss on his own fictional creations. I shall cite three examples of this uniquely Chaucerian exegesis, and follow with my own exegetical remarks on what these examples reveal about his attitude to the Bible and its place in his art.

For the first I leave *The Canterbury Tales* for a moment and turn to *Troilus and Criseyde*:

> I passe all that which chargeth nought to seye.
> What! God foryaf his deth, and she al so
> Foryaf, and with here uncle gan to pleye . . . .

(III 1576-1578)

These are the words of the Narrator the morning after Troilus and Criseyde have spent their first night together. Criseyde is still in bed, Pandarus has lifted her sheet, jokingly offered her a sword to cut off his head, and kissed her. As Robinson notes (p. 827, n. 1577), the phrase "God foryaf his deth" had become proverbial, to express the limit to which forgiveness might be carried. Its ultimate source is Luke 23: 34: "Iesus autem dicebat: Pater, dimitte illis: non enim sciunt quid faciunt . . . ." The Narrator's daring analogy makes Criseyde into Christ, betrayed by Pandarus, put to "death" by Troilus. To explicate all the implications of this analogy—the various ways in which it does or does not hold true—would require too lengthy a digression. Suffice it to say that it is at once playful and profoundly serious; approached from one direction it appears frivolous, nearly blasphemous, while from another it seems weighted with pathos and sober religion.

My second example comes from the *General Prologue*, where Chaucer anticipates objections to some of the stories he is about to tell and answers his imagined critics in advance:

> For this ye knowen al so wel as I,
> Whoso shal telle a tale after a man,
> He moot reherce as ny as evere he kan
> Everich a word, if it be in his charge,
> Al speke he never so rudeliche and large,
> Or ellis he moot telle his tale untrewe,
> Or feyne thyng, or fynde wordes newe.
> He may nat spare, althogh he were his brother;
> He moot as wel seye o word as another.
> Crist spak hymself ful brode in hooly writ,
> And wel ye woot no vileynye is it.

(I 730-740)

---

12. See Grace W. Landrum, "Chaucer's Use of the Vulgate," *PMLA*, 39 (1924), 75-100; and W. Meredith Thompson, "Chaucer's Translation of the Bible," in *English and Medieval Studies Presented to J. R. R. Tolkien*, ed. Norman Davis and C. L. Wrenn (London, 1962), pp. 183-99.

Literalism is defended here on moral grounds. To be literal is to be honest. As in the passage from *Troilus and Criseyde*, Chaucer once again invites extraordinary comparisons: Christ spoke *brode* ('freely, frankly') in the Bible, and so will he, Chaucer, in *The Canterbury Tales*. In what sense is *The Canterbury Tales* comparable to Scripture? Are Christ's frank words in the New Testament like the Miller's or Shipman's?

In the link between *Sir Thopas* and the *Tale of Melibee*, Chaucer again uses the Bible to explain his poem:

> ... ye woot that every Evaungelist,
> That telleth us the peyne of Jhesu Crist,
> Ne seith nat alle thyng as his felawe dooth;
> But nathelees hir sentence is al sooth,
> And alle acorden as in hire sentence,
> Al be ther in hir tellyng difference.
> For somme of hem seyn moore, and somme seyn lesse,
> Whan they his pitous passioun expresse—
> I meene of Mark, Mathew, Luc, and John—
> But doutelees hir sentence is al oon.
> Therfore, lordynges alle, I yow biseche,
> If that you thynke I varie as in my speche,
> As thus, though that I telle somwhat moore
> Of proverbes than ye han herd bifoore
> Comprehended in this litel tretys heere,
> To enforce with th' effect of my mateere,
> And though I nat the same wordes seye
> As ye han herd, yet to yow alle I preye
> Blameth me nat; for, as in my sentence,
> Shul ye nowher fynden difference
> Fro the sentence of this tretys lyte
> After the which this murye tale I write.

(VII 943-964)

Melibee, Chaucer asserts, stands in relation to its source as the Gospel narratives of the Passion to one another: not identical in every detail, but in the "sentence." And the author of *Melibee*, Chaucer himself, stands analogically in the role of Evangelist.

In each of the preceding three passages, Chaucer uses the Bible to gloss his poetry in a way that is playful and at the same time profoundly serious. Playful because rhetoric properly applied is supposed to lead to the true meaning of Scripture, and not vice versa; serious because the literal truth of the Bible and its normative authority in all man's affairs—poetry included—is a commonplace of Christian belief—everything human is ultimately subject to judgment in light of biblical precedent. The combination of these two approaches to the Bible in *The Canterbury Tales* is a neglected aspect of Chaucer's profundity and originality. That he was able to use the Bible in both these ways was in large part due, as I suggested earlier, to the accessibility of the Bible in fourteenth-century England, to new translations and a topical interest in the literal sense. To be sure, interpreting the Bible literally was not a fourteenth-century invention. Anselm of Laon spoke with the weight of tradition behind him when he said: "If a man does not bring his common sense to bear upon Scripture, the more subtle, the madder, he is."[13] This describes Chaucer's approach to the Bible as well as any maxim of exegesis possibly can.

---

13. Quoted by Smalley, p. 67.

The Significance of Marginal Glosses in the Earliest Manuscripts of *The Canterbury Tales*

GRAHAM D. CAIE
University of Copenhagen

One of the most frustrating problems still confronting the student of medieval literature is the difficulty in *recognizing* quotations or paraphrases from scriptural, patristic, or classical authors. We are aided by editorial notes, concordances and collections of sources and analogues, and critics continually uncover hitherto unnoticed sources of phrases and concepts, but there frequently remains the nagging doubt "how do we *know* that Chaucer, for example, expected his audience to catch that particular reference?" Students today are often either dismayed by their own lack of biblical knowledge, or skeptical when confronted by so many quotations, paraphrases and echoes that critics claim Chaucer's contemporaries would have recognized. If one is to follow an historical approach to Chaucer studies, however, it is important to consider this question, especially in terms of how the quotation or adaptation of a text might have been interpreted in Chaucer's own era.

We have seen that Chaucer presents us with a number of exegetes in *The Canterbury Tales*, the best known being the so-called "false exegetes," the Wife of Bath, the Pardoner and the Summoner, while the Parson propounds the orthodox interpretation of Scripture.[1] The Wife of Bath on the other hand partially quotes or persuasively misquotes biblical, patristic and astrological authority, and literally applies the "Old Law" to suit her worldly purposes, thus excusing her immoral conduct. An interpretation of her "Prologue" and therefore of her character depends on our ability to *recall* the text abused and so to appreciate the significance of the Wife's deafness to its fourteenth-century interpretation. Professor Robertson has suggested that "those who deny the validity of spiritual exegesis in the fourteenth-century are in effect implying that the Church was dominated by exegetes like these."[2] Chaucer seems to use the Wife (and others) in such a way as to suggest that he expected his readers to have so easy a

---

familiarity with biblical texts that much of his originality could arise from inter-textual play. The fine shade of irony and the subtle implications which so often both create the tone of the tale and guide our evaluation of the teller are frequently appreciated only if one is aware of the source material.

The Wife says, for example, that Paul "bad oure housbondes for to love us weel" (D 161); and even today many would recognize this partial quotation from 1 Cor. 7: 3 and complete it with "and likewise also the wife unto the husband." An allusion less obvious to modern readers might be the Wife's statement "The dart is set up for virginitee" (D 75) in which the Wife's twisting of the text in 1 Cor. 9: 24 and the interpretation in Jerome's *Contra Jovinianum* 1.12 amply illustrate her skill as a "false exegete."[3] But would the contemporary reader have caught these references? In both of the cases cited, and in many others throughout the *Tales*, there is more concrete evidence, requiring no leap of faith: namely, the glosses in the earliest manuscripts of *The Canterbury Tales*.

We know that the glosses must have been written either during Chaucer's lifetime or just after his death, as they appear in manuscripts such as Ellesmere, Hengwrt and Cambridge Dd. 4.24, dated around 1400. There is also strong evidence to support the theory that many were written by Chaucer himself.[4] Such speculation is indeed tempting, but what is important for our interpretation of the *Tales* is the fact that someone—either Chaucer or a contemporary—saw fit to guide our reading, and that scribes throughout the fifteenth century thought these notations sufficiently important not only to copy them but to give them a prominent position on the page, usually in the same size of hand as the text itself.

It is also important for us to consider the function of these glosses. Were they included merely for decoration, to give the *Tales* an aura of authority, or because a medieval scribe enjoyed quoting the Latin source?[5] Were they source references which an astute scribe noticed and wrote down? Were some of them Chaucer's notes to himself, against which to

3. These examples are explained in context in my article "The Significance of the Early Chaucer Manuscript Glosses (with special reference to the *Wife of Bath's Prologue*)," *The Chaucer Review*, 10 (1977), 354-55. All quotations from Chaucer are from F.N. Robinson, ed., *The Works of Geoffrey Chaucer* (2nd ed.; London: Oxford University Press, 1957).

4. E.g., the dating, the importance given to the glosses by contemporary and later scribes, the nature of the comments, the tradition for authorial glossing in the later Middle Ages, and the fact that the Latin text of the gloss, e.g., from Innocent III's *De miseria humane conditionis*, appears to be nearly identical with the text Chaucer must have used when translating quotations for his *Tales*. To support this point and Chaucerian authorship of the glosses, see Robert Enzer Lewis, "Glosses to the *Man of Law's Tale* from Pope Innocent III's *De Miseria Humane Conditionis*," *Studies in Philology*, 64 (1967), 1-16. The first suggestion that Chaucer wrote the glosses is made by Aage Brusendorff, *The Chaucer Tradition* (Copenhagen, 1925), p. 127 and is supported by J. S. P. Tatlock in "*The Canterbury Tales* in 1400," *PMLA*, 50 (1935), 103; Germaine Dempster, "Chaucer's Manuscripts of Petrarch's Version of the Griselda Story," *Modern Philology*, 41 (1943), 10; and Daniel S. Silvia, Jr., "Glosses to the *Canterbury Tales* from St Jerome's *Epistola adversus Jovinianum*," *Studies in Philology*, 62 (1965), 31-33.

5. This view is put forward by J. S. P. Tatlock, "*The Canterbury Tales* in 1400," 103 and partially shared by Robert Enzer Lewis, "Glosses to the *Man of Law's Tale* . . . ," 15-16.

check his "translation" at a later date?[6] Were some "authorial memoranda"—Chaucer's own notes to himself about texts or *exempla* he might add later but never did?[7] A further possibility might be considered, namely that they were in fact comments on the tale to guide the reader's interpretation. Even to note a source reference has the effect of arresting the reader and drawing his attention to the original when he might otherwise pass on with no more than a hazy flicker of recognition. By boldly placing the glosses (side by side with the text) in as large a hand as the text, the glossator prompts the reader to compare the interpretive context of the quotation, perhaps remembering its usual application. In many cases, for example, in the *Wife of Bath's Prologue*, the scriptural gloss is not taken from the biblical source directly, but from a patristic passage (in her case, Jerome) in which the gloss is paraphrased. One might therefore assume that the glossator is deliberately turning our attention to the application of the text, and forcing us to compare that application with the teller's own use of it.

The importance of glossing in the late Middle Ages cannot be sufficiently stressed. The Biblia Pauperum and *bibles moralisées* presented visual commentary which stressed the typological and tropological interpretation of the text, while the important collections of glosses, such as the *Magna Glosatura* of Peter Lombard and the *Glossa ordinaria* (simply called *Glosa* in the Middle Ages) provided most of the common patristic exegesis of the day from, for example, Augustine, Origen, Jerome, Raban, Strabo and John the Scot.[8] Indeed it would be prudent for modern scholars to look first in the *Glosa* for a source of patristic quotation in late medieval texts, rather than going directly to the patristic work itself, which would likely have been less accessible to the medieval writer. Beryl Smalley stresses the use in the later Middle Ages of glossed texts in teaching subjects such as canon law as well as theology, and reminds us that authors such as John Donne in the seventeenth-century used the *Glosa* "without recourse to the *originalia*."[9] The glosses, therefore, formed "an indispensable minimum for the teaching of 'sacra pagina.'"[10] It is therefore not surprising to find that a number of vernacular texts in the late Middle Ages were also glossed, and that they would have been used by the reader in the same way as the scholastic glossed texts, namely as a commentary, as well as for source and cross references. It is in this context that we must approach the glossing in *The Canterbury Tales* manuscripts, remembering that they provide contemporary—if not authorial—comment, and were considered as an integral part of the text by scribes for a hundred years.

It becomes clear, after a cursory glance at the Chaucer glosses, that they have no one single function, and possibly no single author. Some are

---

6. Robert Enzer Lewis, "Glosses to the *Man of Law's Tale* . . . ," 15.
7. Daniel S. Silvia, Jr., "Glosses to the *Canterbury Tales* . . . ," 38.
8. See Beryl Smalley, *The Study of the Bible in the Middle Ages* (Notre Dame: University of Notre Dame Press, 1964), pp. 56 and 66. See also her conclusions on pp. 366-67.
9. *Ibid.*, p. 367.
10. *Ibid.*

explanations of complex words and expressions; for example, "foore" in *Wife of Bath's Prologue* is glossed by the more common "steppes,"[11] and in the *Man of Law's Tale* (1. 185) the unusual "ceriously" is glossed by the low Latin *ceriose* to explain its sense of 'minutely'.[12] We have also some cynical asides. For example, when the Wife states that no man can swear and lie as well as a woman (*WBProl* 1. 228), there appears the cryptic comment *Verum est* (MS Camb. Dd. 4, 24).[13] Other glosses appear to be direct comments on the text, such as biblical quotations which are definitely not source references, but criticism. For example, when the Wife with great pleasure remembers her youthful adventures (11. 469 ff.), the Egerton glossator adds the admonition from 2 Tim. 2: 22: "Flee also youthful lusts."

Finally, there are glosses which are indeed quotations of Chaucer's source, but, because the teller has misquoted or quoted out of context, these glosses are also interpretative. For this reason, it is necessary to know the precise wording of the gloss, when all too often editors, if they mention it at all, give the biblical reference without pointing out that the original is a patristic paraphrase.[14] It is this final group of glosses I should like to concentrate on here, as the function of the other types is more obvious and less ambiguous. For this purpose I shall take the *Man of Law's Tale* as an example.

The first major gloss in the *Man of Law's Tale* occurs at 1. 197 and is taken from the mid-twelfth century *De mundi universitate sive megacosmus et microcosmus* of Bernardus Silvestris.[15] Although this gloss has no direct biblical reference, it is significant as an indication of the methods used by the glossator.

At this point in the tale the Man of Law has introduced his characters and described how rich merchants returned from Rome to Syria where they sang the praises of Custance, the Emperor's daughter, to their Sultan who

---

11. In the Ellesmere Manuscript.

12. In MSS. Ellesmere 26, Hengwrt 154, Christ Church 152.

13. A similar, laconic *Verum est* occurs in the same manuscript at line 930 when the Wife in her *Tale* states that it is flattery and attention that some women like best.

14. Only a selection of glosses is given in the Explanatory Notes of the Robinson edition, while Manly and Rickert reproduce a selection of glosses "when they seem important" at the conclusion of Vol. III of *The Text of the Canterbury Tales* (Chicago: University of Chicago Press, 1940), pp. 483-527.

15. Completed c. 1147-48, according to Peter Dronke, ed. *Bernardus Silvestris: Cosmographia* (Leiden: E. J. Brill, 1978), p. 2. Until the appearance of this excellent edition, that by C. S. Barach and J. Wrobel, eds., *De Mundi Universitate* (Innsbruck, 1876) was used. The best study on this work is by Brian Stock, *Myth and Science in the Twelfth Century: A Study of Bernard Silvester* (Princeton, N.J.: Princeton University Press, 1972). See also T. Silverstein, "The Fabulous Cosmogony of Bernardus Silvestris," *Modern Philology*, 46 (1948-49), 92-116; Peter Dronke, *Fabula: Explorations into the Uses of Myth in Medieval Platonism* (Leiden, E. J. Brill, 1974); E. Gilson, "La cosmogonie de Bernardus Silvestris," *Archives d'histoire doctrinale et littéraire du Moyen Age*, 3 (1928), 5-24; and Chauncey Wood in *Chaucer and the Country of the Stars: Poetic Uses of Astrological Imagery* (Princeton, N. J.: Princeton University Press, 1970), pp. 208-19.

          caught so greet plesance
To han hir figure in his remembrance,
That al his lust and al his bisy cure
Was for to love hire while his lyf may dure.

(186-189)

The merchants tell of her "greet noblesse" (185), but it is her physical form that the Sultan lusts after, and, captivated by the thought of her, he plots how to possess her. His counsellors advise him how to find a "remedye" (1. 210) for his love sickness. Like evil counsellors in hagiography they suggest "magyk and abusioun" (1. 214) and, as a final solution,

They kan nat seen in that noon avantage,
Ne in noon oother wey, save mariage.

(216-217)

Magic and rape being discarded, only marriage remains. It is in this context that the Man of Law interpolates an astrological digression:

Paraventure in thilke large book
Which that men clepe the hevene ywriten was
With sterres, whan that he his birthe took,
That he for love sholde han his deeth, allas!
For in the sterres, clerer than is glas,
Is writen, God woot, whose koude it rede,
The deeth of every man, withouten drede.

In sterres, many a wynter therbiforn,
Was writen the deeth of Ector, Achilles,
Of Pompei, Julius, er they were born;
The strif of Thebes; and of Ercules,
Of Sampson, Turnus, and of Socrates
The deeth; but mennes wittes ben so dulle
That no wight kan wel rede it atte fulle.

(190-203)

The Man of Law's attention during this entire episode is focused on the Sultan and his emotional problems, with little reference to Custance. He laments his fate like a love-sick Troilus or Arcite, convinced that he would die without Custance, but, as the teller eagerly informs us in this quotation, it is ironically his possession of her that causes his death.

The word "deeth" is repeated no less than four times in these few lines, creating dramatic anticipation and thus enlisting our sympathy for this tragic character. The teller lists the tragic deaths of "historical" characters that were predestined, and laments man's lack of foresight.

At this point in the vast majority of manuscripts there is a marginal gloss from the first part, the "Megacosmus," of Bernardus' *Cosmographia*, Book III, lines 39-40 and 43-44. [16]

---

16. In the following *Canterbury Tales* manuscripts: Additional 35286, Corpus Christi, Lansdowne, Sloane 1686, Christ Church, Cambridge Dd., Ellesmere, Egerton 2863 and 2864, Hengwrt, Harl. 1239, and 7335, Lichfield, Petworth, Rawl. Poet. 141, 149, 223, Hatton, Barlow, Cardigan, Manchester, Paris, McCormick, Royal 18, Fitzwilliam, Holkam, Physicians.

Ceptra Phorenei fratrum discordia Thebe fflammam Phetontis Deucalionis Aque
In stellis Priami species Audacia Turni Sensus Vlixeus Herculeusque vigor. [17]

(There are the scepter of Phoroneus, the conflict of the brothers at Thebes, the
flames of Phaeton, Deucalion's flood. In the stars are Priam's pomp, the bold-
ness of Turnus, Odyssean cleverness, and Herculean strength.)

There are, evidently, only a few parallels between the vernacular passage
and the gloss. Bernardus in fact mentions thirty names in this section of his
work, but only four are in common with the Man of Law's list of nine
names, and there is no similarity in the order of presentation. (The four in
common are Achilles, Thebes, Hercules and Turnus.) [18] Apart from these
few names there is no other similarity. The Man of Law mentions only the
deaths of his characters, while Bernardus explicitly stresses the ruling
qualities of the individuals he lists—Priam's pomp, Hercules' strength and
finally Christ's advent when "earthly existence realizes true divinity." [19]
"For that sequence of events which ages to come and the measured course
of time will wholly unfold has a prior existence in the stars," while "the
firmament prefigures all that may come to pass through the decree of
fate." [20]

It becomes increasingly obvious, when comparing the philosophy
presented by Bernardus and that of the Man of Law, that they are diamet-
rically opposed. Bernardus' views would be attractive to Chaucer; as Peter
Dronke points out, both were "deeply concerned with what 'in
sterres . . . was writen' about human affairs, with how human actions are
determined, and how this determinism leaves room for the affirmation of
freedom." [21] Bernardus' list of natural phenomena, historical events, individual characteristics and talents reaches a conclusion and climax with the
birth of Christ, and cosmic order and rationality are stressed throughout.
Dronke quite rightly denies that Bernardus is deterministic and quotes Tul-
lio Gregory: "if the stars prefigure the future, man can free himself from
them and shape his own destiny." [22] The Man of Law, on the other hand,
presents a deterministic and fatalistic world view, akin to that of a despair-
ing Troilus. "The joy at the beauty of creation that marks Bernardus' work

---

17.   This section appears as the following in Peter Dronke's edition, p. 105:
Sceptra Phoronei, fratrum discordia Thebe,
Flamme Phetontis, Deucalionis aque;

. . . .

In stellis Priami species, audatia Turni,
Sensus Ulixeus, Herculeusque vigor.
Translation by Winthrop Wetherbee, *The Cosmographia of Bernardus Silvestris* (New York:
Columbia University Press, 1973), p. 76.
18.   There is in fact as much similarity between the Man of Law's list and the Wife of
Bath's list of men deceived by women (*Wife of Bath's Prologue*, lines 720 ff.): Samson, Socrates and Samson being common to both.
19.   Wetherbee, p. 76.
20.   *Loc. cit.*
21.   Dronke, ed., *Cosmographia*, Introduction, p. 15.
22.   Dronke, *Fabula*, p. 143, n. Gregory is in fact referring to Bernardus'
Mathematicus, but the discussion of the problems of the human situation is fundamentally
similar in both works.

is turned to despondency at the inevitability of astral determinism by the Man of Law. A passage of birth has been changed to one of death.''[23]

A number of questions arise about Chaucer's intentions in this passage and about the significance of the gloss. Did Chaucer intend his audience to catch the faint echo of Bernardus in the Tale? Did he hope we would note the misquotation and contortion of the meaning? Did the glossator add the quotation to ensure that the discrepancy would be noticed, or is the gloss purely a source reference?

The influence of the *Cosmographia* is clearly seen in other medieval writers, such as Neckam, Jean de Meun, Vincent of Beauvais, Dante and Boccaccio, who himself annotated a copy, while Chaucer also displays the influence of Bernardus in the *Knight's Tale*. [24] What is probably more revealing is the fact that this work was to be found in the same manuscript as the more popular *Poetria Nova* of Geoffrey of Vinsauf, a work frequently referred to by Chaucer, and written soon after the death of Richard I. [25] The work is therefore not as obscure as one might first imagine, yet it is hard to state with confidence, as all previous critics have done, that the Man of Law's astrological periphrasis here is *based* on Bernardus, because the text is so contorted. [26] The vernacular passage does in fact recite a common, albeit dangerous, view of life repeated by many of Chaucer's characters who find themselves at the foot of Fortune's wheel, namely that their tragic fate was predestined.

I believe that it is not essential to establish whether or not the contemporary reader would have known the source. The sentiment is easy enough to catch. The gloss acts more as a *commentary* on the Man of Law's philosophy, warning the reader to be suspicious of the way in which the teller makes us sympathize with the lovelorn Sultan.

The Man of Law, in fact, has much in common with Chaucer's other false exegetes, deliberately misinterpreting a source to justify his own "philosophy." In the *General Prologue*, the *Introduction* and the *Prologue* to his tale, we have already been told of the Man of Law's good memory, the fact that he hated poverty and that he gave the impression of being wise and discerning (*GenProl* 312-13). [27] Yet he appears to be confused about the works written by Chaucer, and is incorrect in the list of women about whom Chaucer wrote in *The Legend of Good Women*, omitting two and

---

23. Wood, *The Country of the Stars*, pp. 217-18.
24. For the influence of the *Cosmographia* on later writers see Dronke, ed., *Cosmographia*, pp. 8-15 and Brian Stock, *Myth and Science*, p. 12.
25. This information was conveyed to me by Karin Margareta Fredborg, Institut for græsk og latinsk middelalder filologi, University of Copenhagen. See also Dronke's text, p. 66.
26. Robinson, for example, simply states in the explanatory notes to his edition (p. 693) that this passage is "from the Megacosmos of Bernardus Silvester," and other critics follow suit.
27. See the *General Prologue*, lines 312-13, 323-27 and the *Prologue* to the *Man of Law's Tale*, lines 99-126. See William L. Sullivan, "Chaucer's Man of Law as a Literary Critic," *Modern Language Notes*, 68 (1953), 2-3.

adding a spurious eight. [28] His good memory is therefore suspect, and this is confirmed by the mangled and partially remembered quotation from Bernardus. What is important is to see how he has consciously or otherwise twisted the meaning to suit his own purposes. The wisdom and discretion also attributed to him in the *General Prologue* (especially when Chaucer adds "He semed swich" (*GenProl* 313)), are therefore also suspect, and this is confirmed by a careful reading of the text and underlined by the glosses.

The shift from sympathy for the conventional heroine to an immoral pagan (although he embraces Christianity in order to marry Custance) is more clearly seen if one compares this section with Chaucer's source, Nicholas Trivet's *Anglo-Norman Chronicle*, where the heroine possesses the typical "militant, self-assured, often unpleasant proselytizing fervor not uncommon in the early Saints' Lives." [29] Custance is a "Christian bluestocking," according to Yunck. Here the Sultan is the pagan persecutor trying to force himself on the proprietous Christian maiden. Yunck's conclusion, however, is that this tale was not meant for the Man of Law but for the more sedate Prioress, because Custance's zeal is toned down. But in fact Custance's lack of missionary fervor fits in perfectly with the way in which the Man of Law has twisted his story away from a didactic Saint's Life and shifted the sympathy to the Sultan, thus creating a world where "woe follows joy." If we had missed the clues already presented to us by Chaucer, then the gloss should arrest our attention and make us compare the flawed philosophy of the teller with that presented by Bernardus Silvestris, itself akin to that of Chaucer. The *Prologue* to the tale, therefore, stressing the miseries of poverty, is far from lacking any connection with the tale itself, and admirably prepares us for a questionable view of the world in which only the dangers of poverty, and not those of riches, are stressed.

The majority of glosses in the *Man of Law's Tale* are taken from Pope Innocent III's *De miseria humane conditionis*, and provide the source references for the five passages from Innocent (about 50 lines altogether) that the teller inserts in his tale. There is no doubt that Chaucer was not only well acquainted with this work, but also may have translated it himself, as he had done the two other works on which he most relied, namely Boethius' *De consolatione philosophiae* and *Le Roman de la Rose*. [30] The

---

28. See Sullivan, pp. 4-5. He concludes that the Man of Law's error is included by Chaucer as deliberate misrepresentation. The condemnation of "moral Gower" implied in lines 77 ff. simply shows the Man of Law's own folly and is, according to Sullivan, "perhaps the most self-revealing remark the Man of Law makes" (p. 7). These factual errors simply reverse the Man of Law's impression of himself regarding his memory and wisdom and therefore ought to serve as subtle warnings when later he quotes from other sources.

29. John Yunck, "Religious Elements in Chaucer's *Man of Law's Tale*," *Journal of English Literary History*, 27 (1960), 250.

30. There is a reference in *Prologue G* to *The Legend of Good Women*, lines 413-15, to Chaucer's own translation of Innocent's work:

> He hath in prose translated Boece,
> And of the Wreched Engendrynge of Mankynde
> As man may in pope Innocent yfynde.

influence and popularity of this work, which circulated in over 500 manuscripts, is indisputable, as illustrated, for example, in *Piers Plowman* and *The Pricke of Conscience*.[31]

In the *Prologue* to his tale, lines 99-121, the Man of Law quotes from Book I, Chapter 15 of this work, concerning the miseries of both poor and rich. Significantly, the Man of Law, as a typical false exegete, mentions only the "hateful harm, condicion of poverte" (1. 99), while the rich merchants are praised: "O riche merchauntz, ful of wele been yee, / O noble, o prudent folk . . . ." (11. 122-23), omitting Innocent's "the rich man is debauched by his own abundance, an unbridled boaster who runs about at will, and so runs afoul into immorality."[32] This section in Innocent concludes with the Matthew 6:21 text: "Where your treasure is, there will your heart be also." In another section of his work (2. 4) Innocent particularly berates lawyers who "neglect the poor man's case with delay, promote the rich man's with dispatch; to the poor you are harsh, to the rich mild."[33] Such a partial quotation and corruption of Innocent's text, akin in methods to those of the Wife of Bath, sets the tone for his later application of "authority," and it is on these occasions that the glosses play a significant role, not only as source references, but as reminders of the meaning of Innocent's text.

The tale, he says, was told to him by a merchant, and the initial part, as seen above, is narrated through the eyes of the Syrian merchants. In the tale itself he is at pains to tell us about the great reception that Custance received on her arrival in Syria; terms such as rich, joy, gay, mirth, glad, distinguished ("solempne"), royally, set the tone of the passage, yet do not at all reflect the mood of the heroine. In spite of his repeated comments that he will avoid extraneous material (e.g., 11. 428, 990), he interpolates, as if angrily and morally aroused to comment, a passage from Innocent (11. 421-27):

O sodeyn wo, that evere art successour
To worldly blisse, spreyned with bitternesse!
The ende of the joye of oure worldly labour!
Wo occupieth the fyn of oure gladnesse.
Herke this conseil for thy sikernesse:
Upon thy glade day have in thy mynde
The unwar wo or harm that comth bihynde.

The passage follows very closely the source in Innocent, *De miseria* 1. 22 on *De inopinato dolore*: The gloss reads as follows (sections omitted by the Man of Law are in brackets):

See also Robert Enzer Lewis, "Chaucer's Artistic Use of Pope Innocent III's *De Miseria Humane Conditionis* in the *Man of Law's Prologue and Tale*," *PMLA*, 81 (1966), 485. Like Yunck he concludes that "it seems almost certain that the tale of Custance was not the tale originally intended for the Man of Law, that it was only later assigned to him" (485).

31. See Donald R. Howard, ed., *On the Misery of the Human Condition*. The Library of Liberal Arts (Indianapolis: Bobbs-Merrill, 1969), pp. xiii-xiv.
32. Trans. Margaret Mary Dietz in the above edition, p. 17.
33. *Ibid.*, p. 35.

Nota de inopinato dolore Semper mundane leticie tristicia repentina succedit Mundana igitur felicitas multis amaritudinibus est respersa extrema gaudii luctus occupat Audi ergo salubre consilium In die bonorum ne immemor sis malorum

On Unexpected Sorrow: For sudden sorrow always follows worldly joy: [what begins in gaiety ends in grief.] Worldly happiness is besprinkled indeed with much bitterness. [He knew this who said, "Laughter shall be mingled with sorrow, and] mourning takes hold of the end of joy." [The children of Job experienced it when they ate and drank wine in the house of their first-born brother, for suddenly a strong wind rushed out of the desert and struck the four corners of the house, which fell in and crushed them all. Rightly then did the father say, "My harp is tuned to mourning and my organ into the voice of those that weep." "It is better to go into the house of mourning than to go into the house of feasting."] A wise counsel: "In the day of good things, be not unmindful of evil things." ["In all thy works remember thy last end and thou shalt never sin."][34]

Lewis notes how closely Chaucer translates the text of Innocent as found in the gloss. Yet viewed in their separate contexts, and especially in respect of the consequent interpretations implied by Innocent and the Man of Law, there is a vast difference in effect. The context in the vernacular story is one of feasting and joy at the prospect of the Sultan's marriage, whereupon the Man of Law once more introduces a note of dramatic foreshadowing by lamenting that this revelry is to be followed by sorrow—another fatalistic warning that all pleasure will end in sadness. But if we once more remember the nature and faith of the revellers and the condition of the Christian "martyr," Custance, then the pleasure becomes highly suspect.

What the Man of Law omits from his source, as one can see from the translation, are the *biblical* quotations from Job, Ecclesiastes and Ecclesiasticus. The *exemplum* omitted from Job 1: 13 stresses the transience of worldly joys, by describing how a great wind struck the house of feasting and killed the children of Job. But it is a text that concludes with a strong affirmation of faith: "The Lord gave and the Lord taketh away. Blessed be the name of the Lord." The stress is on the need to trust in divine providence and the way in which all things work together for good for those who love the Lord. Ironically, then, this is indeed the case when one considers the feasting from the viewpoint of the heroine in the tale. Innocent wishes to show the dignity of the human race, to humble the proud and weaken our reliance on worldly vanity, whereas the Man of Law uses the text to lament the break-up of a good party and a nominally equitable marriage bargain.

In the same section Innocent quotes from Ecclesiasticus 7: "Better to visit the house of mourning than the house of feasting." This is an extremely apt text in the circumstances, but one that would not have aided

---

34. *Ibid.*, pp. 25-26. The text edited by Michele Maccarrone, *Lotharii Cardinalis: De Miseria Humane Conditionis* (Lugano, 1955), pp. 29-30, reads: "Semper enim mundane lelitie tristitia repentina succedit.... Mundana quippe felicitas multis amaritudinibus est respersa... et extrema gaudii luctus occupat. Salubre consilium: 'In die bonorum ne immemor sis malorum.'"

the Man of Law's case. This text continues: "Wise men's thoughts are at home in the house of mourning but a fool's thoughts in the house of mirth." The Man of Law, wishing the mirth to continue, would classify himself amongst the worldly fools if he had not omitted this passage. Patristic morality is now used to shift our sympathies from the Christian saint to the pagan "persecutor." Custance is left out of the picture and the farewell feast for her is silently passed over (lines 246-52). We have, however, a glimpse of her feelings in these lines:

> Custance, that was with sorwe al overcome,
> Ful pale arist, and dresseth hire to wende;
> For wel she seeth ther is noon oother ende.

(264-66)

She has much in common with Job; continually abused, but forever saved from ultimate tragedy as her faith is tested. Like Griselda she is a symbol of endurance, of Christian acceptance of the ways of the world. There is no feeling of "Blessed be the name of the Lord" after this "tragedy" on the part of the Man of Law; he simply sees the plans of the rich merchants and powerful Sultan thwarted, a royal and magnificent marriage and a frustrated trade contract.

The gloss, therefore, does not add any new material to point out the omitted passages, but by reminding us of the well-known source, it invites a comparison of the *application* made of it. The concept of woe after joy was very popular, but not with the interpretation the Man of Law makes. [35] The picture that seems to emerge is one of a worldly lawyer, attracted by the pleasures of this life in such a way as to vitiate in him any just interpretation. [36]

A third source of glosses in the majority of the *Man of Law's Tale* manuscripts comes from astrological works, as is also the case in the *Wife of Bath's Prologue*. [37] The first of these glosses occurs at line 295. Custance laments her departure from Rome to the "Barbre nacioun" (1. 281) and the

---

35. Cf. lines 1132-38 and the gloss which has its source in *De miseria* I. 22: "Quis unquam unicam diem totam duxit in sua dileccione iocundam quem in aliqua parte diei reatus conscience vel impetus   Ire vel motus concupiscencie non turbauerit quem liuior   Inuidie vel Ardor Auaricie vel tumor superbia non vexauerit quem aliqua iactura vel offensa vel passio non commouerit et cetera." See also Robert Enzer Lewis, "Chaucer's Artistic Use ... ," 489-92. He concludes: "because the alternation of "wo after gladnesse" and "joye after wo" is the pattern of action in the *Man of Law's Tale* ... I would suggest that it becomes the organizing principle on which the Tale is based." (492).

36. There are further glosses from *De Miseria* at lines 771 and 925 which quote the source of the Man of Law's outbursts against the sins of *gula* and *luxuria*. Once more our attention is drawn to the source work and the general admonition by Innocent III to spurn all things of this world. Edward A. Block has suggested that these citations were added to the Trivet narrative "to impart a high moral seriousness ... and heighten the formal poetic effect." ("Originality, Controlling Purpose, and Craftsmanship in Chaucer's *Man of Law's Tale*," *PMLA*, 68 (1953), 585, n. 36); this view is also held by Lewis, "Chaucer's Artistic Use ... ," 488-89.

37. At lines 609 and 705 of the *Wife of Bath's Prologue* there are glosses from astrological treatise *Almansoris Propositiones*.

Man of Law melodramatically launches into a list of comparable events in epic and tragedy when one might have heard such "tendre wepyng for pitee" (1. 292). Thereupon he angrily turns, to the reader's surprise, to blame the "first moevyng! crueel firmament" (1. 295) that has caused the death of this marriage. He describes in great detail how the "First Moving" hurls the planets from east to west against their natural tendency, thus causing Mars to slay the marriage (301).

The glossator at this point quotes from Ptolemy's *Almagest* Book 1, Chapter 8:

> Vnde Ptholomeus libro 1° capitulo 8° Primi motus celi duo sunt quorum vnus est qui mouet totum semper ab Oriente in Occidentem vno modo super orbes et cetera Item alter vero motus est qui mouet orbem stellarum currencium contra motum primum videlicet ab Occidente in Orientem super alios duos polos et cetera. [38]

The normal movement of the stars is explained: the Primum Mobile (the First Moving) moved from east to west daily, while the annual motion of the planets was from west to east. The function is orderly and normal: "the motion of the First Moving is regularly associated with rationality," [39] while the movement of the planets from west to east is traditionally associated with an irrational desire, according to Platonic and Aristotelian thought. The Man of Law implies precisely the opposite, and appears to be confused about the basic laws of the Ptolemaic universe, and—perhaps a worse failing—dangerously blames the First Mover and thence God for causing a tragedy. Theseus in the *Knight's Tale* states:

> The Firste Moevere of the cause above,
> Whan he first made the faire cheyne of love,
> Greet was th'effect, and heigh was his entente.
>
> (*KT* 2987-89)

The passage is based on Boethius' hymn to the First Mover and clearly shows the equation of God and First Mover: "[God's] power turns the moving sky . . . . All things obey their ancient law / And all perform their proper task . . . . " [40] To blame the First Mover for being cruel and causing tragedy is indeed a questionable and dangerous statement. Ironically, of course, the "tragedy" ought to have been applauded by the Man of Law, but his attitude to this excellent marriage bargain is not, as we have seen, that expected of a Christian.

The gloss from *Almagest* corrects the error that the Man of Law makes and stresses the natural and orderly nature of the motions of the planets. It is interesting to see that this passage is Chaucer's own invention, and not to be found in Trivet. The glossator, one might assume, was aware of the way in which Chaucer the astrologer frequently places incor-

---

38. This gloss appears in all the manuscripts mentioned in note 16 above with the addition of Phillipps 8137 and Trinity Camb. R. 3. 15 and the exception of Holkham and Physicians.

39. Wood, *The Country of the Stars*, p. 231.

40. *De consolatione philosophiae* 1, m. 5. See also 2, m. 8; 4, pr. 6 and m. 6; 3, pr. 10.

rect astrological assertions in the mouths of his characters to highlight their mistaken thought, and he might well wish to ensure that those less well acquainted with astrology would catch this gross perversion of the *Almagest*.

The illogical thought continues in the next two stanzas of the tale, which are presented in an equally emotional way (11. 302-15). The Emperor is accused by the Man of Law of being imprudent, as he did not take an astrological election to find out the most favorable time for his daughter's departure from Rome. One might initially ask how an election concerning the time of *departure* from Rome would affect the events surrounding the marriage some time later. As it happens, the election would have proved unfavorable, according to the Man of Law, but the journey appears to have been successful, without shipwreck or storm. One might then ask if a drastic configuration would imply tragedy for Custance or the Sultan, as the one is saved a tragic marriage and the other killed. The Man of Law's conclusion that "we been to lewed or to slowe" (1. 315) to bother consulting the stars before acting rebounds on himself, just as his previous statement that "mennes wittes ben so dulle" (1. 202) that they cannot read their deaths in the stars tells us more about the lack of wisdom of the teller. We begin, therefore, to see the implications of the subtle warning in the *General Prologue*, namely that he *seemed* wise, while criticizing others for their lack of forethought.

At this point in the tale the glossator adds a very subtle quotation (at 1. 309) which in many manuscripts is appended to the *Almagest* quotation.[41] It comes from the ninth-century Arab astronomer Zael's *Liber Electionum*:

> Omnes concordati sunt quod elecciones sint debiles nisi in diuitibus habent enim isti licet debilitentur eorum elecciones radicem .i. natiuitates eorum que confortat omnem planetam debilem in itinere et cetera.

> All agree that elections are uncertain except concerning the rich. Although elections concerning them are uncertain (in themselves) as well, these persons possess a fundament in their nativities which serves to conform all planets in their uncertain courses.[42]

The gloss concludes with an "et cetera" which might suggest that we should continue the quotation from Zael: "On the other hand, I should not make any pronouncement on elections for lowly persons or merchants . . . ." It is perhaps amusingly significant that the Man of Law should omit from his paraphrase the reference to any connections between merchants and lowly persons in a tale that praises wealth and is told to the Man of Law by a merchant (1. 132).

---

41. This gloss appears in the manuscripts mentioned in note 16 above with the addition of Phillipps 8137 and Trinity Camb. R. 3. 15 and the exception of Holkham, Physicians, Fitzwilliam and Barlow.

42. I am grateful to Fritz Saaby Petersen, Institut for græsk og latinsk middelalder filologi, University of Copenhagen, for this translation.

Elections are uncertain, the glossator tells us, although the chances are improved for the rich. The edge of the accusation that all this might have been averted is therefore blunted. Elections cannot be trusted; had one been made for the voyage, what validity would it have had concerning the marriage? Finally, in whose interests was it to have a successful marriage? The contemporary reader might well have remembered Paul's admonitions to Christians concerning marriage to non-Christians: "Be ye not unequally yoked together with unbelievers: for what fellowship hath righteousness with unrighteousness? and what communion hath light with darkness?" (2 Cor. 6: 14).

The Man of Law, therefore, blinds us with his astrological "wisdom," creating a complicated astrological configuration which critics have long disputed. However one interprets the details (e.g., the hotly disputed "atazir" (1. 305) and "ascendent tortuous" (1. 302)), the overall meaning is the same, namely that the voyage occurs at a dangerous configuration of the planets with "crueel Mars" to the fore. The resulting interpretation made by the Man of Law, who blinds us with *scientia* and impressive scriptural quotations delivered in an emotional manner, might well convince us and win our sympathy for the poor Sultan who is deprived of his heart's desire, were it not for the glosses that remind us of the manner in which the teller twists his quotations. The glosses may indeed indicate the source of the teller's quotation or allusion, but their presence interrupts the rhetorical flow of the teller's argument and lessens the possibility that the illogical statements or misquoted texts couched in poetic language might lull our reasoning power and make us uncritical of the teller.

Chaucer's *Canterbury Tales* and Nicholas of Lyre's *Postillae litteralis et moralis super totam Bibliam*

DOUGLAS WURTELE
Carleton University

It has been observed that some of the subtlest ironies in Chaucer's *Canterbury Tales* are those produced by the pilgrims' habit of making copious use of biblical quotations, allusions, and resonances. To illumine further the methods and purposes underlying this achievement in irony, the *postillae* on the literal and moral senses of Scripture compiled by the fourteenth-century Franciscan scholar, Nicholas of Lyre,[1] are of considerable importance. Closer attention to this biblical expositor, so nearly contemporaneous with the poet, is also called for by the fact that the exegetical approach to Chaucer's work has proved so fruitful. To be sure, it has been questioned whether all or only some of the components making up the whole *Canterbury Tales* should be interpreted according to the methods of "fourfold" scriptural exegesis. It can be argued that a technique originally designed to reveal the hidden senses implanted in the *pagina sacra* by the *auctor principalis* through the medium of the *auctor instrumentalis*[2] may or

---

1. On the nomenclature suitable for Nicolas de Lyra's work, there has always been some uncertainty. Henri Labrosse, *Études Franciscains*, 35 (1923), 175, 424, refers to the *Postilla litteralis* and the *Postilla moralis* as if citing plural forms. The *New Catholic Encyclopaedia*, 10 (1967), 453-54, refers to the *Postillae perpetuae sive brevia commentaria in universa Biblia*. There seems to be some uncertainty whether "postilla" is a singular or plural form; the title of the 1492 Strassburg edition, *Postilla super totam Bibliam*, is sometimes referred to as a singular "collective," hence "postillae" are the separate parts taken together as a plural noun; but in the *Cambridge History of the Bible*, R. L. P. Milburn writes that the *postilla* "were" recognized as a supplement to the *Glossa* (II, 305-4). Hans Rost in *Der Bibel im Mittelalter* (Augsburg, 1939) also employs "postilla" as a plural form, describing the word as a short term for "post / illa verba" of the "textus Evangeli" (p. 354). These usages raise the problem of how to refer to any one single piece of the commentary on some passage. To avoid confusion the present discussion will follow the coinage adopted by Beryl Smalley in *The Study of the Bible in the Middle Ages* (Oxford, 1964), 270, using the singular form "post-ill' and plural "postills;" I also adopt her usage of referring to the author simply as "Lyre." Margaret Deanesly in *The Lollard Bible and other Medieval Biblical Versions* (Cambridge, 1920) also uses this form. See also M. D. Chenu, *Toward Understanding St. Thomas*, trans. A. M. Landry and D. Hughes (Chicago, 1964), 241, where this usage receives approval.

2. St. Thomas Aquinas makes the distinction between the Holy Spirit as *auctor principalis* of Scripture and man as *auctor instrumentalis* in *Quodlibet* VII, q. 6, art. 1 ad 5.

may not offer a suitable method to apply to a secular poem. Yet the explicit instructions of Dante in both his *Convivio* and his letter to Can Grande afford a warrant for adopting such a procedure at least in reading the Divine Comedy and also, it may be, for the human comedy presented by Chaucer.

Intention aside, of Chaucer's knowledge of Scripture there can by now hardly be any doubt. The evidence for his biblical study is manifest throughout *The Canterbury Tales*, for most of the direct and indirect scriptural citations come not from the various sources drawn on for the pilgrims' prologues and tales but constitute the poet's own interpolation. Even in the *Parson's Tale*, not all of the numerous biblical references are extracted from the Parson's chief manual, St. Raymund of Pennaforte's *Summa casum poenitentiae*. In the nature of things, the acquisition of so firm a grasp on the Vulgate would have exposed Chaucer also to the riches of the interlinear and marginal exegesis supplied in the *Glossa ordinaria*, to which an intensive study, probably over many years, seems to have been devoted by the poet. In that period a strong interest was growing in the precise explication of Scripture's *sensus litteralis*. This need not mean that attention to the traditional sub-surface typological, tropological, and anagogical senses had beem abandoned. Indeed, Wyclif himself upholds the traditional fourfold interpretation for the sake of promoting *caritas*, citing as authority St. Augustine's prescriptions and the Venerable Bede's classic exegesis of "Jerusalem."[3] Preachers are enjoined to search out the "thre goostly vndirstondings" of the allegorical (or typological), the moral (or tropological), and the anagogical levels for which the literal level provides the "ground and foundament." Wyclif's complaint is not against this orthodox method but against clerks who pursue it negligently or sophistically. This much at least links the late medieval period, of Wyclif and Chaucer, Nicholas of Lyre and John Bromyard, to that of a millenium earlier in the exercise and encouragement of what J. B. Allen has called the "analogical sensibility." Throughout this long and heterogeneous period, "the sensibility of the educated medieval man was based on a Latin which distanced his ego into definition, which provided him with a highly cultivated and poeticized corpus of literature as the container of received truth, and which encouraged allegory as the dominant mental procedure for dealing with interior and exterior reality."[4]

If then in Chaucer's century a greater emphasis began to be placed on the extraction of biblical teaching out of the literal level, that does not mean that the allegorical levels fell into desuetude. It is also the case, of course, that by Chaucer's time what might be called the mystical or

---

3. See *Prologue to the Wycliffe Bible*, ed. Forshall and Madden, 4 v. (Oxford, 1850) I, Chap. xii and xiii (pp. 43-52). See also H. Hargreaves, "The Vernacular Scriptures," in *Cambridge History of the Bible*, II, 412, where it is noted that the exegetical marginal commentaries in the Wycliffite Bible are apparently drawn from Nicholas de Lyra as well as St. Augustine and the *Glossa*.
4. "The Education of the Public Man: A Mediaeval View," *Renascence*, 26 (1974), 180-81.

spiritual senses had been very thoroughly analyzed. The original commentaries reproduced in the marginal glosses were by now of some antiquity. Frequently recurring names are those of St. Jerome, St. Augustine, St. Ambrose, of St. John Chrysostom and Origen, of Isidore of Seville and the Venerable Bede, of Gregory the Great and Rabanus Maurus, of Eusebius, Sedulius, Tertullian; those of the Victorines are relative latecomers. Even as early as Aquinas we find, in his *Expositio in Job ad litteram*, the reflection that as Gregory's commentary has adequately explored the allegorical meanings, Aquinas will concentrate on the literal.[5] It should not be surprising, then, to find after the lapse of another century a continuation of that emphasis. Detecting this tendency in mid-fourteenth century thought, W. A. Pantin mentions the "deliberate use of Scripture instead of Scholastic arguments" in the writings of an orthodox thinker like Richard Fitzralph as well as in the appeals to Scripture so important in the system of John Wyclif.[6] One should keep in context the depth and range of scriptural citation in *The Canterbury Tales* by recalling not only that theology "had always been conceived of as based on Scripture, as *pagina sacra*," but also that in Chaucer's time thinkers such as these "seem disposed to take that more literally than usual." In particular, it was also in the century of Fitzralph and Wyclif that the Norman Franciscan, Nicholas of Lyre, devoted his immense labour to the elucidation of the literal sense of Scripture.

Given Chaucer's evident interest in the *pagina sacra*, or more precisely his interest in showing how biblical ideas have penetrated the consciousness of his pilgrim-narrators, there are several reasons why the explanations by the *Doctor planus et utilis*, as Pantin and others describe Lyre, would have commended themselves to the London poet. One of these is the remarkable popularity and accessibility of Lyre's postills. Another is the lucidity of Lyre's textual expositions at the literal level and the tolerant wisdom of his discussions at the moral level. The perspicuity of these expositions can make for ironic contrasts when placed beside the distortions, deliberate or unwitting, found in the pilgrims' brash demonstrations of biblical knowledge. Still another reason for Lyre's possible appeal to Chaucer is the commentator's delight in occasionally expanding on unusual pieces of natural lore suggested by the sacred text.

In a definitive study of Lyre's work, Henri Labrosse gives 1322-1331 for the composition of the *Postilla litteralis* and 1339 for that of the *Postilla moralis*.[7] By 1309 Lyre (c. 1270-1349) had become professor at the Sorbonne, where he taught for many years. He has been described as "one of the best equipped biblical scholars of the Middle Ages;" a master of Hebrew and familiar with rabbinic scholarship, and also particularly indebted

5. See *Prologus* to *Expositio in librum Sancti Job* (Paris, 1876), 18. 2.
6. *The English Church in the Fourteenth Century* (Cambridge, 1955), 132-34.
7. See "Sources de la biographie et œuvres de Nicolas de Lyre," *Études Franciscains* 16 (1906) 383-404; 17 (1907) 489-505, 593-608; 19 (1908) 41-52, 153-75, 368-79; 35 (1923) 171-87, 400-432; see also C. V. Langlois, "Nicolas de Lyre, frère mineur," *Hist. Litt. Franc.* 36 (1927), 355-400.

to Aquinas.[8] His chief work, the *Postillae perpetuae sive brevia commentaria in universa Biblia*, explains and expands upon the literal sense, which he regarded as the foundation of all mystical interpretations. The verdict of the present age, that his "exposition was lucid and concise and his observations, always original, were judicious and sound," seems to have been shared by his own age, and these qualities, again, are precisely those likely to have earned the respect of Geoffrey Chaucer; Herman Hailperin, noting how frequently in Lyre's running commentary on the Old and New Testaments occur references to the medieval Jewish scholar, Rabbi Rashi, or "Rabbi Solomon" as Lyre calls him, expresses the conviction that Lyre was "not only a person of great scholarship but also a man of integrity," who, for all that the postills occasionally display anti-Jewish invective, can be described as "serious, loyal, courteous, positive, and truly scientific."[9]

Qualities of this order may well have served to attract a mind like Chaucer's to Lyre's commentaries; they certainly drew the approbation of others in his day and beyond it. In the Prologue to the Wyclif Bible (Ch. XIII) Lyre is quoted on the manner of explaining the levels of understanding in Holy Writ. In *De veritate sacrae scripturae* (1378) Wyclif describes him as a "copious and ingenious commentator of scripture,"[10] and in the second version of the Wyclif Bible Lyre's own prologue is liberally cited. Some years after Wyclif, Chancellor Gascoigne, one of the Lollards' most formidable opponents, mentions "Doctor Nicholas de Lyra" several times in his *Dictionarium theologicum*.[11] An impressive claim for Lyre's influence is made by Margaret Deanesly, who argues that his commentaries became "the universal text-book for scholars in the fourteenth and fifteenth centuries."[12] Similarly, Rost comes to the conclusion that Lyre's postills provided, next to the *Glossa ordinaria* itself, the most influential and widespread Bible commentary in the later Middle Ages and beyond it into the age of print; in fact, Lyre's was one of the first to be so reproduced.[13]

What Lyre does in examining the *sensus litteralis* is supply an extraordinarily detailed opening out of the meaning of events, places, and pronouncements in the sacred text, as if taking with total seriousness the standard tag, "Littera gesta docet." These "gesta" he makes it his business to analyze thoroughly, for which purpose he had made "a special study of the Hebrew language and of the Jewish commentators."[14] It was no mere antiquarian zeal that impelled him to undertake his task; nor did he discredit

---

8. *New Cath. Ency.*, 10, 453-54.
9. *Rashi and the Christian Scholars* (Pittsburgh, 1963), 137-45. There is a great deal of information on Lyre in this indispensable work.
10. Deanesly (n. 1 above), 241-42, 265-66.
11. E.g., s.v. "Deus" (I. 251) and s.v. "Praedicator" (II. 447) in *Loci e Libro Veritatum*, ed. J. E. T. Rogers (Oxford, 1881).
12. (N. 1 above), 166. Elsewhere she refers to Lyre's work as being after 1340, "the commentary most in demand by what we should call 'scientific scholars'" (p. 175).
13. (N. 1 above), 87.
14. Milburn (n. 1 above), II, 304-5.

the moral and mystical sub-surface meanings of the text. He believed, however, that only by fully grasping all the implications of the literal could the allegorical be comprehended. Hence, as Milburn continues, "though prepared to allow that the student requires the assistance of symbolism and allegory in the task of biblical interpretation, Nicholas made it his prime concern to arrive at an exact understanding of the literal sense." Every page of Lyre's vast work offers examples of this concern; let three suffice. One comes from St. Mark's description of Christ's baptism, one from the account in Genesis of the creation of man and woman, and one from a particularly rich passage in the Song of Songs, that text upon which, relative to its brevity, probably more typological and tropological exegesis was performed than upon any comparable book.

The incident that the Apostle describes was indeed one of the most important "gesta" of history, and in this light Lyre applies to it his technique of opening out the text and asking the right kind of question: "And forthwith coming up out of the water, he saw the heavens opened and the Spirit as a dove, descending and remaining on him. And there came a voice from heaven: Thou art my beloved Son; in thee I am well pleased" (Mk. 1: 10-11). [15] The postill begins with a generality: "In the baptism of Christ appeared the whole Trinity, the Father in the voice, the Holy Spirit under the form of the dove, and the Son in the flesh" (*Glossa*, V, fol. 91r). A distinction is drawn between the flesh being in unity with the Son and the voice and the dove having a unity only "in representatione signi." Lyre then looks into the practical matters raised by the text, such as the basis for baptizing in the name of the Trinity in contrast with apostolical baptism in the name of Christ only, as well as the utility of the text in refuting the error of those who attributed the virtue of baptism to its ministers. In contrast to the marginal glosses drawn, in this instance, from St. Jerome and the Venerable Bede, here there is in Lyre's commentary nothing mystical; he deals on firm ground with an incident explained in its historicity and not as typology; he is interested in the reasons for things, not their hidden senses. Here, typically, his postill is concerned to expose errors of the past and obviate those of the present.

Concerning the single phrase "in te complacui," he not only devotes a postill of well over two hundred words to a literal discussion of the divine pronouncement but also, in scholastic fashion, raises quasi-hypothetical points about the event. He puts the question, for example, "whether it was fitting for the heavens to be opened when Christ was baptized and the voice of the Father to be heard." Here Lyre is not questioning the truth of the narration. This Lyre never does, accepting the text's authenticity without reservation. But by the very fact of taking the text literally instead of figurally and by raising such points as this with respect to concrete

15.   Throughout this paper the Douai-Reims translation is used. References to Lyre's postills will be from the *Glossa ordinaria* as follows: Vols. I, II, III, VI (Paris, 1590), Vols. IV, V (Lyons, 1545). On the question of translation, I should like to record my gratitude to my colleague, Professor R. C. Blockley, for his unfailing assistance and advice.

difficulties, rather as Aquinas did on more abstract issues, he is in fact adding to his audience's sense of the credibility of Holy Writ rather than detracting from it. The lengthy analysis called for by the questions he asks here in a sense combines rationalism and fideism, for in true scholastic fashion he first answers his own proposition by arguing against it. For several reasons it is arguable, then, that the opening of the heavens was not fitting. One is that such an opening was not according to natural law; the celestial bodies are incorruptible, hence the heavens cannot be broken open. Nor could it be merely an apparent opening, for this would mean a falseness in the divine words and that also is not fitting. Moreover, the gates of heaven were not opened to Christ in his baptism but in his passion. Lyre's analysis proceeds in this quasi-scientific style until he can adduce the exact reason why, nevertheless, the opening of the heavens at Christ's baptism was indeed "conveniens." Though an event different in kind from the passion, there was a similarity with the transfiguration, for at that time the voice of the Father was again heard, giving approbation to Christ's preaching. This is the key. Lyre notes that Christ did not begin preaching immediately upon being baptized, but only after the incarceration of the Baptist. His baptism evidently had to come first, not that he stood in need of it but so that he might confer the virtue of rebirth, as is made clear by the Baptist's words. Lyre argues, then, that as it was fitting for the heavens to open so as to bestow divine approval upon Christ's preaching, so also it was at the moment of John the Baptist's testimony concerning the baptism to be bestowed by the newly baptized Christ. The human testimony of the Baptist was in fact the testimony of God the Father on Christ's forthcoming ministry, and on that account "conveniens sit caelum aperiri." What makes this kind of exposition so effective is that the tropological implications then become almost self-evident. Hence in the "postilla moralis" appended to the "litteralis," Lyre need not expand. In the first part of the passage it was signified by Christ's baptism that the baptized soul receives the Holy Spirit and becomes the adopted son of God; in the passage following the voice from heaven, "And immediately the Spirit drove him out into the desert," it is made known, Lyre explains, that those who thus become the adopted sons of God must follow the inspiration of the Holy Spirit. As tropological exegesis this is not perfunctory; it is simply all that he finds necessary to say.

Lyre's combination of rational, detailed explication of the plain words with economical cogency on the "quid agas" sense strikes one as a procedure likely to appeal to any layman devoted to close, intelligent reading of a text, as well as to a respect for language in general and that of God's book in particular—in short, a poet like Chaucer. Lyre's attitude on the *sensus moralis*, moreover, should strike a familiar note for students of Chaucer; it has been defined by Hailperin as meaning, for Lyre, "to be, or to do, like something; to take as a pattern, in its firmness, or kindness, or excellence." [16]

---

16.   (N. 9 above), 142.

There is another side to Lyre's work that also associates him with Chaucer: intellectual curiosity. In our second example this quality stands out. Lyre is postillating on the lines "And God created man to his own image; to the image of God he created him. Male and female he created them" (Gen. 1: 27). In the verse that follows occurs the injunction to be fruitful and multiply. The inherent ambiguity Lyre attempts to unravel partly by rational discussion and partly by reference to a contemporary scientific marvel (*Glossa*, I, cols. 33-34). To explain the crucial phrase "masculum et feminam creavit eos" he refers to the dicta of "certain Hebrews," that human nature was designed in both sexes in the first form; the bodies of the man and the woman were so joined at the sides as to make a single continous form, but afterwards they were separated by divine power. After a lengthy discussion of the Hebrew word for "side" or "rib," Lyre quotes the apparently contradictory account later given of the woman's subsequent creation (Gen. 2: 22). After an elaborate explanation of Eve's birth, he reverts to the "masculum et feminam" crux. It is phrased in anticipation of what Scripture wishes immediately to ordain concerning the multiplication of human nature, "which is done through the co-mixture of male and female." Before giving this explanation, however, Lyre permits himself an excursus into contemporary medical history. In the year 1322, when Philip was King of France, there occurred, he relates, what the glossator to the postill terms a "monstrum mirabile in Normania"—the birth of two females having one body. This phenomenon, evidently a case of Siamese twins, he describes in some detail—how sometimes when one was sad, the other was happy, how when one was sleeping, the other was awake. Finally, he writes, one of the twins died more than a year before the second one, upon which "ex pondere et fetore cadaveris mortua est." Lyre's desire to expand on this piece of natural philosophy is not entirely extraneous, however, for he can use it as evidence against the wrong interpretation of the crucial passage before him. It is, he declares, "per accidens" for a monster of this sort to happen in nature, and therefore it is not reasonable to believe that the "artifex omnium," as he chooses to term God in this context, would have made a monster at the very beginning of creation. Hence there must be an explanation for the literal sense of "masculum et feminam" other than the joining of Adam's body and Eve's followed by a severance. This he supplies by reference to the "crescite et multiplicamini" command. [17] The entire postill, much longer than any summary might suggest, serves very well to encapsulate the various qualities in Lyre's work that, one feels, would have commended it to Chaucer: respect for the *littera*, scholastic argumentation by refuting assumed support for an erroneous view, knowledge of the Hebrew language and Rabbinic scholarship, curiosity over the natural world, and the ability to propel the reader to a certain belief through a logical analysis of the text instead of a reliance on fine-spun analogy.

---

17. For a fuller account of Lyre's postills on these passages from Genesis, particularly with respect to his "acceptance and approval of Rashi's *peshat* interpretation," see Hailperin (n. 9 above), 148-51.

In the third example, Lyre's postill has to compete with typological exegesis that finds, in the words between the *Sponsus* and *Sponsa* of the *Canticum*, the most sacred expressions of love between Christ and Mary or Christ and his Church. The section (Cant. 4: 7-16), too long to quote in full, contains passages deeply venerated in the medieval church; for over the centuries the *lectiones* for the numerous feast days of the Blessed Virgin, to say nothing of such devotional books as the Little Hours, had drawn upon the imagery of the Song of Songs. Its *auctor instrumentalis* was deemed to be Solomon, himself regarded as an antetype of Christ. Upon all of the well-loved exotic phrases, such as "Tota pulchra es, amica mea, et macula non est in te, . . . Veni de Libano, sponsa mea, . . . Vulnerasti cor meum, . . . Quam pulchrae sunt mammae tuae, . . . Hortus conclusus soror mea, . . . fons signatus," Lyre brings to bear his lucid and sensitive literality (*Glossa*, III, cols. 1849-54). The postills on a few phrases will serve to show how sturdily he appends his straight-forward exactness to the most exalted allegorizing, being confident, one feels, that none of it is undermined but rather is strengthened by his method. On "Veni de Libano" he comments: "This Libanus is not the name of the mountain lying in Judaea but the name of another place beyond the Jordan, whence came the sons of Israel into Judaea. For frequently different places are given the same names. And here 'veni' is uttered three times for the sake of greater arousal, as in Jeremiah [22: 29] 'Earth, earth, earth.'" When Lyre writes in this way, showing an alertness to rhetorical effect as well as to geographical precision, it is surely not too much to claim for him that a poet equally sensitive to language would have found in him a kindred spirit. Consistently he refrains from going outside the text in search of significance while at the same time drawing on other parallel texts for reciprocal illumination. Thus on the succeeding phrase, "Come . . . from the dens of lions, from the mountains of leopards," he leaves aside the allegorical explanations of lions as persecutors and leopards as heretics, and explains, again combining the scientific with the historic, "For in those mountains there were lairs of lions and of leopards. They, however, did not harm the children of Israel, just as the hideous serpents living in the desert did not harm the children of Israel who passed through it [Deut. 8: 15]."

As for the "hortus conclusus," perhaps the richest metaphor in the passage, it too receives in Lyre's postill an explanation strictly historical and geographical. For the allegorical expositors, the garden, cited twice, can signify the two holy states of active and contemplative life, each of which is "conclusus." True to the Old Testament setting, in preference to any prefigural sense, Lyre relates the enclosed garden to the land promised the "Ecclesia Israel" which had been betrothed to God in the law given on Mount Sinai. This, for Lyre, is a kind of typology, but one that in no sense implies an antetype. Much more space is devoted to the physical aspect of the promised land: it is a "hortus" because of its fertility; it is "conclusus" because of its security, for the promised land is closed in ("clauditur") on the west by the Mediterranean Sea and on the east by the Jordan River, on the north by Mount Lebanon and on the south by the Egyptian Desert, which, Lyre points out, is not easily crossed. His procedure in this passage is worth scrutinizing, being admirably representative of his method. The enclosed garden has to be given a kind of figural value. But this is to be neither mystical nor anachronistic; it must stand for some actual piece of land in a context falling within the time-frame of the text, hence relative to the Mosaic Law. The garden stands for the promised land, then, and that land has a cartographic locus. For anyone who had studied, with admiration not untinged with exasperation, the extremes of mystical glossing on *Canticum* imagery, as possibly Chaucer had, the plain sense of Lyre's postills must have come as both refreshment and enlightenment.

That such was the response of biblical students of his own age and succeeding ages seems to be confirmed by the widespread dissemination that his commentaries, both *litteralis* and *moralis*, enjoyed among the educated laity and clerics in the late Middle Ages. The Labrosse biography identifies some 800 manuscripts of the full commentary and some 700 of the partial. [18] In Rost's view, the "plenarien," as he terms portions of Scripture that include the postills, were more influential than manuscripts of complete or partial Bibles because with their aid laymen could follow up the literal explication of the text. Rost's survey of this extensive circulation, as one might call it, of Scripture and commentaries in the later Middle Ages is confirmed by inquiries as to England made by Deanesly, who notes that in addition to Scripture itself, "every library contained also a large number of commentaries on the different biblical books." [19] After 1340 the commentator most in demand was Lyre, and "the wills of medieval scholars often record possession of the postill." Included among the lists of manuscripts throughout Western Europe reported by Stegmüller are some at Oxford, including Ralph Strode's college, Merton. [20] Manuscripts of *Lyra super Bibliam* contemporary with Chaucer are recorded in the library lists of Lambeth library and also in those of St. Augustine's Abbey at Canterbury. [21] Such are the facts on the distribution in Chaucer's age of this postillator's bulky work. Whether or not it would have been available to Chaucer's contemporaries as part of the *Glossa ordinaria*, with all the accumulated interlinear and marginal glosses, in the compactly collated form that has come down to us from sixteenth-century printed editions, or whether Lyre's postills were annexed separately from but adjacent to the *Glossa*, is not easy to determine; but this relates mainly to a matter of convenience. Any scholar, cleric or lay, interested in the typological, tropological, and (rarely) anagogical glosses to the *pagina sacra* would

---

18. See Rost (n. 1 above), pp. 87, 353-55.
19. (N. 1 above), 166-68, 174-75.
20. *Repertorium Biblicum Medii Aevi* (Matriti, 1940) IV, 52, 90. See also P. Glorieux, *Répertoire des Maîtres en Théologie de Paris au XIIIes.* (Paris, 1933), 216. Chaucer seems to have had connections with Merton; see J. A. W. Bennett, *Chaucer at Oxford and at Cambridge* (Toronto, 1974), 15, 58, 64-69.
21. See M. R. James, *A Descriptive Catalogue of the Manuscripts in the Library of Lambeth Palace* (Cambridge, 1932) and *Ancient Libraries of Canterbury and Dover* (Cambridge, 1903).

have had equally ready access to the explanations in Lyre's postills against which to compare the exegetical speculations and the textual facts. [22]

Our concern is to determine in what way these explanations were of service to Chaucer. As to the simpler question of Bible study in general, the old notion that there was little reading of Scripture by laymen of the late Middle Ages has long since been discarded. In *The Literature of Medieval England*, for example, D. W. Robertson, Jr., refutes the charge that the Bible was kept away from medieval users and explains the ways men could and did learn from it. [23] As Jean Leclercq has remarked, "it is no longer necessary to prove that medieval laymen knew the Bible as well as clerics, and that everyone capable of doing so was encouraged to read it," [24] and Rost's evidence demonstrates that throughout the Middle Ages the focus of studies was upon the Bible. [25] There is no reason to doubt that Geoffrey Chaucer's own studies also benefitted from this focus. Would he then have found in Lyre's biblical commentaries material not only of value to him as a *viator* through the "wildernesse" of life but also of utility to him as an ironic observer of the human comedy? To the points already raised that suggest a natural affinity between postillator and poet, let there be added a final comment on Lyre by his biographer. For him the *Postilla moralis* reveals Lyre as a

> psychologue avisé, un prédicateur discret, un censeur toujours plein de bonhomie, qui ne craint pas de blâmer les grands, les chanoines et même les prélats. Son imagination s'y donne parfois libre carrière et sait trouver des allégories ingénieuses et délicates, qui ne pouvaient trouver place dans le cadre austère et scientifique de la *Postilla litteralis*. [26]

In some of its particulars this tribute could virtually be made about Chaucer himself, the ironist blessed with *bonhomie*. Labrosse's comment should remind us, moreover, that not only the *Litteralis* but also the *Moralis* should be consulted when one seeks to detect those nuances that run through the texture of Chaucer's special brand of irony.

Incongruity is, in general, an ingredient of irony. A particular kind of Chaucerian incongruity arises from the contrasts between the fully glossed senses of certain scriptural references and their brash exhibition by the

---

22. In addition to the Lyons 1545 and Paris 1590 editions cited above, Rost (n. 1 above, 371-72) mentions the *Biblia cum Glossa interlineari et cum postillis Nicolai de Lyra* in a number of earlier editions, namely, Strassburg 1481, Venice 1495, Basel 1498. Of Bible commentaries he finds over 1,000 editions (1465-1520) and of editions of the Latin Bible with commentaries to the whole of it he finds 13 before 1501, including 9,500 copies. Of the whole *postilla* of Lyre he finds 61 before 1501 (pp. 90-91). In the preparation of this paper I have also used the Strassburg 1492 edition of Lyre (rpt. Frankfurt, 1971). On the question of MSS and printed editions of the *Glossa* I should like to record my gratitude to Miss Beryl Smalley, St. Hilda's College, Oxford, and to Rev. Osmund Lewry, O. P., Blackfriars College, who has also given generous assistance on several other points in this paper.

23. *The Literature of Mediaeval England* (New York, 1970), 25.

24. "The Exposition and Exegesis of Scripture" in *Cambridge History of the Bible*, II, 193.

25. (N. 1 above), 115-20.

26. H. Labrosse (n. 7 above), 35, 175.

pilgrims, sometimes in the self-depiction of a prologue, sometimes in an exemplary tale. Ironical effects are achieved, to cite a notorious case, when the Wife of Bath parades her citations from Genesis and Corinthians, possibly aware of their true import and possibly not. Here the ironical author makes a kind of compact with his real audience to undermine the Wife by a shared perception of knowledge that she either fails to grasp or else willfully distorts.

Other pilgrims besides the Wife deploy biblical knowledge in this distorted fashion. For each one the ironical effects differ. The Merchant offers an example of a narrator whose biblical resonances produce savagely corrosive irony. In uncovering the hidden senses of Scripture that contrast with the narrator's context, the glosses are, of course, essential. Yet so rich is this body of exposition that one can easily overlook the more prosaic discussions in Lyre's postills. Nevertheless, for a number of reasons these supplements to the *Glossa* may very well have influenced the poet in his implantation of certain biblical dicta within the pilgrims' displays of incongruous learning. In those displays the effect is not always what the narrator expects; he reveals a degree of folly or worse. Sometimes the undermining irony thus produced merely strikes a note of absurdity; sometimes it is disturbing. Essential as is allegorical exegesis to the revealing of these biblical incongruities, the lucid interpretations of Nicholas of Lyre seem no less to have stirred Chaucer's imagination when devising these various degrees of irony.

One that probably cuts no deeper than the satirical comes from the Sergeant of the Law's habit of alluding to scriptural personages and events as if supporting a plea in court. That the *pagina sacra* should be familiar to this narrator is not itself incongruous; according to Fortescue, members of his profession were expected to be scholarly and devout. Hence the irony arises from the Sergeant's imperfect or confused knowledge. His prologue contains several citations that show, in collation with Lyre's postills, how this display of knowledge makes him appear ridiculous: two will suffice, and from his tale two more. In the outburst on the hateful "condicion of poverte" (II. 99-133) he declares: "'Bet is to dyen than have indigence.'" [27] It is beside the point that this quotation from Ecclesiasticus (40: 29) exists also in Innocent III's *De Miseria humanae conditionis* (I. 15); the fact that the Sergeant garbles Innocent's argument suggests that he misunderstands as well the scriptural proofs illustrating that argument. [28] The full passage itself reads, "My son, in thy

---

27. All quotations from *The Canterbury Tales* are from the edition of F. N. Robinson, 2nd ed. (Boston, 1957).

28. The Sergeant is partly right that in the *De Miseria* poverty is deplored, but he fails to see that it is deplored in order to deter the unwise from seeking wealth, a vain pursuit bound to lead to misfortune and the calamity of unexpected poverty. Hence Innocent III preaches *contemptus mundi* not only as a shunning of false goods out of a proper fear of *cupiditas*, but also from a practical desire to avoid the misery that wealth-seeking leads to. By being depicted as one who misconstrues this treatise and fails to perceive how its ironies reflect on his own case, the Sergeant becomes the victim of the author's irony.

lifetime be not indigent: for it is better to die than to want." In Lyre's postill (*Glossa*, III, col. 2179) the adjuration "ne indigeas" is explained as "be not idle" or "be not without occupation" ("ne sis otiosus"), for from idleness follows spiritual and temporal poverty. Again, in the second part of the verse, "quam indigere" is explained as literally meaning "than to be idle." It is, after all, the Latin phrase that the Sergeant knows, and if he had absorbed the postill accompanying it he should know that its essence concerns idleness in good works and not shortage of money. Lyre thus expands on his "[quam] otiosum esse" phrase by warning, "through which one dies spiritually." Naturally, he then restores even this modest tropological abstraction to the concrete by adding, "And sometimes physically, for frequently a man is turned by idleness towards robbery—for which he is hanged." Idleness, whether spiritual or corporeal, is Lyre's keynote, not "indigence" in the sense bemoaned by the Sergeant. Has this impressive fellow, who "semed bisier than he was," not been busy enough in essential work? At any rate, he seems to be set up as an example of one who understands the "letter" but not the "spirit," even though that can be extracted, as Lyre shows, directly from the proper sense of the literal.

A little farther on, the Sergeant again draws on Scripture, this time the Book of Proverbs (19: 7):

> If thou be povre, thy brother hateth thee,
> And alle thy freendes fleen from thee, allas!

(II. 120-1)

Here the contrast between the Sergeant's bald citation and the explanatory postill comes out, as often is the case with the irony in biblical resonances, only within the full context of the passage. The Sergeant has left out the second half of the *sententia*, which reads in full: "He that followeth after words only shall have nothing." It is upon the latter sentence that Lyre places the main emphasis (*Glossa*, III, cols. 1685-86). On the first part he gives only a brief explanation: the impoverished man is hated by brothers and shunned by friends because often they are ashamed of his presence and fear lest he come on them to be relieved of his poverty. [29] But on the more significant *Qui tantum* maxim, he thinks well, unlike the Sergeant, to ponder further: "It has two senses. The one concerns the learner ('de discipulo') who, delighting more in ornateness of diction than in beneficial knowledge, receives from his teacher no truth, or so little as to count for nothing. The other concerns the teacher who is good with words but not with substance; he too will receive, from God, nothing of profit." When one reflects upon the pompous rhetoric and the banal sentiments with which the Sergeant smothers some potentially valuable teaching in his exemplum on constancy, a kind of secular saint's life, one notes in Lyre's postill an appropriately personal application on the distinction between surface and substance.

In that exemplum scriptural echoes abound. One of the more vivid is implanted in the *sermocinatio* by which Constance is made, quite incon-

---

29. Reading "relevari" for the *Glossa*'s "revelari."

gruously, to bewail her fate on being sent by her father the Emperor to the "Barbre nacioun" for marriage to the Sultan. Another, equally vivid, occurs in one of the Sergeant's *exclamationes*, directed at the wicked "Sowdanesse" who has her son and his fellow converts slain and Constance, her son's bride, set adrift. In the first Constance laments that "Wommen are born to thraldom and penance, / And to been under mannes governance" (II. 286-87). The commonplace, which does not appear in the Trivet and Gower analogues, finds its clearest echo in the curse laid upon Eve: "I will multiply thy sorrows, and thy conceptions. In sorrow shalt thou bring forth children, and thou shalt be under thy husband's power, and he shall have dominion over thee" (Gen. 3: 16). On this passage the marginal glosses are very full, drawn from the various commentaries on Genesis by Augustine, Procopius, and Rabanus Maurus. They tend to be mainly typological, although one of Augustine's glosses (from *De Genesi ad litteram* XI. 37) looks also at the more practical side of husband-wife relations: her subjection after the Fall is due to the penalty; in the prelapsarian state it would have been by nature. It is this practical focus that Lyre sharpens, and as a consequence we can see how utterly out of keeping with the original sense is the context of Constance's lament. She is complaining here of parental authority, even, indeed, of divine will, for she is made to plead, before bewailing woman's lot in general, "But Crist, that starf for our redempcioun / So yeve me grace his heestes to fulfille!" (II. 283-84). Nevertheless, she is not yet a wife and, in marriage to the ill-fated Sultan, never will be a mother. Lyre explains the passage as implying a twofold penalty ("punitio") in the joining ("coniuncta") of woman to man: in having to bear children in pain and in having to be subject. There follow a few details on parturition, Hebrew sources being used, and the assurance that the violent pains ("vehementes angustiae") did not exist ("non fuissent") in the state of innocence, for then copulation was without disgrace ("absque turpitudine"). Characteristic of Lyre's balanced outlook on life is his statement that even though disgrace may attach to the act of generation "post peccatum," it is lawful that it should have delight. Whether, however, Lyre's down-to-earth explanation of the passage or the glossators' more mystical ones be preferred, the phrase being placed in Constance's mouth marks one of the Sergeant's lapses from decorum. The lapse is made worse by his subsequent apology for mentioning Constance's wedding night, this time after marriage to King Alla: though wives "be ful hooly thynges," he declares, they must accept patiently at night "swiche manere necessaries as been plesynges" to their husbands (II. 709-12).

In the other passages, where the Sergeant steps before the audience, as it were, to denounce the Sultan's mother, the echo is not as directly obvious as the one from Genesis. The outburst, "O serpent under femynynytee, / Lik to the serpent depe in helle ybounde!" (II. 361-62), seems to collate imagery from the revelation that the angel of God "laid hold on the dragon, the old serpent . . . and bound him for a thousand years" (Apoc. 20: 2) with the Apostle's reminder that God delivered the fallen angels, "drawn down by infernal ropes to the lower hell, unto torments, to be reserved unto judgment" (2 Pet. 2: 4). Here it is interesting to find Lyre's postill providing not an ironical reflection on the Sergeant's obtuseness or tactlessness but rather a thematic concordance. Perhaps this is because in denouncing evil-doers the Sergeant's voice sounds more authoritative than in his pietistic outbursts on sanctified behavior. Hence Lyre's postill on the Petrine verse concurs very well with the theme of iniquity being punished, which the Sergeant not very successfully tries to subordinate to that of saintliness being rewarded. The ropes ("rudentibus" in the Epistle, "funes" in the postill, both with nautical overtones) are, Lyre explains, sins, "which are for dragging away into hell." The idea that the sinner is drawn into hell by his own iniquities, bound up in them as a kind of slave, Lyre supports with a citation from Solomon: the wicked man is "fast bound with the ropes ('funibus') of his own sins" (Prov. 5: 22). Appropriate though this notion is for the Sultaness, here being denounced, and later for the equally iniquitous Donegild, the story's possibilities for dilation on the nature of evil and its retribution are largely missed by the Sergeant, who provides rhetorical denunciations of vice and commendations of virtue but little understanding of their nature.

More sombre than the ironical effects produced by a juxtaposition between the Sergeant's rhetorical treatment of Scripture and Lyre's postills is the contrast between the distortions found in the Monk's treatment and the clarification Lyre places on corresponding passages. One example stands out, that of a major figure in the Monk's catalogue of supposedly tragic cases. Though a number of blunders over scriptural history are made by this cloisterer, who asks, whether defiantly or apologetically, why he should drive himself mad by studying books, none is so egregiously wrong as the one he makes about Samson. Even the most perfunctory glance at any *Allegoria*, such as Isidore of Seville's, or any commentary, within or without the *Glossa*, would have reminded the Monk of a commonplace: Samson is an antetype of Christ. "Samson Salvatoris nostri mortem et victoriam figuravit," Isidore states.[30] In the Monk's hands the story of the Nazarite's triumph over God's enemies becomes what the commentators never deemed it to be—a depressing rather than uplifting story. The Monk also treats the annunciation of Samson's coming and the prophecy of his task in perfunctory fashion. Yet these events provide the indispensable context for Samson's death, showing it to be no act of despair but rather the fulfillment of the prophecy—in God's terms, however, not man's. Significantly, then, after Lyre's literal postills on Judges 13 to 16 (*Glossa*, II, cols. 239-62), which explain the implications of "nazaraeus Dei ab infantia sua" and the factual meaning of the messenger's description, "habens vultum angelicum," his moral postills are, for him, exceptionally full. Because Lyre, not usually given to typological and spiritual discussion, here finds it necessary to do this, there is all the more reason to look askance at the Monk's determinedly cursory and gloomy treatment. Not that Lyre's typological version lacks his unfailing scientific sense, in this case evoked by etymology. In stating, on Samson's conception, "Per Samsonem vero qui interpretatur sol eorum," which is a sign for Christ, and

---

30. *Allegoriae quaedam sacrae scripturae*, PL 83, col. IIIC.

later, on Samson's death, "In hoc loco, per Samson Christus significatur," Lyre is being no less definite than the exegetes before him. Even his specific reasons for establishing the prefigural senses are the same as those of, for example, the Victorine school in whose *Allegoriae in Vetus Testamentum* Samson is said to prefigure Christ in the manner of his annunciation and his choice of Gentile bride—the church, not the synagogue.[31] These and other central incidents in Samson's history are blurred or distorted by the Monk, such as the riddle of the honey and the lion, the breaking off of the nuptials, and the expedition to Gaza, on all of which Lyre's postills alone would have shown the Monk his omissions and distortions. None of these is so blatant as the Monk's reiterated implication that Samson committed suicide. In his proem he declares that Samson "slow hymself for wrecchednesse" and again at the end he relates that Samson "slow hymself, and eek his foomen alle" (VII. 2022, 2086), from which his moral comes down only to a warning to men never to reveal essential secrets to their wives. The crucial phrase in the Bible is Samson's plea, "Moriatur anima mea cum Philisthiim" (Judges 16: 30). Upon these words Lyre expends two of his longest literal and moral postills. In the former he is at pains to follow the long-established tradition of exculpating Samson from any taint of suicide. The Monk, who of all the pilgrims should know better, brands Samson's death as deliberate, but Lyre makes clear that Samson did not intend to slay himself ("se occidere") for the sake of suicide but did so only by "accident," that is, in unavoidable consequence of an event whose primary intention was not his own death at all ("non . . . per se sed tantum per accidens"). For this Lyre's logical mind can grasp one good reason: Samson was unable to slay the blasphemers of the Divine name without also slaying himself with them. There are other points in Lyre's closely reasoned argument, but this is the essential one. The Monk appears to ignore it, and for that he has no excuse. But not only does irony at his expense result from a comparison with Lyre's literal explications but also from the moral postill. Samson the Nazarite stands for the man consecrated to the Lord by baptism, as indeed the Monk himself is by his vows. Delila stands for the sensuality by which a man's carnal voluptuousness leads to his fall from that consecration. To judge from the hints dropped by the *General Prologue* narrator, to say nothing of the Host's jokes, the Monk might well have derived discomfort from this tropology had he absorbed it—as perhaps he had.

If the ironies reflected by the Sergeant's scriptural bunglings strike an absurd note, those evoked by the Monk's treatment of Samson cut more deeply. The result is also comedy, perhaps, but of a mordant kind. From the ironies derived from the Wife of Bath's biblical flourishes, there comes comedy sharper than the Sergeant's absurdities, yet less grim than that, found in the Monk's possibly willful errors. With Alisoun such irony serves to extend the ambiguities that surround this "oxymoron in the flesh."[32]

31. In *Exegetica dubia in Sacram Scripturam* (School of St. Victor), *PL* 175, col. 680B.
32. In the phrase of B. J. Whiting in *Sources and Analogues of Chaucer's Canterbury Tales*, ed. Bryan and Dempster (Chicago, 1941; rpt. 1958), 207.

The complexity of her character is seen to have even deeper layers when the biblical ironies are pursued from the *Glossa* into the postills. On the one hand, it arises from her blatant manipulating of Scripture, especially 1 Corinthians, an exercise in distortion convincingly exposed by Robertson.[33] On the other hand, it is a different sort of irony from that which undermines the Monk and the Sergeant. Unscrupulous she may be in exegesis, but unlike them she probably lacks firsthand access to the truth. She makes the *sensus litteralis* mean what she wants it to mean, but very likely does not know what it means to Lyre. Hence when his clarifications on key points are contrasted with her obfuscations, the resulting ironies take on an idiosyncratic subtlety. Where there is willful distorting, they can point to obvious disapprobation. But if the contrast between Lyre's truth and her impercipience brings out a literal and moral sense of greater comfort than Alisoun realizes, then the irony is of a more poignant order. Both kinds, and other shadings as well, emerge from a comparison between the Wife's outbursts and the postills.

One example is her declaration, "For sothe, I wol nat kepe me chaast in al" (III. 46). This calls up no specific citation from Scripture, but the sentiment resonates, as Robinson's note suggests, with St. Paul's adjuration to the unmarried and the widowed to remain, like him, chaste. "But if they do not contain themselves," he states, "let them marry. For it is better to marry than to be burnt ('uri')" (1 Cor. 7: 9).[34] Lyre explains why it is that by contracting marriage one does better than by not marrying. When concupiscence is supreme it is like a fire; consequently, since it is purely bad so to be burnt, it is therefore good to marry, even though this is less good than containing oneself (*Glossa*, VI, cols. 247-48). Here lies some comfort for the Wife, did she but know it. Lyre's implication is that because the fires of concupiscence are bad, the remedy, marriage, is therefore a good. Continence is not so much a remedy as a higher state, an absolute good totally opposite to the purely bad state of concupiscence. Marriage is not, then, as Alisoun seems inwardly to fear, any kind of "malum"; it is, like continence, an opposite to concupiscence, though not as good an opposite. Nor does it mean that this higher good is necessarily something Alisoun should and could have preferred to marriage. Lyre's postill on St. Paul's concession begins with a clear recognition of what continence means. It is a gift one has or has not from God: "si donum continendi non acceperint a Deo." His comment is not entirely free from ambiguity; he may mean that if the gift was not accepted when proffered, it is better to marry than be burnt, or simply that it was not proffered at all and, hence, not received. No ambivalence attaches, however, to the notion of a "donum." Moreover, the whole postill puts a more generous light on St. Paul's rather grudging concession than would be gathered from that favorite treatise of Alisoun's fifth husband, St. Jerome's *Epistola adversus Jovinianum*.

---

33. See *A Preface to Chaucer* (Princeton, 1962), 317-31.
34. The Vulgate "uri" is so rendered in Douai-Reims; most modern translations prefer "than to burn."

The equally noticeable touch of generosity in Lyre's postill on the immediately preceding concession by St. Paul might also have given the Wife some food for less anguished thought. When she argues, "And for to been a wyf he yaf me leve / Of indulgence" (III. 83-84), she is now making an unmistakable reference to St. Paul's qualification on his apparent approval of marriage: "But I speak this by indulgence, not by commandment" (1 Cor. 7: 6). Willy-nilly, she has to repeat the grudging term "indulgence." On this Lyre's comment is both lengthy and instructive. He has to explain that when St. Paul declares husbands and wives can resume relations after a period of intermission, this is not meant as a requirement. Married couples can or may ("possent") by common consent go on abstaining ("continere"). This explication shows up the Wife's distortion by which she tries to claim as a right what St. Paul only says may, not must, be granted. Yet Lyre's reasonable "de communi consensu" once again hits the mark. Furthermore, he feels compelled to object to St. Paul's term "indulgentia." This it cannot be, the postill argues, unless relating to something evil. But as the matrimonial act is not evil, "indulgence" can only be taken to mean "permission." His argument against St. Paul is no mere scholastic quibble; it is grounded in his characteristic hard sense. The conjugal act is without any guilt when it is ordained for procreation of children in God's faith and for the sake of rendering the marriage debt. The first stands on grounds of religion, the second on justice. His postill then adds a declaration that might have vindicated much of Alisoun's case—providing she could meet its fundamental and indispensable condition. "Et si," Lyre writes, "fiat [sc. the conjugal act] ex charitate non solum est sine culpa sed etiam meritorius, quia omnis actus virtutis ex charitate meritorius est" (*Glossa*, VI, cols. 245-46). Of course, Lyre must qualify this declaration by the correct reminder that the act, if undertaken merely to satisfy concupiscence, does have venial guilt even within matrimony, and, if outside it, moral guilt. Yet the key words "ex charitate" and "meritorius" have been announced for all to ponder. Were Alisoun to ponder them, what would be her response?

Lest she find undeserved gratification in this postill, however, let her ponder another, this time concerning a figure whose example she rashly cites as justification for remarriage:

> Lo, heere the wise kyng, daun Salomon;
> I trowe he hadde wyves mo than oon.

(III. 35-36)

Indeed he did: "King Solomon loved many strange women. . . . And he had seven hundred wives as queens, and three hundred concubines" (2 Kings 11: 1, 3). Now the irony tells against the Wife, not for her. Lyre makes it clear that this passage deals with the sins of Solomon and their consequences. The very things seized on by the Wife as evidence in her favor are, Lyre shows, the cause of Solomon's downfall (*Glossa*, II, cols. 781-82). The sins of idolatry that incurred God's wrath were induced by his sins of lechery, for the former arose in an effort to gratify the latter. The Wife's choice of Solomon is almost comically ill-advised. Even Lyre, for all his broadmindedness, has to fall in with the views of Tertullian, Augustine, Theodoretus, Gregory, Ambrose, and other Fathers: women were to blame for Solomon's fall.

Nevertheless, the Wife of Bath's deepest concern centers not, despite her grumblings, so much on the determination of clerks like these to blame women for their pernicious influence, as on their insistence that virginity is a higher state than marriage. "The dart is set up for virginitee," she sighs, drawing a metaphor from running contests; and a moment later, "Virginitee is greet perfeccion" (III. 75, 105). The counterclaim that Alisoun at once appends to the first complaint, that virginity is a counsel of perfection and not meant for everyone, seems to echo Christ's own words on his being questioned about the expediency of marriage: "All men take not this word, but they to whom it is given" (Matt. 19: 11). Yet her second complaint clearly reflects a hard saying of Revelation, which suggests not at all that virginity is a special gift from God, bestowed only on men who have the strength to remain continent "for the kingdom of Heaven," but rather that its opposite is a pollution: "These are they (sc. 'those hundred forty-four thousand who were purchased from the earth') who were not defiled with women: for they are virgins" (Apoc. 14: 4). Lyre's postill on the Gospel passage would have helped to confirm the Wife's effort at reassurance (*Glossa*, V, fol. 59r). Christ's words mean that upon those men who have voluntarily remained chaste—"eunuchi" by their own will—a special gift from God has been granted, "ex speciali munere." For support, Lyre turns back to Solomon (Wisdom 8: 21), this time in his status of *auctor instrumentalis*. "No man can be continent unless God gives it," Lyre declares, at once adding the proviso that because not all continence is praiseworthy, Christ wishes here to explain in what sense it is or is not. Lyre's postill then branches out into a scientific excursus relating to the absence or the amputation of genitalia. But what is bestowed as the "special gift from God" is voluntary continence, which means repression of concupiscence. Moreover, it is bestowed for a particular purpose—liberation to contemplate the divine.

These explanations might not especially placate the Wife of Bath, but they would not make matters worse for her. Would Lyre's postill on the much more disheartening passage from Revelation have assuaged her uneasiness? In some measure, perhaps. Even the interlinear gloss seems to temper the severity of the "cum mulieribus non sunt coinquinati" phrase by inserting "cum aliquibus sordibus mundi," even though conceding "vel ad literam" (*Glossa*, VI, cols. 1607-8). As if with his eye on the interlinear, Lyre appends as expansion: "or simply in preserving the innocence of the flesh ('integritatem carnis') or at least keeping chastity after taking a vow." Thus without inconsistency, for this portion of the *pagina sacra* is unlike any other, does Lyre's seldom-failing good sense soften, or at any rate mitigate, the harshness of the literal by resorting to the figural. Here as elsewhere the Wife of Bath would have found Lyre's *Postillae super totam Bibliam* a somewhat easier fireside book than Jankyn's strange *florilegium*.

The internal evidence of *The Canterbury Tales* discloses an impressive command of Scripture that goes far beyond manipulation of source material. Does this also presuppose knowledge of the glosses and, more important, Lyre's postills? The bibliographical evidence suggests that the poet would have had to make a deliberate effort to avoid these ancillary writings, and that seems unlikely. Chaucer was not the man to deny himself the benefit of learning which in this case was not only essential to comprehension of the sacred text, but was also intellectually and indeed esthetically stimulating in itself. Furthermore, the reflections of this scholarly Franciscan, a man spiritually and intellectually akin to Chaucer in more ways than one, provided the poet with a norm of charity and sanity to juxtapose for ironic effect against the biblical insertions that emerge from the consciousness of his Canterbury pilgrims.

Chaucer and Wyclif: Biblical Hermeneutic and Literary Theory in the XIVth Century

DAVID LYLE JEFFREY
University of Ottawa

The most imaginatively synthetic and controversial biblical scholar in Geoffrey Chaucer's England was John Wyclif. There are a number of arguable social reasons for associating Chaucer with Wyclif. Among the most obvious is that they share a common patron, John of Gaunt. While Gaunt's championing of Wyclif speaks at least as much of self-interest in the controversies of church-state politics as it does of commitment to any of Wyclif's ideas, and although Gaunt's patronage of Chaucer includes a somewhat different set of special concerns, it is nonetheless clear that the two protégés fit within an establishable pattern of values which are common with those of Gaunt and, more especially, substantially mutual to each other. We need not speculate overly much in this connection on the character of self-interest expressed in Gaunt's patronage of the two men. The facts of the patronage, and Gaunt's famous readiness to defend both Wyclif and Chaucer in inauspicious circumstances, are sufficient to taint both professor and poet with the *odium* of distinctive court politics, to enable them in respect of politics—including ecclesiastical politics—to be seen until 1378 or 1379 in largely the same camp. [1] Moreover, it is evident that there was a wider circle of sympathy for Wyclif and his ideas amongst a very substantial and influential group at court, several of whom Chaucer counted as close friends.

I. WYCLIF AND CHAUCER'S SOCIETY

Wyclif was by no means—especially until 1379—the inconsiderable heretic he is sometimes now construed to have been. As May McKisack has observed, "There can be no doubt that he dominated the Oxford of his own day; he was *flos Oxoniae*, 'holden of full many men the greatest Clerk

---

1. Bishop Usher thought Wyclif had dedicated a collection of his early works to John of Gaunt—an explicit association preserved in the catalogue of manuscripts in the Library of Trinity College. The source of the attribution, however, is now lost. See also Anne Hudson, *Selections from English Wycliffite Writings* (Cambridge, 1978), 6; also Joseph Dahmus, *William Courtenay: Archbishop of Canterbury, 1381-1396* (Pennsylvania, 1966), 57.

that they knew then living.'''[2] At the University he was easily the most famous of lecturers. Knighton records in his *Chronicon* that he was there "in philosophia nulli reputatabur secundus, in scholasticis disciplinis incomparabilis."[3] Though Ockham's nominalism had set the dominant trend at Oxford, Wyclif achieved his reputation despite being openly a realist. It is clear, moreover, that even at the height of his philosophical and theological struggles, not even his "worst and most spiteful adversaries" called into question "his excellent piety"; he was regarded at the University, as elsewhere, to be a sincere 'cristen' man.[4] In London, because of his views on tithes and dominion and, correlatively, on the central authority of Scripture, it may be, as Armitage Smith has observed, that "more than half of London openly sympathized" at one point—this despite their hatred for his all too visible patron, Gaunt.[5] But the centre of his popularity was first the University, then the court. In the midst of the 1377 troubles, Princess Joan, widow of the Black Prince, was openly an adherent, and support for Wyclif's general ideas was much wider at court than has been, I think, properly acknowledged.

Derek Brewer has been at pains to revise our impression of Wyclif's courtly influence, and to précis the point I am able to defer to his summary. First, it is clear that one did not have to identify with Wyclif in the extremes of his struggle with Roman control to approve his general theological arguments: in Brewer's words, "many who might better be described as orthodox evangelical Christians shared the Lollards' general concerns without their extremism."[6] Second, it is clear that the so-called 'Lollard Knights,' definitely associated with Wyclif's commitments at court, were men of central prestige and influence. Of the ten 'Lollard Knights' Brewer identifies at court, six were especially important: Sir Richard Sturry, Sir Lewis Clifford, Sir Thomas Latimer, Sir William Neville, Sir John Montague, and Sir John Clanvowe. Added to these were powerful associates, including Sir William de Beauchamp and Sir Philippe de Vache, son-in-law to Clifford who, like Sturry, Clifford, Neville and Clanvowe, was a knight of the King's Chamber. All of these men, it should be noted, were important friends of Chaucer.[7]

One of them, Clanvowe, was a notable poet, authoring not only the "Boke of Cupide" but also "one of the earliest religious tracts by a layman in English."[8] This latter book condemns war and the luxurious life of the courts, rehearsing the Ten Commandments, the Great Commandment, and the poverty of Christ. Though Clanvowe applies the term 'loller' to him-

---

2. May McKisack, *The Fourteenth Century* (Oxford, 1959), 510. The citation is from the *Eulogium* (Rolls Series), III, 345.
3. H. Knighton, *Chronicon*, ed. J. Lumby (Rolls Series, London, 1889-95), 2 vols: II, 151.
4. John Stacey, *John Wyclif and Reform* (London, 1964), 13-14.
5. Armitage Smith, *John of Gaunt* (London, rpt. 1964), 149.
6. Derek Brewer, *Chaucer and His World* (London, 1963), 165-66.
7. Margaret Deanesly, *The Lollard Bible* (Cambridge, 1920), 277.
8. Brewer, 172.

self, he does not expound any extreme doctrines, but rather a simple, literal New Testament Christianity of the sort which characterizes Chaucer's *Parson's Sermon* or *Tale of Melibee*. The streak of what might be called 'pacifism' in the document is reminiscent of the same theme in writings of other court figures (such as Otto de Grandson, associated with the Order of the Passion of Our Lord[9]) and parallels Wyclif's own opposition to the Hundred Years' War and his advocacy of a 'Christian Peace.'[10]

Richard Sturry was in Gaunt's patronage by 1374, at which time Wyclif and Gaunt were becoming acquainted at a conference in Bruges, where Wyclif was a 'clerc' and second in a list of royal commissioners sent to confer with papal legates in a dispute between Edward III and Rome.[11] (Wyclif was clearly valued already at court for such offices.) Sturry, who was close to Princess Joan throughout her life, was in 1391 made Justice of South Wales, and participated in peace missions during 1390-1391. A member of the Order of the Passion of Our Lord, Sturry was commonly associated with Lollardry even in the late 1380s, when it was, following Wyclif's death, a more dangerous identification. Yet his position at court was quite unaffected by the charge.[12] He was interested in literature, and owned a copy of the *Roman de la Rose*.[13]

Of the other 'Lollard Knights,' Sir John Montague, third Earl of Salisbury, was a poet in his own right, although he probably composed in French, and was tutor for the son of Christine de Pisan, whom Robertson describes as "a lady of rather meticulous tastes."[14] Vache was recipient of Chaucer's moral ballad, "Truth," which Brewer suggests exhorts Vache according to his own spiritual values.[15] Neville, along with Clanvowe, died as an image of old chivalric values on a crusade near Constantinople in 1391, and both were mourned as "famous and worthy noblemen among the English," exemplary antetypes for Chaucer's Knight. Clifford, executor to Princess Joan and the agent of Wyclif's release at the Lambeth trial in 1378, could still be associated, along with Sturry, Latimer and Montague, as late as 1395, with the affixation of Lollard manifestos to the doors of Westminster and St. Paul's.

Even Ralph Strode, the poet and philosopher who was to oppose a number of Wycliffian views after 1375, was from early in their Merton days a close friend of Wyclif.[16] Wyclif himself refers to Strode as "reverend master and dearest friend,"[17] and even the later controversy between them was apparently carried out with all courtesy. (Strode's poem, which the

9. D. W. Robertson, *Chaucer's London* (New York, 1968), 209.

10. *Select English Works of John Wyclif*, 3 vols., ed. T. Arnold (Oxford, 1871), III, 138.

11. Kathryn Hoye Pichette, *Chaucer's Lollard Friend, Sir Richard Stury* (Ph.D. dissertation, University of Colorado, 1968), 79.

12. Pichette, 13-25; 80.

13. Robertson, 209.

14. *Ibid.*

15. Brewer, 174.

16. H. B. Workman, *John Wyclif*, 2 vols. (Oxford, 1926), I, 242; II, 125.

17. *Opus minorum*, 197.

catalogue of Merton calls "librum elegiacum vocatum *Phantasma Radulphi*," was added to by Bale, an *Itinerarium Terrae Sanctae*, as he calls it. [18]) Strode, of course, with Gower, was dedicatee of *Troilus and Criseyde* and a close friend also of Chaucer.

Finally, Queen Anne of Bohemia is closely identified with Wyclif. Many of her young courtiers, brought over from her native country, became Wyclif's students. To them we owe the preservation of many of Wyclif's works, taken back as lecture notes to Vienna or Prague. But Anne herself was a devout reader of the Wycliffite Bible—at least according to the testimony of Purvey—and it is recorded of Arundel that he was required to make explicit in her funerary sermon that her copy of the Gospels in English (with Wycliffite glosses) was her daily companion and study. [19]

It is clear, then, that Wyclif had important sympathizers at court, and that central among these were some of Chaucer's closest courtly friends, men with interests in ecclesiastical reform, peace, a renewed chivalry, and, not incidentally, a taste for literature. That Chaucer, as a co-protégé of Gaunt and associate of all of these men, should not have been aware of Wyclif's major positions, even if only from the perspective of the court, is virtually impossible.

For all that, it is in matters more bookish than courtly that Wyclif is interesting to our subject. At the University, Wyclif was associated in his lifetime with at least three Oxford colleges: Queens, Merton, and Balliol. [20] A junior at Merton in 1356, he became a Master of Balliol in 1360, and for a brief period from 1365-1367, was warden at Canterbury Hall. He took his Doctor of Divinity degree in 1372, at about 40 years of age. Although he began lecturing earlier, his first important series of theological lectures to become a book was the *De incarnatione verbi*, or *De benedicta incarnatione*, which appeared about 1368 or 1370. [21] In this series, his views on Scripture, translation, and the relationship between human and divine utterance are already formulated. From 1374-1376, he offered the lecture series which eventuated as *De domino divino* and *De domino civili*, his central treatises on the subject of dominion, in which he argues (derivatively from Fitzralph) that the exercise of all human lordship depends upon grace, and that a sinful man has no right to authority, despite the accident of title in either jurisdiction. The argument is familiar to readers of Chaucer in its précis, the moral ballad "Gentilesse."

Chaucer, for his part, leaves us even less record of his personal life than did Wyclif. It has been speculated that during what have been called the "lost years" (1360-1367), Chaucer may have been a student at Oxford,

---

18.   Workman, II, 126.
19.   "Purvey's Determination," from Deanesly, 445.
20.   Joseph Dahmus, *The Persecution of John Wyclif* (Yale, 1952), 2.
21.   Aubrey Gwynn, *English Austin Friars in the Time of Wyclif* (Oxford, 1940), 211-12.

supported there by John of Gaunt. [22] A reasonable case has been made for his having been a student at the Temple after 1361. [23] But Wood, in his *History and Antiquities of the University of Oxford,* argues that Wyclif, while he was warden at Canterbury, lectured to Chaucer, "who, following the steps of his master, reflected much upon the corruption of the clergy." [24] The report is persistent. A. B. Emden, in his *Biographical Register to the University of Oxford* makes the claim again, appealing to other witnesses: he adduces John Leland's claim that Chaucer studied at Oxford, noting that the statement is further credited (and elaborated) by Bale.

Later information is tantalizing, but entirely speculative. Foxe marvels that the bishops who condemned Wyclif and others of his party should have allowed "the works of Chaucer to remain . . . who seemeth to be a right Wicklevian, or else there never was any." [25] Foxe typically has some of his facts wrong: he has Chaucer a resident of Woodstock; we know only that he visited Woodstock in 1357. [26] He, like others, mistakenly believed Chaucer to be author of *The Testament of Love* and *The Ploughman's Tale.* Moreover, we know from other sources that Chaucer's poetry did not, as he believed, escape the bishops' condemnation for being thought "Wicklevian." [27] In his suggestion that Chaucer used fiction to "veil" his spiritual concerns from a "crafty adversary," however, he may not be entirely misguided; when he says that he has considerable information to suggest "that by the reading of Chaucer's works . . . [some] . . . were brought to a true knowledge of religion" he was surely reflecting on portions of Chaucer's established canon to which we now give much less attention than did his fourteenth-century audience.

Thomas Speght, in his 1598 edition, still argues that Chaucer and Wyclif were together at Oxford, but by this time we can place still less faith in the accuracy of the memory. Later, Sir William Vaughan, in *The Golden Fleece* (1626), goes so far as to say that Chaucer, in the pseudo-authored *Ploughman's Tale,* actually inspired Wyclif to begin his attempts at ecclesiastical reform!

Wyclif's own work refers to few contemporaries by name. He does write a special letter to a young "friend in God," evidently a layman, in which he answers questions on the disposition of love, encouraging lay vocation, and concluding with a short lyric, or tag. It would be pleasant to discover, considering the questions and the grace and quality of Wyclif's

---

22. George Williams, *A New View of Chaucer* (Duke, 1965), 156-57; John Gardiner, *The Life and Times of Geoffrey Chaucer* (Knopf, 1977), 136-37. If Chaucer was a student for a year or two after 1360, as seems likely, then his friend in later life, Ralph Strode, at that time also a close friend of Wyclif's, would still have been in residence as a fellow of Merton. Cf. J. A. W. Bennett, *Chaucer at Oxford and at Cambridge* (Oxford, 1974).

23. Edith Rickert, in *Manly Anniversary Studies in Language and Literature* (Chicago, 1923), 20-31.

24. Workman, I, 194.

25. John Foxe, *Acts and Monuments,* ed. J. Pratt, 8 vols. (4th ed., 1870), IV, 249-50.

26. M. M. Crow and C. C. Olson, eds., *Chaucer Life-Records* (Oxford, 1966), 13.

27. See n. 29 below.

answer, that the young layman was Chaucer, but that is unlikely, and we shall probably never know more of the person to whom Wyclif sent his gentle, open letter.[28] There are other tantalizing suggestions, but none of them is really useful. What we are left with is "tradition," venerable hearsay, and a few credible indications that ecclesiastical polity could place the two men squarely in the same camp on a fairly wide range of issues.[29]

We cannot, of course—even on the basis of only these light evidences—avoid the considerable probability that Chaucer was familiar with Wyclif's ideas, or further, that a good deal of Wyclif's thought was evidently congenial to the group of court and literary friends with whom Chaucer most associated himself. At least until after 1378 there would not have been any offence of that *odium theologicum* which modern literary historians sometimes imagine to argue against an explicit interest in Wyclif on the part of anyone with common sense and good manners.

Moreover, we can see close correspondence between Chaucer's apparent thinking and Wyclif's expressed opinions and convictions on a number of quite controversial subjects. A list of these should probably include: 1) Wyclif's ideas on dominion; 2) Wyclif's criticism of the mendicant orders (largely for departure from the spirit and Rule of their founders); 3) Wyclif's so-called 'nationalistic' bias; 4) Wyclif's commitment to vernacular language and translation; 5) Wyclif's approach to grammar and logic; 6) Wyclif's central preoccupation with proper method in the interpretation of texts (especially with respect to authorial intention); 7) Wyclif's views on the role of *reader* intention in interpretation; 8) Wyclif's conviction concerning the relationship between matter and form in interpretation; and 9) Wyclif's arguments concerning truth and time, the use and value of historical authority. Since Wyclif was a popular, forceful voice in fourteenth-century literary theory, and since few of his ideas are readily accessible to Chaucer scholars, it seems that a discussion of some of his views concerning the literary qualities of scriptural text and the theory of reading which arises from it may be helpful in a volume of the present kind. My own discussion will be limited to brief remarks concerning only four items of potential congruence, and I will try to develop these as clearly as I can for Wyclif's own thought, leaving most of the possible Chaucerian connections to the reader. I shall conclude with some suggestions for further application and development.

---

28.   MS New College 95. Wyclif's students preserved copies of this letter, some of which are now held in Prague and Vienna. See Arnold, III, 187ff.

29.   J. A. F. Thomson, *The Later Lollards* (Oxford, 1965), 243, notes that there was at least one occasion on which a person was accused of being a follower of Wyclif simply because he owned a copy of *The Canterbury Tales*. The accusation proves nothing at all concerning Chaucer's connection with Lollardry (with which in any case we are not here concerned). But even the mistaken associations are not entirely misleading concerning a community of common values which might be imagined between Chaucer the poet and Wyclif the professor and scholar of the Bible.

II. WYCLIF'S LITERARY APPROACH TO THE BIBLE

A. "Intention" in the Reader

An outline of Wyclif's views of "authorial intention" has been advanced in a study by A. J. Minnis.[30] With respect to the allied consideration of *reader* intention, an introduction to Wyclif's principles can be had in the inaugural lecture of the *Principium,* which he offered when elevated to his D.D. in 1372. His theory of interpretation is directed, of course, to the text of Scripture. Wyclif argues that one who would interpret Scripture in pursuit of divine "authorial" intention needs three prerequisites: the first of these is a sound moral disposition, informing one's affection; the second is experience in studying philosophy (informing, presumably, one's attention); and the third is the actual practice of virtue. He argues that these three characteristics oppose the evil and opposite trio of obeisances, the world, the flesh and the devil, disposing the soul to acquire true wisdom and theological truth. To cite Beryl Smalley's good précis, the three prerequisites accomplish this "by antecedent necessity: if matter be fully disposed to receive its form, he who imposes the form cannot fail to inform" the matter—i.e., in this case the intellect of the appropriate student, but normally either the text or the reader himself. The outline of his argument affords a framework for appreciating Wyclif's principles as well as his developing method.

He argues first that the reader requires a proper "moral disposition" *(moralis dispositio informans affectum),* that the need for it is proved by reason, authorities, and various examples. Wyclif recognizes that the traditional ordering of faculties places intellect before the will in the order of knowing. He anticipates objections to his somewhat novel structure, therefore, with the following arguments:

(1)   a commitment of the will is necessary to every pilgrim *(in statu quolibet viatoris)* throughout this life if he works to attain to salvation—the more so is this true if he wishes to study that which surpasses human understanding, and is only given to us from above *(ab extra quam studio humano perquiritur)* ;

(2)   it is quite clear that heretics, infidels and persons in mortal sin can all study theology, but they don't, in that state, gain true wisdom by it;

(3)   the will is the highest and conclusive power of the mind *(summa et finalis potentia animi),* as Augustine and others have always argued. The rectitude of the will, which is equivalent to justice *(eius rectitudo debita, que est iustica),* is the foundation for any virtuous activity. It follows, then, that rectitude of the will is needed all the more and from the outset in the

---

30.   "'Authorial Intention' and 'Literal Sense' in the Exegetical Theories of Richard Fitzralph and John Wyclif: an Essay in the Medieval History of Biblical Hermeneutics," *Proceedings of the Royal Irish Academy,* 75, Section C (1975), 1-31. These ideas are advanced further by his *Medieval Theory of Authorship: Scholastic literary attitudes in the later Middle Ages* (London, 1982).

study of Scripture, whose author is the Holy Spirit *(cui voluntas personaliter correspondet)*. In conclusion, the first condition for the student of Scripture, exceeding any capacity he may have for disputation or logical speculation, is a basic godly morality such as will prompt him to seek a just interpretation of the text. One can see in this argument the early influence of the Franciscans upon Wyclif: the precedence of the "affective" over the "intellective" faculty in preparing for "contemplation of the divine mysteries" corresponds to Bonaventuran (or pseudo-Bonaventuran) psychology, but is here applied not to meditation or to contemplation of the Passion, but to a study of Scripture.[31]

Philosophy, the discipline of intellect, comes next. Under this heading Wyclif includes "the arts of speech *(philosophia sermonicalis)*, natural philosophy *(philosophia naturalis)*, and moral philosophy *(philosophia moralis, tam secundum philosophiam speculativam quam practicam)*. In establishing some sense of his hermeneutical principles, it is the first of these with which we should be most concerned. Not surprisingly, this subject is divided into the three disciplines of the *trivium*, grammar, rhetoric and logic, and here, in a relatively early stage of his thinking, the temporal order of Wyclif's categories is traditional.

In the third and last section, on the practice of virtue, Wyclif argues simply that the right end of interpretation is, like the right end of philosophy, a moral life—particularly, he says, right action. One sees, perhaps, the influence of the Hebrew prophets: action is the most perfect function of man, in which he is most *imago dei*. To choose to act according to what has been understood is good. Correspondingly, not to act according to one's insight and talents is sinful. Thus, anyone who has learned to interpret cannot be excused the duty of enlightening (preaching and teaching), perfecting in good counsel, and purging sin in his cure of souls.

The final exhortation is as follows:

> Let each do his duty, not thrusting himself forward, but modestly, according to the measure meted out to him, in praise of God, the giver. One works in the school, another in the church, one in the world, another in the cloister of virtues, one praying, deep in contemplation, with Mary, another ministering to the people with Martha. Let us all go forward as pilgrims, without discord, seeking not our private advancement, but the unity and perfection of Christ's mystical body, until we ourselves come to perfection, are taught all truth, have full knowledge of Scripture, and read unfailingly in the book of life, in proportion to our meritorious acts and habits.[32]

In short, the reader of Scripture will become only as effective an interpreter of text as he is already a 'translator' of the Text in the actions of his or her personal life.

---

31.   Ch. 3, D. L. Jeffrey, *The Early English Lyric and Franciscan Spirituality* (Nebraska, 1975). On Wyclif's sense of 'reader intention', cf. Minnis, 24-27.
32.   Beryl Smalley, "Wyclif's *Postilla* on the Old Testament and his *Principium*," *Oxford Studies Presented To Daniel Callus, O.P.* (Oxford, 1964), 276.

B. GRAMMAR AND THE LOGIC OF NARRATIVES

For Wyclif, as a schoolman, the *pre cursus* for any higher study of spiritual and philosophical matters was still the *trivium*: grammar, rhetoric and logic. Yet in his own canon of priorities, if grammar still comes first in time, for the discipline of interpretation, logic precedes rhetoric (actually, Wyclif never expostulates upon rhetoric in the classical sense at all) and forms the keystone of a solid interpretative edifice. But to grasp anything of the potential implications of Wyclif's theory of interpretation for a contemporary like Chaucer, it remains helpful to approach his thinking in the traditional context of the *trivium* and that portion of the university curriculum grouped around its disciplines.

It is as an anticipation of Wyclif's address to the grammar and logic of Scripture, particularly as it comes to be explored in his *De veritate sacrae scripturae* (1378), that his objective in earlier lectures, *De logica* (begun 1361-62 but not finished until c. 1380) may most clearly be appreciated. The perspective of the traditional approach of scholastic methodology is here particularly helpful. Anselm, for example, acting as a theologian, had prepared his *Monologion* in response to requests by *quidem fratres* to create a set of theological foundations; to do so, he set out to create "proofs" which have no foundations whatsoever in Scripture or doctrine. Wyclif, in his *proemium* to the *De logica,* explains that he has been prompted by academic colleagues ("certain friends of God's law") to expound the logic and structure of the Bible as a logician. [33]

> Motus sum per quondam legis dei amicos certum tractatum ad declarandum logicam sacre scripture compilare . . . propono ad acuendum mentes fidelium ponere probaciones proposicionum que debent elici ex scripturis. [34]

In this work, we see that Wyclif is greatly indebted to the scholastic tradition of Aristotelian philosophy which preceded him, and that he argues his own realist's case against the nominalism which predominated at Oxford in a thoroughly traditional way, except that his premises are biblically derived rather than taken from classical logic. While he holds Aristotle a great philosopher, he repudiates his doctrine of creation, which undermines, he says, much of Aristotle's utility in Scriptural analysis.

In *De veritate,* he argues even more forcefully that interpretation must be founded upon the single authority of Christ rather than upon the plurality of philosophical authorities [35] and, moreover, that Aristotelian philosophy cannot get at ultimate truth questions and is, at the last, ungrounded speculation or even lies. Therefore, *"ad tantum enim quis potest assuefieri ad mendacia, quod vel non discernat vel minus ponderet veritatem?"* [36] Here we see a reflection of Wyclif's own development, from

---

33. S. H. Harrison, "The Philosophical Basis of Wyclif's Theology," *Journal of Religion,* 11 (1931), 90.
34. *De logica,* I, i.
35. *De veritate sacrae scripturae*, 3 vols., ed. R. Buddenseig (London, 1905-1907), 29-32.
36. *Ibid.*

being a schoolman with an interest in Scripture in the *De logica* to being preeminently an interpreter of the text of Scripture, with a background in philosophy, by the time of *De veritate*. It would be good to be at leisure to engage the argument and principal tenets of the earlier book, but in fact the signal achievement of Wyclif's contribution to the history of the theory of interpretation rests with his "last point of armour," the nature of scriptural language manifest in its own relation of logic to grammar, and for that the pages of the *De veritate* remain far the best expositor.

In his *Principium* Wyclif had set the case for grammar in traditional terms, harking back again to the *De doctrina christiana*. Grammar is useful, he argues, because it sets our feet on the ground, enabling us first to understand biblical terms according to the literal sense and subsequently to distinguish figures and tropes according to the mystical sense in whichever of its aspects, allegorical, tropological or anagogical. "Happy is he who knows all these things perfectly," he says, adding "yet happier he who knows how to resolve the Latin text in terms of its Greek or Hebrew originals: *cognoscendo rei proprietatem et rationem secundum quam nomen rei imponitur.*[37]

Grammar came, however, to have a larger implication for Wyclif, one which is tied more closely to the discipline of logic or dialectic. By the time of his major hermeneutical work, *De veritate sacrae scripturae*, he argues that Scripture has its own distinctive grammar and logic and the principles of its grammar ought to be argued from *it* as text as distinct from the typical anthology of classical authors from whom classical grammar was most often taught. As Gregory and others *(alias sanctas)* have shown, he says, Scripture exhibits a *novum grammaticam ac novam logicam*. These true exegetes expounded Scripture accordingly in terms of a *novas sensus terminorum scripture, qui nusquam originantur ex libris gramatice*. Where, except in the teaching of Scripture, Wyclif asks, is it learned that "Terra sit infernus, virgo, deus ac elementum, celica vita, prothoplastum, machina mundi"[38]? While we might choose to understand Scripture according to the childish sense, or simple grammar, he continues, Scripture has a more mature grammar toward which we progress; as Paul taught in 1 Cor. 13, "When I was a child I thought like a child, and I spoke like a child. Now, however, that I am become a man, I have put off these (childish) things."[39] What then is the character of this "mature grammar" of Scripture, in which something apparently may be that which it is not, or may be many things at the same time, and how may it assist us toward the understanding to which Wyclif aspires?

The first thing that strikes the reader is the evidently awkward character of the example ("Terra sit infernus..." etc.) for normal Aristotelian categories. It counters the "A is not non A" premise with an equation: *sit*.

---

37. Smalley (p. 291) suggests that it is not certain that he knew these 'original' languages, especially Hebrew, so well himself.
38. *De veritate sacrae scripturae,* I, 42.
39. *De veritate s.s.,* I, 44-45.

For Wyclif, the whole character of the Gospel depends on an optative refutation of the law of non-contradiction: i.e., death *may* be life.

Wyclif illustrates this stratagem further in one of his early Oxford sermons, where to counter the derivatively Aristotelian reasoning of the "sophists" among his colleagues (i.e., his opponents), he discusses the necessary relation of grammar to theology in what we would take to be logical or dialectical terms. Proceeding from his earlier point that Scripture offers numerous examples of clear, yet far from simple or traditional grammar, he cites as an example the words of Christ: *"Et sermonem quem audistis non est meus, sed eius qui misit me patris* [and the word which you hear is not mine, but the Father's words, who sent me"].[40] In such a statement, he argues, we see that the grammarians are found to consult the theologian, for the evident antithesis in this statement requires defence in terms of the verbal congruity of the larger context, the whole narrative or discourse in which it occurs. We begin here with the observation that as it stands in John's text, the first complete construction in the statement of Christ *(Et sermonem quem audistis non est meus)* is, on the face of it, a grammatical incongruity. Yet by faith we accept that the Holy Spirit does not allow even such a small irregularity without good reason *(iota vel apicem sine notabili racione)*. What therefore is the reason the accusative is where the nominative should be in this saying? It is to be acknowledged that the rules of grammar and logic are necessarily under the dominion of theology, but in good precedent (Augustine) we may utilize characteristics of the subservient art in ways not natural to itself to address theological difficulties—and the clue in the present conundrum is, as it turns out, in fact the grammatical one. We see that the manner in which Scripture here first chooses to express the concept "word" is in the singular (word) rather than the plural (words). Though this is, by rules of conventional grammar, an irregular construct, the grammatical abnormality actually teaches subtly that all the *words* which are true *(decalogi*, that is, divine sayings) are not in the last analysis formally separable, but are *substantially* that same word which is spoken in the *totum integrum,* Christ himself. Therefore these words of the Evangelist ought to be taken to mean:

> That which Christ teaches is not realized or served by the individual words alone, but rather in the context of the Word before all words, the configuration of God's whole discourse with man.[41]

The point John's gospel makes here, according to Wyclif, is indeed everywhere in the book. In another of his favourite texts, it is rendered explicit in a different way: *non potest solvi scriptura quem Pater sanctificavit et misit in mundum* ("It is not possible to fragment the Word which the Father sanctified and sent into the world"—John 10:35-36).[42] "Contradictions" thus arise primarily as a result of ignorance of the whole

---

40. *Sermones,* 4 vols., ed. J. Loserth (London, 1887), I, 209.
41. *Ibid.,* 210; repeated in *De benedictione incarnatione,* 115; see also G. A. Benrath, *Wyclifs Bibelkommentar* (Berlin, 1966), 366.
42. *De veritate s.s.,* I, 102.

textual fabric of Sacred Scriptures, and from consequent attempts to subordinate the text to philosophical novelties of the hour rather than to its own intrinsic logic.[43] In other words, as he argues elsewhere in the same work, the ultimate function of the *words* is merely to lead you to a sense of the *cortex verborum*, and thus in turn, to a relationship to the Word as personal knowledge, as we see: *Christus et multi sancti non scripserant nisi sensum in tabulis cordis, cum hoc sit perfeccius.*[44] This idea is far from limited to the *De veritate*, but figures largely also in the *postilla*, where he refers again and again to John (especially chapter 7 and 14:10) to deal with this same issue.[45]

Wyclif's preoccupation with the indivisibility of Scripture, in which he is so indebted to John's gospel, begins to come into sharper focus when we remember how literal-minded were the syllogistic excesses of some of the logical and grammatical arguments raised against the authority of Scripture in his time. He gives a straw-man series of these "sophistical" questions which help him to clarify how a failure to see beyond the most narrow limits of classical grammar and logic impede the plain or 'total sense' of many kinds of statements in Scripture which simply model a different logic and grammar. Some of these adversarial questions of his Oxford opponents provide him with illustrations: Scripture refers to Christ as a lamb, a lion, and a worm . . . how can these things be true?[46] Christ said he would not go up to Jerusalem for the feast, but he went up—does Scripture lie? John the Baptist denied he was Elias, but Christ says he was—does Scripture contradict itself?[47] Christ says (Matt. 25:29) that from the man who had nothing even that which he had would be taken away—is this not self-contradictory?[48]

Yet as we see from Wyclif's treatment of the first conundrum (John 14:24), as in his whole *postilla* on John, Scripture cannot be false, simply because at its first and most important level, it is Christ—the Word from the beginning. The term *scriptura* has various meanings. Preeminently it signifies the Book of Life described in the Apocalypse, the very person of the Divine Word, and secondly the *decalogi* or expressions of eternal truth which are not really but only rationally distinct from it. Only in the light of these principles, as Father Hurley has pointed out, do we appreciate the "nominal" sense of the term in which, finally:

> Scripture is also taken by Wyclif to mean the codices and the words written in them, but these are mere signs of Scripture *par excellence*; they are not Scripture except insofar as they exemplify the latter; they are sacred if they lead us

---

43. Benrath, 363.

44. *De veritate s.s.*, III, 44.

45. Postil on Luke 9: see Benrath, 362 ff. Minnis discusses what he calls "Wyclif's categorical refusal to regard the Bible as a book *per se*" (p. 14). My emphasis is on Wyclif's seeing it as *liber liberissimus*, the model for all "books," an implicit literary 'theory'.

46. *De veritate s.s.*, I, 1-19; 40-42; see M. Hurley, S.J., "Scriptura Sola*: Wyclif and his Critics," *Traditio*, 16 (1960), 294-96.

47. *De veritate s.s.*, II, 49-51.

48. *Ibid.*, I, 57; 61-62.

to the knowledge of celestial Scripture, insofar as by faith we see and read in them God's will and ordinance in our regard.[49]

It is this "celestial Scripture" which we ought to identify with the *logos,* the person of the divine Word.

Scripture provides a five-piece armour (cf. Ephesians 6) to defend the literal truth of Scripture: the doctrine of eternal ideas, the existence of universals *ex parte rei,* the real unity in diversity of creation, the metaphysics of eternity and the equivocal nature of Scriptural language, so essential to its own particular grammar and logic.[50] It is the last point, as Hurley observes, which becomes the cutting edge of Wyclif's attack on problem texts like the ones pointed to by his opponents. Once we appreciate that the discourse itself of Scripture (and not merely the larger narrative devices such as parable) is not a univocal language, then we can penetrate the surface of that language and apprehend meaning at the level of authorial *intention,* where it is then found to be 'literally' true. To return to our examples: Christ is a lion in the figurative sense and, in the context of the Scriptures concerning his majesty, this is (with respect to signification) 'literally' true; the same may be said of the lamb, in references to his sacrificial atonement, or the worm, in references to his rejection. Further, Christ did decline to go up to Jerusalem for the feast—he meant that rather than go openly at that moment he would go later and secretly. John denied that he was Elias, in his person—Christ affirmed that he was, in his office. As in all metaphor or analogy, there is equivocity in the language here, but not, from the point of view of intention, any contradiction. The ostensibly grammatical and logical objections disappear when we set the text *in situ* and with respect to a biblical rather than secular view of the nature of time and the temporal aspect of discourse. (We will return to this point momentarily.)

It is in this context that we see how the "literary" realism of Wyclif stands against the nominalism in his opponents' methods, leading him to quote the pseudo-Dionysius:

> est irracionable, et estimo, et stultum non virtuti intencionis attendere, sed diccionibus, et hoc non est divina intelligere volencium proprium, sed sonos nudos suscipiencium.[51]

Not merely in the naked sound of the utterance, which is after all only a sign, but in the authorial will itself is the truth to be had. Wyclif quotes Grosseteste to show us that the term "love" can cover a multitude of sins, simply by becoming a name for many of them—the word clearly has a variety of carnal senses. Yet it is used in Scripture to signify also, and unmistakably, Divine Love. Thus, while according to custom (Wyclif puns nicely here on *consuetum*—also "love affair") we take love in vulgar speech to mean one thing, in Scripture it means another, with the meaning referenced not to the limitations of literal denominations but determined, in

---

49. *Ibid.,* I, 107-17; see Hurley, 295; Minnis, 15.
50. *Ibid.,* I, 167-82.
51. *Ibid.,* III, 43. Cf. Minnis, *op. cit.*

fact, by the establishment in the whole text of the author's intention. This is a matter of a sense of genre, in part, and Wyclif assures us that the idea is not entirely new with him by capping his argument with a final polemical quotation from Dionysius:

> ... est quidem, ut estimo, irracionabile et stultum, seu vanum seu pravum, non attendere virtuti intencionis verbi videlicet et autoris, sed diccionibus secundum vulgarem usum acceptis. [52]

Such mundane literality is hardly adequate to an understanding of the Divine intention, for the words of the Lord are spoken consistently with his character and direct us not, of course, to the commonplace, but to wisdom. Let us never forget, Wyclif argues elsewhere, that intention is the critical aspect of interpretation from at least two perspectives: that of the text and that of the reader. This is why commitment of heart, or recitation of the will—placing it in correspondence with the divine will—is of necessity the first requisite of interpretation in any case where the Author's intention is the ostensible goal of the interpretation. How clear it is, he says in his *postilla* on Luke, that the interpreter can falsify the text by ego-centrism in his own intentions, such as the desire for fame *(laudis humane)* perhaps, or, more simply, self-justification. Then, of course, one will see in the text just what he himself wants to see, rather than the vision of his Author. [53]

The way to ensure one is expounding the text after its own values, and not after a logic imposed on it from somewhere else, is to let the *form* of the Scripture govern the form of the exposition (indeed, of *all* exposition). For the Christian, *Christianus debet loqui sub autoritate scripture verba scripture secundam formam scripturam, qua scriptura ipsa explicat.* The inevitable consequence will be an imitation of biblical rather than an alien logic, so that a right vision of the storic sense of the whole text is realized, such as properly can preface any approach to its several parts. [54] But that there can and should be an extension of this principle to language employed by the Christian generally is made explicit at the outset of the *De veritate.* Holy Scripture, Wyclif says, is written according to the pattern of our speech: *forma igitur locucionis scripture est exemplar omni alii modo loquendi probabile,* [55] but also, as he argues, it affords in turn the pattern for all possible Christian discourse: *ut scriptura, que debet esse exemplar omni humano generi ad loquendum, includat in se omne genus loquendie probabile.* [56] In this, as well as in his subsequent extensions of *forma* to the larger shape of discourse and dialectic of the text, Wyclif argues in

---

52. *Ibid.*
53. Q. Benrath, 364. There is a caveat: Wyclif wishes to be very clear that the principle of the equivocity of scriptural language must be related to divine intention. Clearly, also, there are a variety of logical models exhibited by Scripture *(scriptura sacra habet multas maneries logicarum).* But we apply many of these purely interpretatively to text, and to the mysteries of faith—not all of them correspond to the pragmatic logic of daily life, *secundum quod docetur ex spiritu consilii et regula caritatis, ut expondendo-theologiam misticam debet uti logica plana scripture.*
54. *De veritate s.s.,* III, 52.
55. *Ibid.,* I, 6.
56. *Ibid.,* I, 205.

effect for response to an "intrinsic logic" in Scripture as the essential ingredient for any valid theory of interpretation. His insistence on the right governance of the "form" of Scriptural discourse, and, as we shall see, its right to preference over classical forms for Christian discourse generally, is one of the central hermeneutical aspects of Wyclif's theory.

Wyclif observes that Christ did not teach, as far as Scripture shows us, a formal course in logic. He did, however, model these principles in his own conversation, which is rich and multivalent, yet without duplicity or false equivocation. The logical system derived from the "Terra sit infernus . . ." example is the essence of Scripture, the "form" in terms of which the "matter" (of the Old Testament) is to be realized. While in fourteenth-century Oxford a logical system hardly survives twenty years of disputation, and often changes, the logic of Scripture is eternal. Its very goal is interpretation, the achievement of meaning, and it leads toward that ultimate conclusion *(ad finem ultimum)* straightforwardly and without tumultous ambiguity *(tumultuosis ambagibus)* of its contesting and uncertain alternatives. [57]

In disputation itself, we might note, it had become by Wyclif's time clear that the swing was away from logical argument to argument by or from appeal to authorities. It is of more than passing relevance that William Woodford, a friendly colleague of Ralph Strode and Wyclif and one-time neighbour of Chaucer, [58] exemplifies this other late fourteenth-century method, *contra auctor*. Laurence Eldredge has shown that in his later opposition to Wyclif, in Dubium 63 of his *De Sacramento Altaris*, [59] Woodford is typical of the new university method. Rather than debate by "reasoned argument and logical progression" he merely lists and quotes "hundreds of authorities" — curial, theological, and a plenitude of canon lawyers — offering not to win his case by debate but simply attempting to overwhelm Wyclif's position with names and footnotes. [60] (Thomas Netter, early in the fifteenth-century, was to confirm the same approach. [61]) Wyclif, by contrast, was arguing an integral logic based on a single authority, Scripture (or, in his sense, Christ), and proclaiming that logic to be universally authoritative for faith and life. It is precisely this aspect of his argument which must have seemed most attractive to those students who were being fatigued by the confusing plurality of authorities and logical systems contesting in fourteenth-century intellectual life. Wyclif's brand of realism certainly constituted a minority position. But by the late 1370s, he was easily the best-known theologian and schoolman in the England of his day.

---

57. *Ibid.*, III, 54.
58. William Woodford was confessor to the convent of Franciscan nuns at Aldgate at the time Chaucer was living nearby (early 1380s) above Aldgate.
59. Laurence Eldredge, "The Concept of God's Absolute Power at Oxford in the Later Fourteenth Century," in Jeffrey, *By Things Seen: Reference and Recognition in Medieval Thought* (Ottawa, 1979), 223, dates this document in the early 1380s.
60. Eldredge, 224-25. Cf. Stewart Justman, "Medieval Monism and Abuse of Authority in Chaucer," *Chaucer Review*, 11 (1976), 95-111.
61. In *Fasciculas Zizianorum*, ed. W. W. Shirley (Rolls Series, 1858).

C. OF TRUTH AND TIME
(USE AND VALUE OF HISTORICAL AUTHORITY)

Wyclif was far from illusioned concerning the historical problems presented by any attempt at authorial interpretation. He acknowledges, for example, that there are discreet cultural factors to be accounted for, and he acknowledges also that one is always confronted with the exigencies of translation and transmission in approaching the text.[62] But the problem of time in relationship to truth in interpretation is for him still a more essential problem,[63] invoking what we might now think of as a 'phenomenological' distinction. From his *Principium* forward through the debates with Kenningham to the *De veritate* and finally to his last work, the *Opus Evangelicum*,[64] he considers interpretation with respect to two time schemes, the temporal *(tempus)* —particular or successive time as apprehended by men—and *duratio*, God's 'time,' in which all being is eternally present. All things are individuated by their occurrence in time, which God creates with the world, by his ordinance. Whatever has been or will be *is*.

Beryl Smalley, in her excellent treatment of Wyclif's *Principium*, reminds us that it was this doctrine of time which was principally at stake in four separate attacks on Wyclif by the Carmellite friar Kenningham.[65] Kenningham referenced his objections to the *postilla* on Lamentations and Amos, but he could as easily have focussed on the *De veritate*, the *postilla* on John, the Apocalypse, Jeremiah, or the prologue to Isaiah to make the same points. Wyclif's theory of time proves to be critical to his whole hermeneutic. It deserves at least a cursory look here, in particular because of its implications for his understanding of intrinsic genre.

Wyclif's modified realism involves him in using the word *ideae* in such a way that it usually means "archetypes in the mind of God," *rationes exemplares* or patterns which are the means by which God knows and brings into being his creatures.[66] We may therefore speak of all created things as, in their temporal existence, "intuited" by God, but in their essence present to him eternally. From the *De materis et forma*:

> Omnes enim creaturas, quantum libet remotas, preteritas vel futuras, deus intuetur, quia sunt in tempore suo: et solum deus intuetur. Alias autem possibiles, que non existunt in tempore suo, cognoscit noticia simplicis apprehensionis, de quando cognoscit ista habere esse intelligibile et posse existere.[67]

By this "doctrine of possibles," for something to be possible it must have existed, must now exist, or else it will exist at some time in the future, *in tempore suo*.

---

62. ˇCf. Bacon and Lyra.
63. J. A. Robson, *Wyclif and the Oxford Schools* (Cambridge, 1961), 161.
64. Beryl Smalley, "The Bible and Eternity: John Wyclif's Dilemma," *JWCI*, 27 (1964), 84.
65. Smalley, "Wyclif's *Postilla*...," 259-63.
66. See the summary in Harrison's article, p. 96.
67. *Miscellenea Philosophica*, I, 234-35.

There arise two primary implications here. The first is that if everything to be possible has to have a real existence in God's mind, then the Divine imagination is the present and permanent measure of all things, whether they be singular or universal. What seems infinite to the human mind is finite—already "closed" and complete—to God, for whom nothing is infinite in number, space or time.[68] Time as *tempus* is a unit of measurement confined to the limits of the created world—weeks and months are human calculations. But it is precisely the created world which marks the furthest extension of the measurable. At the ultimate points, the moment of creation (and, by implication, the moment of Apocalypse), time and duration, *tempus* and *duratio*, meet. Robson summarizes it in this way:

> The world possessed durative being before the creation and will continue to possess it after the Day of Judgement; but the first moment of Creation was also the beginning of temporality. Time and Creation, therefore, are reciprocally causal, for without Creation there could be no first moment, and its purpose is to cause the first moment. At this point God, the world and Creation are united, and time as we know it begun.[69]

The second implication of the "doctrine of possibles" is equally interesting, focussing not so much on extra-mental reality as upon the mind and imagination itself. In Harrison's summary, "a reality is real by virtue of its existence in God's thought." Intelligibility is synonomous with possibility. In other words, then, the principles of being and intellection are identical[70]—"what is capable of being thought in a real sense is possible."[71] Effectively, imagination "sees" a "real" possibility.

This idea of the "amplification of time" is, in reality, what governs Wyclif's analysis and resolution of some of the "grammatical" problems in Scripture proposed by his colleagues the logicians; it is at the basis of the logic of Sacred Scripture which we have considered briefly here as well. When Wyclif deals with passages such as the first chapter of Genesis, or even the first and fourteenth chapters of John's gospel, he invokes it as a solution to the ostensibly "grammatical" problems seen there. Whereas from the perspective of classical grammar there is always a disjunction between the imperative and the indicative, in the grammar of Scripture there is no comparable tyranny of the temporal—of the purely causal. God speaks, and the Word and the Event are the same thing.[72] It is not that God's Word *causes* Creation; it *is* creation.[73] Moreover, Wyclif seems to have been aware, if not from an intimate knowledge of Hebrew of his

---

68. Wyclif's reference is to Wisdom 11:21: *De Logica*, III, 36-37; 87-89.
69. Robson, 158.
70. *De ente*, ed. J. A. F. Thomson (Oxford, 1950), 62-63.
71. Cf. Harrison, 111.
72. *Postilla* on John 1:3: "Every existing thing is in reality God himself, for every creature which can be named *is*, in regard to its 'intelligible' existence, and consequently its chief existence is in reality the Word of God."
73. Gotthard Lechler, *Johann von Wyclif und die Vorgeschichte der Reformation*, 2 vols. (Leipzig, 1873), II, 243.

own,[74] then at least from familiarity with his favourite *postilla* by Nicholas of Lyra, that the Hebrew verb is tenseless, that it provides no comparable disjunction between the imperative and the indicative, encompassing future with present tense.[75] Thus Wyclif appears to be one among very few medieval scholars who grasped something of the possibility in this feature of Hebrew for an insight into the temporal-durational aspect of scriptural language. He would have been familiar, presumably, with Lyra's famous observation that Exodus 3:14 should not be translated *Ego sum qui sum,* but rather understood as *Ego ero qui ero.*[76] It is in this sense, Wyclif observes, that Matthew can speak of Christ as the "son of David."[77]

Among Wyclif's opponents, Kenningham the Carmellite objected strongly to this view of time in relationship to interpretation. While he could agree that the New Testament was eternally true from its starting point in time (history) he could not agree to its eternal truth before, in the *duratio.* He argues that this position involves Wyclif in a return to the cyclical view of time held by pagan philosophers such as Plato and already condemned by St. Augustine.[78] In fact, as Professor Smalley has aptly observed, Wyclif actually combines this apparently anti-historical point of view with a keen and unusually searching sense of history. We see further that as he develops and builds his arguments he can command a fine historical sense of theological and ecclesiastical tradition, and he has a real sensitivity to phases and changes in its tempo. When he writes about the historical books of the Old Testament, or the Pentateuch, Wyclif expresses a keen appreciation for the form of their historicity as it is expressed in the narratives. He knows well the pilgrimage motif, the journey of the Hebrew people from exile and captivity, ever toward the promised land, and he lends this theme and structure sensitive and progressive historical evaluation in his *postilla* on the prophets.[79] But right alongside of this he also argues for another kind of time in interpretation, another kind of structure.

The grammatical figure for *duratio* is drawn from Wyclif (in the redaction of one of his students) and placed in the prologue to the Wyclif Bible, where it is the fifth rule for reading Scripture.

> The v. reule is of tymes, and this is bi a figure clepid *synodoches,* whan o part is set for oo part.... Bi this kynde of speche, bi which kinde is al singnefied by a part, thilke question of Cristis rising aʒen is asoiled; the last part of the day, wherinne Crist suffride deth, is taken for al the day with the nyʒt passis before, and the first part of Sunday, in whos morewitide he roos aʒen, is taken for al Sunday and the nyʒt bifore goynge; and the Sabot with the hool nyʒt bifore goynge is an hool day and nyʒt. If these nyʒtis and daies be not taken thus, there moun not be iij daies and iij nyʒtis, in which he bifore seide, that he schulde be in the herte of erthe. Also this reule of tymes is taken for lawful

---

74.   Deanesly, 167-68.
75.   Cf. Smalley, "The Bible and Eternity...," 85.
76.   Nicholas de Lyra, *Postilla* on Exodus, in *Biblia sacra cum glossa ordinaria* (Antwerp, 1634), I, 511.
77.   Cf. Lyra, whom Wyclif follows, in *Postilla* on Matt. 22:42; Matt. 1:1.
78.   Smalley, "The Bible and Eternity...," 86, n. 51.
79.   Cf. *De ben. incarn.,* 110 ff.

noumbris, as ben vij, x and xij and such moo, for ofte such noumbris ben sett for
al tyme, as this that Davith seith, "seuen sithis in the day I seide preying, ether
herying, to thee," is noon othir thing. [80]

That is, Scripture abounds in qualitative as well as merely quantitative descriptions of time, and provides ample illustrations of situations where the
part stands for a much larger or more comprehensive whole. At the grammatical level, the *synecdoche* is relative to Wyclif's theory of the mystery
of the Incarnation from which theology much of the preceding passage
derives, [81] but it also allows him to see scriptural numbers (such as the
144,000 blessed) as figurative in the same sense; the numbers are not quantitative, but qualitative. Moreover, linguistically this forms a bridge toward
understanding a biblical phrase such as "the fullness of time" not merely
as a decisive moment in the *tempus,* but as an interpenetration of the
duratio and the *tempus* such as reflects that which occurred at the Creation
(or will occur again at the conclusion) of the world. [82] The Incarnation is
also such a moment, of course, in which the person of God whose being is
in eternity is at once made known in time, and the fullness of time thus can
constitute, for those who enter into it by faith, not just a highly significant
point in the *tempus* (or *chronos*) but a "real" apprehension of the *duratio*
(or *chairos*)—a time of meaning and ultimate interpretation. Scripture, for
Wyclif, is full of a 'mystical' sense of this interpretation; consequently,
many of its statements confound a merely progressive or sequential interpretation altogether. Here too, *littera occidit, spiritus autem vivificat.*

In his treatise on the Incarnation Wyclif summarizes the various aspects of scriptural address to this interrelationship of times by citing a trenchant passage from Matthew (22:41-46) where Christ has responded to a
scrutinous question, "which is the greatest commandment in the law?"
While the Pharisees consider his famous reply, Jesus puts his own question
to them: *Quid vobis videtur de Christo? cuius filius est?* They give the
right answer: "The Son of *David.*" But then Jesus says, "How then in
spirit does David call him Lord, saying, the Lord said unto my Lord, sit on
my right hand until I make your enemies your footstool? If David then
calls him Lord, how is he his son?" And Matthew concludes, in Wyclif's
citation, "no one was able to answer a word, nor dared anyone from that
day on ask him any more questions." [83]

For Wyclif, the 'amplification of time' here models an implied relationship in Christ's interpretation (the form of interpretation suggested in
the reflection of the Word which is borne out in scriptural words), which
provides a key to biblical interpretation generally. He is aware that the
context of this passage in Matthew is a response to the 'matter' of the
law—its numerous precepts—and to a tricky request for judgement upon
them which would establish the most "authoritative" of many laws. He

---

80. Cf. *De ben. incarn.*, 16.
81. *Ibid.,* 56; 98.
82. Isaiah 34:4; also *Postilla* on Luke 9, in Benrath 362-65.
83. Psalm 110:1; *De ben. incarn.*, 16.

sees that, instead, what the Pharisees get is a *qualitative analysis*, or interpretation of the whole law, which "sums it up," not as a series of temporal actions, but as a foundational spiritual attitude: "You shall love the Lord your God with all your heart, with all your soul, and with all your mind . . . and . . . you shall love your neighbour as yourself." That interpretation on the first passage is a question of letter and spirit the whole tradition of Christian exegesis had already proclaimed. What Wyclif does is to regard the counter question as a further illumination with respect to interpretation, *duratio* vs. *tempus*, casting its light back over the whole passage. The inferences drawn lead Wyclif, in a continuing retrospective exegesis of the Psalms which Christ has been using with reference to himself in Matthew, to see the consequences of the interpretation as argument for the consubstantiality of the Word, the Incarnation of the Word, and finally, the extension to mankind of the Divine nature through the Incarnation.[84]

The basic distinction between form and matter, by which the gospel is seen to provide the "form", the law and the prophets (and indeed, all else in Scripture) the "matter" for interpretation, is, of course, in its essentials, familiarly Pauline and Augustinian.[85] Thus, most of Wyclif's many proclamations of the principle, such as the one following, seem at first traditional:

> For lawe of þe Olde Testament techiþ not but charite, for alle stories and prophetis hangen in þes two wordis, love þi God and love þi neiȝbore; and þis is to kepe þe ten commandementis. Alle ceremonyes and judicial lawes in þe Olde Testament oblishen not Cristene men, but ȝif þei moven to þis *eend*. But wel we witen þat þei ben just, and techen at þe laste þis *eende*. And þus moralte of þe olde law, þat stondiþ in þe lore of vertues, lastiþ in þe newe lawe, and *wiþouten eende* in hevene. And þus Crist filliþ þe olde lawe and makiþ a *perfit eende* þerof, for it is purgid bi þe newe lawe, and more liȝt us to kepe.
>
> And þus seyen clerkes, þat as a man is maad of bodi and of soule, so ful lawe of God is maad of þe olde and of þe newe. Þe olde is *mater* of of þis lawe, and þe newe *forme* þerof. And as *mater* and *forme* ben oo þing in substaunce, as þe bodi and þe soule ben o persone, þat is þe spirit, — so þe olde lawe and þe newe ben oo þing in substance. And þis *forme* is charitie, þat was evermore in þe Chirche, bit it toke perfit degree bi charite þat Crist tauȝte. Ȝif we wolen þryve, love we þis lawe, and caste aweie all oþer lawes, but ȝif þei helpen and serven herto, and so myche mai þei suffrid.[86]

But we see that there is a bit more here. When the principle is considered in the light of passages such as the one from Matthew, or John 1, or John 14, it begins to take on a fresh and intriguing character. Matter and form are in this context narrative and structural terms as well as colloquially philosophical: by *form* Wyclif regularly speaks of the intrinsic sense of structure in terms of which the whole of Scripture is to be understood[87]: when he says "Crist filliþ þi olde lawe and makiþ a perfit eende þerof," he

84. Ps. 22, *ibid.*
85. *Sermones*, III, 169-76; *De ver. s.s.*, I, 228-29.
86. *Sermons, Select English Works*, ed. Arnold, II, 171-72.
87. *De ver. s.s.*, I, 4; 6; 205.

doesn't mean a temporal end, of course, but rather "purpose." It is in this sense that he enunciates here what, in his analysis, will be not only the principle and point of interpenetration and understanding of the whole text, but, in effect, its formal principle of closure. When he says that the "new forme" is "charitie" he is recognizably Augustinian; when he says this law of form pertains fully to the Old Testament, and is not to be separated from it, but is joined to it analogously to the principle of the hypostatic union, he is approaching a Greek theology of the Word in which the "form", as an eternal and unchanging governance, will inform and interpret each temporal phenomenon, each text. But he takes the argument still one step further.

In considering the Incarnation, the interpenetration of which involves an incorporation of the eternal *(duratio)* into the temporal *(tempus)* in the understanding as well as in the fact, Wyclif finds this principle of the 'amplification of time' to be fundamentally operative. It is in this sense that we understand the Incarnation, as the Person of Christ, to be an integrative principle, against and across time, redeeming men of all ages, before and after the historical 'event.' Similarly Christ is to be understood, as Word, as identified with the concept of Wisdom (understanding and truth) from the Old Testament itself (e.g. Prov. 8:22)—the connection, he points out, had been made already by Augustine and Jerome.[88] Thus Ephesians 1:20 (cf. Col. 1:19-20) speaks of Christ in whom "God purposed to gather together all things in one." Wisdom is the appropriate goal of every attempt at interpretation, and in fact is *summe mobilis* —in the realm of this 'form' of interpretation we are absolutely freed from the lockstep of purely causal syntax of temporal perception, and can begin, truly, to apprehend wisdom as opposed to mere knowledge, or to put it another way, to recognize the character of Wisdom as transformation, as distinct from mere information. Thus, Wisdom or "the Word," surpasses everything in its "swiftness," Wyclif concludes, moving through spheres and ages with imperceptible speed, so that

> quod eius brevis passio reduxit totum mundum post et ante ad maius temperamentum quam motus perpetuus primi mobilis suffecisset: prima enim secundum Aristotelem sunt quantitite minima.[89]

In the pursuit of Wisdom, time and space collapse. The Wisdom of God the Father, more "moving" than any creature, sums up all temporalities, *thus* is universal. It is the metaphysical subject, the Being which *duratio* may begin to apprehend once *tempus* has been by it surpassed. It perfectly illustrates the principle that to God all things are present, and that *Iesus Christus hodie et cras ipse et in secula* —is the same yesterday, today, and forever.[90] By this we understand how it is that Abraham can be said to know of the Incarnation and that the faith of the Hebrews is, in essentials, the same as ours.[91] There is an aspect of interpretation of Wisdom which

---

88. *De ben. incarn.*, 108.
89. *Ibid.*, 109.
90. John 12:35.
91. John 8:56; *De ben. incarn.*, 111.

simply transcends the consequences of the temporal altogether: God is "lord of time"; he alone has dominion over it.

But it is clear, Wyclif argues, that this very concept is essential to our interpretation for all of Scripture. Unless the time, past and future, could be understood as being present to God, we would regularly be up against insuperable barriers to interpretation, such as when, in Psalm 22:16, David said, speaking in this Wisdom: "they pierced my hands and feet." Such a statement, like many others in Scripture, is impossible to interpret rationally in its own historical context, yet makes perfect sense in connection with the Christ event, in *immensa Dei eternitas coassistit omni tempore preterito et futuro*.[92] In other words, the governing "form" of scriptural text shows itself, again and again, to be not sequentially historical—*extensive loquendo de motu Sapiencia increata movetur obiective a cognitis terminantibus eius actum*. The end of interpretation is not thus to be reduced to the end of historical action, but rather referred to the unfolding purpose of the *Sapientia increata*. When we look again at John 14:24 ("The word which you hear is not mine, but the words of Him who sent me") we now see that the gaining of a right interpretation is more than just a problem of number and case. While synecdoche speaks to the syntax of individual sentences, the formal principle extends, in a much more profound sense, to genre, and to the largest form, the syntax of the whole. Christ speaks his historical message under the regis of the Divine schema, the intrinsic form of which is the very design and compass of all historical truth. Its meaning, and its sense of closure, is to be known truly as Word, not simply words—for that which speaks is the integral structure or intrinsic form apprehended in the whole of God's utterance, *Sapientia et Verbum*, Scripture and Creation.[93]

So the form for Scripture is the form for Creation; God's creative word is spoken, and the void is shaped, drawn to form. But this creative Word, "set up from everlasting, from the beginning, before ever the earth was . . . daily His delight, at play always before him" (Prov. 8:22-30) is the same Word made flesh in the Incarnation. Thus, by "form", Wyclif intends a metaphysical sense. He cites Phil. 2:16: "being in the form of God . . . he emptied himself, taking the form of a servant," and says that clearly this doesn't mean the physical human shape *naturam visibilem . . . Christo ad litteram*, but rather that *Verbo* which he shares with the Father and in which he may truly say: *Ego et Pater unum sumus*.[94] The statement "My Father is greater than I" is not contradictory—it involves, simply, that equivocity concerning the historical humanity of Christ in the *tempus* and his eternal *duratio* as the Word, and it is in this latter sense that He *is* the Form of truth and meaning. It is this form which he translates when he speaks. The governing form of our interpretation will be the Word as form, then, the pattern of divine syntax, and not simply the causal or temporal

---

92. *Ibid.*, 112.
93. *Ibid.*, 113.
94. *Ibid.*, 114.

sequence of historical matter, which is the *vocabulary only* of the text we read.[95]

We may summarize Wyclif's thought with respect to the relationship of time to interpretation in this way: in any analysis which attempts to get at truth or larger issues of meaning, we soon discover that interpretation transcends an analysis of histories as *tempus*. The question we face looking backward for truth, is, in biblical terms, analogous in this respect to the problem we face in looking forward for it. Either way we ask: "in what sense can anything not of this very present be a relevant authority for us today?" The hidden question concerning authority, as Hannah Arendt has said of more recent times, is the question of meaning *in* history. How would we know? How would we validate? What Wyclif says is that this is also the question we bring to the text of Scripture. But there we find that to direct our quest for meaning only to matter (and not to form) is to misinform our question.

Scripture contains, then, besides its evident vocabulary, two syntaxes of disclosure. One is historical *tempus*, by which we understand the sequence of statement and event. The other is in *ymagionem*, a spiritual *duratio* by which we gather in the reflections of memory on the one hand, and the projections of intention and dream on the other, turning them together toward interpretation and meaning. It is in the realm of this second syntax that we apprehend the *form* of scripture—which also becomes the form of its present conversation in our experience in the here and now. "Where am I? Is this my country?"—these are questions, we now see, about truth and time as well as geography. And the answer Wyclif gives to them is that Scripture—in a unique way—meets every man in his own country; its form is more than history alone can limit.

D. INTRINSIC GENRE AND GOVERNING FORM

The question of form, in Wyclif's thought, is one which pertains to the shape of meaning, the intrinsic structure of a textual disclosure. Thus, he argues vigorously for a larger literary sense of scriptural text. The true meaning of Scripture is arrived at not by extracting pieces out of context for a disembodied (or disinherited) disputation, but by a consideration of the whole text.[96] We are to read it therefore for itself, *in sua integra, ex quibus sensus scripture colligitur*.[97] We should distinguish between the literal sense of given statements, or words, and the storic or 'parabolical' sense of the whole work, which is analogous here to the Word of our earlier consideration.[98] While he does not at all argue against the evidence that *partes scripture habeant privatum sensum alique historicum, alique propheticum, et alique sapiencialem vel misticum,* he refers all of these for

---

95. *Ibid.*, 115-18.
96. *De ver. s.s.*, I, 79.
97. *Ibid.*, I, 80.
98. *Ibid.*, II, 70-71; 113; I, 82-83.

larger understanding to their place in the larger order of discourse of the whole text, in which, in the eternal perspective, *tota scriptura sacra est unum dei verbum*. This larger order is the Word, the governing form, the syntax of the narrative:

> quod tota sentencia sua connexa est quasi pars verbi domini, quod deus dixit sibi in spiritu. Sic enim uno ore locuti sunt unum magnum verbum omnes scribe domini.[99]

The fundamental law of a sound interpretation is thus to consider the text as a whole, and to take single elements apart from their connection to the larger discourse is as much a perversion of the text as changing the meaning of its words by false glossing. This is a principle we must hold to in interpretation, he says, heeding the warning in John's gospel: *nolite indicare secundum faciem sed instum indicium indicate*—"judge not according to the superficial appearance, but judge with righteous judgement."[100] There is a sense in which each statement in the text which forms a complete thought is not at all unintelligible: as a true part it reflects not autonomy, but, where the intention is rightly disposed, it suggests a certain kind of whole. Wyclif argues that our sense of imperfection in creation actually attests to the reality of God's perfect expression. Having experienced one aspect, then others of the same type, we generate on this basis a system of expectations with respect to the whole. But there is another sense in which the understanding of any part of Scripture will always remain to some metaphorical extent *syncategorema*, predicated jointly, not only upon the immediate context in specific discourse, but also upon a grasp of the largest context of discourse, the form of the whole text.[101]

Here is a medieval argument for what Hirsch would call the "genre-bound character of understanding...a version of the hermeneutic circle...the interdependence of part and whole."[102] Its model is discerned in the telescoping categories for understanding Scripture as expounded in Wyclif's treatment of the Gospel of John: at the level of *verbum vocale* we understand the text as a weaving of denominative verbal meanings; at the level of *verbum actus mentis* we see it as a fluid property of the imagination. But neither of these forms the Word in itself—it is only the *verbo* of God which does this, the Word whose most elegant translation is the Incarnation and which is reflected in the form of the whole of Scripture—a form kept there in prospect by God's people as the governing aspect of their life, *inseparabiliter a memoria*—the central feature of their collective memory.[103]

The question is: how does this relationship govern interpretation, or indeed, the text? Here the answer seems to be, as in the earlier discussion

---

99. *Ibid.,* II, 112-13.
100. John 7:24. The Greek here, like the Latin, offers a difficult syntax. In the Greek, it is an example of the cognitive accusative, which repeats, in effect, the verb.
101. *De ver. s.s.,* II, 115-18. In Aquinas, "to predicate jointly."
102. Cf. E. D. Hirsch, *Validity in Interpretation* (Yale, 1967), 76-77.
103. John 1:1-5; in Benrath, 366ff.

of the exposition at the level of the "sentence", that holy men of God spoke the words according to the form of the Word, and that this form of the Word is everywhere the determining factor in the ordering of meaning: rightly understood, as an expression out of *duratio,* it affords us a syntax accessible to our own imagination, when the imagination is conformed to the Church's central memory of the Word made flesh in Jesus Christ. At its highest level, as we have seen, the form of Scripture remains the form of the Word expressed in the Gospel; it *is* Christ. [104]

The implications of this model for questions of canon and canonicity are fascinating in Wyclif's thought, but only one or two brief points concern our present study. Arguing against William Woodsford, his old friend, and against a "black hound," who was possibly (not a Dominican, but) the Benedictine John Wellys of Ramsey, [105] he points out that he is not arguing for a narrow self-sufficiency in Scripture. Rather, he is asserting that it has *implicit* as well as explicit content, and that the "whole truth of God's law," as revealed perfectly in the person of Christ, can of course only be revealed in Scripture imperfectly. Therefore, there is room for additions and explanations, as long as these have the "pure Wisdom of God's Law." [106]

Within the term "Holy Scripture," Wyclif does not include any books by purely human writers—i.e., non-canonized books. It is not that he rejects Ambrose ("all truth is the Lord's wherever we find it"); indeed, he takes up the same point about the "temporal truths" of Aristotle, for example, in many places. He is saying, rather, that this sort of writing, especially by non-Christians, is of a completely different class of authority. [107] Yet it is not a dismissable authority. God reveals his thoughts in pagan writers, and *in scriptis poetarum sunt multe veritates scripture sacre, ut patet Homero et Virgilis Marone.* Even Jerome had mentioned these great poets in his prologue to the Bible, and the same virtues he finds in them Wyclif also applies to Ovid, in whose writings are to be found *veritates evangelicas.* There are other supports: Paul in his writing to Titus (1:12) quotes Eumenides with approval. Apocryphal writings, such as the book of Nichodemus, or Enoch, similarly have value. However, none of these outside the 'information' of canon reflect in the same way the form of the Word. Even though they glimpse aspects of eternal truth, in their "form" they remain locked in the *tempus,* in their own time. Thus they have exemplary value, but no ultimate authority. [108]

Wyclif has, in fact, a high view of poetry. Despite his distaste for friars who use vulgar poetry out of context and in such a way as to distract from the Bible, he vigorously defended the major poets on a number of occasions. One of these prompted a debaters' tactic, apparently, in Ken-

---

104. *De ver. s.s.,* I, 4-18; *Opus Evangelicum,* II, 36; *Postilla* on John 1:1-5.
105. Hurley, 312, n. 13.
106. *Sermones,* III, 263-65.
107. *De ver. s.s.,* I, 107.
108. *Ibid.,* I, 236-38.

ningham, who argued against Wyclif concerning whether a document gains in authority by virtue of its greater antiquity. Wyclif replied in the affirmative. Kenningham rejected this, adducing, *vide,* "Orpheus and others, who wrote fables of the Gods: they lived long before Plato, Aristotle and Pythagoras," he notes, "but now it is the latter whose work is held in greater authority, while the ancient poets," he adds scornfully, are *quasi nullius sunt momenti.* [109] Wyclif clearly thought otherwise.

To my knowledge Wyclif does not discuss the "form" or intrinsic genre of the classical poets, nor does he deal in any of his printed volumes with the logic of their interpretation. He does deal with the form which should pertain to contemporary writing, in which, in his simplest version, as we have already seen, "the Christian should express himself under the authority of Scripture in the words of Scripture according to the form of Scripture." That is, we can see that writing for the contemporary Christian would draw its sense of intrinsic genre from Scripture, and not from Vergil or Ovid. But in literary terms, demystified, what would this form look like? What does Wyclif mean, in literary terms, when he says that the Form of Scripture is Christ, the Word, and also the Gospel? And how would the "form" of the Gospel apply to the analysis, let us say, of a text in the Old Testament as an initial example?

Wyclif's treatment of the prophetic books, especially Daniel, Ezekiel, Isaiah and Jeremiah, provides a partial answer to this method of analysis by intrinsic genre, and models, consequently, what may be called the "logic" of their interpretation. Of these, since the text of itself is so evidently non-narrative and resistant to analysis according to expectations based upon classical models, Isaiah is probably the most useful illustration of Wyclif's modelling. We read in the prologue of the Wycliffite Bible:

> Isaye is worthi to be seid not oneli a profete, but more, a gospellere, for he declaireth so opynli ether priutees of Crist and of Hooli chirche, that thou gesse hym not onelt to ordeyne a profess of thing to comynge, but to ordeyne a stori of thynges passid. [110]

That is, the *ordinance* here embraces the 'amplification of time' of the gospel, in which anything past or to come *is* before God, and, in Scripture, in the realm of interpretation described as the Word. We see, as Wyclif says elsewhere, that Isaiah is not in the normal sense a narrative. It is, in fact, an anthology, much as Scripture itself is an anthology, and is made up of many different sub-species: poems, oracles, prayers, historical accounts and direct divine utterances. In his translation, however, Wyclif eschews setting these out in their various poetic and other forms as they appear in the biblical text, because he is afraid it will lead to a false interpretation based upon classical genres.

> No man whan he prophetis he shal seen with ve'rsis to ben discryued: in metreeyme he hem anentis þe ebrues to be bounden & any thing lijc to han of psalmys or of þe werkis of salomon but þat in demostene & tollo it is wont to be

---

109. *Fas. Ziz.,* 4-5.
110. *Wycliffe Bible,* ed. J. Forshall and F. Madden, 4 vols. (Oxford, 1850), III, 225.

don þat bi dyuysiouns & vuder distincciouns þei ben writen: þe whiche forsoþe
in prose & not in vers writen, we forsoþe toþe profit or rederis purueynge: þe
newe remenyng with a newe maner of writing.

He continues in the prologue by observing that Isaiah is *wijs* (wise) and
clearly "a noble man and of curteys fair speche," and that there is therefore a disadvantage in his decision to set the text in prose, that the problem
of the translation generally is that it may not thus preserve "þe flour of his
sermon." But that is better, he implies, than by an attempt to preserve
external form to mislead people concerning intrinsic form, or, as we might
say now, to confuse the hermeneutical model which governs the text. What
he is arguing is surprisingly near to Hirsch, when the latter says: "One
principle . . . remains universally applicable: valid interpretation depends
upon a valid inference about the properties of the intrinsic genre."[111]

In order to get at the form, Wyclif notes, one must first establish the
author's intention.[112] Here, despite all the specific historical prophecy
concerning the captivity and restoration of Israel, Wyclif insists,
nevertheless: "all his bisyness is of the clepyng of hethene men, and
of the comyng of Crist." This suggests an introduction to three general
rules which he says can be commonly applied to "alle the derk places of
the profetis:"

> The firste is this, that the principal entent of the profetis is to declare the
> mysterie of Cristis incarnacioun, passioun, resurreccioun, ascensioun, and then
> comyng too the general doom, and the pupplischyng of the gospel, and the con-
> uercioun of hethene men, and the tribulacioun of hooli chirche in this lijf, and
> the blis of heuene therfor. The secounde reule is this, that the profetis warnen
> the puple of Jewis of her grete synnes, and exciten hem to do penaunce; and
> thanne thei schulen gete remyssioun of her synnes, and grace in presen tyme,
> and glorie with outen end; ellis thei schulen haue tribulacioun in this lijf and
> peyn with outen ende. The thridde reule is this, that the profetis rehersen ofter
> benefices ʒouun of God bifor to the Jewis, to coumforte hem to ʒyue credence to
> goodis bihiʒt in her profesies; and thanne the stories of Moises lawe, ether of
> Josue, Judicum, Regum, and Paralipomenon, and of othere historial bookis
> schule be wel lokid; and schortli to seie, the profetis schulen be expouned bi the
> text of Moises lawe, and of othere historial bookis of the Elde Testament, ether
> bi the text of the Newe Testament.[113]

These three 'rules' (statements of intention) can be set in *précis* as follows:
(a) to apprehend the form of salvation history, the *humana historia sal-
vationis,* as it is seen in the Gospel; (b) to apprehend the function of the
book as a warning against sin and a call to personal choice; (c) to see the
warning in terms of the memory of God's dealings with his people in history, and therefore to recognize the form itself as a comfort, a consolation
to the Jews. Now what is clear here is that Wyclif actually had a keen
historical sense of the book of Isaiah—he doesn't invite his readers to
spiritualize it out of all context with respect to its original intended
audience; in fact, he continually reminds us of the relevance of that particular first audience. But he still calls us to see the book just as much in

111. Hirsch, 121.
112. Prologue, 225.
113. *Ibid.*, 225-26.

the *duratio*, participating in the eternal form of the Word, the Gospel, in which the book becomes for him, as we see, a psychological recapitulation of the mystery of the Incarnation, (etc.) God's ultimate dialogue with man. In other words, if we read it properly (with "informed" intention), interpretation will account for both aspects, the *tempus* and the *duratio*, and will comprise an interpenetration of their two syntaxes of disclosure.

The doubled focus here permits us to understand why it is that the prologue goes on to announce that old shibboleth, the traditional fourfold schema of allegory, in this particular context. Really, we see once again, it is only a twofold schema: the historical (or, in the case of fictions, *literal*) understanding is obviously "the ground of all goostli understondyng therof"; the other understandings (they are *not* levels) "allegorite . . . moralite . . . and anagotite" reside in the *duratio*, and are properties of it. Notably, they parallel exactly the three "rules" for reading the prophets— each is a recognition, really, of the *form* of the whole Word of which the prophets are a partial expression: words.

> The literal vnderstondyng of hooli scripture is the ground of al gostli vnderstondyng therof, that is, of allegorik, of moral, and of anogogik. No goostli vnderstondyng is autentik, no but it be groundid in the text opynli, ether in opyn resoun, suynge of principlis, ether reulis of feith, seynt Austin witnessith opynli in his pistle to Vincente, Donatiste, and in his book of Soliloquies, and Jerome on Jonas, and Lire on the bigynnynge of Genesis, and in many placis of hooli scripture and Ardmakan in his book of Questiouns of Armenyes. Therfor men moten see the treuthe of the text, and be war of goostli vnderstondyng, ether moral fantasye and ȝyue not ful credence therto, no but it be groundid opynly in the text of hooly writ, in o place or other, ethir in opyn resoun, that may not be auoidid; for eles it wole as likyngli be applied to falsnesse as to treuthe; and it hath dissevued gret men in oure daies, bi ouer greet triste to her fantasies. *Literal ether histor vnderstondyng techith what thing is don*; allgorik techith what we for bileue; moral ether tropologik techith what we owen to do to fle vices, and kep virtues; anagogik techith what we owen to hope of euerlastynge meede in heuen.[114]

Allegory, tropology and anagogy are attributes of an exegesis of the durational rather than the temporal syntax of the text, each in turn respecting one aspect of the authorial intention as manifest in the text of the biblical anthology, or of the Word of the Gospel taken as a whole: the pattern of salvation history (allegorik), the analysis of ethical life (moral), and finally, the presentation of the form and purpose of the Book itself as the preparation of a consolation to which men may respond already by affirming the Divine intention which prepares it (anagogik). But if pure fantasy and exegetical extravagance is to be avoided in all of this, the spiritual understanding must be "grounded in the text openly." *Caveat lector.*

*   *   *

---

114. *Ibid.*, 226.

In little enough of all this is Wyclif fundamentally original. He is a synthetist, and most of his thoughts can be found anticipated in his favourite authors—Augustine, Chrysostom, Jerome, "Dionysius," Fitzralph, Bonaventure and Lyra. On the other hand, it was precisely as a conservative champion of tradition that he wished to advertise himself, so as to set himself apart, especially in the shape and intention of his synthesis, from his less summistically inclined colleagues. Wyclif was, in fact, an ingenious reactionary, not an enthusiastic liberal, and in interpretation theory as well as in ecclesiastical theory it was this direction in his thought which seems to have captured the attention of Chaucer's contemporaries.

Wyclif's principal motive in all of his writing is the larger question of authority—political authority, philosophical authority, cultural authority, religious and ecclesiastical authority. His starting point is often to charge that with respect to *models,* the Church has changed into a Roman Law Court, its history and literature into a pale simulacrum of Roman historiography, and that the issue of authority has thus been subverted by the adoption of models whose temporality and determinisms corrode the whole foundation of a Christian identity. He sees methodological compromise everywhere, as well as confusions of terminology, of grammar and logic, even in the very composition of questions. It is in this context, I think, that we can understand his arguments concerning the authority of ancient poets: Vergil and Homer, he argues, contain valid truths, but they do not offer valid models for the exegesis of Scripture. They are, in fact, deficient in themselves for pursuit of their own best questions. The truth of the poets is thus properly to be authenticated by the truth of Scripture. What we can do with the perplexities of the poets, especially as these diffuse, is to re-compose the questions in terms of a unified authority, recognizing that 'solution' lies not in a synthesis or 'logical' reconciliation of authorities, but in the appropriation of an entirely new context or point of asking. The Bible is, in our pursuit of authority, higher than any other book because it is not locked into temporality. This is because its author and finisher is Christ, who stands eternally outside as well as inside the text. Therefore, the authority of Christ will always be above that of his brethren: *ut autor ad autorem, sic autoritas ad autoritatem.* [115] The authority, in other words, is Personal—Christ's person is truth—and this fact underwrites any valid appropriation of Scripture. With respect to "reading," the true meaning of Scripture is not arrived at by exegesis of passages out of context, but rather with respect to a sense of canon, to the largest patterns of scriptural discourse. We are to read Scripture *in sua integra, ex quibus sensus scripture colligitur.* [116] Finally, the authority of the text does not at all depend on the way the text is interpreted: interpretation is not the same thing as the text, and should never be confused with it.

This point, of course, is that of both Dame Prudence in the *Tale of Melibee,* and also the Parson, in his 'conclusive' ingathering of the tales

---

115. *De ver. s.s.,* I, 354.
116. *Ibid.,* I, 80; II, 70-71; 113-14.

and their 'telling' significances. The patient method of Prudence, correcting specious and shallow reading by a careful comparison of scriptural authorities placed in their full scriptural context, and the careful contextual method of the Parson, who shows us from his opening text in Jeremiah 6 to his concluding allusion to John 14 that nothing is said openly in the prophets that is not said in the Gospels as well, are both resonant with an attitude to reading and to Scripture which Wyclif was popularizing among a wide range of Chaucer's contemporaries. When Harry Bailey thought he smelled a "Lollere in the wynd," the Parson meekly stepped down—and whether he was displaced by the Shipman's tale of monastic corruption and cupidity or the Wife of Bath's exemplary decontextualizings and perversions of Scripture, the effect of this displacement must have been to heighten the reader's sense of contrast between those very things which Wyclif and Chaucer in these tales both criticize, and the exemplification of their contrary virtues in *Melibee* and the *Parson's Tale*. Perhaps Harry Bailey's nose (or his instinct for self-protection) did not that much mislead him. Chaucer's Parson need not at all have been a "Lollere," especially in that fifteenth-century context in which we have come to define the term. [117] Wyclif himself was certainly not such a "Lollere." But the principal preoccupations of Chaucer the poet, reading, interpreting Scripture, and characterizing narrowly personal judgement, make of his use and exaltation of scriptural tradition a worthy complement to Wyclif's own writings. For that reason Wyclif, as the leading English scholar of scriptural tradition during the formative years of Chaucer's writing, should be regarded seriously as a source for insight into Chaucer's literary use of the Bible and literary theory adapted to it.

APPENDIX

Obviously there is not space here to commence an adequate application of these ideas to Chaucer's poetry. What I propose to do is merely to suggest areas for possible investigation, into a few of which I have already begun making tentative incursions of my own. For the sake of greater brevity, I shall intemize these as a series of abstracts.

(1) *Wyclif's theory of dominion*: The influence of Wyclif's theory of dominion will be found, I believe, in the short poems and moral ballads, especially "Gentilesse," "Truth," and "The Former Age," and in certain aspects of the concept of "meisterye," especially as it is explored in the *Tale of Melibee*. There is some similarity of idea and tone between the tale and Clanvowe's treatise, [118] but much more explicitly, Melibee relates to

---

117. See Anne Hudson, *English Wycliffite Writings* (Cambridge, 1978) for edited material relating to later Lollard tradition, much of it which was considerably removed from Wyclif and with which Chaucer would not in fact have associated the Wyclif he and his contemporaries knew.

118. Ed. V.J. Scattergood, "*The Two Ways*, An Unpublished Religious Treatise by Sir John Clanvowe," *English Philological Studies*, X (1967), 33-56.

Wyclif's sermons (which form a significant backdrop for the theme of dominion elsewhere in Chaucer as well). A doctoral dissertation has recently been done at Harvard by R. Kendall, concentrating especially on the moral ballads and Wyclif's theory of dominion.

(2) *Wyclif's criticism of the mendicant orders*: The English Wyclif proves to be a closer and, given Chaucer's proximity to his outpourings, a more plausible source than William of St. Amour, for example, for some aspects of the poet's equally enthusiastic anticlerical satire. His thoughts on this subject are also closely compatible with those attributed to that author and to Jean de Meun, of course. (Some of the 'Lollard Knights' had copies of the *Roman de la Rose* in their libraries.)

(3) *Wyclif's peace-seeking*: It is only natural, I think, that Wyclif's so-called 'pacifism' should ally itself to the interests of followers of the Order of the Passion of Our Lord founded by Philippe de Mézières. Members of the Order in England who were also Lollard Knights include Sir Richard Sturry and, most probably, Sir John Clanvowe, both friends of Chaucer. Wyclif preached against the crusade in Flanders of the Bishop of Norwich, comparing it to other more "legitimate" battles for the faith.

(4) *Wyclif's commitment to vernacular language and translation*: Russell Peck's several well-known articles on Chaucer's approach to translation encourage further address to Wyclif's ideas on "diverse translation" and the importance of the vernacular, which for Wyclif has its necessity rooted in a modified 'realist' theory of language.

(5) *Wyclif's restructuring of grammar and logic*: W. S. Wilson's articles relating Wyclif's scholastic logic and exegetical grammar to Chaucer's impatient rejection of the ordinary 'trivial' arts opens up significant questions for the *House of Fame*.[119] Wyclif's work challenges traditional approaches to these subjects in a way parallel to Chaucer's poem, and the challenge has substantial implications for the interpretation theory of both men.

(6) *Wyclif's theory of interpretation*: Alistair Minnis has already directed our attention to some of Wyclif's contributions, especially on the subject of *authorial intention*. It seems to me that Wyclif's central preoccupation with method can be shown to incur reflections of the sort broached by Chaucer both in the *House of Fame* and in the *Canterbury Tales*. In the former poem interpretation is shown to be specious when it has not an adequate sense of authorial intention; qualitative judgement is suggested as the only possible correction for quantitative misjudgement. The debate between *auctors* exposed in Book I of the *House of Fame* is shown to be a struggle of "partial" words within an unfixed continuum in which the only interpretation which could be valid must be appealed to outside of words, in a larger sense of canon, to a *totum integrum*, a word

---

119. William S. Wilson, "Scholastic Logic in Chaucer's *House of Fame*," *CR* (1967, 181-84; "Exegetical Grammar in the *House of Fame*," *ELN* (1964), 224-48; and "The Eagle's Speech in Chaucer's *House of Fame*," *Quarterly Journal of Speech*, 50 (1964), 153-58.

from the beginning which is also the Last Word (see the last essay of this volume).

(7) *Reader intention*: On the primacy of the reader's will in achieving interpretation of a text there is no writer so forceful as Wyclif in the fourteenth century *except* Chaucer, whose whole approach to reader-centred hermeneutical difficulties in *The Canterbury Tales* offers a brilliantly imaginative outworking of Wyclif's synthetic literary theory, a sustention of ideas first essayed in the *House of Fame*.

(8) *Form and matter*: I think it might be argued that Wyclif's thought in this area is paralleled by Chaucer's, if not directly followed. I refer here to the elaboration of a structural model for reading *The Canterbury Tales* as an essentially finished work composed of three general groups or movements of tales, in which the 'matter' (the tales taken both individually and together) may be read best according to the 'form' of the scriptural *coda* to be found in the Knight's Tale, Melibee, and the Canon's Yeoman's tales (for each section), and in the *Parson's Tale* for the whole poem. This coda, like Wyclif's notion of the "gospel" in Isaiah, or Chaucer's "new tydings" in relationship to the *House of Fame,* is essentially a translation of the *evangelium* rather than a valorization of Chaucer's own immediate literary structure.

(9) *Wyclif on Truth and Time*: In his approach to texts Wyclif is concerned with the general epistemological question: "in what sense can anything of the past be a relevant authority for us today?" His attempt to set out prospects in an answer to this question, in work from *De benedicta incarnatione* to *De veritate sacrae scripturae,* bears close relationship to Chaucer's pursuit of this question in his *House of Fame.* I have been exploring this relationship in my own present study, and have essayed a preliminary discussion in the final essay of this volume. Wyclif's sermons on Fame may be, I think, an explicit influence on Chaucer's poem.

IV

The Canterbury Tales

Biblical Interpretation:
St. Paul and *The Canterbury Tales**

RUSSELL A. PECK
University of Rochester

Chaucer's two good priests—the Parson and the Nun's Priest—both cite St. Paul as authority for the kinds of tale they tell. For the Nun's Priest the Apostle provides justification for his use of fable:

> Taketh the moralite, goode men.
> For seint Paul seith that al that writen is,
> To oure doctrine it is ywrite, ywis;
> Taketh the fruyt, and lat the chaf be stille. [1]

                                    VII(B₂ *4630-33

Chaucer's Parson, on the other hand, invokes Paul as authority for rejecting fables:

> Thou getest fable noon ytoold for me;
> For Paul, that writeth unto Thymothee,
> Repreveth hem that weyven soothfastnesse,
> And tellen fables and swich wrecchednesse.
> Why sholde I sowen draf out of my fest,
> Whan I may sowen whete, if that me lest?

                                    X(I) 31-36

Chaucer's juxtaposition of opposing Pauline texts calls attention to conflicting attitudes toward *fabula* (fiction) and meaning hidden in the integuments of metaphor which have characterized discussions of literature from late classical times on. [2] Obviously, Chaucer's attitude as poet is more

---
* A portion of this essay was presented to the Conference on Christianity and Literature at the annual meeting of the Modern Language Association in New York, December 29, 1978. A more complete version was read at Duke University on March 28, 1979. I owe a large debt of thanks to my colleague Thomas Hahn for suggestions on the essay during various stages of its composition.
   1. All references to Chaucer's works are taken from *The Works of Geoffrey Chaucer*, ed. F.N. Robinson (Cambridge, Mass.: Riverside Press, 1957) and will hereafter be cited by fragment and line number in the context of my argument. The Nun's Priest refers in this passage to Romans 15:4.
   2. See Peter Dronke's excellent chapter, "Fabula: Critical Theories," in *Fabula: Explorations into the Uses of Myth in Medieval Platonism* (Leiden: E.J. Brill, 1974), pp. 13-78. Dronke gives special attention to terms relating to symbolism such as *aenigma, fabula, figura, imago, integumentum, involucrum, mysterium, similitudo, symbolum*, and *translatio*, demonstrating that by the twelfth-century such terms are used in fresh ways and with a precision and penetration that is flexible and more subtle than predictable uses one might find in euhemeristic analysis or conventional moral allegory.

in keeping with that of the Nun's Priest and the younger Paul, who see value in enigma as a mode of discourse,[3] instead of the Parson and elderly Paul, who in his last letter to Timothy speaks of putting fable aside.[4] But both attitudes are important in the framing of a perspective commensurate with the idea of pilgrimage which Chaucer builds into the scheme of the *Tales*. Fable (*fabula*) is an indirect manner of speech. For the Nun's Priest, as we shall see, indirection is an essential rhetorical means for continuing along the way amidst such exigent creatures as the domineering Prioress, cheerless Monk, and "witty" Harry Bailly. For the Parson, at the end of the journey, a different mode of expression is appropriate, for the occasion has changed.

That Paul should be Chaucer's pivotal authority in matters of critical perspective in *The Canterbury Tales* is apt, for Pauline material underlies much of the pilgrimage matter in the superstructure of Chaucer's poem. There are more than eighty explicit references to Paul and his Epistles in *The Canterbury Tales* and numerous extensions of Pauline imagery and spiritual concerns. These materials signal hidden dimensions within the narrative in several ways: (1) In the *Nun's Priest's Tale*, indeed throughout the B2 Fragment, Chaucer uses Pauline observations on interpreting language to focus attention on the necessity of using one's critical judgment as part of the pilgrimage process. That judgment entails the winnowing of chaff from fruit. (2) In the Parson's Prologue he then uses Paul to shift the direction of his narrative and to redefine pilgrimage as a spiritual rather than a social journey. (3) This attention to making a conclusion has been anticipated throughout the tales through Chaucer's extensive use of Pauline ideas to develop such themes as the proper use of time and the making of a good ending, themes which lie at the heart of Chaucer's notion of pilgrimage. (4) In several of the tales Chaucer explores ideas adjacent to good use of time through the dilemmas of old men (cf. Paul's *vetus homo*) in their frustrated attempts to secure their heritages. (5) Related to Pauline questions of the *vetus homo* are complex attitudes toward the human body as a vehicle in life's journey. As we shall see, Chaucer develops his liveliest characters in terms of these ideas, creating dramatic implications which bear upon the overall pilgrimage plot as well as the more restricted plots of their individual tales.

---

3. The Scriptural text rhetoricians regularly cite in discussions of *aenigma* is 1 Cor. 13: 12: *Videmus nunc per speculum in aenigmate: tunc autem facie ad faciem*. See Dronke, pp. 34-39.

4. All the Pauline references to avoiding *fabula* occur in his last writings, the Pastoral Epistles (1 and 2 Timothy and Titus) which, according to modern historical criticism, appear to have been composed after Paul's death from notes and fragments. See Ernest Findlay Scott, *The Literature of the New Testament* (New York: Columbia University Press, 1936), pp. 191-97. What is evident to the reader uninstructed in modern historical method, however, is that this group comes from the end of Paul's life, for he speaks of his imprisonment in Rome (2 Tim. 1: 16-17), his trial (2 Tim. 4: 16-18) and approaching execution: "The time of my deliverance is at hand" (2 Tim. 4: 6). The Wife of Bath alludes to the context of this latter passage in her Prologue (III D 75-76).

I

The Nun's Priest's assertion from Paul (Rom. 15:4) that "al that writen is, / To oure doctrine it is ywrite, ywis" comes as culmination to one of the most carefully structured narrative sequences in *The Canterbury Tales*. The B2 Fragment is organized around problems of critical perception and is framed by lines on the winnowing of chaff from fruit (B1 1183 and B2 *4633). We should note at the outset that St. Paul does not, in fact, use the "fruit and chaff" metaphor as part of his critical vocabulary. Chaucer, however, following tradition, regularly uses the terms as if they were Paul's (n.b., B2 4630-33 and I 31-36). St. Augustine and others conflated Paul's idea of the superiority of the spirit to the letter of the law with the fruit-chaff metaphor, using 2 Corinthians 3:6 as their scriptural basis.[5] Gregory the Great, for example, in the Prologue to his Commentary on the Song of Songs, writes: "*The letter kills, as it is written, but the spirit gives life* (2 Cor. 3:6): Thus the letter covers the spirit as the chaff covers the grain; to eat the chaff is to be a beast of burden; but to eat the grain is to be a man."[6] Peter Dronke notes that Paul's "through a glass darkly" passage was also a favorite justification of the use of such figurative wrapping as *aenigma, involucrum, similitudo,* and *imago.*[7] Paul was frequently represented in medieval art as the spiritual miller, who grinds the grain of the Old Law and the Prophets at his mystical mill of allegory to produce the flour of the New Law.[8] The Abbot Suger describes in *De Administratione* how St. Paul is depicted in the so-called "Anagogical Window" of St. Denis turning a mill to which the Prophets carry sacks of grain. The inscription reads: "By working the mill, thou, Paul, takest the flour out of the bran. / Thou makest known the inmost meaning of the law of Moses / From so many grains is made the true bread without bran, / Our and the angels' perpetual food."[9] In the same window Paul is represented as the remover of a veil which covers Moses' face. The window is aptly labeled "anagogical," for it conjoins the two Pauline ideas—the surpassing of the letter and the removal of the veil of the enigmatic—which become the scriptural basis for an important part of medieval rhetorical tradition.

---

5. On the influence of Paul as an exegete see Henri de Lubac, *Exégèse médiévale*, Première Partie (Paris, 1959), pp. 318-28, 373-83, 668-81; and D. W. Robertson, Jr., *A Preface to Chaucer* (Princeton: Princeton University Press, 1962), pp. 52-75 and 292-305, where Robertson traces features of St. Augustine's theory of enigma and aesthetics to Paul's distinction between interior and exterior man.

6. *Super Cantica Canticorum Expositio: Proemium*, P. L. 473-74: "*Littera occidit,* sicut scriptum est, *spiritus autem vivificat* (II Cor. III, 6); sic enim littera cooperit spiritum, sicut palea tegit frumentum; sed jumentorum est, paleis vesci; hominum, frumentis." Cf. Robertson, *Preface to Chaucer*, pp. 57-58.

7. *Fabula*, p. 34.

8. See Alois Thomas, "Die Mystische Mühle," *Die Christliche Kunst*, 31 (1934-36), 129-39; and Robertson, *Preface to Chaucer*, pp. 290-92. The trope is doubtless an extension of the fruit-chaff metaphor.

9. Abbot Suger, *On the Abbey Church of St.-Denis and its Art Treasures*, ed. and trans. Erwin Panofsky (Princeton: Princeton University Press, 1946), pp. 74-75: "Tollis agendo molam de furfure, Paule, farinam. / Mosaicae legis intima nota facis. / Fit de tot granis verus sine furfure panis, / Perpetuusque cibus noster et angelicus."

Chaucer's first use of the fruit and chaff metaphor in *The Canterbury Tales* occurs in the introduction to the *Shipman's Tale*,[10] where it stands as the frontside of a frame for the B2 Fragment which concludes with the Nun's Priest's maxim. Harry Bailly has called on the Parson to speak. The Parson tries to reform Harry's language, at which point the Shipman intrudes, asserting:

> ". . . . heer schal he nat preche;
> He schal no gospel glosen here ne teche . . . .
> He wolde sowen som difficulte,
> Or springen cokkel in our clene corn."

II(B1) 1179-84

The incipient squabble focuses attention on what constitutes appropriate language and, in the Shipman's reversal of values behind the Pauline idea (for him "cokkel" equates with moral reform and "clene corne" with deceit), amusingly shows just how slippery language can be. The usefulness of such double talk becomes evident in the Shipman's tale, where language is used perversely to hide the truth (or to reveal a hidden meaning for the amusement of those in on the secret). The dispute over proper speech also calls attention to the problem of understanding the enigmatic (of getting the right gloss), which had been a main theme in the *Man of Law's Tale*, immediately preceding the link, with its heavy emphasis on the difficulty "lewed men" have in understanding events which Fortune imposes on them. (In fact, the problem of correct interpretation is prominent from the beginning of the *Tales*, where, in the *Knight's Tale*, the lovers try to interpret the signs of the gods and Theseus tries to understand Saturn's dark actions; the idea is then picked up in the *Miller's Tale*, where Nicholas pretends to read signs in the heavens and Absolon to gloss the itching of his mouth, and in the *Reeve's Tale*, where Mrs. Symkyn and Aleyne misread in the darkness what they thought was a certain sign, namely the cradle with its "propre page." It even occurs in the General Prologue, where Geoffrey fusses about making his words "be cosyn to the dede," despite his "short" wit.) For Custance, understanding is more a matter of faith than intellect, a point Paul reiterates throughout his writings.[11] She fares well because she brings faith to whatever she finds. But faith covers a wide range of postures, and interpretation is contingent upon a great many things. Glossing may reveal hidden truth, but if misapplied it may also increase confusion.

The Shipman begins with what would appear to be the very kernel of Custance's story—"We leven alle in the grete God" (B1 1182). But as he intends it, faith and constancy are twisted into an excuse for silencing the Parson. Had the Parson succeeded in holding forth, he would perhaps,

---

10. I am assuming, as most modern editors do, that the Man of Law endlink is supposed to introduce what is now the *Shipman's Tale*. But see John H. Fisher's edition to the contrary.

11. See especially Rom. 4: 1-5: 1 (justification by faith), Eph. 2: 8 (by grace saved through faith), and Gal. 5: 6 (faith working through charity). Over two-thirds of the references to faith in the Bible (Old and New Testaments) occur in Paul's letters.

even so early, have asserted his austere linguistic reform which would put an end to the tale-telling. [12] But the Shipman's twist to the Pauline maxims on faith and "clene corne" keeps the company in the realm of *fabula* and saves *The Canterbury Tales* for coarser appetites, simply by changing the meaning of some words. This is not the kind of change Paul advocated (he would have changes of heart), though, as we have seen, the Shipman uses the Parson's own Pauline preference for wheat over draff to justify his stance.

Like the *Nun's Priest's Tale* at the end of the fragment, the *Shipman's Tale* is a *tour de force* of double talk and pious winking. [13] The progression of tales between the Shipman and the Nun's Priest explores the difficulty of discerning rightly when true and false are intermingled. The group is centered around Geoffrey's defensive assertion between his Sir Thopas attempt and the *Tale of Melibee* that tales of many forms may contain the same idea (a variant on Paul's statement in Romans 15: 4 which Chaucer gives to the Nun's Priest at the end of the fragment). [14] The Prioress follows the Shipman. Her vision is marred by sentimentality—a sort of faith without good works, where pity (a virtue apt to her office) gets transmuted to tears over trapped mice. This is not to say that she has done anything wrong; rather the problem lies in what she has left *undone*. Her prologue offers an admirable definition of the value of pious instincts, but in her effort to be childlike and innocent she ignores the counterbalancing admonition to put away childish things. Her piety is more decoration than perception. The vision in her tale, like the Shipman's, depends upon an aura of sanctity which winks at right reason and careful examination. (E.g., though she insists that monks are "hooly" men, she seems to have trouble reconciling her premise with the facts which surround her, both in the flesh and the previous tale—cf. 643, 670.)

The structural opposite to the Prioress in the fragment is the Monk, not exactly a "hooly" man. He has his vision blocked by an absence of faith which leaves him sweating and self-swallowed outside his cloister, brooding on the evil effects of Fortune. The Knight attempts to break him out of his funk by changing the words of his definition of tragedy to make a mockery of the position. [15] But there is no changing him through word-

---

12. See Christian Zacher's interesting study of real-life pilgrimages and the conflict between curiosity and true meditation to which the Parson seems so sensitive: *Curiosity and Pilgrimage: The Literature of Discovery in Fourteenth-Century England* (Baltimore: Johns Hopkins University Press, 1976). Zacher observes, "The Canterbury pilgrims begin their journey with a spiritually impertinent kind of sworn pact, and thereafter they break more pacts than they make or keep" (p. 100).

13. For a brilliant discussion of biblical double-talk (from Proverbs) in the *Shipman's Tale*, see Theresa Coletti's essay, "Biblical Wisdom: Chaucer's *Shipman's Tale* and the *mulier fortis*," in this volume.

14. See Glending Olson's discussion of the rhetorical tradition behind this passage in "A Reading of the Thopas-Melibee Link," *Chaucer Review*, 10 (1975-76), 147-53.

15. By substituting opposites into the Monk's *de casibus* definition of tragedy (B₂ *3165-67) the Knight does not offer a medieval definition of comedy, as some have thought, but rather defines mock-tragedy: the man who "stood in greet prosperitee / And is

play. He remains cheerless—"I have no lust to pleye. / Now lat another telle, as I have toold" (B₂ *3996-97).

At the center of the fragment, between the Prioress and Monk, Chaucer places Geoffrey's double effort. Though faith is not a primary issue in either of Geoffrey's attempts, right reason and proper use of rhetoric are. Sir Thopas' pretense to chivalry reveals ludicrously misapplied values—both moral and rhetorical—the incongruity of a bourgeois masquerading as a knight. Undergirded by Geoffrey's too-pompous rhetoric for so insubstantial a hero, the travesty brilliantly fractures all such misapplication, whether it be money-grabbing in the guise of benevolence and cousinage in the *Shipman's Tale* or the Prioress' courtly manners which she confuses with piety—"cokkel for clene corn," to be sure. The *Tale of Melibee*, on the other hand, works through the painstaking process of removing cokkel by the exercise of Prudence (right reason).[16] By carefully removing the husk of Melibee's misprisions Prudence averts disaster so that Sophia, Melibee's daughter and heir, might be restored.[17] That is good fruit indeed. In the process all of the key concepts get redefined—counsel, friends, vengeance, and even enemies—until Melibee is able to see what happened in a new way. The crux seems to lie in the process of change itself, in reinterpretation. As Prudence explains: "And take this for a general reule, that every conseil that is affermed so strongly that it may nat be chaunged for no condicioun that may bityde, I seye that thilke conseil is wikked" (B₂ *2421). The paradox here is that through change Melibee is restored (made sane again). In the introduction to the *Tale of Melibee* Chaucer plays with this paradox, reiterating three times over the Pauline idea of doctrinal uniformity in diverse writings (B₂ *2136-38, 2141-44, 2150-54).[18] To get at the sentence behind (or within) the diverse but unchanging letter of the text, the reader must be able to play with meanings and judge their potential value as contexts change. Success will depend upon the flexibility and discretion of the interpreter. Such an admonition as

---

yfallen out of heigh degree / Into myserie, and endeth wrecchedly" becomes "a man . . . in povre estaat / And clymbeth up and wexeth fortunat, / And there abideth in prosperitee" (B₂ *3965-67). The Knight's effort offers a stunning example of an attempt to alter an effect by changing the words. The physicians in the *Tale of Melibee*, who would cure by administering opposites, would surely approve of the Knight's method, as would Dame Prudence.

16. "Right reason" is the scholastic gloss on "Prudence"; see my "Chaucer and the Nominalist Questions," *Speculum*, 53 (1978), 756.

17. Remigius of Auxerre's commentary on Martianus Capella's *De Nuptiis Philologiae et Mercurii* provides a gloss on Sophie which might be applied to the *Tale of Melibee* and its sources: "By Sophie is meant human wisdom, not any wisdom but that which contemplates *Nous* and perceives God," *Excursus*, Text II, as cited by Dronke, *Fabula*, p. 108.

18. See Robertson, *Preface to Chaucer*, pp. 367-69, for discussion of this notion of a single sentence applicable to the whole of the Tales. (Olson, note 14 above, takes issue with Robertson's interpretation.) When Geoffrey says that a tale may be "told somtyme in sondry wise of sondry folk" (*2131-32) his phrasing reminds one of the nine and twenty "sondry folk . . . and pilgrimes were they alle" with their tales told "in sondry wise" (A 24-26), perhaps to suggest some uniformity of motif even throughout *The Canterbury Tales*.

Blameth me nat; for, as in my sentence,
Shul ye nowher fynden difference
Fro the sentence of this tretys lyte
After the which this murye tale I write,

B_2 *2151-54

is essentially the same as that of the Nun's Priest at the end of the fragment; both require that all in the audience become rhetoricians, glossers of the word and not hearers only, engaged in a sort of speaking in tongues through word-play. [19]

Chaucer's strong emphasis on interpretation and the discovery of truth hidden within the letter in this section of *The Canterbury Tales* implies a subsidiary pilgrimage both for the pilgrims, who are audience to the tales, and for the reader. [20] Though the links between tales mark stages along the way to Canterbury—"Loo, Rochestre stant heer faste by"—keeping the reader mindful of the spatial passage in that journey, Geoffrey and the Nun's Priest use Paul to remind us that we are involved with two kinds of journeys—one on horseback and another in the mind. The two journeys merge in the *Parson's Tale*, when fable is put aside, roles change, the enigmatic shadow for measuring time becomes Geoffrey's own, and the mind is confronted with the interpretation of its own life. [21]

19.　Paul devotes 1 Corinthians 14 to the problem of speaking in tongues, by which he apparently means any form of indirect speech, whether fable, enigma, or allegory, as well as babbling sounds understood only by God and the utterer. He stipulates that such obscurities should be sufficiently glossed that their meanings can be shared. See Aquinas' seven lectures on the chapter in *Super Epistolas S. Pauli*, especially Lectio I. 812 on prophetic kinds of speech which use indirect methods of discourse for hidden purposes, and Lectio IV. 258 on the Old Testament as a sort of speech in tongues with the New Testament as the clarification.

20.　It is noteworthy that several of the MSS of *The Canterbury Tales* contain marginal glosses citing biblical allusions, evidently to help guide the reader on this subsidiary pilgrimage. Daniel S. Silvia, "Glosses to *The Canterbury Tales* from St. Jerome's *Epistola Adversus Jovinianum*," *SP*, 62 (1965), 38, makes a strong case for Chaucer's authorship of some of these glosses, especially those taken from St. Jerome. Graham D. Caie, "The Significance of the Early Chaucer Manuscript Glosses (with Special Reference to the *Wife of Bath's Prologue*)," *Chaucer Review*, 10 (1975-76), 350-60, takes a more general approach to conclude: "For purposes of interpretation it is not vital to prove conclusively the authorship of the glosses . . . . We do know, however, that a well-educated person or persons who may have seen Chaucer's fair copy soon after the composition of *The Tales* thought it necessary to guide the reader's interpretation of the poem by adding the glosses which appear prominently in the early fifteenth-century Ellesmere manuscript . . . . The glosses were recognized to be of such importance by the early scribes that they copied the glosses with great care, and they were recognized by later scribes to be sufficiently important that they perpetuated them through the century. Whether they were written by Chaucer . . . or by some learned contemporary who had less confidence than Chaucer in the moral acumen of his fellows, the glosses appear to form a contemporary commentary and should provide a reliable authority and aid to historical approach to *The Canterbury Tales*" (pp. 357-58). I am indebted to Chauncey Wood for directing my attention to Mr. Caie's useful essay. See also Caie's chapter in the present volume.

21.　On Geoffrey's contemplation of his shadow see "Number Symbolism in the Prologue to Chaucer's *Parson's Tale*," *English Studies*, 48 (1967), 211-215; on change in narrative tone see "The Ideas of 'Entente' and Translation in Chaucer's *Second Nun's Tale*," *Annuale Mediaevale*, 8 (1967), 34-37.

II

Throughout his Epistles Paul stresses the importance of change—of the old being made new, of the trivial giving way to the meritorious, of truth coming out of obscurity.[22] Such redemptive changes entail recognition through faith of the Christian pilgrim's true goal, that is, the holy city with its cenacle feast. In *The Canterbury Tales*, as the pilgrims approach the entrance to the holy city and the Parson is called on to speak, the poet Chaucer introduces a structural change in the dramatic relationship of the pilgrims which is even more startling than his introduction of the Canon's Yeoman, two tales earlier. When the Parson is called this second time to speak, there is, we are told, but one tale left to tell. The Parson then introduces his shift in rhetorical principles with Paul's exhortation against "fables and swich wrecchednesse." But the shift in rhetorical mode is not the most important change effected here. Not only is the Parson called upon to "knytte up well a greet mateere" (I. 28); now, collectively, the pilgrims themselves of their own volition ask him to speak of virtue (I. 38), and all voluntarily agree to listen to him:

> Upon this word we han assented soone,
> For, as it seemed, it was for to doone,
> To enden in som vertuous sentence,
> And for to yeve hym space and audience;
> And bade oure Hoost he sholde to hym seye
> That alle we to telle his tale hym preye.

X(I) 61-66

This new agreement seems to anticipate the new covenant spoken of in the last chapters of Hebrews,[23] a new covenant purchased by Christ's sacrifice

---

22. E.g., Rom. 6: 5-6, on changes through the resurrection; Rom. 12: 2, on being transformed in newness of mind; 1 Cor. 2: 6-16, on true knowledge beyond what eye, ear, or heart yet knows; 1 Cor. 15: 51-57, on the corruptible putting on incorruption; 2 Cor. 3: 2-18, on new covenant revealed beyond the letter of the old; Ephes. 4: 21-24, on putting off the old to put on the new (cf. Col. 3: 9-10); Col. 1: 13, on being translated from darkness into the kingdom of Christ; Phil. 3: 17-21, on awaiting the end when all will be refashioned in Christ.

23. Though Hebrews was probably not written by Paul it has traditionally been part of the Pauline canon. Despite reservations of authorship expressed at the Council of Nicea, Jerome included it with the other Pauline epistles, suggesting that Paul wrote it in Hebrew to his fellow Jews and that what we have is Luke's translation of it into Greek after Paul's death. Medieval manuscripts of Hebrews usually included some form of Jerome's Prologue explaining this history and noting that Paul did not follow his usual opening formula because of his humility (which commentators often stress). E.g., "This is the cause, that he writynge to hem that of circumcisiouns bileueden, wroot as the apostle of hethene men, and not of Jewis; and he knowynge her pride, and schewinge his owene humblenesse, nolde not putte bifore the dissert of his office" (*Wycliffite Versions of the Holy Bible*, ed. Josiah Forshall and Frederic Madden [London: Oxford University Press, 1850], IV, 480 [the later version; the early version contains a similar statement]). St. Thomas Aquinas includes Hebrews in his commentaries *Super Epistolas S. Pauli*, noting the authorship controversy in his prologue, but siding with Jerome. So, in *Paradiso* 24. 62 ff., Dante attributes the words of Hebrews to Paul. For all practical purposes, then, Chaucer and his contemporaries viewed Hebrews as a Pauline work, and thus I will include it in my discussion. The notion of a new covenant which displaces the old is prominent throughout Paul's letters (see especially Gal. 3), though it is especially pronounced in Hebrews.

which displaces the old. The old, which took Israel out of Egypt, is but a "figure" or "schadewe" of the new (Heb. 8: 5) which, maintained by "a verray herte in þe fulnesse of þe feith" (10:22), encourages men to seek that "dwellande cyte... þat is to come" (13:4).[24] The Middle English wording in this translation in the Parker manuscript (14th century) seems particularly apt for this context in Chaucer, as the poet-narrator, just outside Canterbury, contemplates his shadow while the Parson begins his sermon on penance (cf. X[I] 5-9). Likewise, the shift in rhetorical style from *integumentum* to *fructum* reflects Paul's notion of the unveiling of the old law to reveal a new. For Chaucer's pilgrims, their old agreement upon leaving the tavern had promised a free supper as reward for the best-told tale. Their new agreement, through the Parson's guidance, will offer a eucharistic supper available to all who confess truly and are changed in their hearts (cf. Heb. 8: 10 and 10: 16; also 1 Cor: 5: 7-8).

Chaucer deliberately sets the Parson's notion of pilgrimage in opposition to Harry's, not only here in the Parson's prologue, but earlier, as we have seen, in the link between the B fragments. Though Harry's scheme has brought the group to the very gates of Canterbury and has provided a good deal of amusement, it has not brought much peace of mind.[25] Always the host is worried about time getting away from the company, leaving them bereft as Malkyn of her maidenhead (B₁ 30). Nor have the tales with which he would pass the time brought him much consolation. In fact, he himself becomes increasingly distraught by the tales as they proceed, first being forced to arbitrate disputes, then upset by the scandalous behavior of churchmen within the stories and even provoked by none other than the elvish Geoffrey himself to think on his shrewish wife (B₂ *3081 ff.), and then so overwrought by the Physician's depraved story of the slaughter of Virginia that he fears a heart attack and has to seek treacle—some cake or

---

24. Here I have followed a fourteenth-century translation found in the Parker 32 MS of *Pauline Epistles*, ed. Margaret Joyce Powell, EETS, e.s. 116 (London: Oxford University Press, 1916), because of its expansion of metaphors in the Vulgate almost to the point of glossing. Usually I will follow the Douai translation in my text, while occasionally preferring a "Wycliffite" version. The Latin text, in this instance, reads: "cum vero corde in plenitudine fidei" (Heb. 10: 22) and "hic manentem civitatem sed futuram inquirimus" (Heb. 13: 14). My text for the Vulgate is that edited by Fischer, Gribomont, Sparks, and Theile, revised by Robert Weber (Stuttgart: Wurttembergische Bibelanstalt, 1969), 2 vols.

25. Harry's pilgrim compact, with its qualified success, is similar in some ways to that of the old covenant, which in Pauline thought is "a figure of present time" (quae parabola est temporis instantis—Heb. 9: 9), which does not perfect conscience but only supplies food and drink and various ablutions and bodily regulations "imposed until a time of reformation" (ad tempus correctionis impositis—Heb. 9: 10). That is, Harry is a sort of law keeper (bailly) and supplier (host) as he tries to regulate his pilgrims and look after their various timely needs. Cf. Aquinas on Gal. 4: 24-27, where he equates things temporal with the Old Law and things eternal with the New (*Super Epistolas S. Pauli: Lectura*, ed. Father Raphael Cai [Rome: Marietti, 1953], cap. 4 Lectio VIII. 256-258, I, 621). Paul variously discusses the Old Law as a figure or allegory of the New (Gal. 4: 24), a tutor or keeper of children (Gal. 3: 24-25), or as the flesh or womb or mother (Gal. 4: 4) which conveys men to their true end amidst travail and frustration. I do not wish, however, to suggest any direct allegorical connection between the Canterbury pilgrimage and the progress of Old-New Testament history.

ale to sweeten his thoughts.[26] He calls on the "beel amy" Pardoner to restore his mirthful spirits, but instead of reassuring him, the Pardoner makes him so angry that the whole journey comes to an impasse, until the Knight intervenes. Though Harry Bailly remains spokesman to the end, he too seems glad enough to hear what the Parson would say.

III

But Chaucer uses Paul as more than a signalling device to turn attention toward the new covenant at the journey's end and as an authority on interpretation. Paul's letters are frequently cited, especially in the marriage group and by the Pardoner and Second Nun, to monitor ethical considerations of all kinds. I had never recognized how pervasively ideas of pilgrimage are built into *The Canterbury Tales* until I began to notice the intricacy of Chaucer's Pauline allusions.

Paul was traditionally viewed as the first great Christian pilgrim, a man who exemplified in his life story the translation from old to new, from death to life, from blindness to divine vision. His ministry took him throughout the Mediterranean world and even, by his own admission, to the third heaven (2 Cor. 12: 2-5) to be instructed by Christ Himself. Of that journey St. Thomas Aquinas writes, "Truly, just such a person [as Paul] ought the proclaimer of wholesome wisdom to be—an Israelite in his contemplation of God, a Christian in his religious faith, and an Apostle in his duteous counsel."[27] Elsewhere the Angelic Doctor glosses Paul's title "the Apostle" to mean "sent" (*missus*), the one who leads men to the source of authority, the Author Himself.[28] We get some indication of how a medieval writer might regard Paul as a figurative pilgrim in Dante's *Inferno*, when the wandering persona, upon encountering Virgil, wonders why he should be permitted to make the journey: "Io non Enëa, io non Paulo sono."[29] Aeneas is, of course, the classical pilgrim seeking his true home. Paul is the model Christian journeyman. A fourteenth-century English translator of St. Jerome's Vulgate singles Paul out as "a pilgryme and a dyscyple" and example for Jerome's own "pylgrymage."[30]

---

26. My discussion follows the modified order of *The Canterbury Tales* advocated by Bradshaw and reiterated by Robert Pratt, "The Order of *The Canterbury Tales*," *PMLA*, 66 (1951), 1141-67 (i.e., A, B₁, B₂, D, E, F, C, G, H, I). I find that order more compelling thematically than that of the Ellesmere MS because of the placement of the B₂ fragment toward the beginning of the journey and the juxtaposition of the Physician-Pardoner fragment (C) with the *Second Nun's Tale* at the beginning of the conclusion.

27. Talis debet esse praedicator sapientiae salutaris, scilicet *Israëlita* quo ad contemplationem Dei, *Christianus* quo ad religionem fidei, *Apostolus* quo ad auctoritatem officii. (*Super Epistolam ad Ephesios: Lectura*, Prologus 1 [ed., Cai, II, 1]).

28. *Super Epistolam ad Galatas: Lectura*, Cap. I, Lec. 1.3-4 (ed., Cai, I, 565); and *Super Epistolam ad Philippenses*: Lectura, Cap. I, Lec. 1.4 (ed., Cai, II, 91).

29. *Inferno* II. 31. *La Divina Commedia*, ed. C.H. Grandgent; rev. Charles S. Singleton (Cambridge, Mass.: Harvard University Press, 1972), p. 22.

30. Prologus, or "epistil of seynt Ierom prest of alle þe bookis of goddis storie," *MS Bodley 959*, ed. Conrad Lindberg (Stockholm: Almqvist & Wiksell, 1959), pp. 26-36 (1.17-18 and 4.8). In his commentary on Galatians, Aquinas stresses Paul's sanctity by noting that

Quite evidently, a successful pilgrim—one who reaches his goal—knows how to use time well, to redeem the time, as Paul says. Men must go as "wyse men, aȝen byinge tyme" (Eph. 5: 16; Col. 4: 5) and keep watch against the time when "the Lord schal come, as a theef in the niȝt" (1 Thess. 5: 2).[31] Sleepy-headed stewards must awake, be prepared, and remain sober. Men who redeem time through alert watchfulness may hope to be redeemed in good time. Chaucer's Custance, Prudence, Griselde, and Cecile exemplify the watchful who remain alert and use time fruitfully.[32] More often, however, one encounters characters living in a stupor, like the drunken Cook falling from his horse into the slough or Januarie in his imperturbable fantasy. Blindness metaphors in Chaucer usually are tied up with problems of using time idly and getting lost in some vagrant fantasy. The *Nun's Priest's Tale* offers one of the more elaborate comic vignettes on this idea, when Chauntecleer's winking and idle play in his barnyard almost cost him everything, until he wakes up, starts using his wits, and escapes to keep watch from his tree.[33]

Harry Bailly is the main timekeeper on the pilgrimage—"oure aller cok" (A 823). He has a practical alertness which enables him to get on remarkably well. His love of good fellowship includes an appreciation of both wisdom and delight, and he is admirable in the orderly way he hustles the pilgrims along toward their intended goal. He chides the Clerk and Prioress for holding back at the outset and with much dispatch gets the lots cast to see who will tell a tale first. When the drunken Miller interrupts, he protests, "Abyd, Robyn, my leeve brother . . . Abyd, and lat us werken thriftily" (A 3129-31). Though he is forced to make virtue of necessity and let the Miller speak or lose him, he keeps the pace moving. When the loquacious old Reeve starts "sermonyng" on old age Harry quickly interrupts:

> "what amounteth al this wit?
> What shul we speke alday of hooly writ? . . .
> Sey forth thy tale, and tarie nat the tyme

Peter traditionally is placed at Christ's left, since he was called by Christ in the flesh, while Paul is placed on the right, since he was called by Christ glorified (*Super Epistolas ad Galatas*, I. 1.7, ed., Cai, II, 566).

31. From *Wycliffite Versions of the Bible*, ed. Forshall and Madden. The Ephesians quotation is from the "earlier version" (collated from 18 mss) and the 1 Thessalonians verse is from the "later version" (collated from 37 mss). The Vulgate reads: "ut sapientes redimentes tempus" and "quia dies Domini sicut fur in nocte ita veniet."

32. It is noteworthy that Chaucer emphasizes right use of time for each of these heroines: N.B., Custance's patience and waiting until the time is right to reveal her full identity; the recurrent phrase "and whan she saugh hir tyme" used to describe Prudence's dialogue with Melibee; Griselde's biding her time even in exile until her lord reveals his true intent; and Cecile's fortitude which so measures her life that she brings many to fruitfulness even "in tyme and space."

33. See Charles Dahlberg's informed reading of allusions to the passion in Chauntecleer's timely escape in "Chaucer's Cock and Fox," *JEGP*, 53 (1954), 287-90. The taking refuge in the tree might be likened to adherence to the "beem" or cross, as it does in the story of St. Kenelm, which Chauntecleer learnedly cites as part of his oration on dreams. See also Bernard S. Levy and George R. Adams, "Chauntecleer's Paradise Lost and Regained," *Mediaeval Studies*, 29 (1967), 192.

Lo Depeford! and it is half-wey pryme.
Lo Grenewych, ther many a shrewe is inne!
It were al tyme thy tale to bigynne."

I(A) 3901-3908

He even has the audacity to interrupt Geoffrey:

"By God . . . for pleynly, at a word,
Thy drasty rymyng is nat worth a toord!
Thou doost noght elles but despendest tyme."

VII(B₂) *2119-2121

The problem of "despending time" is one of the most complex on the
whole pilgrimage. Paul would probably think Harry short-sighted in his insistence upon mirth as the best way to pass time—"Telle us swich thyng
as may our hertes glade. Be blithe" (B₂ *4001), he cries; "Telle us som
myrthe or japes right anon" (C 319). Yet the Parson too will promise a
"merye tale," for what is more merry than the new song of salvation? For
the most part, Harry has a different kind of mirth in mind. And it is true, as
we have seen, that frequently Harry's attempts at finding mirth—treacle for
his debilitation—miscue as he gets the depressing Physician and the Pardoner for his pleasure. Yet Harry Bailly ultimately turns out to be a pretty
good watchman, despite the fact that the Monk's lamentable tragedies almost put him to sleep. Though he may not be the world's greatest intellect,
he has enough goodwill and common sense to ward off the fiendish canon,
that daylight thief who would rob his pilgrim band of its possessions even
in the suburb of the holy city. Harry not only gets the pilgrims to Canterbury safely, but even into the Parson's care, at just the right time—that is,
the last moment!

That is good plotting on Chaucer's part, for it reflects the essence of
any good plot, even that of history with all its enigmas and suspense,
where up to the last hour, as Paul points out, the antichrist waits to make
his final play before the last veil is removed (cf. 2 Thess. 2). The whole
point of using time well is to make a good end. And in a good ending the
best is saved till last. (Cf. the Marriage of Cana, referred to in the Wife of
Bath's Prologue, where the best wine, that transformed by Christ himself,
is served at the end of the feast. [34])

The problem of making a good ending is a prominent topic throughout
The Canterbury Tales, from the *Knight's Tale* on. Some of the pilgrims,
like the Shipman, rely on deceit to make their endings work. Others, like
the Wife of Bath, rely on trickery. Some, like the Physician, Miller, and
Reeve, end in barrenness and debauchery. Some endings are forced, like
the Franklin's; others backfire, like the Summoner's, or are abortive like
the Pardoner's. Some (the interrupted ones) have no ends at all. Within the
tales, characters, troubled by their dilemmas, frequently cry out—"Is
there no grace, is there no remedy?" But everywhere, both in and out of

---

34. St. Augustine, *Tractate IX on the Gospel of John*, glosses the six vessels as the
six ages which have been fulfilled and transformed through the revelation of the Trinity to
both Jews and Gentiles. See also Aquinas, *Catena Aurea*, the glosses for John 2: 5-11.

the tales, Chaucer's characters worry about making a good end. Even the inept, whose tales do not get finished, consider the problem. The Squire gets Canacee walking in her garden; then, pressed for matter and plot, he observes:

> The knotte why that every tale is toold,
> If it be taried til that lust be coold
> Of hem that han it after herkned yoore,
> The savour passeth ever lenger the moore . . .[35]
> And by the same resoun, thynketh me,
> I sholde to the knotte condescende
> And maken of hir walkyng soone an ende.

V (F) 401-408

It is an amusing moment as the narrator, having got his heroine walking, ponders how to get her stopped. But the problem has serious ramifications for more wanderers than Canacee. Discovering the knot to perambulation, whether of young ladies or sage pilgrims, may be no easy matter. Though he brings Canacee's walking to a rhetorical cease, the Squire does not find a knot for his own wandering tale, which, rather than revealing its meaning, becomes lost in loose threads.

Chaucer, as part of the structuring of his ending to the whole of *The Canterbury Tales*, introduces two alchemists to alert us to the final changes about to take place.[36] The alchemists' endeavors to multiply always end in frustration: "We faille of oure desir," the Yeoman laments, "For evere we lakken oure conclusion" (G 671-72). The Canon tries to silence his apprentice, saying, "Thou sclaundrest me . . . and eek discoverest that thou sholdest hyde" (G 695-96). The ending he imagines depends upon deceit. But in a good ending, one which redeems time rather than wastes it, truth is revealed, as in the apocalyptic conclusions of the stories of Custance and Griselde, when all veils have been removed. It is that kind of ending, a good conclusion with nothing hidden, which the Parson, in his new agreement with the pilgrims, hopes to discover as he puts fable aside to knit up the matter.

I have written elsewhere of the two time-telling passages which Chaucer builds into the Canterbury pilgrimage, the first in the Introduction to the *Man of Law's Tale* where Harry Bailly exhorts the pilgrims to make haste, for already it is ten o'clock, and the second in the Parson's Prologue where Geoffrey tells time by contemplating his own shadow, that parable of himself in the time world which the Parson will help explicate.[37] Both passages seem to be part of Chaucer's Pauline design to accentuate within the pilgrimage frame the need to use time well if one would reach a satisfactory conclusion. Chaucer juxtaposes lists of his works with each of

---

35. Harry Bailly makes a similar point about spoiling the end when scolding the Monk for his wearisome tragedies (B2 *3980-92). Cf. Pandarus' concern in his dealing with Criseyde (*T&C*, II. 255-63; 267-73).

36. See note 21.

37. "Number Symbolism in the Prologue to Chaucer's *Parson's Tale*," *English Studies*, 48 (1967), 205-15.

these time-telling passages, first as the Man of Law complains that Chaucer has told all the rhymes, and second in the Retraction. The effect calls attention to ways in which the poet himself has mis-spent his time. That the poet puts aside his "enditynges of worldly vanitees" in his Retraction seems in keeping with the Parson's guidelines from St. Paul that fables are ultimately a form of idleness and that redemption comes "not after [according to] oure werkys; but after his purpos and grace þe whiche is gyfen to vs in crist iesu bifore þe seculer worldys [existed]" (2 Tim. 1: 9); "not of þe werkys of riȝtwisnes þat we han don but after his myche mercy he has maad vs safe" whereby we receive grace and "ben heyrys after the hope of þe euerlastande life" (Tit. 3: 5-7).[38] Yet even so, in the Retraction Chaucer thanks "lord Jhesu Crist and his blisful mooder" (l. 1088) for his translation of Boethius and his moral writings. Geoffrey insists in the Retraction that in telling "this litel tretys" his wit may have been deficient but not his will, and he hearkens one last time to that by now familiar passage from Romans, "For oure book seith, 'Al that is writen is writen for oure doctrine,' and that is myn entente" (l. 1082). Thus the Retraction, though it follows the Parson and Paul's letter to Timothy in rejecting fable, once again places the burden of understanding upon the explicator. The paradox here is that Chaucer has slyly returned to the Nun's Priest's Pauline text, which gets the last word after all.[39] What becomes clear, once fable is put aside, is a deeper enigma still, for in the Retraction Chaucer does not see God face to face; he only makes himself naked through an artful manifestation of faith.[40] With that passive assertion there is a release, for the present at least, a kind of meditative openness which is perhaps the beginning of pilgrimage, rather than its end. In the Retraction Chaucer, like Harry Bailly in the Parson's prologue, fulfills his covenant by getting his reader to the goal he promised, then turns him over to another host. It has troubled some readers that in making his ending Chaucer takes the matter not only out of the poet's hands but out of man's hands altogether. But that is where the essential matter of the pilgrimage rests. In his ending Chaucer makes artfully clear precisely what the limits of art are. The Retraction provides him a kind of linguistic innocence which, in the putting aside of his old words, allows a release from that long labor and a nakedness out of which new beginnings can grow.

---

38. *The Pauline Epistles: Parker 32 MS*, ed. Margaret Powell. Vulgata: "non secundum opera nostra sed secundum propositum suum et gratiam quae data est nobis in Christo Iesu ante tempora saecularia" (2 Tim. 1: 9); and, "non ex operibus iustitiae quae fecimus nos sed secundum suam misericordiam salvos nos fecit [per lavacrum regenerationis et renovationis Spiritus Sancti quem effudit in nos abunde per Iesum Christum salvatorem nostrum ut iustificati gratia] ipsius heredes simus secundum spem vitae aeternae" (Tit. 3: 5-7).

39. I am indebted in part to Edmund Reiss and Kathleen Ashley of Duke University for this part of my discussion of the Retraction.

40. Regardless of whether one approaches truth directly or through enigma, Paul's point is that one must be guided by the right spirit (what Chaucer would call "good entente"). See Robertson, *Preface to Chaucer*, pp. 290 ff., on Paul's method. Also his interesting note on the Retraction (p. 369), which emphasizes the concluding rhetoric which Chaucer uses.

IV

Related to these ideas of redeeming time and making a good end are two other Pauline notions which Chaucer draws upon extensively to develop his pilgrimage: (1) the idea of the *vetus homo*, that ancient unredeemed man burdened by time and in need of release,[41] and (2) the idea of becoming heir to God's grace. The Reeve and Januarie offer excellent examples of the old man worrying about his heritage and provide fascinating insights into Chaucer's subtle understanding of Paul's concepts. As the Reeve boasts of his agedness, insisting all the while upon his sexual prowess, he seems to demonstrate, as D. W. Robertson, Jr., has pointed out,[42] a quite unredeemed attitude toward time. His "holy writ" is little more than time-serving. Nevertheless, there is an ambiguous side to the Reeve's lechery which Chaucer seems willing to consider, namely that even in old age man is still afflicted with desire.[43] In some respects, the Reeve's lechery makes him foolish, perhaps even contemptable. In another, it is a sign of hope. (So it would seem to him, at least!) The same might be said of Januarie. There is life in these old boys, even if perversely oriented. Usually the old men express their desire in some ludicrous fantasy; they seek some fancied good, some "feeste." But so do the virtuous. Desire may hinder as well as help the wanderer's progress, but it must be there.[44] Chaucer is a master at exploring the dialogue between an essentially good desire and a perverse *entente*.

The opposites to these old men are Chaucer's saintly and fertile heroines, like Custance and Griselde, who, though burdened at first with toil and grief, have their children restored to their rightful inheritances. They follow that Pauline model whereby "the Spirit himself gives tes-

---

41. Several excellent studies have been made of Chaucer's use of the *vetus homo*; see especially the entries indexed under "New Man vs Old Man" in Robertson's *Preface to Chaucer* and Robert P. Miller, "Chaucer's Pardoner, the Scriptural Eunuch, and the Pardoner's Tale," *Speculum*, 30 (1955), 180-99. Christopher Dean, "Salvation, Damnation, and the Role of the Old Man in the *Pardoner's Tale*," *Chaucer Review*, 3 (1968), 44-49, offers an interesting opposition to Miller's argument.

42. *Preface to Chaucer*, pp. 379-82.

43. At the conclusion of Gower's *Confessio Amantis*, VIII. 2771-2779, Amans makes the same discovery, namely "that the wylde loves rage / In mannes lif forberth non Age" (*The English Works of John Gower*, ed. G. C. Macaulay [London: Oxford University Press, 1901], II, 461). That simple fact offers small consolation, but enough, it seems, for him to redirect his affection to something more worthy, once Cupid's dart has been removed.

44. Desire (*cupiditas*) is not in and of itself a bad thing; on the contrary, it is essential to man's nature. The problems derive from man's perverting of desire toward a false good. As Boethius' *Philosophia* explains: "est enim mentibus hominum ueri boni naturaliter inserta cupiditas, sed ad falsa deuius error abducit" *Consolatio Philosophiae* III. pr. 2.4, ed. L. Bieler (Turnholt: Brepols, 1957), p. 38 (Corpus Christianorum Series Latina, 44). Cf. Chaucer's translation: "Forwhy the covetise of verray good is naturely enplaunted in the hertes of men, but the myswanderynge errour mysledeth hem into false goodes" III, pr. 2, 11. 22-25. Chaucer's Parson makes a comparable point when he emphasizes the "seed of grace, the which seed is mooder of sikernesse" implanted in man, "egre and hoot." the "heete" of which is the "love of God and the desiryng of the joye perdurable" I(X) 115-120. Old Januarie has a compelling sense of this drive, albeit blindly misdirected.

timony to our spirit that we are sons of God. / But if we are sons, we are heirs also: heirs indeed of God and joint heirs with Christ, provided, however, we suffer with him that we may also be glorified with him'' (Rom. 8: 16-17—Douai).[45] The old men in the fabliaux, like John the carpenter, Symkyn the miller, and old Januarie, have something of the same inspiration. They would secure their heritages, sometimes at the expense of great labor, perhaps even sensing something sacred in the endeavor, but their orientations are confused, and they lack faith in proper ends. Thus their hopes come to naught; old John Carpenter, though he would save his ''swete Alisoun'' and become lord of the whole world ''al his lyve,'' becomes a laughing-stock; Symkyn's daughter ''that is come of swich lynage'' is disparaged despite Symkyn's sneaky attempts to advance his heritage by outwitting the clerks. Only Januarie succeeds (or thinks so) as he fondly strokes the pregnant May's womb ''ful softe,'' while we lasciviously watch and deem him fool. What he will be ''joint-heir'' to even Justinus could not predict, though Paul probably could. (Certainly Damian could![46])

V

Chaucer's exploration of the *vetus homo* and his enfeebled heritage is not restricted to the old men of *The Canterbury Tales*. The mere mention of Chaucer and St. Paul brings instantly to mind the Wife of Bath who, in her search for maistrye, establishes herself as Paul's formidable opponent. The Wife's concern is well met, for the Apostle is indeed the opponent of aggressive women. Yet in an odd way the Wife and Saint are on the same side, at least in terms of shared concerns: both assertively speculate on man's sovereign rights, both worry over the nature of inheritance and possessions, both consider what proper use of the flesh might be, both talk about marriage and being well-chosen vessels, and both reflect upon ways in which the old can be made new. That the Wife audaciously demands equal time with Paul on such points as chastity seems amusing, since Paul is so hallowed and Alisoun, despite her age, so fresh. But I do not think Chaucer means us simply to laugh at Alisoun; nor is she meant to be the object of pious scorn. Chaucer uses her, as he uses other willful pilgrims, to fracture received ideas as a way of getting at the spirit within them. Her perception of her problems and her solutions are in their limited way both profound and revealing, even though opposite to Paul's. In fact, from our position along the way in the world of fabulous experience, Alisoun's perceptions, despite their ludicrous incongruities, may provide more accessible avenues into the issue than Paul's more true, yet more austere formulations.

---

45. Vulgata: ''ipse Spiritus testimonium reddit spiritui nostro quod sumus filii Dei / si autem filii et heredes quidem Dei coheredes autem Christi si tamen conpatimur ut et conglorificemur'' (Rom. 8: 16-17).

46. See Milton Miller's witty note, ''The Heir in the Merchant's Tale,'' *PQ*, 29 (1950), 437-40.

One of the most frequently cited biblical passages in *The Canterbury Tales* is Ephesians 5: 21-33, where Paul exhorts: "Wives be subject to your husbands as to the Lord; because a husband is head of the wife, just as Christ is head of the Church, being himself savior of the body. But just as the Church is subject to Christ, so also let wives be to their husbands . . . . Husbands, love your wives, just as Christ . . . . Thus ought husbands also to love their wives as their own bodies" etc. (Douai trans.).[47] For Paul, women, as women, are emphatically the second sex. They are subject to men and in that respect enjoy a more limited freedom than men. As Christian souls they are, of course, equal: "For you are all the children of God through faith in Christ Jesus. For all who have been baptized into Christ have put on Christ. There is neither Jew nor Greek, neither slave nor freeman, neither male nor female. For all are one in Christ. And if you are Christ's, then you are the offspring of Abraham, heirs according to promise" (Gal. 3: 26-29—Douai).[48] But that is not a promise which much concerns Alisoun, for all her Scripture quoting. She would be woman, and as woman resents the secondary role. She will speak out on theological issues, despite Paul's admonitions for silence.[49] In dealing with her attitude Chaucer is astoundingly perceptive. Rightly sensing the need for sovereignty in her life (and, if Paul is right, it is not a sovereignty that men can give her, only Christ, who is beyond male and female), the Wife tries to resolve the problem not by claiming maistrye over herself, though she allows that maistrye is what women most desire, but by taking possession of the men who possess her. The dilemma as she perceives it revolves around rule of the body. Oddly enough she sees her-

---

47. Vulgata: "subiecti invicem in timore Christi / mulieres viris suis subditae sint sicut Domino / quoniam vir caput est mulieris sicut Christus caput est ecclesiae ipse salvator corporis / sed ut ecclesia subiecta est Christo ita et mulieres viris suis in omnibus / viri diligite uxores sicut et Christus dilexit ecclesiam et se ipsum tradidit pro ea / ut illam sanctificaret mundans lavacro aquae in verbo / ut exhiberet ipse sibi gloriosam ecclesiam non habentem maculam aut rugam aut aliquid eiusmodi sed ut sit sancta et inmaculata / ita et viri debent diligere uxores suas ut corpora sua qui suam uxorem diligit se ipsum diligit / nemo enim umquam carnem suam odio habuit sed nutrit et fovet eam sicut et Christus ecclesiam / quia membra sumus corporis eius de carne eius et de ossibus eius / propter hoc relinquet homo patrem et matrem suam et adherebit uxori suae et erunt duo in carne una / sacramentum hoc magnum est ego autem dico in Christo et in ecclesia / verumtamen et vos singuli unusquisque suam uxorem sicut se ipsum diligat uxor autem ut timeat virum" (Eph. 5: 21-33).

48. Vulgata: "omnes enim filii Dei estis per fidem in Christo Iesu / quicumque enim in Christo baptizati estis Christum induistis / non est Iudaeus neque Graecus non est servus neque liber non est masculus neque femina omnes enim vos unum estis in Christo Iesu / si autem vos Christi ergo Abrahae semen estis secundum promissionem heredes" (Gal. 3: 26-29).

49. I Cor. 14:34-35: "Let women keep silence in the churches, for it is not permitted them to speak, but let them be submissive, as the Law also says. / But if they wish to learn anything let them ask their husbands at home, for it is unseemly for a woman to speak in church" (Douai). Then, as if to answer possible objections or objectors, Paul goes on to assert: "Let him recognize that the things I am writing to you are the Lord's commandments./If anyone ignores this, he shall be ignored" (I Cor. 14:37-38—Douai). But despite the authority, such words are offensive to Dame Alyce, who will let no clerk "naille" her tongue, but "evere answereth at the countretaille," as Chaucer advises her to do in his envoy to the *Clerk's Tale* (E 1183 ff.). See also 1 Tim. 2: 11 ff.

self ruled by the planets Mars and Venus, without control over her body. Yet that seems preferable to the subjugation to husband which Paul would require of her. But in either instance the implication is that her body is not her own. Apparently denied control of her body by both husbands and stars, Alisoun seeks other bodies to control. To make up for the loss she feels she would rule her possessors. And it is easier to rule men than stars.

Her tale presents women dealing with men in a male-oriented world. Though the king is titular head of the court, it is the queen who determines the rules of the game. In dealing with the rapist knight the queen demands control over his body:

> And suretee wol I han er that thou pace,
> Thy body for to yelden in this place.
>
> III(D) 911-12

The answer to the question she poses—"What thyng is it that wommen moost desiren"—is the most un-Pauline notion that they themselves would be their own heads, both over their desires and their husbands (D 1038-40). Though the answer suggests a vindictive settling of accounts (you husbands have ruled us in the past—now we would rule you), the Wife's interpretation of regained sovereignty in the actual workings of the tale has its sympathetic moments. In her argument on gentilesse, poverty, and old age, the loathly hag, unable to make herself young, would change the mind of her husband through her brilliant reasoning. She is a sort of siren, Bernard Levy suggests,[50] who, unable to find the new woman by some Pauline journey toward a new spirit, relies on a more pagan means. She asks, in effect, to be admired for her wisdom, an admiration not easily come by for a medieval woman. It is evident from the Wife's Prologue that men do not usually think of wisdom when they think of the Wife of Bath, or if they do it is "wisdom" with a variant gloss. To make up for that emptiness she thus craves to be filled in other ways. She would use her "sely instrument" to control her husbands—be their shoe, grind their grain (though hardly at some mystical mill), and provide baths of bliss—but all for purposes of control.

The Wife's discourse on her body and its instrumentality generates a nexus of related images in this section of the Tales, ranging from wells, mills, shoes, and tuns to rebekkes and widows, all of which are vessels or instruments for man's use. It may be that for Chaucer the origin of this rather salacious configuration of images is none other than the Apostle.[51] Paul talks at length about the body as vessel of the flesh. He was himself one who tried to make up for his own unredeemed emptiness by being

---

50. "Chaucer's Wife of Bath, the Loathly Lady, and Dante's Siren," *Symposium*, 19 (1965), 357-73.
51. Graham Caie, "The Significance of the Early Chaucer Manuscript Glosses," notes that many of these metaphors are accompanied in the Ellesmere MS by scriptural glosses, the largest number of which pertain to the Wife's "perverse literal interpretation of the Old Law to suit her purposes" (353); he also notes that "the largest flood of indignant glosses in all glossed manuscripts" (355) pertain to the Wife's observations on uses of vessels!

purgatory for others—"som Cristen men," doubtless—who failed to uphold what he thought the spirit of the old law to be. In his conversion Paul became God's chosen vessel (*vas electionis*), filled with the Holy Spirit, God's "sely instrument," indeed.[52] As oft-widowed pilgrim, Alisoun has likewise suffered the burden of emptiness. But although her vessel has often been elected and she has been much transported, she remains quite untranslatable. Gladly would she serve, if only with instruments of tree. Paul comments (2 Tim. 2: 20-26) on the value of wooden vessels, noting that they should be clean, honorable, sanctified and useful to the Lord for good work; the vessel of the body, he says, should not be an excuse, however, for cravings of youth[53] or foolish controversies or quarrels. Alisoun would, of course, agree with the letter of nearly everything Paul says. She is not dirty, and she is always ready to help in that perfect maker the Lord's work, by using her instrument as freely as he gave it to her; and she perceives that it is foolish for men to dispute with her. When she was young she preferred old men. Like Paul, she would have the old man die, but in order that his gold be left to her, not that he be born again. But if a new man should come she would have that new man for herself.

Now that she is old she has a different view of old men. She also has a different view of herself. She would be young, if only in young men's eyes. As much as Paul scorns the *vetulus*, she scorns the *vetula*, even though experience has often made her a widow. For Paul, the widow should remain empty of men (i.e., chaste)[54] to leave room for Christ (N.B., the Latin pun on *vidua*—widow and empty); for Alisoun her widowhood would eagerly be refilled, or rather refreshed in the sense that when we take a refreshment we fill the tun. Like the Woman of Samaria with her five husbands, she would gladly serve from the well of waters which whet one's thirst; and she would welcome a sixth husband. But she does not recognize the gloss that would make the sixth husband Christ.[55] She might be a shrewish rebekke, skilled in the old dance of husband deception, but not a Rebecca to secure the heritage despite her old husband's blindness. (Cf. Romans 9: 10, where Paul compares Rebecca to Sara as divine instrument for securing Abraham's heritage.)

In the *Friar's Tale*, which follows the *Wife of Bath's Tale*, Chaucer explores this configuration of Pauline ideas in a different way. In this tale a summoner, having misdefined his sovereign obligations to his lord (that is,

---

52. The epithet "vas electionis" bestowed on Paul by Luke (Acts 9: 15) became a conventional way of alluding to the Apostle. E.g., Dante refers to him as "Vas d'elezione" (*Inferno* II. 28), and the Wycliffite translator speaks of him as "þe vessel of eleccioun" (MS Bodley 959, prol. 2.2 and 4.21), explaining that the epithet means Paul was full of God's wisdom.

53. Caie notes that the Egerton MS glossator cites 2 Tim. 2: 22—"Flee also youthful lusts"—when the wife reminisces about her lost youth.

54. 1 Cor. 7: 7-9, 40; also 1 Tim. 5: 3 ff.

55. St. Augustine, Tractate XV on John, suggests that Christ becomes the woman's sixth husband when she believes in him and drinks from the cup of living water; immediately she becomes instrumental in the converting of others, that is, fruitful in a most sacred way. Augustine's glosses are repeated in St. Thomas' *Catena Aurea*.

his "rente," as David Jeffrey has explained the term),[56] sets his whole
entente on robbing a widow. (The widow is a conventional figure of Holy
Church, God's holy vessel through which he channels his grace for
mankind.)[57] As churchman, the summoner should care for the widow; that
is his obligation. But he perverts his office to rob the widow. It is as if he
would make up for some emptiness in his soul by getting money. As he sets
out with this entente he meets the fiend in a wood. The fiend explains that
he is God's instrument despite himself. Having lost his created form
through his perversity, he now has no body of his own. Instead, he must
try to possess the bodies of others. That is, he suffers the effect of lost
sovereignty which was the Wife of Bath's dilemma. The fiend ends up with
the summoner's body as a consequence of the summoner's own perverse
entente to rob the widow. The summoner refers to the widow as a "rebekke," meaning a "shrew," but in doing so he reminds us of Isaac's
bride. Isaac's marriage was commonly glossed to signify Christ's marriage
to Holy Church, the bride keeping the well. Her name was given to a
stringed musical instrument often used in paintings of the Virgin Mary as a
sign of her being God's special instrument.[58] The summoner in the
Friar's Tale abuses the "rebekke" and in the process loses his only
heritage, himself. Possessed by the fiend, he is dispossessed of himself, an
empty vessel. The *Friar's Tale*, with its insights into right possession,
God's chosen instruments, widows, and rebekkes, thus stands as an extension of concerns first explored in the *Wife of Bath's Tale*. It offers a concise moral vignette on the care and possession of the body and the progressive emptiness and degenerate craving which result when that care is ab-
sent.

The idea of sacred vessel takes a somewhat different turn in the
Summoner's Tale, but it is still there. Now we encounter a literal church
and a friar preoccupied with raising funds for the building of it. Though the
friar would appear to be a well-filled vessel (he is very fat and continues

---

56.   "The Friar's Rent," *JEGP*, 70 (1971), 600-606.
57.   St. Augustine glosses the much widowed Woman of Samaria as a type of the
church not yet justified. But Bede's comments on the widow Anna, who awaits the presentation of Jesus in Luke 2: 36-37, provide the model gloss: "According to the mystical meaning,
Anna signifies the Church, who at present is indeed a widow by the death of her Husband; the
number also of the years of her widowhood marks the time of the Church, at which established in the body, she is separated from the Lord. For seven times twelve make eighty-four,
seven indeed referring to the course of this world, which revolves in seven days; but twelve
had reference to the perfection of Apostolic teaching, and therefore the Universal Church, or
any faithful soul which strives to devote the whole period of its life to the following of Apostolic practice . . . ." St. Thomas Aquinas, *Catena Aurea*, trans. J. H. N. (Oxford: John Henry
Parker, 1843), III (pt. 1), 93. (Cf. glosses on widow of Sarepta, Luke 4: 26, by St. John
Chrysostom, *Cat. Aur.* III pt. 1, 161). Mortimer J. Donovon, "The *Moralite* of the Nun's
Priest's Sermon," *JEGP*, 52 (1953), 504-506, cites glosses by Isidore, Alcuin, and St. Augustine on the widow as a type of Holy Church. Cf. Dahlberg, "Chaucer's Cock and Fox,"
JEGP, 53 (1954), 286, for additional references.
58.   See especially pictures of the nativity or childhood of Jesus. But for a more in-
volved treatment of the music-instrument metaphor, see David L. Jeffrey, "Bosch's
'Haywain': Communion, Community, and the Theater of the World," *Viator*, 4 (1973),
312-15, 325-29.

eating through much of the tale), his activities and the church he hopes to tile as soon as he can get enough money are as empty of the Holy Spirit as the mock-pentecostal dispute over the fart and first fruits which ends the tale.[59]

The *Clerk's Tale* continues the sacred vessel motif in the character of Griselde, who is a Rebecca-type set in opposition to the rebekke Wife of Bath.[60] Griselde fulfills Paul's idea of woman's office. Like Rebecca, serving at "a welle" (276), she is elected to be her lord's chosen vessel. Chaucer doubles the biblical typology, adding ox-stall imagery to the waterpots and wells to suggest the Virgin Mary, whom Rebecca prefigures. In her marriage Griselde leaves the rule of "this olde man" Janicula (303), only to find trials under her new lord. But armed with faith she never subverts her husband's plans, even though she does not understand them. When cruelly cast out she remains "a wydwe clene in body, herte, and al" (836). Though she is transported here and there at her husband's command, her heart is steadfast. As she explains to Walter, when he calls her back to be chambermaid:

> "Nat oonly, lord, that I am glad," quod she,
> "To doon youre lust, but I desire also
> Yow for to serve and plese in my degree
> *Withouten feyntyng*, and shal everemo."
>
> IV (E) 967-70 (Italics mine)

Griselde seems mindful of the Pauline exhortation from Job in Hebrews 12: 5-6: "Despise not thou the chastening of the Lord, nor *faint* when thou art rebuked of him, / For whom the Lord loveth he chasteneth." Griselde does not faint in her trials and is ultimately translated a second time (cf. 385, 379, 1114 ff.) into a prosperous "heritage" (1135), according to promise.

Griselde's serving at the well might be understood as a metaphor of the proper keeping of time.[61] Indeed, the *Clerk's Tale* is a study in the uses of time, where Chaucer combines Pauline material on keeping time with Ecclesiastes, for remarkable effect. When Harry Bailly calls on the Clerk to speak, he re-emphasizes their old covenant: "For what man that is en-

---

59. See Bernard S. Levy, "Biblical Parody in the *Summoner's Tale*," *TSL*, 11 (1966), 45-60; and Alan Levitan, "The Parody of Pentecost in Chaucer's *Summoner's Tale*," *UTQ*, 40 (1971), 236-46.

60. Several excellent studies have dealt with biblical motifs in the *Clerk's Tale*: see especially James Sledd, "The Clerk's Tale: The Monsters and the Critics," *MP*, 51 (1953), 73-82; Charles Muscatine, *Chaucer and the French Tradition* (Berkeley, 1960), pp. 192-97; S. K. Henninger, Jr., "The Concept of Order in Chaucer's *Clerk's Tale*," *JEGP*, 56 (1957), 382-95; John P. McCall, "The *Clerk's Tale* and the Theme of Obedience," *MLQ*, 27 (1966), 260-69; and Lynn Staley Johnson, "The Prince and his People: A Study of the Two Covenants in the *Clerk's Tale*," *Chaucer Review*, 10 (1975-76), 17-29.

61. See glosses on the Woman of Samaria (*Catena Aurea*, IV, 134-162), who first served the water of temporality but through Christ became servant of the living water of everlasting life. Griselde is a keeper of this second kind; she drinks and serves "ofter of the welle than of the tonne" (215), in contrast to the Wife of Bath, who serves from the tun (D 177).

tred in a pley, / He nedes moot unto the pley assente'' (10-11), reminding him, as Solomon says, that "every thyng hath tyme" (6; cf. Eccles. 3: 1). The Clerk assents to tell a tale, but it is evident that he, in his quiet meditation, has, from the beginning, had his thoughts on other matters (cf. A 840 and E 4-8). Harry compares him to a "mayde . . . newe spoused, sittynge at the bord" (2-3). The comparison is apt, for that is exactly what he is as he prepares for his marriage to Christ. His tale is more than an answer to the Wife of Bath; he sees himself in Griselde, as he prepares to become God's chosen vessel. Notice the wording as he accepts Harry's invitation:

> "Hooste," quod he, "I am under youre yerde;
> Ye han of us as *now* the governance,
> And therfore wol I do yow obeisance,
> As fer as resoun axeth, hardily."

IV(E) 22-25 (Italics mine)

The word which resonates is *now*, for evidently he has another time scheme and his obligations to it well in mind. He picks up Harry's reference to Ecclesiastes, to give it a Pauline gloss, noting that everything, indeed, has its time, witness even his good author Petrarch and the philosopher "Lynyan" whom death "that wol nat suffre us dwellen heer, / But as it were a twynklyng of an ye, / Hem bothe hath slayn, and alle shul we dye" (36-38). Death is the fullness of time (old time) which Paul speaks of in the same section of 1 Corinthians in which he discusses the first fruits (the ancient patriarchs [old men]), to be resurrected according to new time. (Cf. the end of the *Summoner's Tale*, with its mockery of the first fruits [D 2277] which, in the legal-minded friar's keeping, become an obligatory fart, mystifyingly difficult to apportion). For Paul, the mystery of the first fruits is that in the fullness of time "We shall not all sleep, but we shall all be changed / In a moment, in the twinkling of an eye, at the last trump . . . and the dead shall be raised incorruptible, and we shall be changed" (1 Cor 15: 51-52).[62] The tale the Clerk tells presents Griselde as the perfect vessel, abiding time according to her lord's will even though she does not understand it. When the right time comes, in the twinkling of an eye, she is changed from chambermaid to queen, raised to an eminence even higher than that of her initial marriage (1126-27), as she "riseth up abaysed from hire traunce" (1108; cf. 1079, 1086) to receive her children, lord, and worthy heritage (first fruits, indeed).[63]

---

62. Vulgata: "ecce mysterium vobis dico omnes quidem resurgemus sed non omnes inmutabimur / in momento in ictu oculi in novissima tuba canet enim et mortui resurgent incorrupti et nos inmutabimur" (1 Cor. 15: 51-52). This chapter of 1 Corinthians also discusses man's true heritage in ways which, if there were time, might be tied in with the earlier section of this essay dealing with covenants and heirs.

63. The Clerk's double time sense of new coming out of old and of vessels fulfilled even in time is built admirably into the structure of his tale with its six parts, which correspond roughly to the six ages (cf. Augustine's glosses on the six vessels at the Marriage at Cana mentioned in note 34). The correspondences work out roughly as follows:
1. Age of Adam: Adam's supplication for a wife and his marriage to Eve, prefiguring Christ's marriage to Church, the latter being a redeemed marriage insuring man his inheritance.
   Part One: The people of Saluzzo beseech Walter to marry to be assured of inheritance. He grants the request providing that they obey his commandments and do not question his actions.

As Chaucer's Envoy to the *Clerk's Tale* makes clear, Griselde's sense of stewardship is quite opposite to the Wife of Bath's, despite the Wife's wealth of practical experience. Yet, it is to Alisoun's world that the narrative returns. The *Merchant's Tale*, which follows the Clerk's, turns the Wife of Bath's situation around, offering a comic presentation of the quintessential old man in Januarie who, wanting all his time now, puts himself into a self-sustained limbo. Paul, as noted above, exhorts man to love his wife as Christ loves his church. Januarie is crazily literal in his piety as he worships at his wife's shrine, hoping to have his paradise on earth. Paul defines blindness as the rejection of knowledge and faith in Christ, despite clear evidences of the way to salvation (2 Cor. 4: 4). This is precisely Januarie's kind of blindness as he repeatedly goes to Scripture for guidance and twists its meaning to his desires. Thus it is fitting that as May helps the blind old man regain his sight she does so through a delicious travesty of Pauline maxims. May answers Januarie's literalism with her own. She has heard that the way to restore the blind is to "strugle with a man upon a tree" (E 2374). That is, in effect, what Paul exhorts every Christian to do (i.e., to struggle with Christ on the Cross) if he hopes to see God face to face. May has gladly embraced this struggle and Januarie's sight has been restored, even if only as through a glass darkly — "Ye han som glymsyng, and no parfit sighte" (2382). May continues her Pauline analogy, noting that Januarie is like "a man that waketh out of his sleep" (2397), who is not yet accustomed to what he sees (cf. Eph. 5: 13 ff. and 1 Cor. 2: 9-11).

Chaucer anticipated the cross-tree analogy in the *Nun's Priest's Tale*, where St. Kenelm and Chauntecleer make their escapes through the tree. [64] The apocalyptic analogy of removing the veil he anticipated in the *Wife of Bath's Tale*. There the old hag removes the curtain to allow the knight to see face to face her true beauty, that new lady to which he was previously

---

2. Age of Noah: The covenant given, with God's promise not to forsake man.
   Part Two: The marriage of Walter and Griselde, concluding with the birth of a daughter and proof of her fertility.
3. Age of Abraham: The proving of Abraham by the mock-sacrifice of Isaac.
   Part Three: Growth of the daughter and the proving of Griselde by the mock-sacrifice of the daughter.
4. Age of David: Reassurance of inheritance with the promise of a Messiah to spring from the root of Jesse.
   Part Four: Assurance of inheritance with the birth of the son, yet further delay because of the disappearance of the son.
5. Age of Daniel: The exile in Babylon.
   Part Five: Griselde is cast out of the palace, stripped of her glory; the people turn from her.
6. Age of John the Baptist: The revelation of Christ and the Holy Spirit. The true character of history is seen through the reunion of Heaven and Earth.
   Part Six: The reunion of Walter and Griselde and the revelation of the true motives behind the lord's treatment of his bride.
In this context it is amusing to juxtapose the seventh age, Judgment, when the Lord puts an end to history, with Chaucer's seventh part, Lenvoy de Chaucer, where the author steps forward to pass his ironic judgment on the Wife of Bath and all her sect.
   64. See note 33.

blind. Paul equates removing the veil with transcending the letter of the old law to enjoy the spirit of the new (2 Cor. 3:6-18; cf. note 8). Both of Chaucer's clever ladies (Alisoun and May) seem to commend the soundness of Paul's idea, for in both instances the difficult husbands under their guidance transcend the letter and come to see in a better spirit!

In view of Januarie's happy resolution one must conclude, along with the friar in the *Summoner's Tale*, that "glosynge is a glorious thyng, certeyn, / For lettre sleeth, so as we clerkes seyn" (D 1793-94; cf. 2 Cor. 3:6). In their ancient wisdom, both the Wife and Januarie study the letter carefully. They seem to recognize that the letter kills and the spirit keeps alive. Both distort the letter magnificently as they spring toward a new spirit capable of maintaining their fantasies. Indeed, for all their confusion, they remain the lively adversaries. Januarie, undaunted, continues to love his wife as his own flesh and with his lordly strokes honors her as his church (that shrine where he would place his relics), and the Wife will continue to recall the words of the Apostle that "the dart is set up for virginitee: Cacche whoso may, who renneth best lat see" (D 75-76). If Paul, in his last days, thought the prize his, for he had fought the good fight and run the good race (2 Tim. 4:7), his achievements in no way belittle Alisoun's. Doubtless, to her, his "gentil dedis" would seem "frail" by comparison with her own (cf. D 93).

The next focal point for Pauline ideas occurs in the *Pardoner's Tale*. Like the summoner in the *Friar's Tale*, the Pardoner does not care that he robs widows. He too would avoid emptiness by filling his purse. Earlier Chaucer linked the Pardoner dramatically with the Wife of Bath, where, in her Prologue, the Pardoner interrupted to discuss taking a wife, which is a joke, for if he is the eunuch critics have thought him to be,[65] it would be a barren marriage. Like the Wife, the Pardoner is an exhibitionist, who makes up for his deficiencies by tyrannizing others. Such behavior is a paradigm of sin and its effects on the psyche. The Wife used God's sexual gifts as her instrument of power. The Pardoner draws his bitter strength from the lack of them. He uses his wit to get goods, as if in retribution for God's monstrous gift of deformity to him, twisting to his advantage another text from Paul—"Radix malorum est cupiditas." But the Pardoner carries us more deeply into Paul than even the Wife of Bath had done. It does not matter, he says, if by chance he is God's instrument (cf. C 429 ff.). Paul speaks explicitly against the Pardoner's stance here in Romans 3:7-8, when he considers the question of good coming out of the errors of others: "But if through my lie the truth of God has abounded unto his glory, why am I also still judged as a sinner? / And why should we not, as some calumniously accuse us of teaching, do evil that good may come from it?" The answer Paul gives to such specious questions is that the presumptuous shall be condemned and become worthless: "Their throat is an open sepulchre; with their tongues they have dealt deceitfully. The venom of asps is beneath their lips; / their mouth is full of cursing and bitterness"

---

65. See Miller, note 41.

(Rom. 3: 13-14).[66] The Pardoner seems quite aware of Paul's admonition as he boasts about spitting out his "venym" (C 421) and is deliberately perverse as he quotes this same passage from Paul to accuse his pitiful audiences of making sepulchres of their throats (558). Rather than glossing to support his fantasies, as Alisoun did, the Pardoner breaks off fragments of Paul purposefully, as if to damn himself and all mankind as well. His attitude is wound up in the figure of the Old Man in his tale, whom critics have frequently explained as the *vetus homo*, wishing he could be unborn rather than reborn.

Claiming to be a "ful vicious man" (459), the Pardoner seems dedicated to death, as if knowing, with Paul, that the "last enemy to be destroyed will be death, for he has put all things under his feet" (1 Cor. 15: 26).[67] In his sinister sermon he follows Paul's notion that sin is a living death (Rom. 8: 6):

> But, certes, he that haunteth swiche delices
> Is deed, whil that he lyveth in tho vices.
>
> VI(C)547-48

But ignoring the conclusion to the passage, where Paul offers man great reassurance (Rom. 8: 9-13), the Pardoner projects the most depraved view of human nature in *The Canterbury Tales*. He would besmirch all mankind as he spits out "venym under hewe / Of hoolynesse" (421-22). His sermons give him opportunity to defile human nature, heap filth upon the heads of his victims. His diatribe against gluttony, for example, turns the human body into a stinking codpiece, a privy, a stuck swine, a sepulchre—altogether foul things.[68] Several of his images are taken from Paul, but for a most depraved effect. He quotes quite accurately part of 1 Cor. 6: 13: "Of this matiere, o Paul, wel kanstow trete: / 'Mete unto wombe, and wombe eek unto mete, / Shal God destroyen both,' as Paulus seith" (521-23). What the Pardoner does not note is that the passage is part of Paul's argument on the *sacredness* of the body, not its natural depravity. Paul's verse concludes, "The body is not for immorality, but for the Lord, and the Lord for the body." He then continues, "Do you not know that

---

66. Vulgata: "si enim veritas Dei in meo mendacio abundavit in gloriam ipsius quid adhuc et ego tamquam peccator iudicor / et non sicut blasphemamur et sicut aiunt nos quidam dicere faciamus mala ut veniant bona . . ." (Rom. 3: 7-8).

Vulgata: "sepulchrum patens est guttur eorum linguis suis dolose agebant venenum aspidum sub labiis eorum / quorum os maledictione et amaritudine plenum est" (Rom. 3: 13-14).

67. Vulgata: "novissima autem inimica destruetur mors omnia enim subiecit sub pedibus eius" (1 Cor. 15: 26).

68. The idea that the obstacles to man's earthly happiness lie in nature goes back to the *Franklin's Tale*, where Dorigen complains of the black rocks. The *Physician's Tale*, which (in both the Bradshaw-Pratt and Ellesmere orderings) separates the Franklin's and Pardoner's tales, praises the power of nature but argues that nature's beneficence is no guarantee of happiness. In fact, quite the opposite, as Virginia's beauty provokes her destruction. At least so it seems to Harry Bailly, who cries out in despair, "Allas . . . [the] yiftes of Fortune and of Nature / Been cause of deeth to many a creature" (C 295-96). The Pardoner's circumstance, it would seem, is opposite to Virginia's—nature has made him ugly—but the effect is the same. He would be his own assassin.

your members are the temple of the Holy Spirit, who is in you, whom you have from God and that you are not your own? For you have been bought at a great price. Glorify God and bear him in your body" (1 Cor. 6: 19-20).[69] The Pardoner selects only that which damns man, ignoring the part which speaks of man's pardon and of his body as God's chosen vessel. Immediately the unforgiving Pardoner follows the condemnatory quotation with another, this time taken from Philippians 3: 18-19. Again his quotation is accurate as far as it goes; there is no glossing, but he gives us only the depraved part:

> The apostel wepyng seith ful pitously,
> "Ther walken manye of whiche you toold have I—
> I seye it now wepyng, with pitous voys—
> That they been enemys of Cristes croys,
> Of whiche the ende is deeth, wombe is hir god!"

VI(C) 529-33

But the part is not the whole. The Pardoner's selection mutilates the intent of the passage, which reads in full: (17) "Brethren, be imitators of me, and mark those who walk after the pattern you have in us. (18) For many walk, as I have told you often and now tell you even weeping, who are enemies of the cross of Christ. (19) Their end is ruin, their god is the belly, their glory is in their shame . . . . (20) But our citizenship is in heaven from which we eagerly await a Savior, our Lord Jesus Christ, (21) who will refashion the body of our lowness, conforming it to the body of his glory . . . ."[70] In view of Paul's assurance, the Pardoner's natural deformity can be of no harmful significance. For all bodies will be refashioned, even the deformed, to conform to God's glory, that is, if they walk in imitation of Christ and the Cross, as Paul does. But the Pardoner ignores God's creative pardon to dwell instead on the corruption:

> O wombe! O bely! O stynkyng cod,
> Fulfilled of donge and of corrupcioun!
> At either ende of thee foul is the soun.

VI(C) 534-36

The Pardoner's perverse attitude toward human nature comes to its inevitable conclusion when he invites destruction upon himself by attacking the Host, accusing him of being "moost envoluped in synne," and telling him to come forth and "kisse the relikes everychon" (944). This time the

---

69. Vulgata: "corpus autem non fornicationi sed Domino et Dominus corpori" (1 Cor. 6: 13), and "an nescitis quoniam membra vestra templum est Spiritus Sancti qui in vobis est quem habetis a Deo et non estis vestri / empti enim estis pretio magno glorificate et portate Deum in corpore vestro" (1 Cor. 6: 19-20).

70. Vulgata: "imitatores mei estote fratres et observate eos cui ita ambulant sicut habetis formam nos / multi enim ambulant quos saepe dicebam vobis nunc autem et flens dico inimicos crucis Christi / quorum finis interitus quorum deus venter et gloria in confusione ipsorum qui terrena sapiunt / nostra autem conversatio in caelis est unde etiam salvatorem expectamus Dominum Iesum Christum / qui reformabit corpus humilitatis nostrae configuratum corpori claritatis suae" (Phil. 3: 17-21). The Pardoner's situation is like that of his own rioters who, directed by the old man up the crooked way to the tree—"God save yow, that boghte agayn mankynde" (766), fail to struggle eagerly with the man in the tree, as Paul advised, and thus be reformed; rather, he, like his rioters, turns to the gold and death—"who wende / To-day that we sholde han so fair a grace?" (782-83).

dung-flinging misfires as Harry replies that he would have his "coillons in myn hond," cut them off, and enshrine them "in a hogges toord" (955). Harry's revenge is stunningly just, for it is in the dung of an unclean animal that the Pardoner has already set his talents.

Chaucer brings his configuration of Pauline materials on sacred vessels, the body, old men, heritage, and the redeeming of time to a climax in the *Second Nun's Tale*, where the unforgiving, graceless disposition of the Pardoner is displaced by St. Cecile, with her Pauline view of the body as the sacred dwelling place of God. Cecile is a full person, as her name implies, a "hevene of peple," full of "wise werkes alle" (G 105-106). Her tale is loaded with Pauline material. In sovereign control of her body, Cecile conjoins both the fleshly and divine natures of man. Her body is not her own, but her husband Christ's, who gives her true sovereignty. She is both bride and husband—a woman turned into a man, as Jeremiah puts it[71]—as she helps Valerian come into his own life. She truly understands that text—"Be fruitful and multiply"—which the Wife of Bath so blatantly misunderstood; in "lastynge bisynesse" she is perpetually pregnant with "the fruyt of thilke seed of chastite" (193) sown in her by Christ, "hierde of us alle." Through example of her life she helps remove the curtain for all believers who, by her help, come to see, even in time and space, the angel of God. "Wey to the blind," she sends Valerian to a baptismal bath of bliss which is surpassingly sweet. The old man who appears at Valerian's conversion is the antithesis of the *vetus homo*. Radiant, full of the Holy Spirit, this shining old man is none other than St. Paul himself, the *vas electionis*, come from his third heaven[72] to read from his letter to the Ephesians:

> "O Lord, O feith, O God, withouten mo,
> O Cristendom, and Fader of alle also,
> Aboven alle and over alle everywhere."

> VIII(G) 207-209; cf., Eph. 4:5-6

The sanctity and fruitfulness of the new marriage is marked by the scent of roses and lilies. Though Chaucer is following closely his source in his translation, the inspiration behind the idea of Tiburce's smelling the "soote savour" (247) is again St. Paul (2 Cor. 2: 14-16): "But thanks be to God who always leads us in triumph in Christ Jesus, manifesting through the odor of his knowledge in every place. For we are the fragrance of Christ for God . . . an odor that leads to life."[73] As Cecile draws many to oneness

---

71. Jeremiah 31: 22: "I have seen a new thing in earth: a woman turned into a man." The passage was glossed to prefigure the Virgin Mary. See the *Biblia Pauperum* (40 Plate Block Book), plate A of the Annunciation, which presents Jeremiah's words as an anticipation of the angel's salutation to Mary.

72. So he has been variously identified (e.g., John H. Fisher, *The Complete Poetry and Prose of Geoffrey Chaucer* [New York: Holt, Rinehart & Winston, 1977], p. 314, note to l. 201). I imagine the third heaven, that being the place Paul visited in his famous dream, and thus his traditional resting place (1 Cor. 12: 2 ff.).

73. Vulgata: "Deo autem gratias qui semper triumphat nos in Christo Iesu et odorem notitiae suae manifestat per nos in omni loco / quia Christi bonus odor sumus Deo [in iis qui salvi fiunt et in iis qui pereunt / aliis quidem odor mortis in mortem aliis autem] odor vitae in vitam" (2 Cor. 2: 14-16).

in Christ, it is evident that her earthly body, even like the "cloistre blisful" of Mary's sides, is "perpetuelly a cherche" (546).

In summary, we see that Paul lurks at the heart of Chaucer's idea of spiritual pilgrimage in *The Canterbury Tales*.[74] The idea of pilgrimage is maintained throughout the tales, even in the most unlikely places, through configurations of Pauline imagery, often in parody and travesty. The Apostle's presence lies behind such *topoi* as old men and new men, doctrine hidden amidst enigma, full and empty psyches with attendant iconography of wells, vessels, widows, rebekkes or other kinds of instruments, concepts of redeeming time, heritage, and the search for grace. He lurks in the background of that poetic which espouses the use of enigma in the exploration of man's journey, and provides the text for the withdrawing of such curtains at the end in an effort to approach truth directly. Without the richness of perspective and language he contributes to *The Canterbury Tales* that work would be diminished in both its wit and wisdom.

74.　Paul is not, of course, the only biblical author Chaucer draws upon. In fact, the most extensive single biblical source in his writings is Proverbs. He makes frequent use of the Gospels and also Job, Ecclesiastes, and other New Testament epistles besides those of Paul, especially James. But the emphasis one finds on Pauline comments is prominent in *The Canterbury Tales*, mainly because of the pilgrimage matter.

Biblical Wisdom:
Chaucer's *Shipman's Tale* and the *Mulier Fortis**

THERESA COLETTI
University of Maryland

The search for sources and analogues to the *Shipman's Tale* has uncovered its notable similarities with versions of the "lover's gift regained"
story in folktales and in the works of Boccaccio and Sercambi;[1] yet few
people would dispute that Chaucer's adaptation of that plot far surpasses
its counterparts in richness of poetic texture and meaning. Comparisons of
the *Shipman's Tale* with its acknowledged analogues have only lent further
support to several truisms of Chaucer studies: that the stories our poet
read or heard and remembered at second hand were but grist for the mill of
his poetic imagination; that the achievement of his works lies principally in
their departures from, rather than their likeness to, the stories that inspired
them; that the whole is indeed greater than the sum of its parts. But while
Chaucer's treatment of his sources stands as one of the hallmarks of his
unassailable originality, this very originality often depends upon his precise
manipulation of other texts whose presence in his works, if muted for
twentieth-century readers, doubtless kindled the admiration of his first audience because they provided delightful recognition of the familiar. One
such text lies behind much of the "originality" of the *Shipman's Tale*: the
famous passage in Proverbs 31: 10-31 that describes the *mulier fortis*.[2]

---

* This essay appears by special permission of *The Chaucer Review*, where it has
previously appeared in vol. 15, no. 2 (1982), pp. 236-49.
1. John W. Spargo, *Chaucer's Shipman's Tale: The Lover's Gift Regained*, Folklore
Fellows Communications, No. 91 (Helsinki, 1930); "The Shipman's Tale," *Sources and
Analogues of Chaucer's Canterbury Tales*, ed. W.F. Bryan and Germaine Dempster (New
York: Humanities Press, 1958), pp. 439-46; Robert A. Pratt, "Chaucer's *Shipman's Tale* and
Sercambi," *MLN*, 55 (1940), 142-45; Richard Guerin, "*The Shipman's Tale*: The Italian
Analogues," *ES*, 52 (1971), 412-19; *The Literary Context of Chaucer's Fabliaux*, ed. Larry
Benson and Theodore M. Andersson (Indianapolis and New York: Bobbs-Merrill, 1971), pp.
280-337.
2. The presence of other biblical resonances in the *Shipman's Tale* has been noted by
Gail McMurray Gibson, who argues that the tale alludes to Resurrection motifs, particularly
Christ's encounter with Mary Magdalene: "Resurrection as Dramatic Icon in Chaucer's
Shipman's Tale," forthcoming in the volume of collected papers from the 1977 University of
Alabama Symposium on "Signs and Symbols in Chaucer." See also my article on Chaucer's
manipulation of the apocryphal legend of Anne and Joachim in the *Shipman's Tale*: "The
Meeting at the Gate: Comic Hagiography and Symbol in the *Shipman's Tale*", *Studies in*

One of the *Shipman's Tale*'s most significant departures from its analogues is its sympathetic portrayal of the wife. For unlike nearly all her counterparts in the tales of the "lover's gift regained," the wife of Chaucer's *Shipman's Tale* emerges triumphant in the end.[3] We may credit the difference to Chaucer's ingenuity if we wish, but this and other facets of the wife's character can be accounted for in more specific ways. What lies behind them is an allusive pattern of meaning, a chain of reminiscences that hark back to Proverbs 31: 10-31, which tells of the ideal wife who is praised for her domestic talents and her conjugal virtue. In the *Shipman's Tale* Chaucer gives us a topsy-turvy dislocation of the ideal of the *mulier fortis*, a parodic mirroring of traits and behaviors that correspond to the letter, if not the spirit, of the scriptural text that describes her.

That this biblical passage has been overlooked in studies of the Shipman's fabliau is not surprising; its presence in the tale, though far from obscure, is hardly obtrusive. Rather, its function is akin to what V. A. Kolve has observed of Chaucer's use of "controlling images," which "do not call attention to themselves in specifically symbolic ways but are instead discovered in—uncovered by—the narrative as it moves naturally from its beginning to its end." These images, according to Kolve, "create a certain residue in the mind" and endow Chaucer's narratives with "intellectual, artistic, and imaginative coherence."[4] Though not iconographic in an explicitly visual way, Proverbs 31: 10-31 lends to the *Shipman's Tale* just such a coherence. From it Chaucer subtly appropriated a cluster of words, images, and ideas that bear a dramatic and dynamic relationship to the more worldly substance of his domestic comedy.

Reading the *Shipman's Tale* in light of Proverbs 31: 10-31 results in a "mental residue" that retrospectively illuminates some notable features of the tale (besides its portrayal of the wife) that references to its known analogues fail to explain. An examination of the tale's appropriation of the *mulier fortis* passage also provides further evidence that Chaucer originally intended the story for the Wife of Bath, a creature with whom he clearly associated the playful manipulation of the scriptural text. Finally, a close look at Chaucer's adaptation of the biblical ideal of the *mulier fortis* in the *Shipman's Tale* sheds some light on the method and purpose of a significant aspect of Chaucer's poetic technique, his delicate weaving of the sacred text into the profane fabric of his poetic substance.

Before examining the *Shipman's Tale*'s peculiar congruence with Proverbs 31: 10-31, we ought briefly to review the ample evidence attesting to the popularity of the passage in the Middle Ages and hence to the strong

---

Iconography, 3 (1977), 47-56. Addressing aspects of Chaucer's use of biblical allusion that I was unable to develop in that article, the thesis of the present essay complements the argument of the earlier piece.

    3. Benson and Andersson, p. 278; William W. Lawrence, "Chaucer's *Shipman's Tale*," *Speculum*, 33 (1958), 59.

    4. "Chaucer and the Visual Arts," in *Geoffrey Chaucer*, ed. Derek Brewer (Athens, Ohio: Ohio University Press, 1975), p. 309.

likelihood that it was well-known to Chaucer and his audience. The *mulier fortis* was a favorite subject of medieval commentators, whose glosses on the passage reached even wider audiences through their inclusion in works like the *Bible moralisée*.[5] Robert P. Miller observes that the scriptural ideal of the *mulier fortis* helped establish the medieval stereotype of "womanly virtue,"[6] as appears, for example, in the work of Chaucer's contemporary John Gower, who refers directly to Proverbs 31: 10-31 in his *Vox clamantis* to explain how the behaviors of good and bad women affect men.[7] Still closer to home, Chaucer's own widely acknowledged familiarity with Scripture can be adduced as further testimony to his awareness of the *mulier fortis* passage. Though the extent of Chaucer's firsthand knowledge of the Bible has provoked some debate, impressive evidence, based on the availability of the scriptural text in the fourteenth-century and convincing illustrations from his own work, establishes that the poet's acquaintance with Scripture was far from casual and that he sometimes worked directly from the Vulgate.[8] And even though Chaucer doubtless acquired many of his biblical references and quotations from redactions of Scripture, the sheer bulk of these quotations, particularly from the Book of Proverbs,[9] suggests that his ignorance of a passage that had achieved the status of a scriptural commonplace would have been the more surprising eventuality.[10]

Why the ideal of the *mulier fortis* offers itself as a likely subtext for the *Shipman's Tale* is apparent from a close look at the biblical passage.

---

5. Robert P. Miller, ed., *Chaucer: Sources and Backgrounds* (New York: Oxford University Press, 1977), p. 391. Miller includes illustrations which indicate the standard allegorical reading of the *mulier fortis* as a type of the Church: pp. 392, 394. The significance of the *Bible Moralisée* illustrations will be discussed below.
6. *Ibid.*, p. 391.
7. *Vox clamantis*, Bk. 5, ch. 6 in *The Complete Works of John Gower*, ed. G. C. Macaulay, Vol. 4, *The Latin Works* (Oxford: Clarendon Press, 1902), 209; for a translation of the passage see *The Major Latin Works of John Gower*, trans. Eric W. Stockton (Seattle: University of Washington Press, 1962), pp. 202-203.
8. Thomas R. Lounsbury, *Studies in Chaucer*, 2 vols. (New York: Harper and Brothers, 1892), II, 389; Margaret Deanesly, *The Lollard Bible and Other Medieval Biblical Versions* (Cambridge: Cambridge University Press, 1920), p. 224; Dudley Johnson, "Chaucer and the Bible," Ph.D dissertation, Yale University, 1941; Grace Landrum, "Chaucer's Use of the Vulgate," *PMLA*, 39 (1924), 75-100. Daniel S. Silvia Jr. suggests that glosses from the Vulgate in the most authoritative manuscripts of *The Canterbury Tales* may be Chaucer's own: "Glosses to *The Canterbury Tales* from St. Jerome's *Epistola Adversus Jovinianum*," *Studies in Philology*, 62 (1965), 28-39. Although not ruling out the possibility that Chaucer wrote the glosses, Graham D. Caie maintains that they are probably the work of learned contemporaries who added them to guide a reader's interpretation of the text: "The Significance of the Early Chaucer Manuscript Glosses (with special reference of the *Wife of Bath's Prologue*)," *Chaucer Review*, 10 (1975-76), 350-60.
9. *The Complete Works of Geoffrey Chaucer*, ed. Rev. Walter W. Skeat, 7 vols. (Oxford: Clarendon Press, 1894-97), VI, 381-82.
10. The Wycliffite translation of Proverbs, which Chaucer may also have known, shows no significant departures from the Vulgate text in the passages on which the following discussion is based. I cite the Wycliffite version when the Middle English rendering appears to reflect directly upon the *Shipman's Tale*; see *The Earlier Version of the Wycliffite Bible*, ed. Conrad Lindberg (Stockholm: Almquist and Wiksell, 1959—), IV, 274-75.

(For the sake of convenience I quote it here from the Vulgate and its Douay translation.)

VULGATE

Proverbs Chapter 31

10 Mulierem fortem quis inveniet?
    Procul et de ultimis finibus pretium eius.
11 Confidit in ea cor viri sui, et spoliis non indigebit;
    12 reddet ei bonum et non malum, omnibus diebus vitae suae;
13 quaesivit lanam et linum
    et operata est consilio manuum suarum;
14 facta est quasi navis institoris,
    de longe portans panem suum,
15 et de nocte surrexit deditque praedam domesticis suis
    et cibaria ancillis suis;
16 consideravit agrum et emit eum,
    de fructu manuum suarum plantavit vineam.
17 Accinxit fortitudine lumbos suos
    et roboravit bracchium suum;
18 gustavit et vidit quia bona est negotiatio eius,
    non exstinguetur in nocte lucerna eius.
19 Manum suam misit ad fortia,
    et digiti eius apprehenderunt fusum;
20 manum suam aperuit inopi
    et palmas suas extendit ad pauperem,
21 non timebit domui suae a frigoribus nivis;
    omnes enim domestici eius vestiti sunt duplicibus.
22 Stragulatam vestem fecit sibi,
    byssus et purpura indumentum eius;
23 nobilis in portis vir eius, quando sederit cum senatoribus terrae.
    24 Sindonem fecit et vendidit
    et cingulum tradidit Chananaeo;
25 fortitudo et decor indumentum eius,
    et ridebit in die novissimo.
26 Os suum aperuit sapientiae,
    et lex clementiae in lingua eius;
27 consideravit semitas domus suae
    et panem otiosa non comedit.
28 Surrexerunt filii eius et beatissimam praedicaverunt,
    vir eius et laudavit eam.
29 Multae filiae congregaverunt divitias,
    tu supergressa es universas.
30 Fallax gratia et vana est pulchritudo,
    mulier timens Dominum ipsa laudabitur.
31 Date ei de fructu manuum suarum,
    et laudent eam in portis opera eius.

DOUAY TRANSLATION

Proverbs Chapter 31

10 Who shall find a valiant woman? far and from the uttermost coasts is the price of her.

11 The heart of her husband trusteth in her, and he shall have no need of spoils.

12 She will render him good, and not evil, all the days of her life.

13 She hath sought wool and flax, and hath wrought by the counsel of her hands.

14 She is like the merchant's ship, she bringeth her bread from afar.

15 And she hath risen in the night, and given a prey to her household, and victuals to her maidens.

16 She hath considered a field, and bought it: with the fruit of her hands she hath planted a vineyard.

17 She hath girded her loins with strength, and hath strengthened her arm.

18 She hath tasted and seen that her traffic is good: her lamp shall not be put out in the night.

19 She hath put out her hand to strong things, and her fingers have taken hold of the spindle.

20 She hath opened her hand to the needy, and stretched out her hands to the poor.

21 She shall not fear for her house in the cold of snow: for all her domestics are clothed with double garments.

22 She hath made for herself clothing of tapestry: fine linen, and purple is her covering.

23 Her husband is honourable in the gates, when he sitteth among the senators of the land.

24 She made fine linen, and sold it, and delivered a girdle to the Chanaanite.

25 Strength and beauty are her clothing, and she shall laugh in the latter day.

26 She hath opened her mouth to wisdom, and the law of clemency is on her tongue.

27 She hath looked well to the paths of her house, and hath not eaten her bread idle.

28 Her children rose up, and called her blessed: her husband, and he praised her.

29 Many daughters have gathered together riches: thou hast surpassed them all.

30 Favour is deceitful, and beauty is vain: the woman that feareth the Lord, she shall be praised.

31 Give her of the fruit of her hands: and let her works praise her in the gates.

We can first observe a general feature of the biblical text that corresponds to the thematic preoccupations of the *Shipman's Tale*. Proverbs 31:10-31 details the characteristics of an ideal wife and speaks of the ennobling effects these characteristics have upon her husband. So too does the *Shipman's Tale* focus particularly on the behavior of its wife in relation to her husband's "honor." That Chaucer conceived the tale, at least in part, as a statement about and perhaps humorously on behalf of wives is indicated by the problematic feminine persona of the opening lines as well as the merchant's spouse's own detailed account of her marital tribulations (VII, 145-47; 161-172).[11] That the couple in the tale are referred to, not by name, but only as "housbonde" and "wyf" further suggests that Chaucer wished to emphasize their conjugal roles and obligations.[12]

---

11. All line citations are from F. N. Robinson's *The Works of Geoffrey Chaucer*, 2nd ed. (Boston: Houghton Mifflin, 1957). The problem of the implied female speaker of the opening lines will be discussed below.

12. On this point see V. J. Scattergood, "The Originality of the *Shipman's Tale*," *Chaucer Review*, 11 (1977), 217.

We might easily pass over such a basic similarity if it were not for a more specific thematic congruence between the two texts. Proverbs 31:10-31 emphasizes the ideal wife's industry, modesty, and dedication; it explains how a wife contributes to the dignity of her husband, how, to borrow a phrase from the Shipman, she "keeps his goods." This manifest concern for the wife's domestic management is twice echoed in the *Shipman's Tale*, briefly at the conclusion (432) and with scripturally resonant detail in the speech in which the departing merchant charges his wife with overseeing their household:

> "... my deere wyf, I thee biseke,
> As be to every wight buxom and meke,
> And for to kepe oure good be curious,
> And honestly governe wel oure hous.
> Thou has ynough, in every maner wise,
> That to a thrifty houshold may suffise.
> Thee lakketh noon array ne no vitaille;
> Of silver in thy purs shaltow nat faille." (241-48)

Of course, the merchant's entrusting of his "goods" to his wife not only ironically anticipates his cuckolding by Daun John, whom he invites to take freely from his "chaffare" (285), but also relates to the whole tale's playful equation of sexual and financial actions and rewards. But more important for our purpose here is the merchant's significant mention of two things—"array" and "vitaille"—in which the *mulier fortis* enjoys a corresponding prosperity; the biblical passage stresses how the ideal wife's household is well provided with both clothing and food. Though the *Shipman's Tale* concerns itself only secondarily with "vitaille" (252-54), its attention to "array," a subject of incidental interest in only one of the tale's analogues (Boccaccio, *Decameron*, 8.2), is paramount; and, as I shall argue, it is a central element through which Chaucer incorporates into his tale allusions to the ideal set forth in Proverbs 31:10-31.

This respective concern of the scriptural passage and the poetic tale for the wife's household management calls our attention to other more explicit details of character, action, and imagery in the biblical text that, when viewed in light of the *Shipman's Tale*, strike a familiar chord. Besides its statements about the ideal wife's "array," Proverbs 31:10-31 comments on the value of a wife, the payment she renders her husband, and his consequent trust in her; it also speaks of the quality of the wife's business dealings, of the transience of attractive physical appearances, and of the strong woman's laughter and accumulation of riches—details whose reverberations in the Shipman's fabliau clearly point to its subtle evocation of the biblical passage. [13]

An attempt to uncover the *Shipman's Tale*'s veiled allusion to Proverbs 31:10-31 must begin with the opening lines of the story, which give

---

13. It should be noted that both the scriptural text and the poetic tale associate wives with merchants. The similarity is probably accidental, for it is just as likely that here Chaucer may be following Boccaccio and Sercambi in making the cheated husband a merchant; see Lawrence, "Chaucer's *Shipman's Tale*," p. 63.

us the noteworthy juxtaposition, unaccounted for by any of the tale's analogues, of a wife's worth with the idea of payment:

A marchant whilom dwelled at Seint-Denys,
That riche was, for which men helde hym wys.
A wyf he hadde of excellent beautee;
And compaignable and revelous was she
Which is a thyng that causeth more dispence
Than worth is al the chiere and reverence
That men hem doon at festes and at daunces.
Swiche salutaciouns and contenaunces
Passen as dooth a shadwe upon the wal;
But wo is hym that payen moot for al! (1-10)

The first verses of the scriptural passage harmoniously speak to similar concerns, observing the high price (*pretium*) of the ideal wife and the good she pays (*reddet*) her husband. Though the fictional tale and the scriptural passage begin on the same note, the tale ironically reduces the meaning of the biblical language to vulgar terms. Thus the great *pretium* of the *mulier fortis* is translated into the great "dispence" that a wife's maintenance costs her husband. The reference in Proverbs 31:12 to the good the wife renders her husband is inverted to suggest the "wo" that attends the husband who pays. Of course, the tale's initial concern with the idea of payment (as well as its elaborate punning on sexual and monetary debts) also clearly reflects the Pauline maxim that enjoined husbands and wives to pay their marriage debts (*Uxori vir debitum reddat: similiter autem et uxor viro*, 1 Cor. 7:3). But both the tale and Proverbs 31 uniquely link the subject of payment to what the wife herself is worth.

In the *Shipman's Tale* everyone pays, but the wife's payment merits the most attention. And although the tale is hardly as unequivocal as the biblical text in assessing the upright moral nature of its wife's payment—indeed the tale is a *tour de force* of moral equivocation—the manner in which the merchant's wife pays her husband resembles that of her scriptural counterpart, who renders *bonum et non malum omnibus diebus vitae suae*. In responding to her husband's gentle reproof for her failure to report Daun John's return of the hundred franks, the tale's wife declares her commitment to pay her husband regularly, "wel and redily / fro day to day" (414-15). His capitulation and final entrusting of his household to her—"Keep bet my good, this yeve I thee in charge"—may also implicitly and ironically reflect the attitude of the *mulier fortis*'s husband, whose heart *confidit in ea*.

Both the idea of a wife's value and the emphasis on payment in the *Shipman's Tale* are solidly connected to the wife's need to "arraye" herself with finery that will make her a credit to her husband. [14] The husband's

---

14. The laudable conjunction of a wife's array with her husband's honor was a commonplace of medieval feminine deportment; see, for example, the selections from the book on wifely conduct by the Ménagier de Paris, quoted in Eileen Power's *Medieval People*, 9th ed. (London: Methuen, 1963), p. 102. In the context of the other reminiscences of Proverbs 31:10-31, Chaucer's use of this timely theme in the *Shipman's Tale* takes on added significance.

conjugal obligation to "paye" for his wife's "array" and the consequent
benefit of doing so are admonished at the tale's outset:

> The sely housbonde, algate he moot paye,
> He moot us clothe, and he moot us arraye,
> Al for his owene worshipe richely,
> In which array we daunce jolily. (11-14)

and reiterated by the wife herself, first to Daun John and later to her
husband:

> "But by that ilke Lord that for us bledde,
> For his honour, myself for to arraye,
> A Sonday next I moste nedes paye
> An hundred frankes, or ellis I am lorn." (178-81)

> "And I shal paye as soone as ever I may.
> For by my trouthe, I have on myn array,
> And not on wast, bistowed every deel;
> And for I have bistowed it so weel
> For youre honour . . . ." (417-21)

A similar association of husband's honor with wife's array appears in the
mulier fortis passage, which describes a wife who spends her best efforts
providing clothing for others. But it also makes significant reference to the
garments of the ideal wife herself. She is clothed with fine fabric (22) and
with *fortitudo* and *decor* (25); such array, the passage implies, contributes
to the good name of her husband, who is *nobilis* because of her.

The conjunction of good repute and fine clothing thus applies to both
the merchant's wife and the *mulier fortis*, but the woman of St. Denis uses
her ostensibly reputable goal of enhancing her husband's honor to further
her own personal gain. Indeed, the wife's desire to "arraye" herself
prompts her to borrow the hundred franks from Daun John, thereby incur-
ring a debt that she happily pays him in the currency of sexual favors:

> And shortly to the point right for to gon,
> This faire wyf accorded with daun John
> That for thise hundred frankes he sholde al nyght
> Have hire in his armes bolt upright;
> And this acord parfourned was in dede.
> In myrthe al nyght a bisy lyf they lede . . . . (313-18)

The manner in which the wife contracts this agreement reflects the tale's
abiding concern with mercantile values and its consistent reduction of important human relationships to matters of business. But the merchant's
wife's "deal" also points out once again a congruence between her conduct and that of the ideal wife of Proverbs 31:10-31. As both the poetic tale
and the scriptural text make clear, one of the more salient aspects of the
wives' characters is their ability to do business: the *mulier fortis* buys land
and sells fine fabric (Prov. 31:16, 24), while the merchant's wife sells her
body to win the money to buy fine fabrics to adorn it. She would doubtlessly have agreed with the *mulier fortis*, who *gustavit et vidit quia bona est
negotiatio eius* (18).[15] Moreover, the wives' business ventures result in

---

15. The Wycliffite translation mirrors the language of the *Shipman's Tale* even more
distinctly: "she tastede & sawȝ: for good is þe chaffaringe of hir."

similar behaviors. These dealings occupy their energies well beyond the daylight hours: the *mulier fortis* keeps her lamp burning at night; the "bisy lyf" of the merchant's wife finds her "in myrthe al nyght."

The thematic and verbal correspondences linking the *Shipman's Tale* with Proverbs 31:10-31 that I have proposed thus far—their shared emphasis on a wife's value and payment, on honor, array, business, and domestic management—gain further support from the inclusion in both texts of an admonition on the fragility of attractive appearances, especially ones that seem to redound to the credit of a wife. Proverbs 31:30 warns that appearances are deceptive—*Fallax gratia et vana est pulchritudo*—while the opening lines of the *Shipman's Tale* assert that the "salutaciouns and contenaunces" a beautiful wife receives "passen as dooth a shadwe upon the wal." The mention of false favor and the vanity of beauty in the scriptural text serves further to highlight the passage's depiction of the ideal wife whose *pretium* resides, not in pleasant appearances, but in industrious and virtuous action. In the *Shipman's Tale*, however, quite the opposite is true. Despite the tale's initial suggestion that the worth of a beautiful wife costs too much, the husband proves willing to pay the price for such appearances. [16]

These veiled hints of the scriptural subtext scattered throughout the tale converge as the story draws to its close, and we learn that the fabliau wife once again lives up to the qualities of her ideal counterpart. Her response to her husband's request that she always report payments made by his debtors shows that she, whose strength lies in her cunning and in her clever tongue, is truly a *mulier fortis*: "This wyf was nat afered nor affrayed, / But boldely she seyde . . ." (400-401). Still more comic mirroring of the ideal wife of Proverbs 31, who laughs *in die novissimo* and who surpasses all such women who *congregaverunt divitias*, occurs in the tale's final lines. For the merchant's wife quite literally has the "last laugh"—she even enjoins her husband to share in her mirth (422); and she has indubitably gathered together riches.

On the simplest level the *Shipman's Tale* gives us a comic reduction of a commonplace of virtuous wifely conduct; it presents for our scrutiny the very idea of the *mulier fortis*: the "strong" woman who merits a high price, pays her trusting husband well, adorns herself to his honor, manages the household, succeeds in business, and triumphs in laughter—and in riches. However familiar the attributes of the biblical *mulier fortis* may have been to Chaucer and his audience, they take on a new and consistently developed ironic pattern of meaning when viewed through the fabliau lens of the *Shipman's Tale*. Before considering the precise nature of this irony, I would like to suggest the extent to which its general configuration might relate to Chaucer's original design for *The Canterbury Tales*, particularly the relationship of teller and tale. To be sure, the subtle

---

16. On the importance of appearance and illusion in the *Shipman's Tale* see A. Booker Thro, "Chaucer's Creative Comedy: A Study of the *Miller's Tale* and the *Shipman's Tale*," *Chaucer Review*, 5 (1970), 109.

reminiscence of the biblical ideal in the story of the scheming middle class couple serves as an ironic and humorous sub-text for the portrait of its far from ideal wife. But it would have been even more appropriate if, as so many critics now believe, Chaucer originally intended the *Shipman's Tale* for the Wife of Bath.[17]

Ample evidence in the Shipman's fabliau—its echoing of significant passages from the *Wife of Bath's Prologue* and *Tale* (III, 235-40; 337-47; 409-12; 1258-59); its focus on the marriage debt; the implied female persona of its opening lines—suggests that the tale could well have been first conceived for the outspoken Dame Alys of Bath. Indeed many readers of the tale would argue it is far better suited to the character of the robust wife than to the Shipman. If we assume, as so much in the *Shipman's Tale* invites us to do, that Chaucer did intend it for the Wife of Bath, that attribution takes on a new and delightful significance in view of the tale's covert allusion to the biblical ideal of the *mulier fortis*. For her demonstrable antitype is Dame Alys herself, whom Chaucer uniquely fashions in terms that resonate thematic and iconic correspondences with the *mulier fortis*. Both women are specifically characterized as wives; from this role each derives her principal identity. Furthermore, both the scriptural woman and the fictional wife are occupied with the business of clothmaking. Proverbs 31:10-31 speaks several times of the good wife's industry in this labor; illustrations of the passage in the *Bible moralisée* show the *mulier fortis* at work with her distaff.[18] The professional activities of Dame Alys, who in "clooth makyng . . . passed hem of Ypres and of Gaunt,"[19] doubtlessly serve to place her within the iconographic and interpretive tradition that designated spinning as woman's post-lapsarian labor. But the peculiar configuration of her clothmaking, her business, and her special mastery of the skills of "wifehood" ironically link her more specifically to the scriptural *mulier fortis*, who, incidentally, like Dame Alys is clothed in fine garments. Indeed, as Robert P. Miller suggests, the very idea of the *mulier fortis* may lie behind Chaucer's description of the Wife of Bath as a "worthy woman" in the General Prologue.[20]

---

17.   See Robinson, *The Works of Geoffrey Chaucer*, p. 732. The most thorough and useful discussion of the attribution of the tale to the Wife of Bath appears in Lawrence's article, cited in note 3 above.

18.   Bibl. Nat. MS. lat. 11560, fol. 59, reproduced in Miller, *Chaucer: Sources and Backgrounds*, p. 394.

19.   In a recent article Mary Carruthers argues that the Wife of Bath was a capitalist clothier, one who supervised the whole process of cloth manufacture, and not herself a maker of cloth. However accurate Carruthers' socio-economic evidence may be, I doubt that many in Chaucer's audience would have made this distinction, especially given the rich iconographic resonance of Dame Aly's occupation: "The Wife of Bath and the Painting of Lions," *PMLA*, 94 (1979), 210.

20.   *Chaucer: Sources and Backgrounds*, p. 391. The association of the Wife of Bath and the *mulier fortis* by Chaucer's contemporaries gains further support from the inclusion of Proverbs 31:10 as a gloss on 1. 689 of the *Wife of Bath's Prologue* in certain manuscripts of *The Canterbury Tales*; see Caie, "The Significance of the Early Chaucer Manuscript Glosses," p. 353. The inverted ideal of the *mulier fortis* in the character of the Wife of Bath may also be implied by the Clerk's envoy (IV, 1177-1212), which enjoins "archewyves" to be "strong as is a greet camaille" and echoes significant traits of the woman of Proverbs 31:10-31.

The playful association of the one clothmaking wife with the other would probably not have been lost on Chaucer's audience, especially if Dame Alys were to hold forth with the tale now assigned to the Shipman. For that tale, with its quiet delineation of the qualities of the *mulier fortis* lurking beneath the surface of the narrative, would have provided her the opportunity to reveal still more her ironic kinship with her scriptural alter ego. But for some reason Chaucer deprived us of that irony, possibly because he saw in the character of the Wife of Bath even greater potential for the comic inversion of scriptural lore on wifely behavior and for the debunking of all ideals of feminine conduct. Nevertheless, the *Shipman's Tale* is laden with irony, and we do not need to hear it from the mouth of the Wife of Bath to recognize how its undercurrent of biblical allusion is appropriate to its subject, which, like Proverbs 31:10-31, addresses in no small way how a wife may best conduct herself to bring "honor" to her husband and rewards to herself.

This ironic yoking together of the scriptural ideal and the comic fiction that undermines it is by no means unique to the *Shipman's Tale*. We might briefly recall, for example, that the *Miller's Tale* invites us, however momentarily, to see John and Alisoun's incongruous congruence with Joseph and Mary (the other cuckolded old carpenter and his young wife). Or we might consider how Chaucer's weaving of Edenic associations in the *Nun's Priest's Tale* permits us to view Chaunticleer and Pertilote as a neo-Adam and Eve about to enact a second fall while never letting us forget that they are but a rooster and a hen. To these playful renderings of scriptural plot and character in contexts thoroughly unsuited to them we may add other more sophisticated manipulations whose import and impact, implied rather than stated, depends upon an aping of the scriptural text. Thus in the humorous words and deeds of January and May in the *Merchant's Tale*, in the Wife of Bath in her *Prologue*, and in the portrait of the Pardoner we find the literal translation of the pious maxims of St. Paul into the realm of everyday experience.[21]

This literal appropriation of the scriptural text governs Chaucer's use of Proverbs 31:10-31 in the *Shipman's Tale*. The biblical details are secularized and transposed into a worldly, bourgeois context that renders the ideal remarkably incongruous. For the honor and rewards won by the fictional husband and wife depend, not upon demonstrated virtue, but upon shady business deals, fine clothes, and extra-marital affairs successfully concealed. But what, we must ask ourselves, is the final effect of these scriptural reminiscences? Is their purpose fulfilled simply in our humorous

---

21. Russell A. Peck, "Biblical Interpretation: St. Paul and *The Canterbury Tales*," in the present volume; Hope Phyllis Weissman, "The Pardoner's Vernicle, the Wife's Coverchiefs, and Saint Paul," *Chaucer Newsletter*, 1, no. 2 (1979), 10-12; Theresa Coletti, "The Pardoner's Vernicle and the Image of Man in the *Pardoner's Tale*," *Chaucer Newsletter*, 1, no. 1 (1979), 10-12. Along similar lines John V. Fleming has argued that Chaucer regularly appropriated exegetical details from medieval scriptural tradition, radically transplanting them into the far more worldly fabric of his poetic Canterbury fictions; see below, "Gospel Asceticism: Some Chaucerian Images of Perfection."

recognition of their presence, or do they provide a serious moral backdrop against which the fictional characters of the tale are to be viewed—and judged?[22] Chaucer rarely provided such comic juxtapositions purely for the sake of embellishing his fictions, and he is rarely so openly didactic as to point to a particular "moral" to any of his stories. Rather, the richness and the meaning of Chaucer's poetry more often resides in the tension that exists between the comic and its moral implications; his aim was not, I think, to show us what people should be, but to tell us instead what they in fact are.

In the *Shipman's Tale* the biblical ideal of wifely conduct and its ribald incarnation in the fleshly fabliau world qualify each other. If the allusions to the *mulier fortis* cast a few reprehensible shadows upon the merchant's wife, so too does her conduct provoke a reassessment of the ideal. It is laudable, to be sure, but at least for some neither possible nor desirable. The pull that the sacred text and the profane fiction exert upon each other endorses neither of them; it enjoins us instead to be tolerant of differences and to see the familiar scriptural ideal in the equally familiar fancy-dress guise of human fallibility. It is in this double consciousness, this capacious respect for variety, that much of the irony—and the originality—of the *Shipman's Tale* resides.[23]

---

22. On the subject of moral standards in the *Shipman's Tale* see Janette Richardson, "The Facade of Bawdry: Image Patterns in Chaucer's *Shipman's Tale*," *ELH*, 32 (1965), 303-13. For a more generous view of the "morality" of Chaucer's fictions see Kolve, "Chaucer and the Visual Arts," pp. 315-18.

23. After this article was accepted for publication, James Boren's essay, "Alysoun of Bath and the Vulgate 'Perfect Wife,'" *Neuphilologische Mitteilungen*, 76 (1975), 247-56, came to my attention. Boren argues that Chaucer's characterization of the Wife of Bath is enriched by allusions to the *mulier fortis* of Proverbs 31:10-31, whose exemplary behavior provides a spiritual antithesis to that of the Wife of Bath. Boren's provocative analysis of the Wife of Bath in light of the *mulier fortis* treats in greater detail the similarities between the two I suggest in this essay. More important, his discussion tacitly points to the possibility of still other connections between the Vulgate wife and the wife of the *Shipman's Tale*, whose characterization parallels that of the Wife of Bath. Boren's article as a whole reinforces my argument that Chaucer intended a cluster of associations between the scriptural ideal and her fictional antitypes, associations he playfully developed and even more playfully veiled in the *Shipman's Tale*.

Gospel Asceticism:
Some Chaucerian Images of Perfection

JOHN V. FLEMING
Princeton University

Virginitee is greet perfeccion,
And continence eek with devocion,
But Crist, that of perfeccion is welle
Bad nat every wight he sholde go selle
Al that he hadde, and gyve it to the poore
And in swich wise folwe hym and his foore.
He spak to hem that wolde lyve parfitly;
And lordynges, by youre leve, that am nat I.

Thus Magistra Alicia de Bath *in Matt. 19*. As with so much else that is delightful and outrageous in her prologue, this particular "sentence" is arresting because it manages at once to be both right and wrong. By the middle of the fourteenth-century an energetic collector, if he so chose, could have gathered together a small library devoted to the question of "perfection" in Matthew 19, the question being, of course, whether the injunction to perfection was a precept or a counsel. A precept was a moral rule binding on all Christians (required reading, so to speak); a counsel was sound and valuable advice—but not absolutely required.

The answer to the question was in a sense latitudinarian: perfection was *both* a precept *and* a counsel. It was a counsel insofar as it spoke to one's station in the moral hierarchy of the religious life, but it was a precept in terms of one's obligations within one's chosen or allotted state. In concrete terms this meant that there was no general requirement that all Christians be "evangelically poor," but that if one had taken a friar's vows, evangelical poverty was indeed required. Marriage was, clearly, not a "perfect" state; yet it was possible to live "perfectly" in marriage. Such perfection was more than a possibility; it was a requirement. All Christians were required to be perfect within their own vocations. That was the pellucid teaching of the Sermon on the Mount (Matt. 5:48).

The Wife of Bath adroitly adduces a correct argument about perfection as precept, but, as numerous other parts of her *lectio* comically demonstrate, she is much less orthodox on the question of perfection as counsel. We owe to D. W. Robertson our appreciation of the complexity of the Wife's use of Latin exegetical materials, mainly though not exclusively from the *Adversus Jovinianum* of Jerome, and of the apparent expectations which Chaucer's reliance upon them implies about his readers.[1] There has by no means been universal critical agreement concerning the interpretive conclusions Robertson draws from the materials adduced, but such controversy as there has been is irrelevant to the point of this essay. What concerns me here is the *fact* of Chaucer's repeated use of what I call "ascetical images." My argument is that Chaucer's most artistically fruitful contact with exegetical ideas and images often involves the poetic mediation of formal documents of *ascetic* theology.[2]

That the most robustly secular and intellectually generous of medieval English poets should repeatedly turn for the materials of his art to crabbed Latin texts monkish in their aspirations and unworldly in their doctrines presents what is at least an apparent paradox which, though it proves to be apparent only under scrutiny, nonetheless merits attention and speculation. If we think of the growth of the "vernacular" cultures of late medieval Europe, as we often do, in terms of the emergence of increasingly "secular" attitudes and art forms created by "lay" artists for "lay" audiences, we are telling less than half the truth, for the process which we too easily call "vernacularization" involved, at every significant level of western culture, the appropriation of essentially monastic patterns of thought adapted to the purposes of an increasingly self-confident secular society. That a number of the most worldly or "secular" of Chaucer's pilgrims, those who rush after the world and its goods with the greatest zest and passion — that such literary creations should be heavily mortgaged to the literature of *de contemptu mundi* is, however unexpected, entirely predictable.

Chaucer's depraved clerics, of whom there are a disturbing number, present the most poignant examples. That the Friar or the Pardoner is "worldly" is the mere *donnée* of their artistic conception. That Chaucer's primary appeal in presenting their worldliness is not to an experience of the actual world but to a reading of unworldly texts is another matter. His treatment of the Summoner presents a particularly stunning example of what I mean. As a social phenomenon, the summoner belongs distinctively to Chaucer's own time and even, one might argue, to his own place, England, where the structures of ecclesiastical justice had taken on both unique forms and a unique importance. He is, accordingly, one of the most "realistic" of Chaucer's pilgrims, if we mean by that that we could credibly attribute his invention to the literary quest for "local color." He has no very precise models or analogues in the religious life of classical Christendom, certainly. Yet scholars have demonstrated with increasing conviction that the most salient features of his description, the most arresting details of his literary portrait, details of physiognomy, of diet, of apparel, have at least as much connection with traditions of scriptural exegesis already an-

---

1. *A Preface to Chaucer* (Princeton, 1962), pp. 317 ff.
2. I am grateful to the editors of *Christianity and Literature* and *The Chaucer Review* for permission to use materials which first appeared in those journals in two articles of mine: "Chaucer's Ascetical Images," *C & L* 28 (1979) 19-26, and "Daun Piers and Dom Pier: Waterless Fish and Unholy Hunters," in press at *CR*.

cient in the fourteenth-century as they possibly could have with empirical observation. Thus the Summoner loves garlic, onions, and leeks not because it is a "realistic detail" to love garlic, onions, and leeks, but because it is an appetite which identifies him immediately as a reprobate pilgrim lusting after the fleshpots of Egypt.[3]

If we turn from the Summoner's portrait in the General Prologue to his own tale, the fact of scriptural authority becomes even more remarkable. The *Summoner's Tale* has, as a primary focus, an explicitly ascetical subject, the religious life of friars. Its satire is so persistent, unrelenting indeed, as to become in fact a sustained essay in literary caricature.[4] The vanity, the carnality, the unbridled hypocrisy of the friar who is the tale's central character are underscored with a variety of brilliant but hyperbolic poetic techniques, so that the portrait becomes, as Robertson has put it, a kind of anthology of all the charges that had ever been made anywhere in Europe during more than a century of anti-fraternal polemic. That this creation has been hailed as a triumph of "realism"—and indeed Friar John has more than once been called a "typical" fourteenth-century English friar—is a testimony to the alchemical powers of art rather than to those of empirical observation.

The clear and demonstrable fact is that the friar in the *Summoner's Tale* walked into *The Canterbury Tales* not from the dusty roads of fourteenth-century England but from the pages of a literary tradition of scriptural inspiration, a tradition already becoming "classic" in Chaucer's time but nonetheless learned and in many respects even arcane. Some of what Chaucer does in the *Summoner's Tale* had already been done by Jean de Meun in the creation of Faussemblant in the *Roman de la Rose*, but many specific details in Chaucer's text make it clear that he was familiar with Jean's own primary source, the opaque polemic of William of Saint-Amour entitled *De periculis novissimorum temporum*. To put the matter another way, the *Summoner's Tale* has as its very foundation—not a mere decorative detail but its very foundation—the specialized tradition of scriptural exegesis associated with the ascetical texts of the mendicant controversy at Paris in the 1250s. The very materials for the vibrant and tactile secularity of one of Chaucer's earthiest characters have been appropriated from the exegetical traditions of Christian asceticism. And in this, we may say that Chaucer is the rule for vernacular poets rather than the exception. In France we have the clear models of Jean de Meun and Rutebeuf before him, in England his own contemporaries Langland and Gower. Each of these poets, in his own way and in varying degrees, has "secularized" privileged ascetical texts, but with Chaucer the process is radical, fundamental. One can no more understand the strategies of the *Summoner's Tale*

---

3. There is a clear reference to Numbers 11:5. See the illuminating note by R. E. Kaske, "The Summoner's Garleek, Oynons, and eek Lekes," *MLN*, 74 (1959), 481-84; also Chauncey Wood, above.
4. See Penn R. Szittya, "The Friar as False Apostle," *SP*, 71 (1974), 19-46 and John V. Fleming, "The Antifraternalism of the *Summoner's Tale*," *JEGP*, 65 (1966), 688-700.

without reading the *De periculis* than one can understand the Wife of Bath without reading Jerome against Jovinian.

I have written at length of these matters elsewhere. The Summoner and his tale might be described as secular reflexes of the medieval literature of Christian perfection. So are others, including the Summoner's "freend and compeer," the Pardoner. In a general sense, the Pardoner reflects the literary ancestry of Faussemblant in the *Roman de la Rose* as well. Like the Summoner, he has often seemed to critics to be too closely wedded to the specific ecclesiastical conditions of late medieval England to be anything other than a "real-life character," in whose creation observatio must have taken priority over invention. Yet in fact practically every detail in his literary portrait is controlled by one or another strand of medieval scriptural tradition. This fact is in itself not unremarkable; but even more significant is the way in which, even in the act of borrowing, Chaucer makes traditional exegetical details distinctively his own. Consider, for example, the small matter of basket-weaving. The Pardoner, in his prologue, distances himself from the major traditions of medieval ascetic theory in the following terms:

> What, trowe ye, that whiles I may preche,
> And wynne gold and silver for I teche,
> That I wol lyve in poverte wilfully?
> Nay, nay, I thoghte it nevere, trewely!
> I wol nat do no labour with myne handes,
> Ne make baskettes, and lyve therby,
> By cause I wol nat beggen ydelly.
> I wol noon of the apostles countrefete . . . . (439-447)

His general drift is clear, but questions do arise. Why, of all the useful things in the world the Pardoner might not do in order to remain idle, does he choose not to make baskets? And what does this have to do with imitating or not imitating the apostles? F. N. Robinson, in his explanatory note on this passage, finds an allusion to Jerome's *Vita Pauli*. Paul was indeed a basket-maker, but so were many of the desert fathers whose anecdotes were collected into the *Vitae patrum*. Robinson goes on to suggest that Chaucer, like many of his later commentators, may have confused Paul the Apostle with Paul the Hermit. "Whether Chaucer himself was confused (note the apostles, 1. 447) is not clear."[5] In fact, Chaucer is not in the slightest degree confused. His allusion to basket-making does not conflate Paul the Hermit with Paul the Apostle but it does collate an idea of ascetic industry found in the most ancient Christian hagiographic texts with scriptural images of apostolic life; and in doing so he follows a clear but specialized tradition of scriptural exegesis most conspicuously represented in his day in the texts surrounding the "friar question." Arnold Williams noted many years ago an important parallel use of the image of basket-making in an obscure work called the *Protectorium Pauperis* by Chaucer's contemporary, the Carmelite Richard of Maidstone. I myself would cavil at Williams' suggestion only to the extent of pointing out that the passage in

---

5. *The Works of Geoffrey Chaucer* (Boston, 1957), p. 730.

the *Protectorium* is a virtual quotation from a much more famous book, St. Bonaventure's *Apologia pauperum*, a book easily available to Chaucer and undoubtedly well known to many members of his audience.[6] The reason that the Pardoner will not make baskets is that a long tradition of ascetic exegesis, beginning at least with Jerome and actually incorporated into the *Glossa ordinaria*, tells him that is how the apostles made their living!

The Pardoner can provide us with a second example, this time from the description in the General Prologue. In drawing attention to the peculiarly repulsive hair of the Pardoner, Chaucer explains that it was visible because he rode unhooded:

> But hood, for jolitee, wered he noon,
> For it was trussed up in his walet.
> Hym thoughte he rood al of the newe jet;
> Dischevelee, save his cappe, he rood al bare.
> Swiche glarynge eyen hadde he as an hare.
> A vernycle hadde he sowed upon his cappe.
> His walet lay biforn hym in his lappe,
> Bretful of pardoun, comen from Rome al hoot.
> A voys he hadde as smal as hath a goot.
> No berd hadde he, he nevere sholde have;
> As smothe it was as it were late shave.
> I trowe he were a geldyng or a mare. (680-91)

Many of the details in this famous description have attracted illuminating scholarly commentary based on the use of medieval exegetical materials—the animal imagery, the vernicle, the "glaring eyen"; but surely the most exciting such study remains R. P. Miller's brilliant essay on the Pardoner and the scriptural tradition of the spiritual eunuch.[7] Miller has shown that the jarring and somewhat inconsistent references to the Pardoner's want of sexual organs ("I trowe he were a gelding or a mare"), coarsely taken up again at the end of the *Pardoner's Tale* by the provoked Harry Bailly, who wishes he could castrate him and enshrine the results in a "hogges toord," are best understood in terms of the exegetical traditions surrounding the passage in Matthew 19:12: "For there are eunuchs which were so born from their mother's womb: and there are eunuchs, which were made eunuchs by men; and there are eunuchs which made themselves eunuchs for the kingdom of heaven's sake."

The passage in Matthew 19 which gives the central image of the "spiritual eunuch" ("those who have made themselves eunuchs for the kingdom of heaven's sake") is of course a recurrent authority in the major ascetic texts of medieval Christianity, including many of the monastic *regulae* themselves. The idea involves a paradox: that religious chastity is in fact a kind of fecundity. In a similar vein Chaucer underscores, in the

---

6. Arnold Williams, "Some Documents on English Pardoners, 1350-1400" in *Mediaeval Studies in Honor of Urban Tigner Holmes, Jr.*, ed. John Mahoney and John E. Keller (Chapel Hill, 1965), pp. 204-5. Williams refers to his edition of the *Protectorium Pauperis* in Carmelus, 5 (1958), 178; but cf. Bonaventure, *Apologia pauperum*, XII, 14.

7. "Chaucer's Pardoner, the Scriptural Eunuch, and the Pardoner's Tale," *Speculum*, 30 (1955), 180-99.

character of the Pardoner, a cruel victory of flesh over spirit through two contrasting patterns of poetic imagery: on the one hand sterility, on the other increase. The Pardoner is a gelding; yet he amasses silver, and his false relics promise the multiplication of crops and cattle.

The detail to which I should like to draw attention, however, involves what the Pardoner has rather than what he lacks. What does the Pardoner actually have in lieu of his missing members of generation? Here Chaucer indulges his taste, acquired from Dante and Jean de Meun among others, for the cerebrally grotesque. What the Pardoner has instead of sexual organs is a *purse*. "But hood, for jolitee, wered he noon" writes Chaucer; "for it was trussed up in his *wallet*." And he goes on to tell us precisely where the Pardoner wears his purse:

> His wallet lay biforn hym in his lappe,
> Bretful of pardoun, comen from Rome al hoot. (686-87)

The phallic possibilities of the medieval purse thus worn are frequently exploited in medieval visual art, but I think that Chaucer here takes his own cue from literary tradition and, specifically, from the *Roman de la rose*, where the Lover, in a lengthy flight of fancy as remarkable for its rhetorical self-confidence as for its indisputably dubious taste, compares in tedious anatomical detail his shameful members with a pilgrim's script. The Pardoner's purse is stuffed nearly to bursting with the instruments of his dubious multiplication, his "hooly bull," parchment entrails, tubular scrolls from which dangle leaden pendants, the *bullae* themselves, as much a coarse double-entendre in medieval Latin as in modern English.

Within the general economy of the Pardoner's description, the purse is a matte image which draws little attention to itself, claiming only a quiet place in the overall scheme of Gothic decoration which makes up the Pardoner's "portrait." Yet I think it offers us a good example of the kind of privileged exegetical vocabulary which came to Chaucer through the literature of medieval asceticism and which he transmuted for the purposes of a poem profoundly engaged with the realities of *this* world.

For the fact of the matter is that discussions of Christian perfection in the thirteenth and fourteenth-century sometimes seems to be obsessed with what might be called the "purse question."[8] Was it lawful for a Christian to carry a purse? More to the point, was it right for a Christian *who sought to be perfect* to carry a purse? Most to the point of all, perhaps, did Christ himself carry a purse? The scriptural authority on the question seemed ambiguous. On the one hand there was the clear injunction of Christ in commissioning his apostles that they should carry nothing with them for the journey, "neither scrip nor staff." On the other hand there was the equally clear evidence of John 12 and 13 that Judas carried a purse, certainly by Christ's leave and possibly by his command. The Vulgate text has a plural in these two passages, *loculos*, "little purses." Chaucer makes

---

8. See John V. Fleming, *An Introduction to the Franciscan Literature of the Middle Ages* (Chicago, 1977), pp. 87-88.

explicit reference to one of them (John 12:6) in a context which shows he was entirely aware of its significance in ascetical literature. The Friar says of the summoner who is the subject of his tale:

> And right as Judas hadde purses smale,
> And was a theef, right swich a theef was he. (1350-51)

A good deal of ink, and inevitably some blood too, was spilled over the "purse question." In Chaucer's days theories of ascetic perfection centered largely, though by no means exclusively, around the debates concerning the mendicant orders. Both William of Saint-Amour, the antifraternal polemicist, and St. Bonaventure, the friars' most powerful and effective defender, explore the question in some depth. Bonaventure, indeed, habitually identifies the *perfecti* — "hem that wolde lyve parfitly," in the Wife of Bath's translation — simply as "those that bear no purse."[9]

The examples so far adduced show some of the possibilities which Chaucer found in the exegetical vocabulary of Christian perfection. Access to it laid the foundations for a particularly witty and sophisticated kind of clerical satire: David could once more slay Goliath with his own sword. Such images are "simple" in the sense that their primary if not sole intertextual obligation is scriptural. There are, however, more complex examples involving more complex intertextuality. When we read the description of Chaucer's Monk — concerning whose moral character there can be little doubt as to where the poet stands — we note that he is a "modern" churchman whose modernity is nowhere better illustrated than in his *literary* attitudes. He explicitly rejects the authority of ancient ascetical documents. Two examples are especially conspicuous. He regards the Benedictine rule itself as outmoded and impractical — "it was old and somdel streit" — and he rejects with forthright contempt the central doctrine of Augustine's *De opere monachorum*. The one text is explicitly mentioned, the other clearly alluded to. Both were definitive "classics." He also rejects the authority of a mystery "text":

> He yaf nat of that text a pulled hen,
> That seith that hunters ben nat hooly men,
> Ne that a monk, whan he is recheless,
> Is likned til a fissh that is waterlees, —
> That is to seyn, a monk out of his cloystre.
> But thilke text heeld he nat worth an oystre.... (177-82)

The passage is problematical in more than one respect. There is in the first place something of a syntactical puzzle. Chaucer uses the word "text" in line 177 in the singular, yet seems to give *two* texts, one about unholy, and a second about cloisterless, monks. I have found no explicit discussion of this problem, but the implicit solution has been to posit a rather elaborate ellipsis at line 179: "Ne [that text that seith] that a monk...." Edmund Reiss, in an important article, writes thus: "The text that says that 'hunters ben nat hooly men' is what is not worth a *pulled hen*; that which says

---

9. His actual phrase is "religio carentium loculis"; see the *titulus* to *Apologia pauperum*, X.

a monk out of his cloister is like a fish out of water is what is not worth an oystre." [10] That may well be correct, though it is also possible that the *ne* of line 179 has a general conjunctive force, that "pulled hen" and "oystre" are alternative terms for an object of little worth, and that *thilke* (182) has its normal function of reaffirming an object already clearly stated and thus refers to a single text which contains both ideas.

But the syntactical problem, whether "solved" or merely finessed, leads immediately to another layer of difficulty, and that is the question of "source." The two texts, or the two independent clauses of the one text, have been troublesome for different reasons. Scholars have found the one nowhere, the other everywhere. Is there a "text that seith that hunters ben nat hooly men" in so many words? The Bible has some good hints in that general direction, and Rudolph Willard uncovered a very rich vein of relevant antivenatical commonplaces in canon law; but no one has been able to produce an "original" of which Chaucer's text could be said to be a quotation or a translation. [11] The fish out of water is, as it were, from a different kettle. The phrase is a cliché for us, and probably was for Chaucer; and its application to an exclaustrated monk is so common that it can rightly be regarded as proverbial. [12] One can hunt only so long for a text that will say that hunters are unholy, and we should perhaps try another track. Is it possible to identify a text in which Chaucer's three principal ideas—unholy hunters, cloisterless monks, and waterless fish—are linked within a context which can illuminate the spiritual portrait of his Monk?

The answer is that there is indeed at least one such text in the classical repertory of medieval asceticism; it will be found in the prologue to Peter Damian's celebrated essay on the omnipotence of God. Both its actual words and its larger contextual implications are highly relevant to Chaucer's Monk. That Peter Damian is indeed the undiscovered "source" of the troublesome lines, though not demonstrably certain, seems to me likely; what *is* certain is that Chaucer is once again appropriating the imagery of specialized ascetic texts.

Chaucer's monk is an "outridere," a term which Paul Beichner, who wrote something of an apology for him, has nicely translated into the modern idiom as "business administrator." [13] Beichner supplies evidence to show that Chaucer's outrider would not have been alone among fourteenth-century monks in rejecting the old-fashioned ideas of Benedictine tradition in favor of more streamlined and secular ones. What Chaucer himself thought is another matter. What he says is "I seyde his opinion

---

10. "The Symbolic Surface of *The Canterbury Tales*: The Monk's Portrait," *CR*, 2 (1967), 265.

11. "Chaucer's 'Text that seith that hunters been nat hooly men,'" [Texas] *Studies in English* (1947), 209-51.

12. "Monachus extra claustrum est sicut piscis extra aquam." Hans Walther, *Proverbia sententiaeque medii aevi latina*, no. 15026a.

13. "Daun Piers, Monk and Business Administrator," *Speculum*, 24 (1959), 611-19.

was good"—by which he certainly means that he thinks it was bad. So did Peter Damian.

Is it possible for a man to be at once a true monk and a "business administrator"? Peter Damian himself had occasion to ponder that question when he found himself wrenched from monastic solitude and charged with the administrative duties of a cardinal bishop. His answer to his own mute question was to resign the episcopal office to return to a hermit's cell. He describes that moment in his own spiritual biography with an elaborate metaphor of shipwreck. His brief stint as "business administrator" he likens to experiencing a howling ocean storm in a small boat. In his nearly miraculous escape from business administration he is like the shipwrecked mariner providentially thrown upon the beach still alive by the violence of the storm. Likewise it is the answer to this question, thus gained from personal experience, which he offers to the Abbot Desiderius. "Errat, pater, errat, qui confidit se simul et monachus esse et curiae deservire. Quam male mercatur qui comachorum praesumit claustra deserere, ut mundi valeat militiam baiulare." [14] Certain of his phrases (*curiae deseruire, mundi militiam baiulare*) may well find their echo in Chaucer's own wonderfully ironic question—"How shall the world be served?" And the verb *mercatur* has a happy resonance for the kind of trafficking engaged in by Daun John in the *Shipman's Tale*. Peter's whole text reads as follows:

> Qui solus de marini fluctus procellis eripitur, dum sagenam adhuc inter rupes et scopulos, inter minaces atque intumescentes undarum cumulos periclitari considerat, inhumanus est si laborantes in discrimine socios non deplorat. Ego itaque, episcopatu dimisso, me quidem uelut arenis expositum gaudeo; sed te uentis adhuc atque turnibus atteri, ac inter hiantis pelagi fluctuare uoraginem, non sine fraterna compassione suspiro. Errat, pater, errat, qui confidit se simul et monachum esse et curiae deseruire. Quam male mercatur qui monachorum praesumit claustra deserere, ut mundi ualeat militiam baiulare. Vndis erutus sanus est piscis, non ut sibi uiuat, sed ut alios pascat. Vocamur, attrahimur, sed ut uiuamus aliis, moriamur nobis. Amat uenator ceruum, sed ut faciat cibum; persequitur capreas, lepusculos insectatur; sed ut ipse bene sit, illa nichil sint. Amant et homines nos, sed non nobis; sibimet diligunt, in suas non uertere delicias concupiscunt. [15]

The larger contextual congruences which may link the two passages include the emblematic capacities of the two monks, the one addressed by Peter Damian and the one described by Chaucer. Chaucer's monk is "a manly man, to ben an abbot able." Desiderius *was* an abbot, the abbot indeed of Monte Cassino, the premier house of Benedictine monachism, and therefore an almost natural representative of monastic aspiration. That aspiration was to an "angelic" life, not to a "manly" one, which is no doubt one of the reasons why Peter elsewhere addressed Desiderius as "the archangel of monks." [16] The whole point of the prologue, though, is that the "angel" stands in a fair way to becoming a "business administrator," and thus to giving the lie to the monk within him.

---

14. Pierre Damien, *Lettre sur la Toute-Puissance divine*, ed. André Cantin (Paris, 1972), p. 384.

15. *Lettre sur la Toute-Puissance*, ed. Cantin, 384, 386.

16. *Lettre sur la Toute-Puissance*, p. 47.

The actual ideas in the two texts share a kinship of rhetorical wittiness in the use of traditional materials, not a filiation of "source" and "translation."[17] We may note that Peter Damian does not *cite* a text to the effect that a monk out of his cloister is like a fish out of water; he *alludes* to one, and with an intellectual and poetic cleverness that may well have appealed to another poet. We may think of a fish out of water as a creature out of its element, flopping helplessly in a creel, gasping at the gills. That would hardly be an apt description of Chaucer's outrider, however. His "element" is not the cloister, but the world which he serves and in which he is a "fair prelaat," very much alive and pricking.

Peter's text would seem to have prepared such a possibility with its clever reversal of a metaphor already established. For the shipwrecked mariner (the monk burdened with worldly service) to be thrown from the water onto the beach was a providential salvation. For the netted fish, on the other hand (the monk captured by the world), that same journey from water to land has an altogether different meaning. The fish is indeed still alive and unharmed —*sanus* is the word Peter uses —yet "not to live at his own will, but in order to be the food of others."

Peter then moves from waterless fish to hunters. In Chaucer's description the vocabulary of the chase is marked by obvious double-entendres —*venerye, full many a deyntee hors, prikyng* —which suggest a connection between the Monk's passion for the hunt and other sorts of passions.[18] Yet it is clear that he is a "real" hunter too, and that Chaucer dwells on his hunting as a general emblem of his immersion in worldly affairs. The emphasis in Peter Damian is rather different, but he too shows how the relationship of hunter and prey is a "love" relationship. "The hunter loves the deer, but so that he can make him food." (Chaucer's Monk knows something of this love: "A fat swan loved he best of any roost.") But this is also how the world "loves" monks. Hunters are not holy men, merely hungry men. And in Peter Damian's complex image it is in fact holy men —that is to say, true monks —who become their food.

The congruences to which I have drawn attention are substantial, numerous, and to a degree specific. Peter Damian was widely respected in the fourteenth-century, and the *De divina omnipotentia* alone has survived in more than a hundred manuscripts.[19] The hypothesis that Chaucer "used" Damian, directly or indirectly, seems to me both attractive and reasonable, but it is only an hypothesis. Yet we can perhaps push matters further by examining a corollary involving a famous vernacular analogue to Chaucer's text. Chaucer's Monk is not anonymous, as we learn only when the Knight interrupts his mirthless catena of tragedies. The knight calls him Peter —or "daun Piers by your name." Given the demonstrably witty way in which Chaucer often names his characters —Madame Eglantine, hende

---

17.   For a brief rhetorical analysis of Peter's prologue see Angelo Benedetti, *Contemplazione e poesia in Pier Damiano* (Brescia, 1975), pp. 30-31.

18.   Robertson, *Preface to Chaucer*, p. 253.

19.   *Lettre sur la Toute-Puissance*, p. 351.

Nicholas, January, May, Aurelius, and so on—it may well be that Chaucer is amusing himself and at least some of his readers by drawing attention through daun Piers to Dom Pier, an earlier and somewhat more reputable authority on "modern" monasticism.

Certainly he would have had authoritative warrant for using Peter Damian as a literary emblem of traditional monastic aspiration in a vernacular poem. In the twenty-first canto of the *Paradiso* Dante introduces Peter Damian precisely as a rebuke to "modern" churchmen:

> Render solea quel chiostro a questi cieli
> fertilmente; e ora è fatto vano,
> sì che tosto convien che si riveli. . . .
> Venne Cefàs e venne il gran vasello
> de lo Spirito Santo, magri e scalzi,
> prendendo il cibo da qualunque ostello.
> Or voglion quinci e quindi chi rincalzi
> li moderni pastori e chi li meni,
> tanto son gravi, e chi di rietro li alzi.
> Cuopron d'i manti loro i palafreni,
> sì che due bestie van sott'una pelle:
> oh pazïenza che tanto sostieni![20]

The "cloister [that] used to yield abundant harvest" is Peter's own former hermitage at Fonte Avellana. Peter goes on to speak of leaving the hermit's life in much the same terms as those he used in the letter to the Abbot Desiderius. Being an "outrider" is to be dragged to "that hat which ever passes down from bad to worse."

Peter Damian obliquely alludes to Peter and Paul, the authentic emblems of apostolic life, whom he bitterly constrasts with *modern pastors* ("pastori moderni"). The apostles were "lean and barefoot, taking their food at whatsoever inn." Their "modern" counterparts, on the other hand, are so heavy that they must be propped up by attendants. "They cover their palfreys with their mantles, so that two beasts go under one hide." Even while recognizing that these images reflect commonplaces of monastic satire, I should point out that nearly all this material reappears in Chaucerian form, whether in negative or positive image, in the portrait of Daun Piers. He is neither lean nor barefoot. "He was a lord ful fat and in good poynt. . . . His bootes souple, his horse in greet estaat." The parallel phrase "in good poynt" and "in greet estaat" rhetorically link horse and rider in a way which underscores the likeness of the two beasts. The phrase "in greet estaat" probably refers to some kind of ostentatious caparison, like Dante's *manti*, of which the jingling bridle bells are also a part. Finally, though Chaucer rarely uses the word palfrey, he does so here: "His palfrey was as broun as is a berye." Palfrey is Dante's word too: *palefrini*.

My suggestion would be that Chaucer has followed Dante in seeing in Peter Damian an appropriate emblem of that "sacred zeal," often savage in

---

20. *Paradiso*, xxi, 118-120, 127-135. The text and translated phrases are from the edition of Charles S. Singleton (Princeton, 1975).

its rhetorical expression, which both poets share in their handling of ecclesiastical corruption.[21] Among the several strands of imagery and invective which interlace in the textured portrait of Daun Piers in the General Prologue is one that leads back through the twenty-first canto of the *Paradiso* to "that text that seith that hunters ben nat hooly men," in the prologue of another famous book by another famous man, who, by his very person no less than by his writings, might suggest a monastic ideal sharply distinct from that of business administration.

The Summoner, the Pardoner, and the Monk are, of course, official religious, and it is in a sense logical that their literary antecedents come from the pages of "religious" literature. What of Chaucer's "secular" characters? That his use of ascetical imagery is not confined to the clerisy is demonstrated most conspicuously and most delightfully by the Wife of Bath, but one can adduce other examples—and yet others would probably be revealed by deeper research. Among the most widely read of medieval ascetic tracts, no doubt admired as much for its style as for its substance, is the "Letter to Eustochium" (*Epistola xxii*) of Jerome. The importance of this essay for the aristocratic art of the late Middle Ages has long been known to art historians, who have found in it the primary source of Hieronymite iconography; its relevance to Chaucer has not so far as I know been explored.[22] One particularly remarkable passage draws a vivid satirical sketch of the worldly clergy of the Urbs, all too much at ease in Zion, whose aspirations are to hobnob (and worse) with elegant society ladies rather than to serve God. Their affectations of dress and foppishness make of them "sponsos magis quam clericos."[23] Jerome's identification of them as the pseudo-apostles of 2 Timothy anticipates William of Saint-Amour, who is in fact writing in a fairly well established satirical tradition, and seems also to have suggested to Chaucer an admirable model of false dandyism.

At any rate his own two most memorable dandies—the Squire of the Prologue and Absolon of the *Miller's Tale*—both seem to have passed through Jerome's scriptorium. The Squire is "a lovyere and a lusty bacheler, / with lokkes crulle as they were leyd in presse" (80-81). This is a fair rendition of Jerome on the monastic fops of Rome: "Crines calamastri vestigio rotantur." Here Chaucer has merely made a feint, and his real masterpiece of the type is the dandy Absolon, who is an almost perfect Hieronymite *poseur*. He is better suited to the task, being a minor cleric, the local thurifer, whose occupation (as Chaucer puts it with a wicked pun) is "sensynge the wyves of the parisshe faste." Like the Squire, Absolon has frizzed hair, and it is further conspicuous for its abundance. His fancy

21.   See Giovanni Cattani, "Il sacro zelo di san Pier Damiani a sostegno del sacro zelo di Dante nell'invettiva religiosa della *Commedia* (*Par.*, c. xxi)," *S. Pier Damiani: Atti del Convegno di studi nel ix centenario della morte* (Faenza [1973]), 43-67.

22.   See Millard Meiss, "Scholarship and Penitence in the Early Renaissance: The Image of St. Jerome," *Pantheon*, 32 (1974), 134-140; reprinted in Meiss, *The Painter's Choice* (New York, 1976), pp. 189 ff.

23.   Saint-Jérome, *Lettres*, ed. Jérome Labourt (Paris, 1949), I, p. 142 (*Epistola xxii*, 28).

shoes (3118 ff.), his golden ring (1704), his perfumes (3690), and several other details echo the fatuities of a man Jerome calls the "prince" of pretenders.[24]

> Whan that the firste cok hath crowe, anon
> Up rist this joly lovere Absolon,
> And hym arraieth gay, at poynt-devys . . .
> He rometh to the carpenteres hous,
> And still he stant under the shot-wyndowe. (3687-89, 3694-95)

"Cum sole festinus exurgit; salutandi ei ordo disponitur; uiarum conpedia requiruntur, et paene usque ad cubilia dormientium senex inportunus ingreditur."[25] There is no question of "translation" here, but of a witty transformation. There are many other claims on Absolon—including those of his long-haired biblical namesake and of Chaucer's own powerfully inventive mind—but one general model is a thumbnail satirical sketch from the *Ad Eustochium*.

Numerous other examples of Chaucer's explicit or covert use of the literature of Christian perfection could be adduced. They may help to remind us of the extent to which poetic learning and ascetic doctrine went together in the late Middle Ages and the Renaissance, and how it could be, for example, that among the most "humanistic" productions of such representatives figures as Petrarch, Valla, and Erasmus are formal *encomia* of monastic life.[26] Chaucer's greatest French debt was to Jean de Meun— the author of the *Testament* no less than of the *Roman de la Rose*. He learned most about Italian narrative from Boccaccio, a man most famous in his own day for a work now little read—the *De casibus*. Though the Knight might "stint" its dreary rehashing by the Monk, he could by no means banish its Boethian truths—or turns of phrase—from the poet's major works. The author of the *Summoner's Tale* was the same man that translated the *De contemptu mundi* of the Cardinal Lothario.

Christian ascetic doctrine was based upon certain powerful traditions of scriptural exegesis, and from John Cassian to Francis of Assisi discussions of Christian perfection in the Latin West are controlled by a number of vivid pictorial images rather than by abstract and discursive formulations. Such images are almost invariably of scriptural origin: the just and rustic Abel, Jacob's ladder, Mount Carmel, Jesus in the desert, the charismatic socialism of the apostolic church of Jerusalem. They were the images which nourished the Christian ascetic imagination for a thousand years, stimulating a desire for new experiences beyond the tumult of the flesh, a new nature, a new creation, a new Jerusalem. What Chaucer discovered, together with other great vernacular poets of his tradition, was that such images could also inform the most powerful description of the imperfect creation which he saw about him.

---

24. *Ibid.*
25. *Ibid.*
26. See Robert Bultot, "La *Chartula* et l'enseignement du mépris du monde dans les écoles et les universités médiévales," *Studi medievali*, 3rd series, 8 (1967), 787-834.

Scriptural Testament in *The Canterbury Tales*: The Letter Takes Its Revenge

JOHN A. ALFORD
Michigan State University

When the Wife of Bath presumes to preach on the subject "of wo that is in mariage"—enlisting the aid of Scripture at every turn—she provokes a debate not only about marriage but also about exegesis. How should a text be interpreted? Obviously her own practice leaves much to be desired. As Alfred David shows, "It is a fact that practically every reference the Wife makes to Holy Writ twists its meaning and violates if not the letter, then the spirit of the law."[1] As soon as she finishes her tale, the Friar admonishes her to "lete auctoritees, in Goddes name, / To prechyng and to scole eek of clergye"—in short, to professional glossators like himself. But his real quarrel lies with another. Following the direction begun by Dame Alice, he tells of an obtuse summoner whose inability to see beyond the letter to the spirit or "entente" leads ultimately to his own damnation. The Summoner then responds with a tale about a "glosyng" friar whose contempt of the letter is, if anything, even more obtuse.[2]

Seen from this point of view, the three performances that make up Fragment D of *The Canterbury Tales* are a coherent whole. What follows the Wife's *Tale* is not simply, as Kittredge put it, a "comic interlude" in the marriage debate but rather a continuation of the issue raised by her handling of scriptural authority. The pervasive concern throughout is the relation between letter and gloss. Moreover, the impression of unity is strengthened by a steady departure from decorum, which parallels the erosion of romantic idealism in Fragment A.[3] The Wife blithely perverts both the letter and the spirit as it suits her purpose, and yet she does so with

---

1. *The Strumpet Muse: Art and Morals in Chaucer's Poetry* (Bloomington, 1976), p. 138.

2. For the idea that the Friar's Tale exploits the distinction between the letter and the spirit, see D. W. Robertson, Jr., *A Preface to Chaucer* (Princeton, 1962), p. 268. The distinction is further elaborated and extended to the Summoner's Tale by Mary Carruthers, "Letter and Gloss in the Friar's and Summoner's Tales," *The Journal of Narrative Technique*, 2 (1972), 208-14.

3. For a summary of the progressive decline of style, morals, and idealism in Fragment A, see John H. Fisher, ed., *The Complete Poetry and Prose of Geoffrey Chaucer* (New York, 1977), p. 8.

such obvious good humor that no one is really offended. There is a touch of admiration as well as irony in the Pardoner's praise: "Ye been a noble prechour in this cas." But the Friar's performance represents a sharp falling-off. Although the Host reminds him, "A! sire, ye sholde be hende / And curteys, as a man of youre estaat," he presses on with his malicious tale of a summoner who is blind to the spirit. Finally, in the Summoner's angry retort about a friar slain by the letter, we touch bottom. It is the most scatological of all the *Tales*.[4]

This essay focuses on the Summoner's contribution to the debate. Although the Wife first draws attention to the practice of "glosyng," and although the Friar is the most qualified by training to illustrate its proper use, it is the Summoner who exploits most fully and directly the metaphorical possibilities of the distinction between the letter and the spirit. Moreover, in doing so, he clearly suggests the appropriate context for dealing with the scriptural parody at the heart of the tale.

Before identifying the biblical passage in question, I would like to review briefly the importance of "glosyng" as a theme in the tale. This word, as many critics have noted, may be taken in two ways. Well before Chaucer's time it had come to mean not only "commenting on Scripture" but also (an indication, perhaps, of popular cynicism about the method) "perverting the meaning of, lying, deceiving through flattery." In this latter sense of the word, the hypocritical Friar's ability to "glosen" is everywhere apparent. He flatters the old man's wife: "Yet saugh I nat this day so fair a wyf / In al the chirche." Then, in accepting the hoped-for dinner invitation, he makes gluttony sound like a virtue: "Have I nat of a capon but the lyvere, / And of youre softe breed nat but a shyvere, / And after that a rosted pigges heed . . . . / I am a man of litel sustenaunce." When informed of the death of their child, he pretends to have seen his soul carried to heaven in a vision—a privilege granted only to friars because of their clean living. And repeatedly, all the while extolling his own devotion to poverty, he nags sick Thomas for more money: "Youre maladye," he says, "is for we han to lyte":

> Thomas, of me thou shalt nat been yflatered;
> Thou woldest han oure labour al for noght.
> The hye God, that al this world hath wroght,
> Seith that the werkman worthy is his hyre.[5]

---

4. In fact, a sense of personal propriety has kept many critics from giving the tale the attention it deserves. The opinion expressed by G. K. Anderson is not uncommon: "Highly unsavory" and not calling for "further comment" (*Old and Middle English Literature* [Oxford, 1950], p. 159). In his book *The Idea of the Canterbury Tales*, Donald Howard gives barely a page to the tale. The Summoner's response to the Friar is "pre-adolescent filth" and his tale is no better: "As a way of laying down a curse on an opponent it is childish and primitive and shows the Summoner's grossness: his 'scatological vision' may get down to the basics of anal aggression, but that only shows the Summoner's infantile level" (Berkeley, 1976), p. 257. As "criticism" this is not really very helpful. No one doubts the Summoner's "grossness." The more important question—as in the case of the Miller or Pardoner—concerns the ways in which the tale transcends the moral failure of its teller.

5. All quotations of the text are from F. N. Robinson, ed., *The Works of Geoffrey Chaucer*, 2nd ed. (Boston, 1961).

By this time, angry Thomas is quite ready to pay the workman exactly what he is worth.

"Glosyng" is a word not only for the Friar's "false dissymulacioun," however, but also for his own special way of reading Scripture. Hardly has he taken a place beside Thomas's bed when he begins harping on the idea:

> I have to day been at youre chirche at messe.
> And seyd a sermon after my symple wit,
> Nat al after the text of hooly writ;
> For it is hard to yow, as I suppose,
> And therfore wol I teche yow al the glose.
> Glosynge is a glorious thyng, certeyn,
> For lettre sleeth, so as we clerkes seyn.

Later he returns to the superiority of the gloss over the letter in his self-serving praise of friars:

> But herkne now, Thomas, what I shal seyn.
> I ne have no text of it, as I suppose,
> But I shal fynde it in a maner glose,
> That specially oure sweete Lord Jhesus
> Spak this by freres, whan he seyde thus:
> 'Blessed be they that povere in spirit been.'

Of course, this is outrageous. The Friar is poor neither in spirit nor in material goods. In this instance the two meanings of the word *glosyng* converge. Indeed, we may say that one is the exact sign or equivalent of the other. Certainly there is no distinction in practice. Whether the Friar is talking about Scripture or about himself, his natural impulse is always the same—to put on the face that will best serve his own advantage. His "glosyng" distorts the true intent both of the Bible and of his own behavior. He is, in a word, bad exegesis.

From this point of view, the Friar's come-uppance is perfect. Because he has offended against the letter—the literal truth of the Bible and of himself—he is punished by the letter. In the first place, his quotation of 2 Cor. 3:6 ("For the letter killeth, but the spirit quickeneth") is full of self-incriminating irony. Paul is in the very midst of condemning those who, like the Friar, exploit the gospel for private gain: "For we are not as many," he says, "adulterating the word of God," or as *The Living Bible* more vividly translates it, "We are not like those hucksters—and there are many of them—whose idea of getting out the gospel is to make a good living out of it" (2 Cor. 2:17). There is potential irony as well in Paul's description of those who preach with truth and sincerity: "Now thanks be to God," he says, "who . . . manifesteth the odour of his knowledge by us in every place. For we are the good odour of Christ . . ." (2 Cor. 2:15). This is a suggestive metaphor to say the least. We do not need a commentary to tell us what kind of odor belongs to hucksters of the word. Angry old Thomas, I would suggest, gives (or performs) a reasonably accurate gloss. The most pointed irony, however, is that the Friar's use of 2 Cor. 3:6 to support "glosyng" completely overlooks the primary meaning of the text. Paul is not talking about exegesis. By *letter* he means the letter of the law, strict justice, which under the old covenant slays the sinner, in contrast to the spirit of love and mercy, which under the new covenant gives him life eternal. This is the standard interpretation from Augustine on.[6] Even if one took *letter* here to refer to the literal meaning of a text—a secondary interpretation allowed by some commentators—he could hardly conclude that because it "slayeth," it is therefore dispensable. The letter must be given its due.

The downfall of the Friar clearly represents the revenge of the letter in both senses of the word. The old man repays the Friar according to the letter of the law, if not an eye for an eye, then *crepitus* for *crepitus*.[7] At the same time, he reveals the literal truth beneath the Friar's "glosyng," for Friar John leaves hellbent on revenge, torn by the very emotion he had condemned in Thomas just a few minutes earlier. Most obviously, of course, the insult itself is unmistakably, defiantly, unredeemably literal. There's no glossing it. A fart is a fart. Finally, we should credit the literalistic thinking that inspired the insult. When the Friar asks rhetorically—and perhaps with a lisp—"What is a ferthyng worth parted in twelve?," Thomas is tempted to reply not in terms of what the Friar intended, but in terms of what he actually said. (Quite possibly Chaucer is also playing here on the Latin word *divisio*. In one of his letters *ad familiares*, Cicero singles out this word as an absurd example of the length to which the literalist mind will go. He puts the question: Shall we treat the word *divisio* as

---

6. Augustine devotes a whole treatise to the verse. In *De spiritu et littera* (ch. 7), he states his purpose as follows: "For I want, if possible, to prove that the apostle's words, 'The letter killeth, but the spirit giveth life,' do not refer to figurative phrases,—although even in this sense a suitable signification might be obtained from them,—but rather plainly to the law, which forbids whatever is evil," trans. in *A Select Library of the Nicene and Post-Nicene Fathers of the Christian Church*, V (repr. Grand Rapids, 1971), p. 85. Chrysostom gives the same explanation: "And by *letter* here he meaneth the Law, which punisheth them that transgress; but by spirit the *grace*, which through Baptism giveth life to them who by sins were made dead . . . . The Law laid hold on one that gathered sticks on a sabbath day, and stoned him. This is the meaning of, *the letter killeth*. The Gospel takes hold on thousands of homicides and robbers, and baptizing delivereth them from their former vices. This is the meaning of, *the Spirit giveth life*" (Sixth Homily of *The Homilies of St. John Chrysostom on the Second Epistle of St. Paul the Apostle to the Corinthians*, trans. J. Ashworth, in *A Library of Fathers* [Oxford, 1848], p. 83). See also Haymo of Halberstadt's *Expositio in Divi Pauli Epistolas*, *PL* 117:615-18. Denis the Carthusian follows the usual interpretation—"Lex autem Mosaica appellatur lex litterae, quia in libro ac tabulis scripta"—but tacks on the following: "Vel sic: Littera, id est sensus litteralis, vel potius qui litteralis videtur, occidit; spiritus autem, id est intellectus spiritualis ac mysticus, vivificat" (*Ennaratio in Epistolam II Beati Pauli ad Corinthios*, in *Opera Omnia* [Monstrolii, 1901], p. 223).

7. Classical writers, in fact, play on the double meaning of the word: "noise, prattle, boasting" and "a breaking wind." Thus Plautus in *Poenulus*:

> Collybiscus: This door (indicating Lycus' house) just did something perfectly dreadful.
> Counsellors: Dreadful? What?
> Collybiscus: It let out a loud rumble [Crepuerunt clare].

Translated by Paul Nixon, *Plautus*, IV, in The Loeb Classical Library (London, 1932), p. 63. The connection implied by Chaucer between *ructare* (line 1934) and *crepare* is also foreshadowed in Cicero's comment on Stoic usage: "But *they*—why, they go so far as to say that *crepitus* should be just as free as *ructus*! (Epistle IX.xxii, *Epistulae ad familiares*, trans. W. Glynn Williams, The Loeb Classical Library [London, 1928], p. 271).

obscene because it contains another word that is, namely *visium*, "a vile stench"?[8] Here in a word is the chief device of the Summoner's plot, both the idea of dividing and the thing to be divided.) But the letter is not yet through with Friar John. When he storms into the lord's house, sputtering with rage that Thomas has perpetrated "an odious mischief," he runs into a wall of liberalism. He is furious, he says, at "this false blasphemour, that charged me / To parte that wol nat departed be." Immediately everyone puts his mind to thinking how to divide the gift and thus help the Friar to keep his promise. This, of course, is not what the Friar meant at all. But once again it is the letter and not the intent that predominates. Everyone focuses on the literal meaning of his words rather than on the insult behind them—with the clear implication that the Friar has no grounds for offense on any other score.

But let us push the notion of the letter's revenge still further and consider it in the context established by the Friar himself, specifically, biblical exegesis. As we have seen, the Friar is given to the habit of inserting himself into Scripture: *he* is one of the poor in spirit, *he* is the workman worthy of his hire, *he* is a doer and not hearer only of the word. Of course he is nothing of the sort. Ironically every time he describes himself in the words of Scripture, he does so to his own condemnation. By the end of the tale, even the lord of the village has jumped into the game when he reminds the Friar, in the cruelest *double-entendre* of all, "Ye been the salt of the erthe and the savour." The principle at work here is beyond question. But Chaucer, as we know, was quite capable of inverting whole scenes from the Bible in much the same way. Indeed, Alan Levitan, Bernard Levy, and others have suggested that the solution at the end of the tale is a parody of the descent of the Holy Spirit upon the twelve apostles at Pentecost.[9] Whether this is so or not, the suggestion applies less to the original giving of the gift than to the problem of dividing it. Let me propose, therefore, that what happens in Thomas's house is also a parody of a scriptural passage, itself rich in farcical possibilities if interpreted strictly on a literal level.

Compare the scene in the *Summoner's Tale*—an old man lying on his death-bed, alone with an individual who, having taken a solemn oath (to divide the gift), places his hand between the sick man's legs—compare this, I say, with the following scene from Genesis 24:1-4:

Now Abraham was old; and advanced in age: and the Lord had blessed him in all things. And he said to the elder servant of his house, who was ruler over all he had: Put thy hand under my thigh, That I may make thee swear by the Lord the God of heaven and earth, that thou take not a wife for my son, of the daughters of the Chanaanites, among whom I dwell: But that thou go to my own country and kindred, and take a wife from thence for my son Isaac.

---

8. *Ibid.*, p. 271.
9. Alan Levitan, "The Parody of Pentecost in Chaucer's *Summoner's Tale*," *UTQ*, 40 (1971), 236-46; Bernard Levy, "Biblical Parody in the *Summoner's Tale*," *TSL*, 11 (1966), 45-60.

The same ritual is repeated in Genesis 47:29, where Jacob calls his son Joseph to him and says: "If I have found favour in thy sight, put thy hand under my thigh; and thou shalt shew me this kindness and truth, not to bury me in Egypt." There is little question about the literal meaning of these passages. As medieval commentators correctly observed, the phrase "under my thigh" is a euphemism for genitals. [10] This form of oath-taking seems to have been widespread throughout the ancient world, and there are still traces of it in the language, such as in the Latin word *testis*, which means both one who swears and that which he is presumed to have sworn upon. [11] However, Christian exegetes were not very interested in the literal aspects of the custom. Augustine sets the pattern. It was not seemly that a servant of Abraham should put his hand under the patriarch's "thigh"—unless by this act God intended some great mystery. Was not Christ the promised seed of Abraham? Therefore, the oath could be seen as sanctified not only by the sign of the old covenant, circumcision, but also and more profoundly by the hope of the new. [12]

This idea was developed with great ingenuity by medieval commentators. A crucial moment in the historical account of Abraham's succession is transformed suddenly into a living, contemporary drama of the Church. As we would expect, Abraham stands for God the Father; his son Isaac, for Christ; and the bride-to-be, for the Church. But the focus of medieval commentary is on the servant Eliezer. According to Hugh of St. Cher: "Eliezer means 'fellow-worker of my God.' And he is a type of prelates, teachers, and preachers, who are fellow-workers of God in the government of his people, concerning which the apostle says (1 Cor. 3:9), 'We are God's fellow-workers,' who ought to put our hand under the thigh of Abraham, that is, to preach to men the way of Christ through imitating his

---

10. See Hugh of St. Cher, *Opera omnia*, I (Lyons, 1669), 30v. Jewish commentators explain the ritual as a swearing by the circumcision. Thus Rashi: "*Under my thigh*—because whoever takes an oath must take in his hand some sacred object, such as a Scroll of the Law or Tefillin . . . . As circumcision was the first commandment given to him and became his only through much pain it was consequently dear to him and therefore he selected this as the object upon which to take the oath" (*Pentateuch with Rashi's Commentary*, trans. M. Rosenbaum and A. M. Silbermann [Jerusalem, 1929], p. 101). A modern commentary explains: "the reference is to an oath by the genital organs, as emblems of the life-giving power of deity,—a survival of primitive religion whose significance had probably been forgotten in the time of the narrator. Traces have been found in various parts of the world . . . . By Jewish writers it was considered an appeal to the covenant of circumcision . . . , [by others] as a symbol of subjection . . . [and still others] as invoking posterity . . . to maintain the sanctity of the oath" (see John Skinner, *A Critical and Exegetical Commentary on Genesis*, in *The International Critical Commentary*, 2nd edition [Edinburgh, 1930], pp. 341-42.

11. Latin authors frequently play on the double meaning of the word. Plautus writes in *Curculo*, for example, "Caute ut incedas via. Quod amas amato testibus praesentibus" [Be careful—stick to the open road. Love your love, but don't lose your witnesses!], translated in *Plautus*, p. 191. Pat Eberle has reminded me of the mnemonic aid proposed by the *Ad Herennium* for lawyers who wish to remember the idea of *witnesses* at a particular point in their argument: the image of a ram's testicles. See Frances Yates, *The Art of Memory* (London, 1966), p. 11.

12. See, for example, his commentary on Psalm 44, trans. in *A Select Library of the Nicene and Post-Nicene Fathers*, First Series, VIII (repr. Grand Rapids, 1974), p. 149.

works." Concerning the oath itself, Hugh explains: "Our Lord thus adjures prelates and preachers that they not accept for Christ a wife from among the daughters of Canaan, which is interpreted 'negotiatio' . . . . the daughters of Canaan, therefore, are all those who live soft lives in this world, unsteadily following after secular commerce and affairs. Such are not to be joined with Christ in matrimony." Hugh then expounds at great length on the gifts taken by the servant for the bride as the qualities a preacher ought to take before the people. These include, he says, strict poverty, hunger, humility, moral integrity, and zeal of the doctrine, "which things the preacher ought to carry with him as riches to be distributed among the poor, since the more quickly he would persuade his listeners to follow God, the more he must show in himself that which he preaches." [13]

The commentary on the biblical scene reenacted by Thomas and Friar John could hardly be a more exact indictment of the Friar. Although literally he takes the place of Eliezer, the type for preachers, he shares in none of the spiritual meaning of the ceremony. He puts his hand "under the thigh of Abraham" not in order to sanctify his vow as a fellow-worker of God but to violate it; not in order to abjure the marriage of Christ to the daughters of Canaan but actually to preside over it. He is himself a Canaanite. His life, as the tale emphasizes, revolves around *negotiatio*. He is not interested in the spiritual gifts of poverty, fasting, and humility: his mind is wholly on gifts of a more literal nature—and not in giving but in getting. Finally, he does not "show in himself that which he preaches to others." He is a hypocrite.

To all the other ways in which the letter takes its revenge on the "glosyng" Friar, therefore, we may add this. Just as his quotations from Scripture condemn him, so also does his unwitting dramatization of this moment from Scripture. He proves himself an unworthy son of Eliezer. Because he has denied its spiritual implications, he finds himself trapped in a merely literal reenactment of the story, a parody of its true meaning.

---

13. The passages quoted are as follows: "Eliezer interpretatur Dei mei adiutorium: Et est typus praelatorum, doctorum, & praedicatorum, qui sunt Dei coadiutores in regimine populi, secundum quod dicit Apost. I Cor. 3.C. Dei adiutores sumus, qui debent ponere manum sub femore Abraham, i. Christi hominis conversationem, suis operibus imitando praedicare"; "Adiurat n. Dominus praelatos, & praedicatores, ut non accipiant Christo uxorem de Filiab. Chanaan quod interpretatur negociatio, vel motus eorum, Filiae igitur Chanaan, sunt omnes molliter in saeculo viventes, negotia saecularia instabiliter sectantes. Tales Christo matrimonio non coniungentur"; "Bona Domini, sunt paupertas angustia, fames, vilitas humilitas, morum honestas, animarum zelus doctrinae pabulum, quae quasi divitias pauperibus erogandas debet portare secum praedicator, ut tanto citius ad sequendum Deum persuadeat, quanto auditoribus in seipso monstrat quod praedicat" (fol. 30v).

V

The House of Fame

Sacred and Secular Scripture:
Authority and Interpretation in *The House of Fame*

DAVID LYLE JEFFREY
University of Ottawa

As Russell Peck's essay has suggested, allusion and textual interplay between the text of the Bible and Chaucer's own text has its part not only at the levels of characterization, allusion, and literary humor, but at the level of structure as well. In this last essay I want to turn away from *The Canterbury Tales*, where most of our discussion has naturally centered, toward consideration of an earlier Chaucer poem in which some of the larger issues of text and interpretation are placed directly in question, and in which the issue of authority, so basic to medieval assumptions about Scripture, is openly essayed by the poet in respect of two obvious alternatives, personal experience and secular story. It is of more than passing interest to the scriptural aspect of our study that this relatively early poem is Chaucer's most 'eschatological' and visionary, and that, like *The Canterbury Tales*, it is apparently incomplete.

The structure of the *House of Fame* has always seemed to be familiar and enigmatic. The familiar elements are its ordered construction, three parts, and a progressive education of the dreamer such as is characteristic of deliberate invocations of the dream vision genre. Enigma arises initially from the fact that although the poem is ordered, it is formally incomplete, apparently frustrated of any satisfying answer to its persona's last questions. The reader is thus puzzled in attempting to interpret Chaucer's text. The poem follows a traditional pattern of design—a three-stage ascent toward understanding. It invites careful reading according to that traditional framework, and in almost every respect encourages the reader to anticipate such an intellectual journey as he or she might find in Augustine, Bonaventure, Dante, or Chaucer's own *Book of the Duchess*. But by the time one reaches what is merely the 'end' of this poem (rather than a conclusion), something has gone awry with the expected itinerary, and the reader (or 'hearer') is left on an aesthetic precipice. Along with a fair number of sympathetic critics over the years, one might perhaps take the apparently fragmented poem to be a bit of a blight upon Chaucer's reputation, perhaps isolate and catalogue some of its typology, locate it "ortho-culturally," and then abandon concern for its structural meaning. Chaucer, however, assaults us at the outset with a very stern warning against misjudgment of this poem. Calling down a fullsome blessing on those who "take hit wel and skorne hyt noght,"[1] he further invokes a comprehensive curse on those who "misdemen" it:

And whoso thorgh presumpcion,
Or hate, or skorn, or thorgh envye,
Dispit, or jape or vilanye,
Mysdeme hyt, pray I Jesus God
That dreme he barefot, dreme he shod,
That every harm that any man
Hath had, syth the world began,
Befalle hym therof, or he sterve,
And graunte he mote hit ful deserve,
Lo, with such a conclusion
As had of his avision
Cresus, that was kyng of Lyde,
That high upon a gebet dyde!   (ll. 94-106)

The blunt warning against misreading of his poem is unique in Chaucer, and, focused as it is on the "conclusion" of an insensitive exegete, King Cresus (See *Monk's Tale*, 2740 ff.), it is surely intended to focus our own unpresumptive attention on the structure and interpretation of his crafted "avision."

I

It might appear surprising in this light that Chaucer's persona, Geffrey, should begin his dream in an encounter with the story of Troy. The cliché could seem almost to invite the presumption against which we are warned. The history of Aeneas had become fundamental to secular story in western literature, from Vergil himself, and Ovid, but principally through the numerous and varied adaptations, translations and commentaries on the matter of Troy which so dominated secular literature from the twelfth to the fourteenth-centuries. Chaucer recurs to this material for plot or story in a number of his other poems, including, of course, *Troilus and Criseyde* and the *Monk's* and *Knight's Tales*.

In these narratives, the protagonists are ostensibly characters in a Trojan drama; the significances of their pseudo-historical actions for meaning contemporary with Chaucer's audience are inferred, if consciously "read out" at all, as axioms of conventional systems of cultural reference — 'allegorical' or otherwise. It is clear that in the fourteenth century the secular scripture of Rome was still being heavily underwritten by 'Rome's' sacred scripture.[2]

---

1. The allusion is to Proverbs 14:6. All Chaucer references, unless marked otherwise, are to the Robinson edition.
2. The terms are, of course, Northrop Frye's, and inasmuch as the reference is to a kind of 'romance' historiography here, I intend the distinction pretty much in his sense. See his *The Secular Scripture: A Study of the Structure of Romance* (Cambridge, Mass.: Harvard University Press, 1976).

In the *House of Fame*, on the other hand, the reader is not so permitted to enter into the conventional interpretation of the story, as though the poem were another adaptation or 'translation' of the Troy matter—a tale or parable from history. The persona (closely identified with the author, rather than, as is usual in dream-vision, with the reader) intervenes with a self-consciousness calculated to purchase distance from the convention, and he makes the *artifice* of history's telling (more than the 'content' of the history) explicit to reader consciousness. For Geffrey self-consciously encounters the familiar Troy 'history' as *art* external to his own life, just as, from the reader's own perspective, Troy remains external to the narrative in which Geffrey himself is a character. In short, Chaucer presents his protagonist-persona as a fictive 'reader' engaged in reflective exegesis of a text commonly held by his 'actual' readers, allowing them, in turn, to 'over-hear' the fictive reader struggle toward interpretation and meaning. As the actual readers (among whom we are numbered) begin to realize that the "temple of images" containing the Troy story is situated in the desert, as "in the desert of Lybye," and remember that what Aeneas saw in the temple of Dido, before encountering her, is almost the same thing that Geffrey sees in his dream, story and interpretation (*i.e., in this instance Aeneid and The House of Fame*) are forcibly juxtaposed in a novel way.

At the first level, what Geffrey sees is (apparently) what Aeneas saw, history as art, or artifice. The art describes a history with which both he and his author's audience are familiar: Geffrey can speed over a number of well-known details. Because of the fused horizons of narrative and interpretation on which Chaucer has placed him, Geffrey may especially omit the visit to Dido's temple in his retelling. The parallel is more than obvious.

At the other level, the forced juxtaposition of Book I accomplishes two additional functions, separate, yet integrally related in their establishment of Chaucer's argument. First, the poet has made his readers acutely aware of their actual separation from any story—even a story familiar enough to have been welded into their sense of present identity, as unquestioned as cliché. For the story, like historical Troy itself, is other. It is then and there; the reader is here and now. Secondly, the poet has invited his readers to measure against that real distance the apparent close congruence of his own and Vergil's purpose, especially as directed toward questions about art, interpretation, and history. By pitting the device of an unpredictable persona-exegete against his readers' comfortable possession of the Troy story in its traditional modes of interpretation, Chaucer *requires* us to be continuously aware that our present telling is a version according to Geffrey. This deliberate diminishment of his 'own' authorial authority prepares us, accordingly, for exploration of the main Vergilian point about meaning and justification in the representative life of Aeneas. Instead of affirming the conventional conclusion of the story—in which Aeneas is brought on, despite distractions, to his proper achievement as a 'Rome-bearer'—Geffrey himself becomes distracted toward a different and contrasting centre of meaning. What he sees, at least when he reads Ovid's account of the matter, is unanswered questions and unjustified action—the issue of betrayal and false-seeming as manifest in Aeneas' notorious rejection of Dido.[3] At this complication, with the appeal to another text, or another version (another way of reading the story), the central intellectual tensions in Chaucer's poem begin to develop.

It seems possible, then, that the choice of the famous and familiar story of Aeneas as a *status quaestionis* for his poem does not constitute a failure of imagination on Chaucer's part, but that its very status as *cliché* makes it all the more appropriate as a vehicle for the poem's *real* subject, which is, in fact, unusually contextualized in the title of the poem. The word *'fame'* means for us (as it did for Vergil), chiefly 'reputation.' Up to the eighteenth century, as for example in Dr. Johnson's *Dictionary*, the English word still held its ancient meaning, "rumor," as well. Both these meanings are highly visible in Chaucer's poem, and have received a good deal of comment.[4] But in Chaucer's own time, *fame* had another meaning, one which, though now obsolete, gets in fact a primary listing in the OED. It is 'public report', 'story' received, or 'true report'. Thus Trevisa, in translating Ranulf Higden's *Polychronicon*, describes his submission to earlier histories: "Me schall trowe old fame, þat is nought wiþseide" (I. 71). As a verb the word meant to 'record for posterity' (cf. Lat. *famare*), and in medieval Latin *famen* (word or utterance), as in the early Greek, preserved the sense of historical utterance, record, or simply *word*. None of these meanings—reputation, rumor, received history—is singular, nor to be separated from the others in an attempt to understand the title of Chaucer's poem, especially in view of the occasion, or initial matter Chaucer sets before us in Book I.

For one thing, the "fame of Aeneas" had had, to Chaucer's time, an enormous role in the development of Christian historiography. As B. G. Koonce has shown, in the earliest development of the *romans* as a genre, from the translation and adaptations of Roman story represented by *Aeneas*, the *Thebiad* and the *Roman de Troie* in the mid-twelfth century to the characterization of the good *christes milites* in Chrétien de Troyes or other Arthurian romances, there had been a strong component, in these adaptations, of Vergilian *pietas* and concern for *fama*. Among the signal themes in Christian 'histories' of Britain such as Geoffrey of Monmouth's *Historia*, or Laȝamon's *Brut*, these values continued to be observed as 'ideals' in Chaucer's lifetime, as, for example, in *Sir Gawain and the Green Knight*, and after him, even in the collections of Malory. Every student of medieval literature is aware that the story of Troy and Christian 'readings' of medieval history are so intertwined, both in structure and motif, that they remain nearly inseparable from the time of Augustine until the 'rewritings' of history which took place during the Reformation, when men

---

3. Petrarch had anticipated Chaucer in considering, to the point of preference, Ovid's version: see *Fam.* ix,5; *Sen* i,4; iv,5.

4. Especially in Benjamin G. Koonce, *Chaucer and the Tradition of Fame: Symbolism in the House of Fame* (Princeton: Princeton University Press, 1966). For an alternate view, compatible with the present hypothesis, see William S. Wilson, "Exegetical Grammar in the *House of Fame*," *ELN* 1 (1964), 244-48.

such as the appropriately named expatriate Polydore Vergil took pains to explicitate a separation.[5]

It was for quite different reasons that Wyclif and others in Chaucer's time were beginning to question certain implications of the traditional connection. Especially they were questioning whether Christian thought could be thought of as peculiarly given to such an explicit Vergilian historicism in and of itself. Rather, as Wyclif was to ask, could it only sometimes seem to be that way because Christian thought was often refracted through the historicist lenses afforded by Roman culture?[6] Notably expressed in the *Aeneid*, Roman cultural historicism had argued strongly for a transcendent meaning in secular history, a grand design which in early Christian times still proclaimed the victory of Rome (now allegorically, now literally taken) as the right end to all history. "The judgment of history," men said, was that Rome should triumph. All history led up to and found its significance in Rome's glory (*fama*), and thus could all be retrospectively interpreted in terms of stages in the ascent or progress toward that desideratum, *fama romana*. Expressed in the conjoint vocabulary of the two "scriptures," this interpretative model exerted an almost irresistible pressure on Christian writers: Augustine's *City of God*, Orosius' *History*, and Dante's *De Monarchia*, all medieval Christian classics, are evidently historicist in the manner of the *Aeneid*, arguing biblically a spiritual gloria (*fama*) in the New Jerusalem as the ultimate adequation of human history. Subsequently we see this structured representation of the meaning of history taking on literary shapes, patterned evidences of an elaborative hermeneutical model such as is suggested not only in the surface details of a storic plot or narrative, but in such allied conventions as the generic three-stage ascent from the senses through *scientia* to *sapientia* (in Augustine's *De Trinitate* or Scotus' *De Divisione Natura*), and the associated provision Hell/Purgatorio/Paradiso (of Dante's *Commedia*). One of the most widely influential views of the *House of Fame* is that it too, in fact, is structured according to this same interior model, following Dante particularly, with perhaps a few ironic touches.[7]

Indeed, these ideas seem to be never very far from Chaucer, and are important to him in the *Book of the Duchess* and *The Canterbury Tales*, for example. But his use of the Troy story in the *House of Fame* is such as to raise serious questions about whether or not this particular poem is built

---

5. See C. David Benson, *The History of Troy in Middle English Literature* (Woodbridge, Suffolk: D.S. Brewer, 1980). Benson notes the confidence with which "historical truth was ascribed to the Troy versions: "The Middle English historians of Troy affirm their common dedication to both history and poetry in their individual prologues. The expressed goal ... is identical: the historical record must be preserved completely" (35). Cf. *Troilus and Creseyde*, however, where he notes an exception; that while Chaucer expects his readers to know the Troy history, he "feels under no obligation to reproduce this history accurately or in full" (134).

6. John Wyclif, *De veritate sacrae scripturae*, ed. R. Buddenseig (London: Wyclif Society, 1905) I, 228-9; 237; cf. 51-53.

7. I refer here to Koonce especially, whose detailed work on the typology of the poem opens up many of the questions pursued here.

upon the traditional historicist three-stage structure of ascent which the surface structure of the poem may seem to imply.

II

To return to our text: if Chaucer seems to invoke the expectations generated by the identification of secular and sacred scripture which usually accompanied elaborate references to Troy, he certainly complicates his signals to the reader by undermining the authority of the author and principal traditions of interpretation which allowed for the identification in the first place. For Chaucer is less impressed by the traditional justification of Aeneas' 'moving on' (as given in Vergil or Bernard Silvestris) than persuaded by the focus of other authors, such as Ovid and *Ovide moralisé*, respecting the plight of abandoned Dido. Or at least his persona takes this position, and with some energy. In Chaucer's telling, it is the perfidy and truth-breaking of Aeneas which dominates interest: *contra auctorem*, we are led to see in Aeneas' departure from Carthage less a noble parturition than a dimly rationalized divorce. When Geffrey comes to the Vergilian justification by way of Ovid, he finds in it less reason than *excuse* (l. 427). The bidding of Mercury, the sycophant of intellect (that Aeneas should go on to fulfill his destiny) might portray well enough a conventional end in view; the problem for Geffrey as reader is that it leaves something unsaid, 'something' which embodies a potential contradiction of value or justification which might be attributed to the story's ending.

I am aware that at this point in the essay my argument could be misunderstood. I do not at all wish to suggest here that Chaucer is trying to ennoble, as passionate, romantic love, the tryst between Dido and Aeneas, nor that he really wishes us to see her as she would wish to see herself, almost as guiltless. What I think he does wish us to reckon with is that there may be two sides, or many, to a story, rather than one, and that the larger end of the *Aeneid* story leaves completely unresolved the question of betrayal, and of *untrouthe*. In a sense, medieval allegorizations and hermeneutical baptisms of the *Aeneid*, such as are found not only in Silvestris or Fulgentius[8] but in all manner of secular literature (cf. the *Knight's Tale*), mostly read well enough in terms of their typology alone—what Chaucer calls "alle the mervelous signals of the goddys celestials" (*H.F.*, ll. 459-60). But important *value questions* are left very much unresolved by mere mastery of this typology. Whose text is 'right' in its focus? Vergil's or Ovid's? To paraphrase C. S. Lewis: what is the standard of judgment by which we accept that the successful tyrant is more important—or more excusable—than the patience or despair of some one among his victims?[9] Let us speak of Aeneas, Chaucer says, "how he betrayed hir..."

---

8. Especially Bernardus Silvestris, *Commentum super sex libros Eneidos Virgilii*, ed. W. Reidel (Greifswald: J. Abel, 1924).

9. C. S. Lewis, "Historicism," in *Fernseed and Elephants* (Glasgow: Collins, 1975), 59.

(293 ff.)—that is part of the story too, and the long list of analogues to this betrayal (from Demophon and Phyllis through Jason and Medea to Theseus and Ariadne) circumvent our dismissal of his protest as a mere deferential gesture in the direction of the ladies in the court. There is clearly a plausible historical perspective in which Aeneas is a fink, a truth-breaker. What has to be determined now is: which version, Vergil's or Ovid's, really describes the *truth* of the story? What determines the reliability of history? Has it really any *unity* of truth that encompasses each perspective, each experience—including our own experience too? What would be the significance for the authority of history, if, as each of these stories suggest, the problem of sinful or mischievous narration were a significant factor in the history of human affairs? Whom would we trust? Faced with a plurality of authorities, how should we judge?

At the conclusion of his 'reading' Geffrey acknowledges that yes, he is impressed with the "noblesse of ymages" (471), but also that he is still beset by two questions. One appears to be minor and tangential: who was the author? ("not wot I whoo did hem wirche"—474); the other question immediately appears as both crucial and personal: 'Well enough,' he seems to be saying, 'I see the old familiar historiography ... ; But where am I? Or in what country?' (475). In short, he asks: 'is this *my patria*, or not?' It seems to be the lack of a sense of his own place in the scheme that causes him anxiety. Unlike Aeneas (who saw himself in the art of Dido's temple, and thus in the great scheme of things), Geffrey is left without *personal* reference by the history he 'reads', and he runs outside looking for someone, as he says, "that may me telle where *I* am" (479). With respect to narrative development then, the key question is personal, and not purely formal. Geffrey's flight is not to another book or tableau of history. Rather, he runs out to see if he can find "any stiryng man" (478). Yet he sees no living person, and his alienation is made graphic by the desert landscape which confronts him. Ironically, though Geffrey as persona is not aware of it, it is just this landscape, the desert of Libya, which turns us, as readers, back again to the old book, the *Aeneid*, for reference, [10] for we see that Geffrey is still tacitly compared to Aeneas—not as the Roman hero stepping out of Dido's temple, but as we find him later in the *Aeneid*, when he leaves Dido to recommence his pilgrimage. For now, instead of Mercury, but in the very same role, Jove is said to send down an eagle to draw the contemporary pilgrim Geffrey another stage forward on his predestined itinerary.

From this point, the classical story which occasioned the poet's questions seems to fade away. Despite the clear parallel with Mercury, the eagle has often been seen as a biblical, rather than classical, commentary

---

10. It could also invoke biblical counterparts, of course: the desert of Moses' canticle (Deut. 32:10-12), Ezekiel's desert (Ezek. 37:1-14), the desert of Jeremiah (2:6; 17:6-8; 50:12-13), or Isaiah. Cf. Sheila Delany, "Phantom and the House of Fame," *Chaucer Review*, 2 (1967), 67-74.

on the story.[11] As with the eagle image in Isaiah (40:31), the eagle of St. John's apocalypse (or the golden eagle of the *Paradiso*), the bird has been associated with contemplation, "translation," the perspective of intellect, and even the *Word*—one thinks of the eagle bearing up on his wings the *Word* (the carved lecterns for reading the Gospels).[12] We should be cautious: Geffrey's eagle does not act like "The Word" at all.[13] When it comes to snatch Geffrey out of his sluggish malaise and befuddlement in the realm of Venus, it may seem to function well within the conventions of the medieval dream vision. Yet the key is to a somewhat wider genre. The eagle is a kind of parody, first perhaps of Lady Philosophy in her advent to Boethius, imprisoned in his slothful and concupiscent wilderness. It might pretend kinship to Knowledge in the play *Everyman*—"I am thy frend," he says to Chaucer (1. 582). As a symbol for the powers of intellect, as these sometimes grow upon disappointments of concupiscence, the eagle could prepare us to anticipate, accordingly, a Boethian or Dantesque hermeneutic and an appropriate conclusion—perhaps the sort of final revelation we get in *Pearl*. But we do not, despite this intuited expectation and teasing, arrive at such a conclusion. Why?

We might begin to essay an answer, I think, by attempting to get inside the conventional structure of the poem in such a way as to examine further the problem of contradiction in perspective and attribution. We discover this in the narrative voice, particularly that part of it which belongs to the persona. A curious circumstance attends upon Chaucer's invocation, following the proem to Book I, to Morpheus:

> . . . the god of slep anoon,
> That duelleth in a cave of stoon
> Upon a strem that cometh fro Lete,
> That is a flood of helle unswete.   (ll. 69-72)

By convention the reader anticipates that an invocation to Morpheus will be a prolegomena to whatever condition of sluggishness and torpor is sufficient to occasion the necessary dream (cf. *Book of the Duchess*), since Morpheus is notably personification of *forgetfulness*, whose dwelling is beside Lethe and whose floral icon is the poppy.[14] Yet Chaucer has just promised us:

---

11. Cf. W. S. Wilson, "The Eagle's Speech in Chaucer's *House of Fame*," *QJS*, 50 (1964), 153-58; Charles P. Tisdale, "The House of Fame: Virgilian Reason and Boethian Wisdom," *CL*, 25 (1973), 247-61.

12. E.g. St. Augustine, *Harmony of the Gospels*, I, vi, 9. Cf. John M. Steadman, "Chaucer's Eagle: A Contemplative Symbol," *PMLA*, 75 (1960), 153-59. Chaucer may have in mind Ezekiel's eagle. Pierre Bersuire, in Bk. XV of his *Reductorium Morale*, justifies his moralizing of Ovid by arguing that *fabulae* are used in many passages of Sacred Scripture. One of his two exemplary instances is Ezekiel 17:3, "where we read how the eagle with great wings carried away the branch of the cedar. The *poetae*, inventors of *fabulae*, composed in a similar way; by figments of this kind they wished truths to be understood." Petrus Berchorius, *De Formis figurisquae deorum*, naar de Parijse druk van 1509 (Utrecht, 1960), p. 4. The eagle was also heraldic symbol for John of Gaunt.

13. Cf. John Leyerle, "Chaucer's Windy Eagle," *UTQ*, 40 (1971), 247-65.

14. Ovid, *Metamorphoses*, xi, 592ff.

as I kan now *remembre*
I wol you tellen everydel.   (ll. 64-5) (italics mine)

He has carefully labored to tell us that he wants to reconstruct his dream for us with all clarity, and needs memory to help him out. But he invokes Morpheus. Here is a patent contradiction, and it is not in Book I resolved by introducing the problematical variety of ways in which one might remember the Troy story, but in fact only exacerbated by this reminder. The desire the narrator expresses is for memory, but his invocation is curiously opposite, to the influence of Morpheus.

A similar problem persists in the next section of the poem. Though the invocation in Book II is to Venus, the appeal is to Thought, the processes of intellect that "wrot" (wrought, wrote) all that the poet has encountered, and subsequently transmitted it to memory:

O Thought, that wrot al that I mette
And in the tresorye hyt shette
Of my brayn, now shall me se
Yf any vertu in the be
To tellen al my drem aryght.   (ll. 523-27)

With this probable allusion to the beginning of the *Inferno*,[15] we move from memory to its sponsor, intellect, and thereby encounter a progression of interpretation at least as familiar as concupiscence-knowledge-wisdom, or hell-purgatorio-paradiso, but not, however, necessarily to be identified with them. To be sure, the eagle clearly recognizes Geffrey's concupiscent state ("You are a noxious little load to carry, parde," he says), and, in tones all too much like one Chaucer could tell about ("Geffrey—wake up!") he invites Geffrey, but in words also reminiscent of Scripture (Eph. 5:14)[16] and the liturgy (*'Exsurge anima mea'*) to leave off his dispiritedness.

                           "Awak!
And be not agast so, for shame!"   (l. 556)

The eagle, like Mercury, moves the protagonist forward physically as the force of plot: whether Geffrey moves spiritually is a matter not of force, or plot, but of his own will and perspective. The apparent contradictions of appeal in the poems are thus an important continuing reflection of Geffrey's *lack* of solution. Even while the appeal to Thought (the warden of memory) strives to move him forward, his initial invocation to Venus reminds us of the temple in which Geffrey has been sojourning. Venus is his tie to earth—but also, as in the "temple of Venus," his tie to story, and to story with all of its ambivalent possibilities, historiographical and personal.

The eagle, whether we see him as intellect, contemplation or reason, has ostensibly been sent by Jove to provide Geffrey with a bit of

---

15. Dante, *Inferno*, 2. 7-9.
16. "Thus it is said: Awake, you that sleep, and arise from that dead, and Christ shall give you light." (This is the passage, much commented on from Augustine forward, which speaks of "redeeming the time, because the days are evil." See *Confessions*, Bk.10.)

perspective.[17] The poet's problem has been that he spends all of his time up to the *hals* in books, out of contact with experience as such (654-60), and the implication is that he has become one who cannot see the forest for the trees, the structure of things for particulars, because he is so narrowly engrossed with the pursuit of particular authorities. But because he has been a diligent student, has sat up nights and persevered (despite his dullness and intellectual limitations), Jove's will is that he should get some perspective, even on the authorities he has been reading. The intellectual journey thus sets in relationship to the vagaries of human history something of the larger structure of the universe during which a number of authorities, on points of cosmology, philosophy and mythography, are confirmed (e.g. 712; 759-60; 985-89).

The context for this dialectic between scriptures and author, we remember, is a very Boethian discussion (cf. *Boece*, I-III) of the doctrine of natural place, in which the *House of Fame* is reported to be the "natural place" of ingathering for every kind of tiding, news, or human history. Recalling (as does Dido, by the way) the alarming Mediterranean notion that every human word spoken is preserved perpetually (vide Matt. 12:34-37) and thus an *ultimate* subject available for recollection, the eagle concludes his 'philosophy' and asks Geffrey to make a judgment—"How thinketh the my conclusyon?" (1. 871)—i.e., what does Geffrey think o the idea that *every* human story, every utterance, every viewpoint is all recorded, in the entirety, somewhere up in the air as a kind of master library of history? Geffrey's answer is ironically skeptical: "A good persuasion" (i.e. opinion), he says—not entirely swept away either by the rhetoric or the presumed 'confirmation' of authorities on points cosmographical. Miffed, the eagle then retorts:

> "Be God," quod he, "and as I leve,
> Thou shalt have yet, or hit be eve,
> Of every word of thys sentence
> A preve by experience,
> . . . What wilt thou more?"   (ll. 875-9; 883)

Swearing by St. James he urges Chaucer then to confirm, if he can, by personal experience, the "trouth" of his physical and present place, hovering over the terrestrial landscape. What the eagle asks, in short, is a more explicitly empiricist version of Geffrey's own urgent question of himself: *Where are you*? Can you tell? The answer is that Geffrey sees recognizable but only *general* features—cities, fields, seas, ships—and soon he is so high he sees only the whole globe as a tiny point, defying particular discernment (1. 909). When the eagle asks, "Seest thou any token (sign) or aught that in the world of is spoken?" (ll. 911-12 [Fisher]), Geffrey's answer has to be "Nay." Clearly, there is a perspective which is true, yet defeats practical validation by personal experience—is simply beyond it. The story of Phaeton's difficulty in holding the mean between earthly and

---

17. Cf. David M. Bevington, "The Obtuse Narrator in Chaucer's *House of Fame*," *Speculum*, 36 (1961), 288-98.

terrestrial (corporeal and spiritual) inclinations, repeating a motif from the first two proems, follows as a warning to the reader of the persona's instability, of Geffrey's own need to keep these points of reference in balance.

The persona's own (partial) recognition here of the validity of the eagle's instruction embraces both an acknowledgment of God's ultimate authorship and Boethius' philosophy (ll. 970ff), but Geffrey is still lost between the poles of two inclinations, clearly uncertain of the integrating point of his own experience (ll. 980-82). So, to proceed, he refers his insight, habitually, as a reader, to a textual confirmation of typography (e.g. Martianus and Alanus), seeing experiential support for them as authorities. When admonished by the eagle to "let be" his "fantasye" and take a short scientific course on location in astrology, Geffrey acquires the wit to demur. If the eagle protests "How are you going to read poetry without it?" Geffrey can say wisely enough, "hyt is no nede" —he can believe for this sort of thing in the authority of books as easily as his present interplanetary experience.

This statement (especially given Chaucer's scientific interest in astronomy) would seem to suggest a measure of the persona's growing discrimination. It contains two recognitions. First, in view of the fact that one has not time to learn everything, summistically ("For I am now too old"), it suggests that there are some kinds of truth for which authority provides as helpful an adequation as experience. Second, the persona rejects the notion that it is the function of poetry, or its use of typology, to point merely to the 'empirical' validation of received typology in this sense. Typology is one means—at the first level—of systematizing understanding. It serves to identify a group of ideas approximately by situating them within a familiar set. It is absolutely necessary as the first ground of figurative language. But 'true' historical or intellectual understanding, seeking to grasp the way in which a story develops, its central intuition or its organic intellectual structure, begins precisely at the point where these rudimentary identifications are ended. The mere citation of authority on such points of identification does not really speak to the main issues of the dream (or poem). As Geffrey prepares to examine the *House of Fame*, his concerns, like those he had at the end of Book I, are still with the larger issues, and are (in the philosophical sense), personal rather than typological. In Book I the problem had not been merely the abstraction which is history, but establishing a personal relationship to it: "Where am I?" Here in Book II the problem is not merely the availability of information, but "What is the *point* of information?"

> "Now," quod I, "while we han space
> To speke, or that I goo fro the,
> For the love of God, telle me—
> In sooth, that wil I of the lere—"   (ll. 1054-57)

'What am I going to *learn* in all of this?' he asks. 'Give me some unified meaning, the *sentence* of it all.' Suddenly it is the eagle's turn to demur:

"Noo," quod he, "by Seynte Clare,
And also wis God rede me!"   (ll. 1066-7)

'Nothing doing,' he says, swearing by a saint of silence: the perspective of intellect does not of itself yield up that kind of knowing. The eagle is not necessarily discourteous—merely limited: it wishes him God's grace, as assistance for the quest "*some* good to lernen in this place." But the limiting quantifier is a confirmation to us that this scene is more to be distinguished from than paralleled with that moment at the end of the *Purgatorio*, when Vergil hands Dante on to Beatrice for ultimate revelation. In suggesting partial knowledge in its plurality rather than truth in its unity, the eagle's viaticum confirms a growing apprehension that the curriculum in Book III may provide Geffrey anything *but* a glimpse of The Reader's New Jerusalem.

III

The departure of the eagle should not be taken to mean that Chaucer, as a poet, has abandoned or forgotten his appropriate concerns for the schema, or structure, of his poem by the beginning of Book III. In fact, in his request for Apollo's blessing of "science and light," Chaucer as narrator emerges again from behind his persona to tell us that he is far less concerned that his own book illustrate a mastery of "art poetical" (whereby *he* might have "fame") than that it reveal "o sentence" ('only meaning', or, 'unified meaning'); his present object is not to "shewe craft" in skillful effects, but rather to reveal design:

O God of science and of lyght,
. . . entre in my brest anoon!   (ll. 1091-1109)

This proem, though less obviously ambivalent than the others, proceeds to a redoubled invocation in which each aspect of the invocation is more clearly a mirror to the other. The "divyne vertu" to which he prays in the second part of the proem is personally addressed; he now seeks a divine *inspiration* such as can help him to find a shape for what memory and thought have already "ymarked" in his head. Thus, while Apollo's typology of ordered exposition looks backward to the intellectual analysis of Book II, his 'virtue', divine inspiration, looks forward to a dimension of revelation for which the structure of the poem still entices us to hope. As in many dream visions, the advantage to the dream's perspective of divine inspiration is for transformation of the will.[18] For all that, many readers have felt that in Book III the revelation never comes—there appears to be no unified meaning discerned, no key to all mythographies proclaimed. Fame's palace and the bird cage are complete and deliberate inversions of imagery from Ezekiel and St. John's Apocalypse, and instead of unifying truth which answers the dreamer's questions, Geffrey is bombarded with a veritable frenzy of contradictory, patently false, partially true, but all un-

---

18. Cf. *Paradiso*, 1. 13-27.

sortable data without judgment or ordering of any kind. What he gets is simply *more* and *more* histories, not any integration for their reconciliation and understanding. Far more than Book I, it is Book III which parallels Dante's *Inferno*. Certainly here is no *Paradiso*. So for the "o sentence" and design, the reader will still have queries concerning the architecture of the *House of Fame*.

Let us reflect and reconsider Chaucer's structure as if it really were rather like that of Dante's *Commedia*. There, as in Dante's own *De Monarchia*, or Augustine's *City of God*, what we really have is Vergil's historicism 'baptized'. The three stages of a history whose meaning is unified, whose means are all satisfactorily subsumed to the end, are basically exile/via/patria. Since the end of the story had been reached, for Vergil, it was quite possible in his case to reconstruct the details of narrative so that they all achieved their significance in terms of the happy political conclusion. For Augustine, who experimented with these ideas in his *Confessions*, Christian historiography was less well equipped to proceed in the same way, since the Christian end goal had not yet been fully realized, even though it had, at least in shadow and basic outline, been anticipated in biblical prophecy and dream vision (e.g. St. John's Apocalypse.) Dante's organization, on the other hand, more explicitly images the Vergilian promise. In his work we see that the external hermeneutical model (the "grand narrative") was presently available in this way for allegorical readings of history, or the articulation, for history still 'unfolding', of a larger hermeneutical design with full temporal coordinates. [19]

Such an historiography is not, of course, history in the temporal sense, but a model, a metaphor. Dante knew this. Others at the time and up to Chaucer were even more literalist, however, in their temporalizing. From well-known historicists like Joachim da Fiore and Otto von Freising to numerous minor apocalyptic writers in Chaucer's own day, thousands of pages had been devoted (against all the explicit warnings of Scripture) to fixing the literal details of European history to the metaphor as though it were in fact a calendar. The most extravagant reaches of this habit, from certain wild interpretations of the days of Frederick II to incessantly repeated predictions of the year of Christ's second coming (1233, 1260, 1300, 1366, 1400), are far too numerous to mention here, but one can read about them at leisure, as well as see their influence upon other English poets of Chaucer's age, such as William Langland. [20] The effort of such prognostications was to try to provide a unified meaning for history that would allow for the interpretation and justification of mediate events. Their effect was

---

19.   Guiseppe Mazzotta writes that for Dante the providential "...*opus restaurationis* is also of the temporal order, and ... Dante shows how Roman history is constitutive of the redemptive process." *Dante, Poet of Exile* (Princeton: Princeton University Press, 1979), 64. See Mazzotta's 4th chapter, "Vergil and Augustine," and Charles T. Davis, *Dante and the Idea of Rome* (Oxford: Clarendon Press, 1957), where Davis argues that Dante's Vergil becomes "a bridge between the two Romes" (p. 137).

20.   See Morton Bloomfield, *Piers Plowman as a Fourteenth Century Apocalypse* (New York: Knopf, 1963), 66-77.

to place the possibility of a unity of truth *in* history under incalculable strain, to drive some men to despair of meaning in history and authority alike. Supposing one had been told, really believing in Christ's prophesied return, that the demonstrable date of that coming again was last year and it did not happen? Supposing one had been told that the infinitely more significant destiny of the state or the political Church rendered the accidents of personal or national destiny insignificant, and one had lived long enough to wonder?

It is the biblical language, allusion, and direct critical quotation which really point to these questions in the *House of Fame*, not the story of Troy or its panoply of typologies. The secular scripture, Troy, is the initial *matière*, the occasion of his essay. But Chaucer's critical angle comes from the other text. Whereas Dante had used his national poet, Vergil, as an irrefragably 'authoritative' interlocutor, Chaucer uses the 'intellectual' but more ambiguous eagle. For Dante, the point is that poetic history and its historicist schema becomes a confirmation, a guide to the truth of the theological, or of revelation. For Chaucer it is just the other way around, that a revelation—far beyond the sight of intellect—would be needed as a guide to the truth value of history or the historical 'authorities' one reads.

The actual text of Scripture itself does not read according to the historicist model at all, except in the largest sense of expectation, of an openness to the ending known to be coming, but not yet known. Chaucer's contemporary, Wyclif, is sensitive to this point, quoting Christ: "No man knows the day or the hour, not even the angels of heaven, but my Father only" (Matt. 24:36).[21] The reason we can't 'read' the story of history in that definitively literal way is, just as literally, that we do not have the whole text. It may be that the significance of the biblical December 10th date, cited twice at the beginning of the *House of Fame*, is not simply for announcement of apocalyptic insight or revelation.[22] Rather, as the date (10th day of 10th month) in which Ezekiel "saw" in his vision the destruction of Jerusalem, it may signify to Chaucer much what it did to Ezekiel—the end of the illusion of historical security, the death of history, a separation, an ending of the past order. Wyclif in his lectures points out that the vision, as indeed the destruction of Jerusalem itself, is an irrefragable corrective to Israel's tendency to create its own literalist historicism, to expect a heavenly kingdom on its own terms, in the here and now.[23] The destruction of Jerusalem, the prophets argue, cuts off that 'progressive' history and blows the theory away like chaff from the threshing floor. From such a point of understanding the text of Scripture is read

---

21. Wyclif, *Sermones*, ed. J. Loserth (London: Wyclif Society, 1890), IV, 189-90; 206-7. See also T. Arnold, *Select English Works* (Oxford, 1871), II, 407.
22. Cf. Koonce, pp. 181-85. Koonce itemizes medieval allegorizations of the account in Ezekiel 40:1-2 and 2 Kings 25, which identify the captivity of Jerusalem with the siege and captivity of Holy Church by the force of Satan in the last days. This typology for the text may have had some appeal in 1378, the date of Chaucer's poem and the time of the papal Schism.
23. Wyclif, *Comm. in Ezek.*, in Ms. Magdalen Coll., Oxford 117, 176a.

not according to an external and historicist schema, but according to an *internal* hermeneutical model, well known to commentators from Nicholas of Lyra to John Wyclif as a kind of *forma tractatus* for Scripture's consolatory dialogue with its readers. It is relevant to the whole canon of Scripture, but particularly the books we call 'prophecy', the visionary literature of Isaiah, Jeremiah, and Ezekiel. [24]

Several factors invite a recapitulation of the form of Ezekiel's dialogic for comparison with the *House of Fame*. First, there is Chaucer's repeated reference to the visionary date from Ezekiel (40:1-2), the tenth day of the tenth month. Further, there are many echoes of the imagery of that book throughout Chaucer's poem, some elements of which have already been noted by Koonce and others. [25] But there are specific structural relationships between Ezekiel and the *House of Fame* which merit critical consideration. For form, the chapter from Ezekiel which first comes to mind is not in fact the fortieth, but chapter eight, which recounts a much earlier vision. Here Ezekiel is confronted by Yahweh in his desert exile and "lifted up between earth and heaven" (v. 3) to be shown a vision of the historical temple of his day. Corrupted by the unseemly presence of a statue of Ashtoreth, or Venus ("The image of jealousy" (v. 5) because Yahweh's 'jealousy' is thereby aroused), [26] and defiled by distorted vision ("every man in the chambers of his imagery" — v. 12) [27] the temple proves less the prophet's 'true country' than did even the desert wasteland. Whereas Ezekiel's vision was concerned with the parody by which a temple devoted to concupiscence contradicted the ideal Temple of the New Jerusalem revealed at the end of his book, Chaucer's vision begins in such a temple of Venus, also a "chamber of imagery," only to reveal to us a Geffrey who is 'actually' like the historical Ezekiel, in a desert, alienated and unsure of his own country. Then, in a fashion which bears further structural comparison with the continuation of Ezekiel's book, Chaucer's vision proceeds to description of another temple, comprised of two 'courts', the Houses of Rumor and Fame. That the described structure of that 'temple' may invert the "Outer Court" and "Inner Court" of Ezekiel's description is a possi-

---

24. Wyclif argues that the prophetic books have a special form, both in his lectures on Isaiah and in his prologue to Isaiah. See J. Forshall and F. Madden, *Wycliffe's Bible in Two Versions*, 4 vols. (Oxford: Oxford University Press, 1850).

25. Koonce, especially 105, 106; 178-82.

26. Nicholas of Lyra, in his *Postilla* on Ezekiel (in *Biblia Sacra cum Glossa Ordinaria*, etc., Antwerp, 1634. ed. J. Meursium), writes: "scilicet idoli zeli quod erat iuxta introitum portae, et illi idolo erat altare constitutum, a quo denominabatur illa porta" and adds the following point by way of moraliter: "Idolatria secunda, est multorum simulacrum, quae tangitur ibi . . ." (1129). He observes further, of vv. 14-17, that the women are weeping for Adonis, "which is to say, the love of Venus." He notes that Rabbi Solomon identifies the Hebrew *Thammuz* with the idol, as with the sin *luxuria*, saying that such languishing after Venus is a kind of sickness unto death, a form of idolatry. Wyclif makes points on Ezekiel 8:17: "Sic stulti Christiani delusi detergunt pulverem ymaginum ad ungendum oculos male sanos." Elsewhere he refers to v.10: "alle idols of the hous of Israel . . . peyntid in the wall al aboute in cumpas" (Forshall and Madden, 515).

27. The Vulgate is actually: "in abscondito cubilis sui." Wyclif translates: "ech in the hid place of his couch." (Forshall and Madden, 516).

bility which merits more detailed study, especially perhaps in light of fourteenth-century commentary on Ezekiel's temple by Nicholas of Lyra and, subsequently, by Wyclif.[28]

In the present comparison we may concern ourselves primarily with the form of Ezekiel's total narrative, the structure of his book. Despite the conveyance of some aspects of historical sequence, this book is typical of visionary literature in manifesting narrative design as rhetorical and psychological, rather than as 'historical'. Its three-part organization may be capitulated in this way:

Proem: announcing the genre: vision, or prophecy (ch. 1)

   I. The Problem of History (ch. 2-24)

      a) Israel (the reader) exemplifies a sinful history, and goes astray from true understanding because forgetful of its 'Author'.

      b) The result of this forgetfulness is confused and distorted perspective, alienation in the wilderness, diseased interpretation. The parable of the eagle (ch. 17) is a parable of captivity. Israel is shown to need this extreme therapy because she is apparently incompetent to remember without reinforcement the true lessons of history.

  II. Analysis (ch. 25-32)

      a) Human judgment and interpretation, especially of alien authorities (here exemplified by Egypt and her neighbors) are shown to be presumptuous and inadequate.

      b) Yahweh's judgment is that truth comes from another source . . . .

  III. Options: (ch. 33-48)

      a) A conversation with the Author by which our mediate author (Ezekiel) is also tacitly admonished concerning the pitfalls of a visionary vocation by negative examples of his art (the lying prophets [ch. 33-36]) then shown that by itself history is dead—a valley of dry bones (ch. 37).

      b) An answering of questions by action, by event. What can vivify these bones, bringing them to life in coherent fidelity to their history? Only that divine inspiration which the visionary poet (prophet) is commanded by Yahweh to invoke (17:9-10).

---

28. Lyra's Postilla includes a diagram of the historical temple described in ch. 8, which has 3 'frames', and a contrasting diagram of the future temple (ch. 40), in which the structure is seen as significantly changed. Here Lyra draws, as before, 3 'courts' (atrium immundorum circuitus; atrium mundorum; atrium sacerdotum), but structures the diagram in such a way that these constitute a series of frames for a fourth entity which may not be explicitated yet, in history, and which is the true inner sanctum, the templum to be revealed (pp. 1125, 1366). But cf. Helen Rosenau, "The Architecture of Nicolaus de Lyra's Temple Illustrations and the Jewish Tradition," Journal of Jewish Studies, 25 (1974) 294-304. The Wyclif translation calls the outer porch of the temple "the utmer porche, or large hous" (Forshall and Madden, 596). Throughout the prophets the translation regularly employs hous to translate "temple bildid of Salomon" (see gloss in 237).

It reveals that the true temple can only be situated in the 'true country' which transcends history, where the Author's final authority is to be revealed to the reader in person. The name of that place is simply *Yahweh Shammah* (*Dominus ibidem*)—"the Lord is there." [29]

This outline of argument for Ezekiel is almost conventional in terms of modern scholarship. [30] But more to the point, the essential features are all anticipated in fourteenth-century commentaries, notably in Nicholas of Lyra and John Wyclif. [31]

Narratively, the notable thing about 'prophetic' or visionary biblical narrative is its self-conscious address to the reader, one consequence of which is insistence on a conclusion taking place effectually only *outside* the historical text of the story. With respect to Chaucer, what we must try to imagine, I think, is what might constitute the influence of such a hermeneutic in a poetic critique of *historicism* and its kind of justification for poetic closure. Let us suppose that, superimposed on our readers' expectation of the historicist and progressive hermeneutic (signaled by the Vergilian desert, engendered by the temple of Venus, and encompassed by the progression of Morpheus, Venus, Apollo), Chaucer may have skillfully introduced a "second stage" of reference—another design (underwritten by the desert and temple of Ezekiel ch. 8). Let us say that it might be the very simple rhetorical model used by Ezekiel (problem/analysis/option), and that as applied to the problem of history and a possible unity of truth its development might be keyed not by the progression of temporal states of mind (e.g. concupiscence/science/sapience), but by an appeal to *faculties* of mind (to memory/intellect/will). In such a case, a diagram for the structure of the *House of Fame* could look like this:

I. Problem: a) The reader has a fragmented, fallen perspective; he is 'forgetful' of Authority.

Morpheus is invoked;   (ll. 67-69)

b) What the reader sees is a fallen history; his experience is that of everyman, sickness in body, spirit, head, the alienation of a desert;

Memory is appealed to;   (ll. 64-65)

II. Analysis: a) What the reader offers: venal sacrifices, wrong 'readings';

Venus is invoked;   ll. 518-19)

---

29. Lyra comments: "dominus ibidem: non solum per essentiam, potentiam, et praesentiam, sicut est, aliis locis: sed etiam per specialem suorum beneficiorum influentiam" (p. 1467). The Wycliffite translations restrain the copula: "The Lord there" (Forshall and Madden, 620).

30. E.g., G. A. Cooke's volume on Ezekiel in *The International Critical Commentary* (Edinburgh: T. & T. Clark, repr. 1970), xvii; John B. Taylor *Ezekiel: An Introduction and Commentary* (London: Tyndale Press, 1969).

31. Lyra, *Postilla*, 1365-67; The Wycliffite Bible prologue connects Ezekiel directly to St. John's Apocalypse. The prologue to all the prophetic books argues that the first intention of the prophets is to capitulate in their discourse the whole history of salvation.

     b) What Jove wants: "learn to do well, seek judgment";
     Intellect is appealed to (the Eagle);   (ll. 523-28)

III. Option: a) The poem is engaged as a 'conversation' to order perspective on authorship, etc. "Come let us *reason* together ...";
     Apollo is invoked;   (ll. 1091-93)
     b) The poem becomes an invitation to an *act* of acknowledgment (beyond the poem), recognizing the necessity of silence before an ultimate authority. Divine inspiration is sought, for a transformation of the will.   (ll. 1101-1109)

  The dialectic which the biblical model affords would seem to suggest that if the view of the poem as an incomplete fideistic celebration seems finally less than adequate, then so too is the view that the poem is a classicist-humanist attack on faith.[32] Chaucer's skepticism, reflected in the narrative structure of the *House of Fame*, is not in fact directed toward Christian revelation or the notion of ultimate and unified truth, but toward the problem of a reader's human perspective, his overwhelming difficulties in recovering truth from history. *In what sense can anything of the past be a true authority for us today?* That is the question Chaucer poses of his standard models and authorities, and what his intellect gives him back is the answer that trust in them involves as much (or more) an act of will, a leap of faith, as any other he could imagine.

  The plurality of authorities, a series of histories and points of view contradicting each other, naturally leads us in the direction of skepticism. The ambiguous histories that we live with, unfortunately, are our state of asking. We are, in measure, what we remember. Like Aeneas bearing Anchises on his shoulders we carry our history with us. But not all of the way. Or, as Chaucer puts the abstraction: Fame bears upon her shoulders not only the history of the great (1410-13), of nations (1432-36), or universal history (1460-1500 ff.), but also that of the mundane good, of unjudged villains, of sin, and of a veritable host of liars and their lies. Laboring along under this burden, it is unsurprising that the reader should sometimes stagger, and be incessantly prompted to seek a truth whose sign, implicitly, is some ultimate *agreement*, some unity.

  Most readers have at one time or another expected history to have a certain objectivity—what, in the words of one philosopher, "thought has worked out, put into order, understood, and what it can thus *make* understood."[33] The historicist, or revelationist (Joachim, Dante, Hegel,

---

  32. Cf. Sheila Delaney, "Chaucer's House of Fame: The Poetics of Skeptical Fideism," *DA* 28 (1967), 178A-83A (Columbia), and "Phantom and the *House of Fame*," *Chaucer Review* 2 (1967), 67-74.
  33. Paul Ricoeur, in *History and Truth* (Evanston: Northwestern University Press, 1965), 21.

Marx) is one who asks that this objectivity be extended systematically to a universal—and yet literal—history. Chaucer, on the other hand, is one who asks of history a different type of question, one which candidly discloses his *subjective* concern.[34] He is concerned above all with the emergence of values, of the truth of attitudes and states of mind, with knowing, personal action, the mutual encumbrances of life and death—values which, in fact, emerge through the temporal span of human societies but whose point of asking is always (in the Augustinian sense) existential, the arena of the personal question. For Chaucer in the *House of Fame* one's search for truth is thus characterized by being stretched between two poles: our personal situation, and a certain objective intention with respect to being. Our contemporary, Ricoeur, puts the problem in terms proximate enough for comparison:

> The latent parodox is this: we say history, *history in the singular*, because we expect this unique history of mankind to be unified and made reasonable by a human meaning. . . . But we also say men, *men in the plural*, and we define history as the science of past men because we find persons who emerge as radically manifold centres of mankind.[35]

It is well recognized that Chaucer, in most of his poetry, reiterates a suggestion that however much we try to pursue the truth of history objectively, we cannot extract from this pursuit the personal, the subjective. Even the Wife of Bath suggests (ironically) that the study of past men is motivated not just by a desire for *explanation*, but by a will for *encounter*.[36] Of course, as Chaucer shows us with Geffrey, that means that there will always be frustration. We are unavoidably, as readers, limited, for the encounter with history is never a dialogue. Texts do not answer, not even when we cast them in the fire. We have communication, yes, but without reciprocity. (As Ricoeur says, "it's a little like unrequited love.") It is the personal in our own questions which reminds us that though we speak of history as singular, we are always dealing with persons in the plural. And we find that we must acknowledge that the appearance of a great (indeed *any*) human personality is not simply more data, but an *event* which is irreducible to the surmise of reason as that could be transmitted by words alone.

The frustrated conclusion of the *House of Fame* draws attention to itself, and thus, at its first meaning, to a practical necessity. Of history, the poet does not have the complete text. The experience of books—the 'academy' of Fame's household—only makes this reality more evident. Its 'bookish' authority, like the temporal authority of the Court, the House or Rumor, are, as secular scripture, but information and frustration. The very sense we have of incompleteness drives us to search for a unity of truth, for a oneness which we intuit, yet, like the persona, don't know yet nor

---

34. Cf. Owen Barfield, *Saving the Appearances: A Study in Idolatry* (London: Faber and Faber, 1957), 126-33; Barfield, *History in English Words* (Grand Rapids: Eerdmans, 1967), 172; and Ricoeur, 35.
35. Ricoeur, 38.
36. *Ibid.*, 29; 36-40.

can we know—unless there be revealed, face to face, "one" who could compose such a unity, containing and transcending our diverse particularity of vision, our divergent readings—in short, a genuine auctoritee, "author and finisher" of the whole story. Yet that is clearly not the only point of Chaucer's poem. In the midst of all the compounded and all too court-like confusion of Rumor's whirling jumbo ("mischief upon mischief," "rumor upon rumor," as the prophet Ezekiel puts it), there has been little so far to suggest any such possible unity of truth. Geffrey has in fact come hither, he plainly says, neither to seek fame himself (1872-82), nor to merely add to the confusion another tale (1906-9), but to get something categorically different—"newe tydynges for to lere" (1886) and though he cannot, of course, yet specify what that would be, by definition these must be differentiated in *quality*, not merely an addition to the astonishing quantity of contradictory proclamations which make up Fame and Rumor's confusion. In short, having dispensed with the pursuit of *fame* as either reputation or rumor, he is now focused intently on its other meaning, and would like to bring his search to a conclusion. Or, we could say, to a point of judgment.

Tidings, we are reminded, had a primary meaning in Chaucer's time (OED), not of 'report' or 'news' but of 'event', or 'happening'—the *occasion of fame*, not just its happenstance reporting. The request for "newe tidings for to lere" (to be taught) is thus a request for something transformational to happen—in a sense, for history to be *made* rather than simply reported. The *tydings* should be of some different "countre," of which he need not speak, since there are others who can sing its praises better than he (2134-38)—for, as he alludes to that place further, there will one day come a sorting out of the wheat from the tares, the true from the false, "alle the sheves in the lathe" (ll. 2140; cf. Ps. 125:6). And it may be that this penultimate allusion to a final Judgment, authoritative beyond dispute, actually opens up, rather than closes down, the horizons of the poem.

It seems that plurality is not for Chaucer the final reality, nor is misunderstanding the ultimate end of attempts at communication. The last element of the vision is not to be another flood of reports, or even one report, but a concrete event. With everyone scrambling to try to see, Geffrey turns for his frustrated attempts at concluding his search for truth to see what is happening. And what he sees is the first emergence of another human, personal entity in the poem—at last an answer to his initial search—running out of the temple, weighted with the authorities of history, to see if he could find "any styring man" to tell him where and who he was:

Atte laste y saugh a man,
Which that y [nevene] nat ne kan,
But he semed for to be
A man of gret auctorite . . .   (ll. 2155-9)

The reference is, I think, unmistakably to the mysterious One before whom all things are to be uncovered, and from whom nothing is hid—to the ultimate Judge, or interpreter. [37] In the face of the difficulty of determining authority as exposed by the poem, it is in fact only such an open ending, however fearful that openness is, which could provide the reader with any hope. That is, Chaucer puts before his reader the intractable problem of determining truth in a history in which confusion reigns, but as a problem which is at least illuminated by an optional framework for understanding, an eschaton, a "fullness of time" which can hold out hope for a unified and eternal 'reading' for history without presuming to be in any facile sense literalistically coordinate with fragmented history of the moment.

Giuseppe Mazzotta, writing of Dante, asks the pertinent formal question:

> If the journey of writing has not an end where all its promises are fulfilled, how does the poem come to an end? What is the exile with which poetry seems to be synonymous? We must provisionally single out as having a special, revelatory function the ending of the poem, the point which is conventionally given special importance, because it is there that the sense of the poem lies. [38]

Dante's historicist model develops a markedly different form for conclusion than that which emerges from the biblical model by which Chaucer contravenes it in his *House of Fame*. Yet in Chaucer's poem the two models do speak to each other; many of the same questions are put with intensity, and in Chaucer we ought certainly to "single out as having a special, revelatory function the ending of the poem." It is the relationship between revelation and history, truth and poetry, which so distinguishes the form of argument in the two poems by which the two writers are most often compared.

Let me then summarize: What I have tried to suggest in this final essay is: (1) that in his poem Chaucer despairs of a unity of truth based on 'history', or any visible unity of historical meaning; (2) that he thus limits the ambition of the poetic endeavor, and finds unhelpful to its subjective concerns the ostensibly 'objective' structures of 'classical' historicism; (3) that the function of the biblical (as opposed to the classical) component in this poem is not simply a fideistic *oblige*, or merely another descriptive typology, but a means of introducing, amidst the skepticism engendered by a plurality of authorities, a more 'tractable' form of enquiry. The result is a new hermeneutic horizon, opening the way to an authoritative conclusion not yet grasped by individual readings, but possibly to be anticipated by them. In this perspective, "readings," such as the seriously playful reading of a poet, can be truly helpful, if only because the questions, less presumptuous than pseudo-answers, are really proposals concerning a story—a

---

37. It is surely one of the poem's nicer ironies that its ending should carry us back to the occasion of its primary question, the plight of Dido. It was she who said: "O, soth ys, every thing ys wist/ Though hit be kevered with the myst" (11. 351-52), so echoing the Gospel, "there is nothing covered that shall not be revealed; neither hid that shall not be known" (Luke 12:1-2).

38. Mazzotta, 253.

"hidden scripture"—that is still unfolding.[39] (4) The structure which the poem appears to have—and by which it invites its reader into a conventional set of temporal interpretation, Chaucer portrays as the inevitably historicized property of all temporal interpretation, including his own. But by exposing an ambivalence of reader motivation toward this structure, and then by leaving it (temporarily) open, Chaucer underscores the role of will and inspiration in the reader's response. Thus, he opens up a logic for closure in which the formal logic of conventional poetic structure may be traced, but in which that formal logic is also transcended by the silent space of his reader's choosing. (5) Finally, an inference: the problem of (sinful) subjectivity in the reader is for Chaucer the most limiting problem in interpretation—(one which he will explore more fully in *The Canterbury Tales*.) For it, an ultimate *judgment* separating the true from the false is needed. The ending of the present poem is thus not 'apocalyptic,' in the usual or catastrophic sense, but *hopeful* or 'eschatalogical,' in the sense that such an eschaton is not the limitation of a 'historical' conclusion, but rather an *openness* to the final perspective of a full text and Authorial reading.

The "conclusion" to Chaucer's *House of Fame* can be, in this openness, itself a kind of *eschaton*. As a poem, it concludes neither in a pluralistic quandary-skepticism, nor in a dogmatic assertion. Rather, it rests in a simple suspension of the story—"the end is not yet." In what is *not* said there is, perhaps, an invitation to the reader to offer something of his own. Yet in the perspective of the poem's last rejections this invitation is not merely for more information. Rather, almost as it would be in the liturgical context suggested by Ezekiel, the invitation is in silence, to silence, before the unutterable Word.[40]

---

39. Cf. Walter Benjamin, who argues that in a good traditional storyteller, the product is a kind of wisdom literature in which "counsel is less an answer to a question than a proposal concerning the continuation of a story which is just unfolding." *Illuminations*, ed. Hannah Arendt, trans. Harry Zohn (London: Jonathan Cape, 1970), 86.

40. My own imagination suggests to me St. John of the Cross:
The Father utters one Word and that Word is his Son,
and he utters him forever in everlasting silence
and in silence the soul has to hear him.
R.J. Schoeck has offered plausible evidence, on the other hand, to suggest that the poem may have been recited for members of the Inns of Court during an Advent celebration, about the time of the literal Dec. 10th date—which often connected, in fact, readings from Ezekiel with the Advent liturgy. See his "A legal reading of Chaucer's Hous of Fame," UTQ, 23 (1953), 185-92. Schoeck's reading seems to me to add another conceivable context for that implied here. I am less content with his identification of the "man of gret auctorite" as the Master of Revels. At least in the literal sense. One can imagine in such a setting, however, what might come after the unfinished last sentence of the poem. From the Advent liturgy, and originally occasioned by the oppression of that very historicism to which Vergil gave 'fame', it might be: "Fear not, for behold I bring you good tydings, of great joy, which shall be to all people." Or possibly, and also from the liturgy, it might be a succinct celebration of the greatest 'fame': "Glory be to the Father, and to the Son, and to the Holy Ghost. World without end. Amen."

General Index

Aaron 58, 59
Abel 195
Abelard, Peter 9, 14
Abigail 55
Abraham 129, 165 n 63, 201, 202, 203
Absalom 42, 51
Adam 31, 56, 95, 164 n 63
Adam of Halle 22
Adams, George R. 49 n 7, 153 n 33
Adhemar of Puy 5
Aeneas 50, 152, 208, 209, 210, 211, 212, 213
Aeneid 208-213
Ailred of Rievaulx 8-9
Alanus of Insulis 8, 9, 217
Albertano of Brescia 55
alchemy 155
Alcuin 13, 162 n 57
Aldhelm, St. 7
Alexander the Great 47
Alford, John A. intro., [197-203]
allegory 14, 68, 90, 97, 102-103, 118, 131, 145ff,
    et passim
Allen, Judson B. intro., 90
Ambrose, St. 13 n 51, 91, 106, 133
Anchises 224
Ancrene Wisse 21
Anderson, G.K. 198 n 4
Andreas Cappellanus 10
Anne of Bohemia, Queen 112
Annunciation 49, 169 n 71
Anselm of Laon 13, 65, 72, 117
Antiochus 57
Apollo 218, 223, 224
Aquinas, St. Thomas 91, 92, 94, 132 n 101, 152
archetypes 124
Arnold, T. 220 n 21
Aristotle 12, 117, 118, 119, 133, 134
Arnulf of Orléans 9
Arthur, King 11, 47, 210
Arundel 112
Ashley, Kathleen 156 n 39
Aspin, Isabel S.T. 23 n 97
Aston, Margaret 28 n 120
Auer, Johann 4 n 4
Augustine, St. intro., 4, 6 n 10, 7, 10, 13, 15,
    77, 90, 91, 101, 106, 115, 119, 126, 128, 129,
    137, 145, 162 n 57, 200, 202, 207, 210, 219
    City of God 31, 211, 219

Commentary on Psalms 13 n 51
Commentary on the Sermon on the Mount 46
Confessions 41, 215 n 16, 219
De genesis ad litteram 101
De opere monachorum 189
De spiritu et littera 200 n 6
De Trinitate 211
Enchiridion 15
Harmony of the Gospels 214 n 12
On Christian Doctrine intro., 3, 4, 5-6, 13,
    17
Tractate IX on the Gospel of John 154 n 34,
    161 n 55, 164 n 63
Augustine of Canterbury 7
Ault, W.O. 22 n 94
authority 36, 68, 69, 75, 76, 114, 115, 117, 123,
    124ff, 137, 143, 189, 197, 207-228

Babylon 165 n 63
Bacon, Roger 124 n 62
Baker, J.H. 19 n 77
Bale, John 112, 113
Barfield, Owen 225 n 34
Barnie, John 30
Baudoin of Guisnes 14
Beaumont, Robert and Walerin 14
Bede, St. 90, 91, 93, 162 n 57
Beichner, Paul E. 51 n 10, 190
Bellamy, John 25 n 106
Belshazzar 56-57
Beneditti, Angelo 192 n 17
Benjamin, Walter 228 n 39
Bennett, J.A.W. 97 n 20, 113 n 22
Benrath, G.A. 119 n 41, 120 n 43, 122 n 53, 127
    n 82, 132 n 103
Benson, C. David 211 n 5
Bersuire, Pierre (Berchorius) 214 n 12
Beowulf 7
Bernard of Clairvaux, St. 8, 11, 14
Bernard, P. 11 n 37
Bernardus Silvestris 78, 79, 80ff, 212
Besserman, Lawrence L. intro., 49 n 6, 56 n 21,
    61 n 30, [65-73]
Bevington, David M. 216 n 17
Bible Moralisée 77, 173, 180
Biblia Pauperum 77, 169 n 71
Black Death 24-31

234

Scriptural Index

238

Notes on Contributors

JOHN A. ALFORD teaches at Michigan State University. He is author of articles on Chaucer and medieval English literature.

LAWRENCE BESSERMAN is Professor and Acting Chairman of the Department of English at the Hebrew University in Jerusalem. Author of *The Legend of Job in the Middle Ages* (1979), he has also written numerous articles on Chaucer and medieval literature.

GRAHAM D. CAIE teaches at the University of Copenhagen. After his dissertation on marginal glosses in MSS of *The Canterbury Tales* (McMaster), he has published articles in *Chaucer Review* and elsewhere on this subject.

THERESA COLETTI teaches at the University of Maryland. She has published numerous essays on Chaucer.

JOHN V. FLEMING is Professor and Chairman of the Department of English at Princeton University. He is author of *The Roman de la Rose* (1969), *An Introduction to Franciscan Literature* (1977), and *From Bonaventure to Bellini: An Essay in Franciscan Iconography* (1982), as well as numerous articles and studies of Chaucer and patristic tradition.

DAVID LYLE JEFFREY is Professor of English at the University of Ottawa. His published work includes *The Early English Lyric and Franciscan Spirituality* (1975), (ed.) *By Things Seen: Reference and Recognition in Medieval Thought* (1979), as well as articles on Chaucer and medieval literature. Currently he is General Editor for the forthcoming *Dictionary of Biblical Tradition in English Literature*.

RUSSELL A. PECK has authored numerous influential essays on Chaucer. Author also of *Kingship and Common Profit in Gower's "Confessio Amantis"* (1978) and editor of the *Confessio Amantis* (1968), he has for many years been Professor of English at the University of Rochester.

EDMUND REISS is the author of books and articles on medieval literature, including *Sir Thomas Malory* (1966), *The Art of the Middle English Lyric* (1972), and *William Dunbar* (1978). He teaches at Duke University.

D. W. ROBERTSON, Jr. has only recently retired as Murray Professor of English Literature at Princeton University. Author of the landmark study *A Preface to Chaucer* (1962), his writings also include *Chaucer's London* (1968), *Abelard and Eloise* (1972), *The Literature of Medieval England* (1970) and, with B. F. Huppé, *Piers Plowman and Scriptural Tradition* (1951). He is translator of St. Augustine's *On Christian Doctrine* (1958),

242

and a collection of his essays has recently appeared, *Essays in Medieval Culture* (1980).

CHAUNCEY WOOD is Professor of English at McMaster University. His first book, *Chaucer and the Country of the Stars* appeared in 1970. His book on *Troilus* will soon appear, and he is currently projecting a work on Chaucer and the Bible.

DOUGLAS WURTELE is Professor and Chairman of English at Carleton University (Ottawa). He has a forthcoming book on Chaucer, *Voices and Irony in the Canterbury Tales*.

THIS VOLUME WAS
COMPOSED IN TIMES ROMAN
AND PRINTED IN APRIL 1984
BY L'IMPRIMERIE MARQUIS
OF MONTMAGNY, QUÉBEC.
THE COVER WAS DESIGNED
BY GILLES ROBERT.